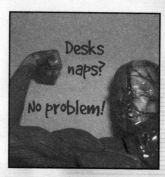

Desks naps? No problem!

Toshiaki Iwashiro

There's so much content I have to fit into each story now, but it's really more fun that way. It makes me a lot more motivated.

So...hanging in there!

Toshiaki Iwashiro was born December 11, 1977, in Tokyo and has the blood type of A. His debut manga was the popular *Mieru Hito*, which ran from 2005 to 2007 in Japan in *Weekly Shonen Jump*, where *Psyren* was also serialized.

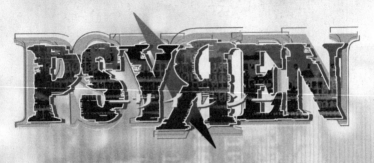

PSYREN VOL. 14
SHONEN JUMP Manga Edition

STORY AND ART BY TOSHIAKI IWASHIRO

Translation/Camellia Nieh
Lettering/Annaliese Christman
Design/Matt Hinrichs
Editor/Joel Enos

PSYREN © 2007 by Toshiaki Iwashiro
All rights reserved.
First published in Japan in 2007 by SHUEISHA Inc., Tokyo.
English translation rights arranged by SHUEISHA Inc.

The stories, characters and incidents mentioned in this publication are
entirely fictional.

Printed in the U.S.A.

Published by VIZ Media, LLC
P.O. Box 77010
San Francisco, CA 94107

10 9 8 7 6 5 4 3 2 1
First printing, January 2014

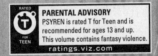
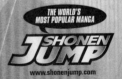

THE WORLD'S
MOST POPULAR MANGA

www.viz.com

www.shonenjump.com

SHONEN JUMP MANGA EDITION

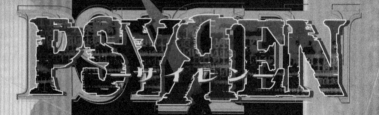

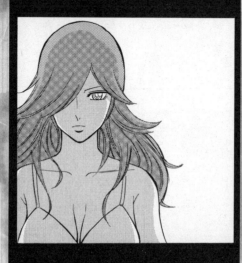

14

NOVA

Story and Art by
Toshiaki Iwashiro

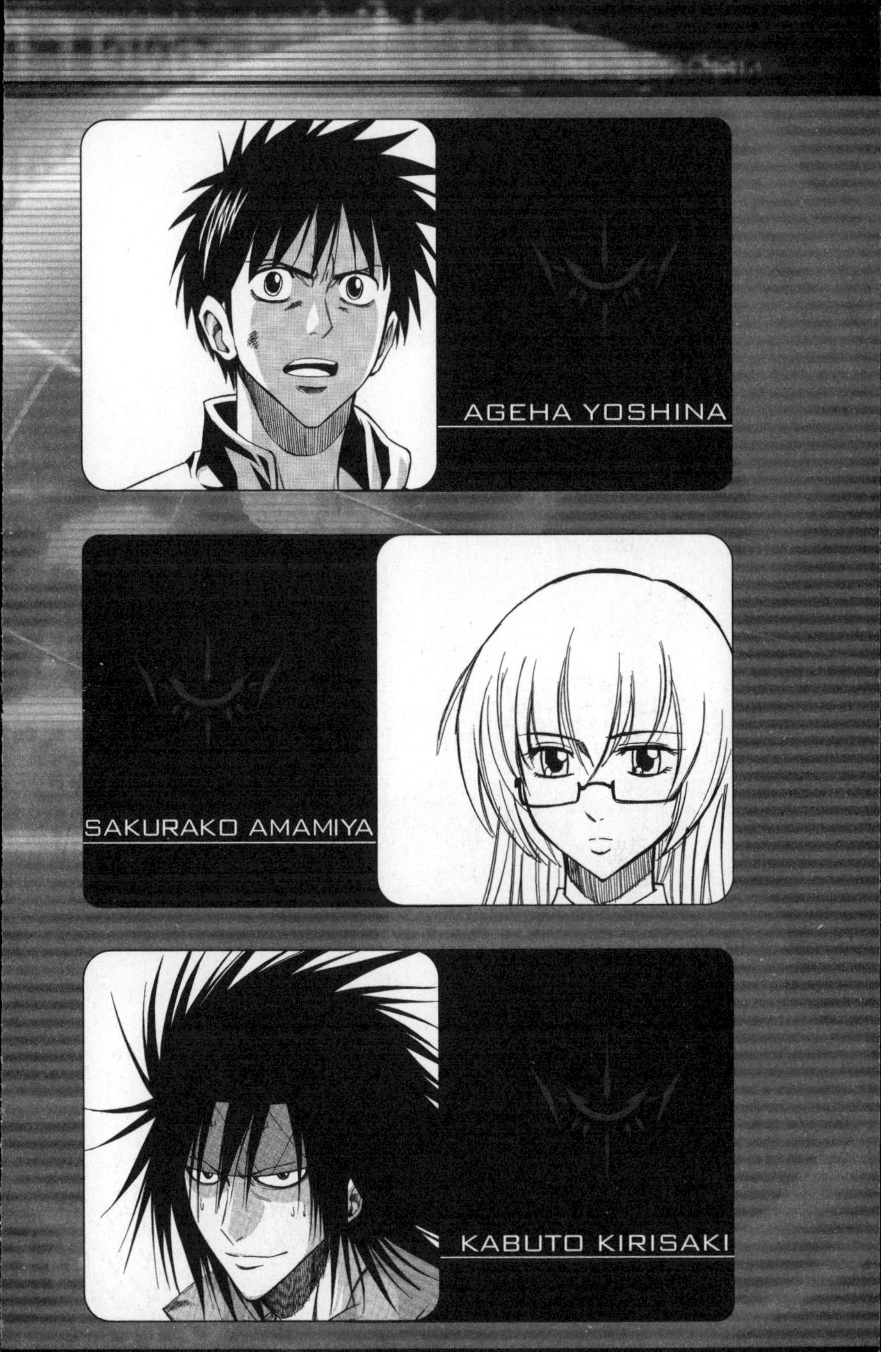
AGEHA YOSHINA
SAKURAKO AMAMIYA
KABUTO KIRISAKI

acters

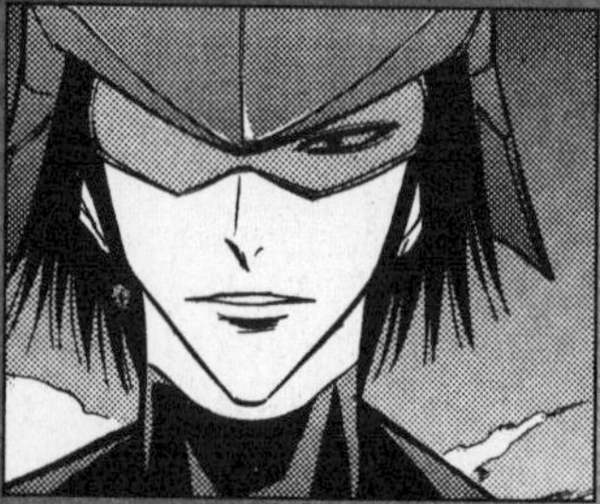

JUNAS

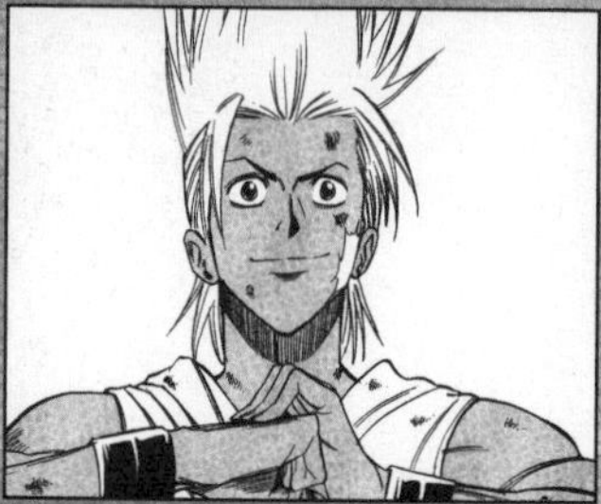

KYLE

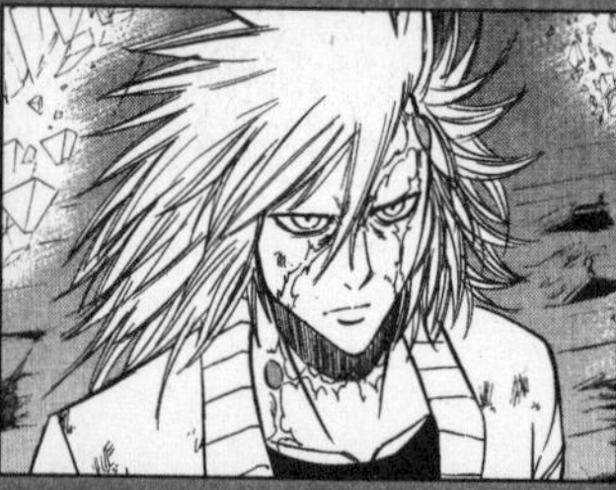

DELBORO

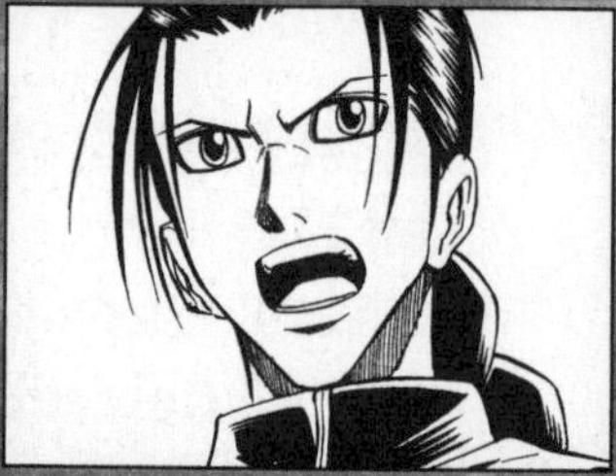

SHAO

Story

THIS IS THE STORY OF A GROUP OF TEENAGERS CAUGHT UP IN A LIFE-OR-DEATH GAME THAT HAS THEM TRAVELING BACK AND FORTH BETWEEN THE PRESENT AND THE FUTURE, IN A DESPERATE BATTLE TO AVERT THE END OF THE WORLD AS THEY KNOW IT.

HAVING SURVIVED THEIR FOURTH TRIP TO PSYREN, AGEHA AND HIS FRIENDS SET OUT TO LEARN MORE ABOUT MIROKU AMAGI. AGEHA PROPOSES INFILTRATING THE PSYREN CAPITAL, ASTRAL NAVA, AND QUESTIONING MIROKU DIRECTLY. SOON AFTER, THE FRIENDS ARE WHISKED INTO THE FUTURE FOR THE FIFTH TIME. THEIR JOYOUS REUNION WITH THE ELMORE WOOD GANG IS RUDELY INTERRUPTED BY W.I.S.E, WHO ATTACK THE ROOT WITH THEIR SPECIAL FORCES TROUPE, OTHERWISE KNOWN AS THE SCOURGE!

PSYREN

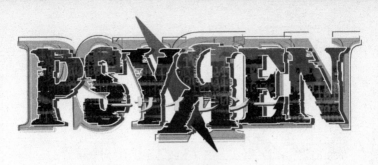

VOL. 14
NOVA
CONTENTS

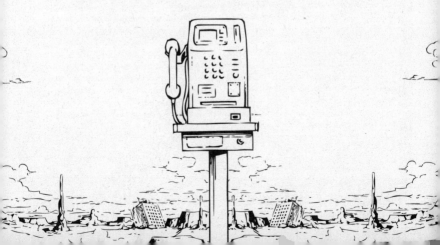

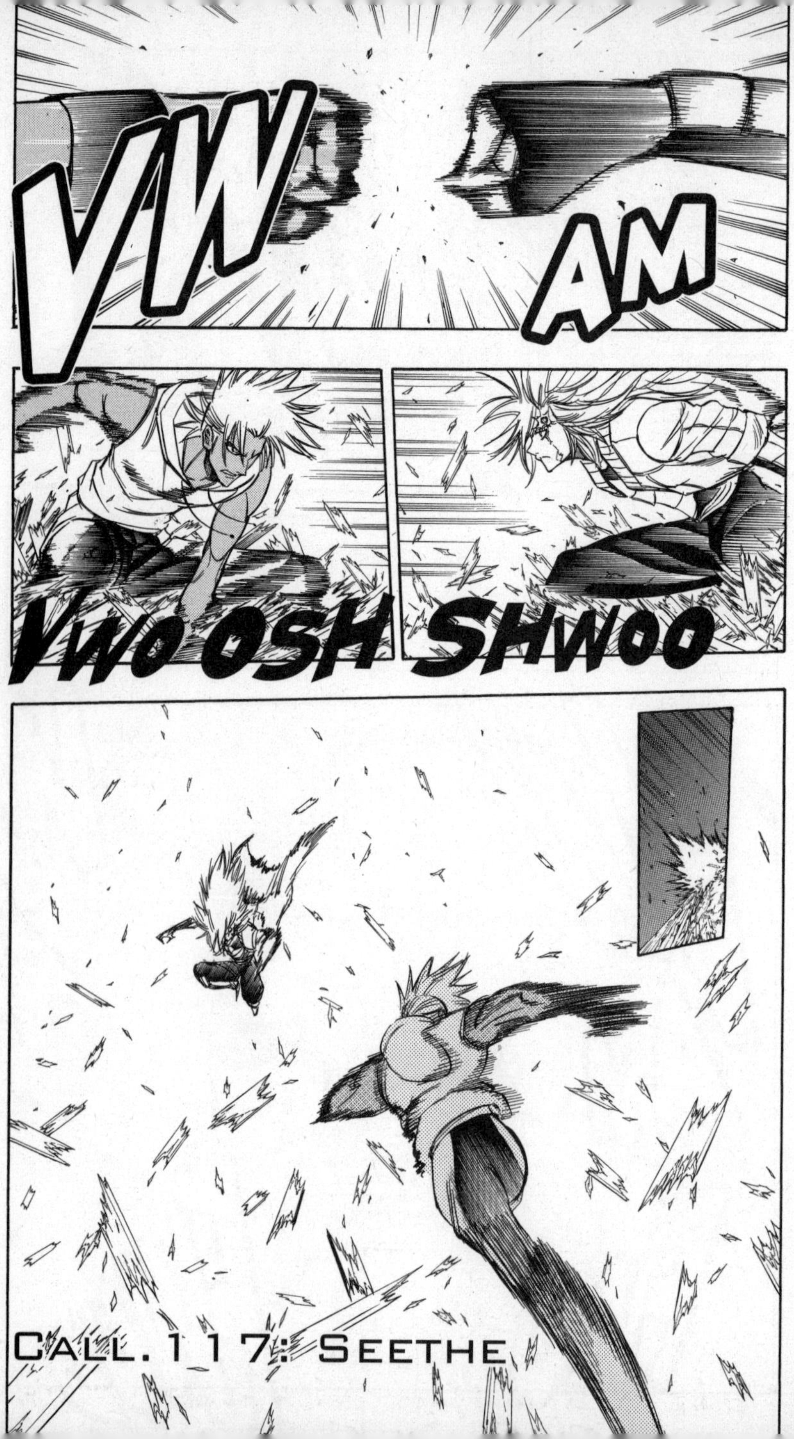
VW
AM
VWOOSH SHWOO
CALL. 117: SEETHE

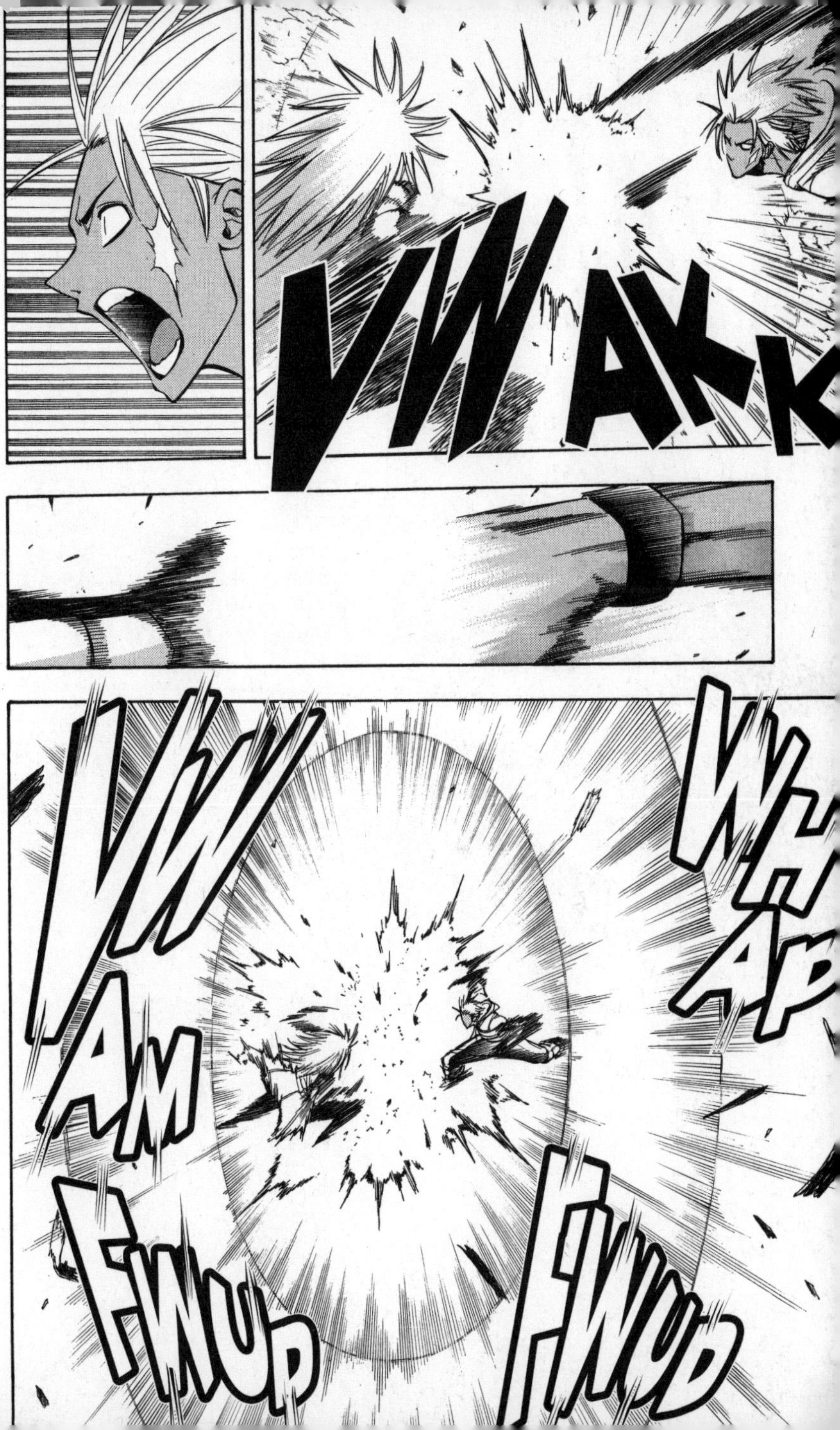
WHAK
WHAP
WHAM
FWUD
FWUD

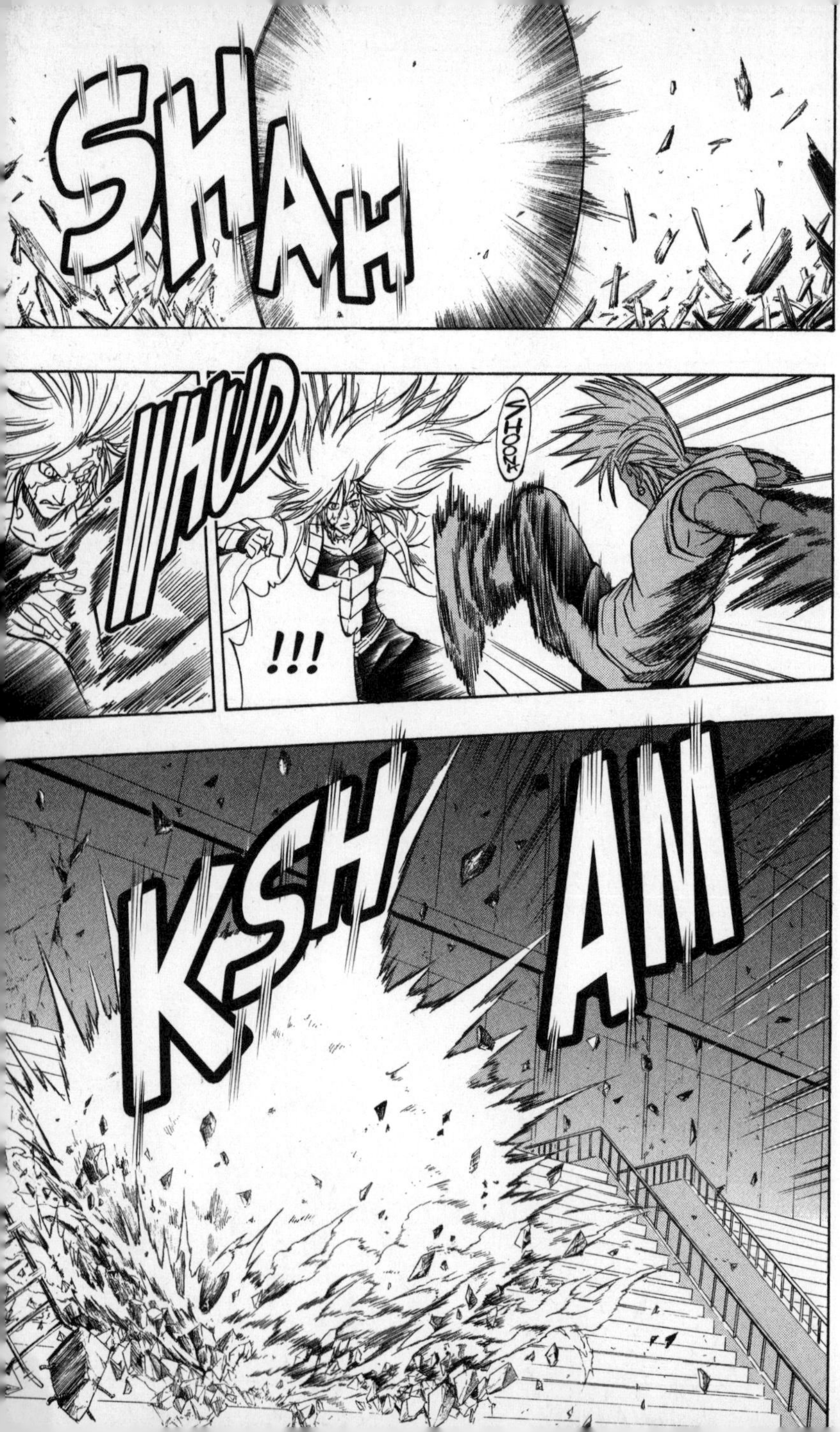
SHAH
SHOOM
!!!
THUD
KSHAM

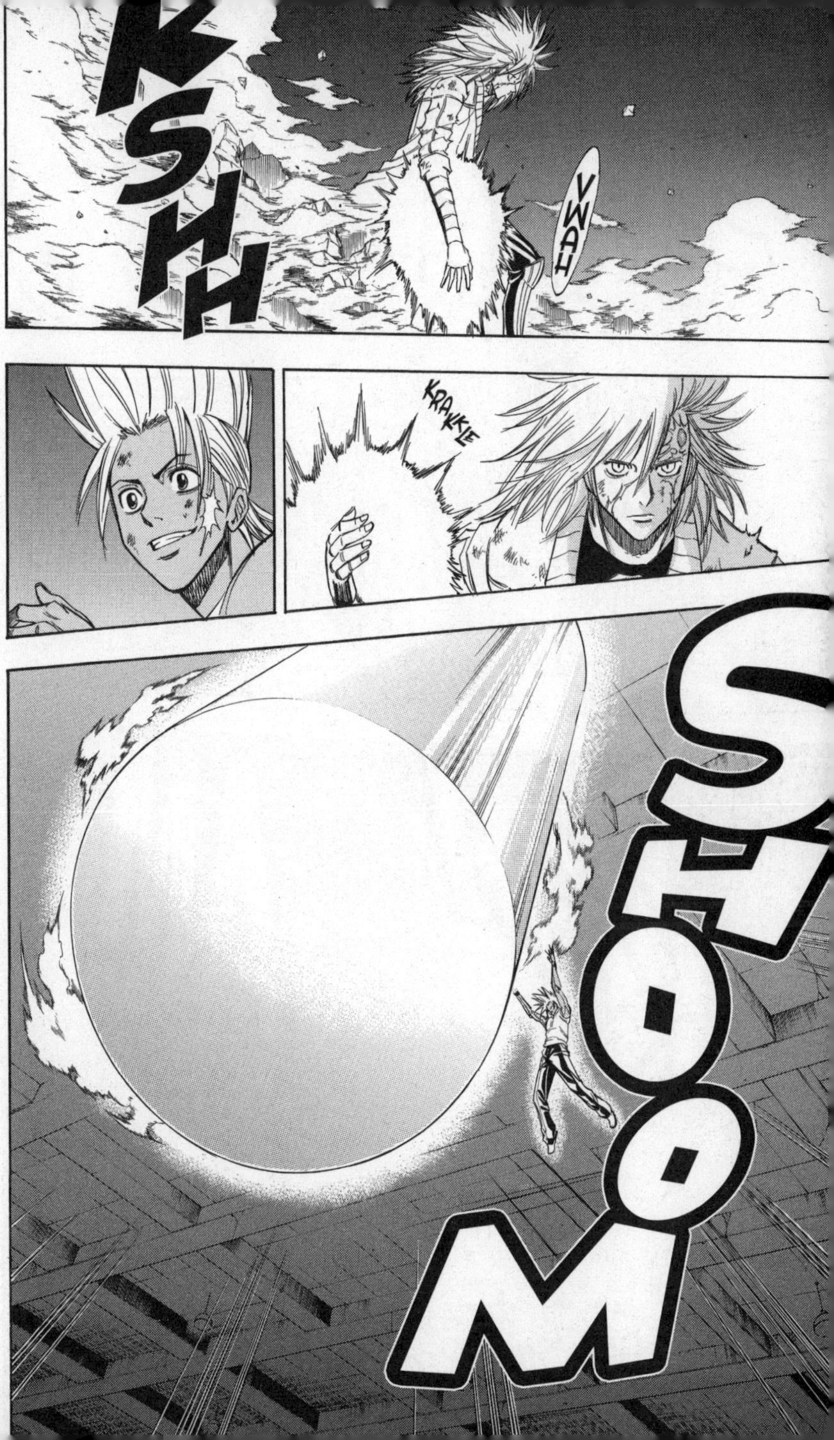
VWAH
KSHHH
KRAKKLE
SHOOOM

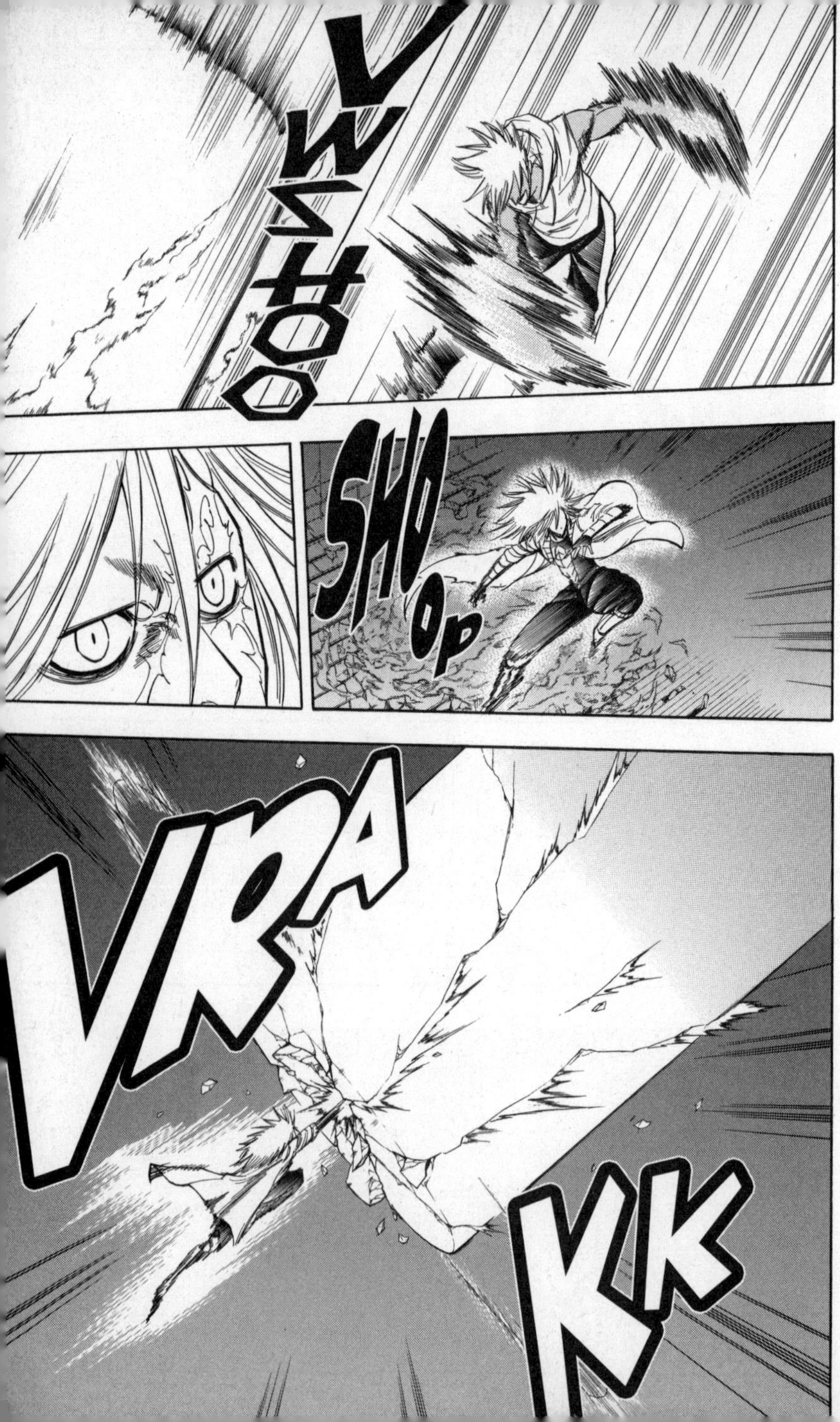
VWSHOO
SHOOP
VRAKK

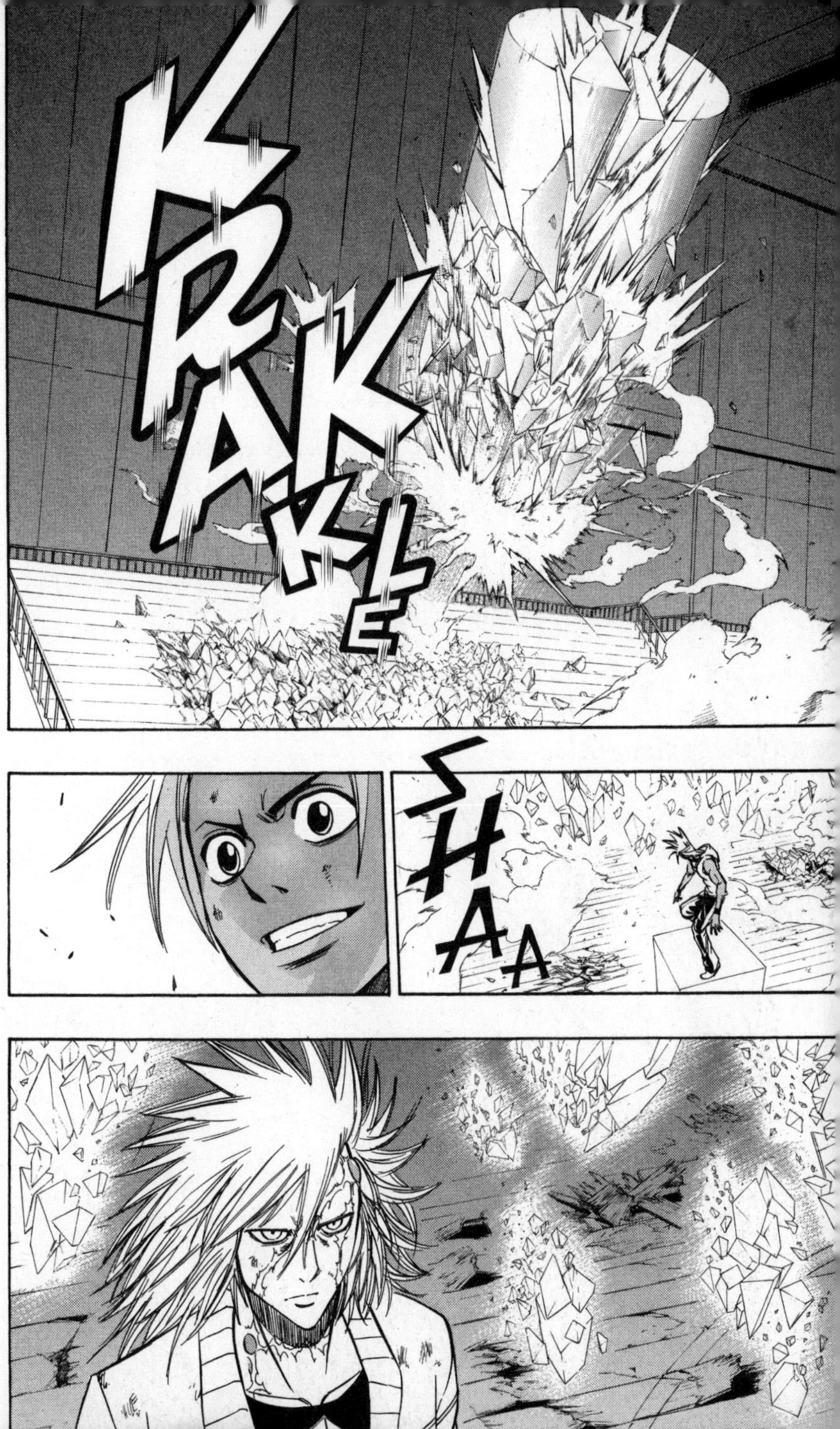
KRAKKLE
SHAA

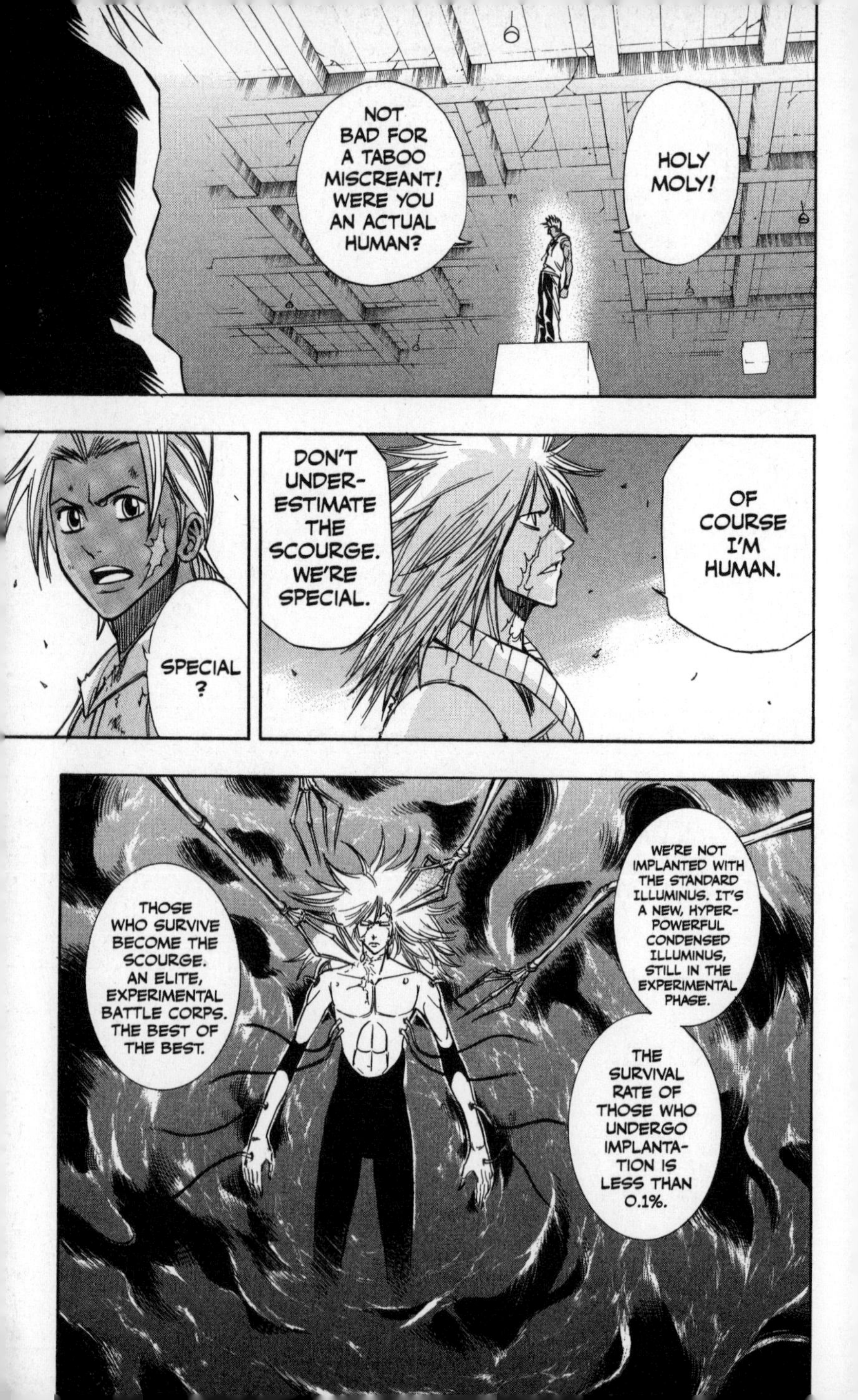
HOLY MOLY!
NOT BAD FOR A TABOO MISCREANT! WERE YOU AN ACTUAL HUMAN?
OF COURSE I'M HUMAN.
DON'T UNDER-ESTIMATE THE SCOURGE. WE'RE SPECIAL.
SPECIAL?
WE'RE NOT IMPLANTED WITH THE STANDARD ILLUMINUS. IT'S A NEW, HYPER-POWERFUL CONDENSED ILLUMINUS, STILL IN THE EXPERIMENTAL PHASE.
THE SURVIVAL RATE OF THOSE WHO UNDERGO IMPLANTA-TION IS LESS THAN 0.1%.
THOSE WHO SURVIVE BECOME THE SCOURGE. AN ELITE, EXPERIMENTAL BATTLE CORPS. THE BEST OF THE BEST.

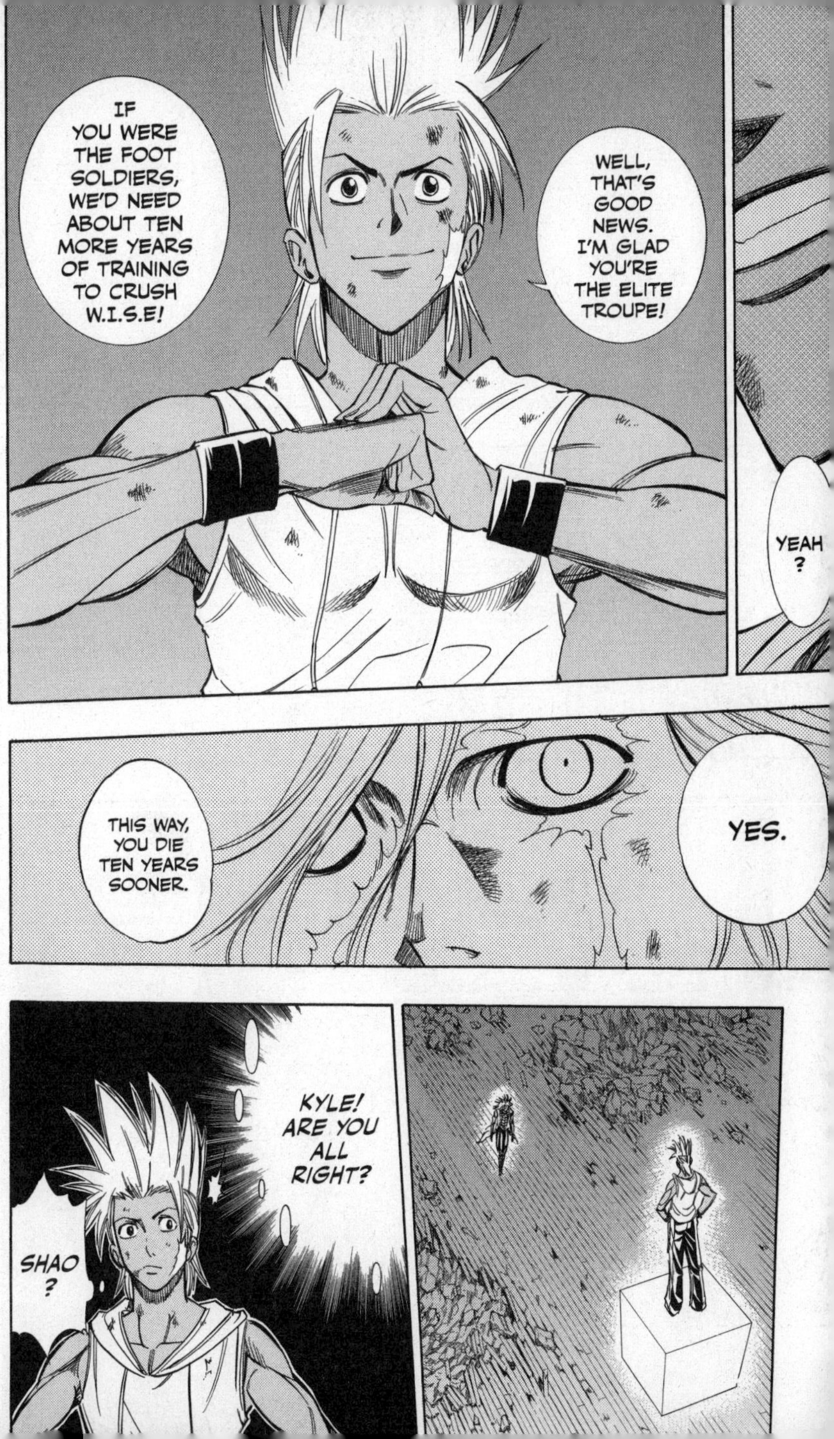
YEAH?
WELL, THAT'S GOOD NEWS. I'M GLAD YOU'RE THE ELITE TROUPE!
IF YOU WERE THE FOOT SOLDIERS, WE'D NEED ABOUT TEN MORE YEARS OF TRAINING TO CRUSH W.I.S.E!
YES.
THIS WAY, YOU DIE TEN YEARS SOONER.
KYLE! ARE YOU ALL RIGHT?
SHAO?

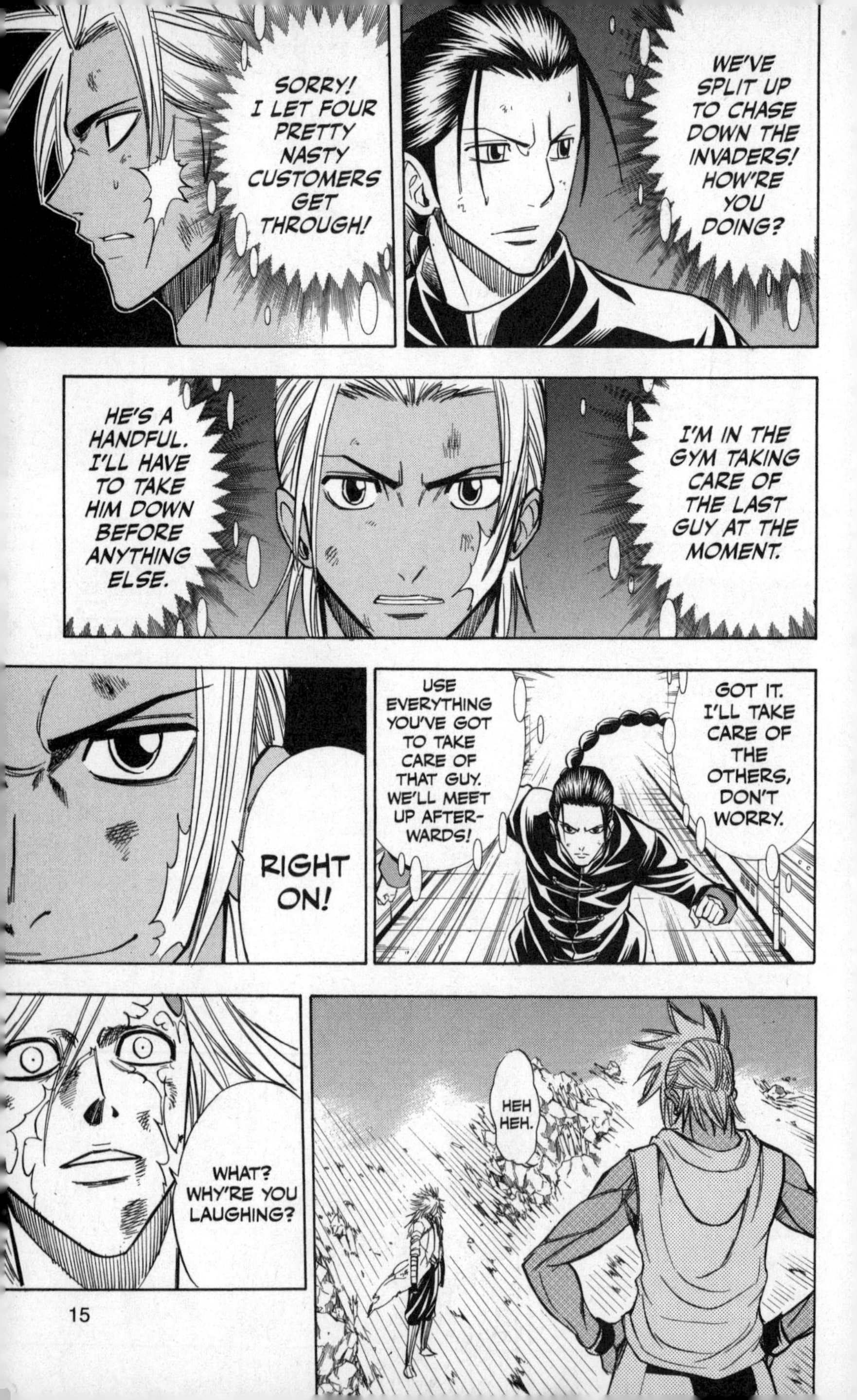
WE'VE SPLIT UP TO CHASE DOWN THE INVADERS! HOW'RE YOU DOING?
SORRY! I LET FOUR PRETTY NASTY CUSTOMERS GET THROUGH!
I'M IN THE GYM TAKING CARE OF THE LAST GUY AT THE MOMENT.
HE'S A HANDFUL. I'LL HAVE TO TAKE HIM DOWN BEFORE ANYTHING ELSE.
GOT IT. I'LL TAKE CARE OF THE OTHERS, DON'T WORRY.
USE EVERYTHING YOU'VE GOT TO TAKE CARE OF THAT GUY. WE'LL MEET UP AFTER-WARDS!
RIGHT ON!
HEH HEH.
WHAT? WHY'RE YOU LAUGHING?

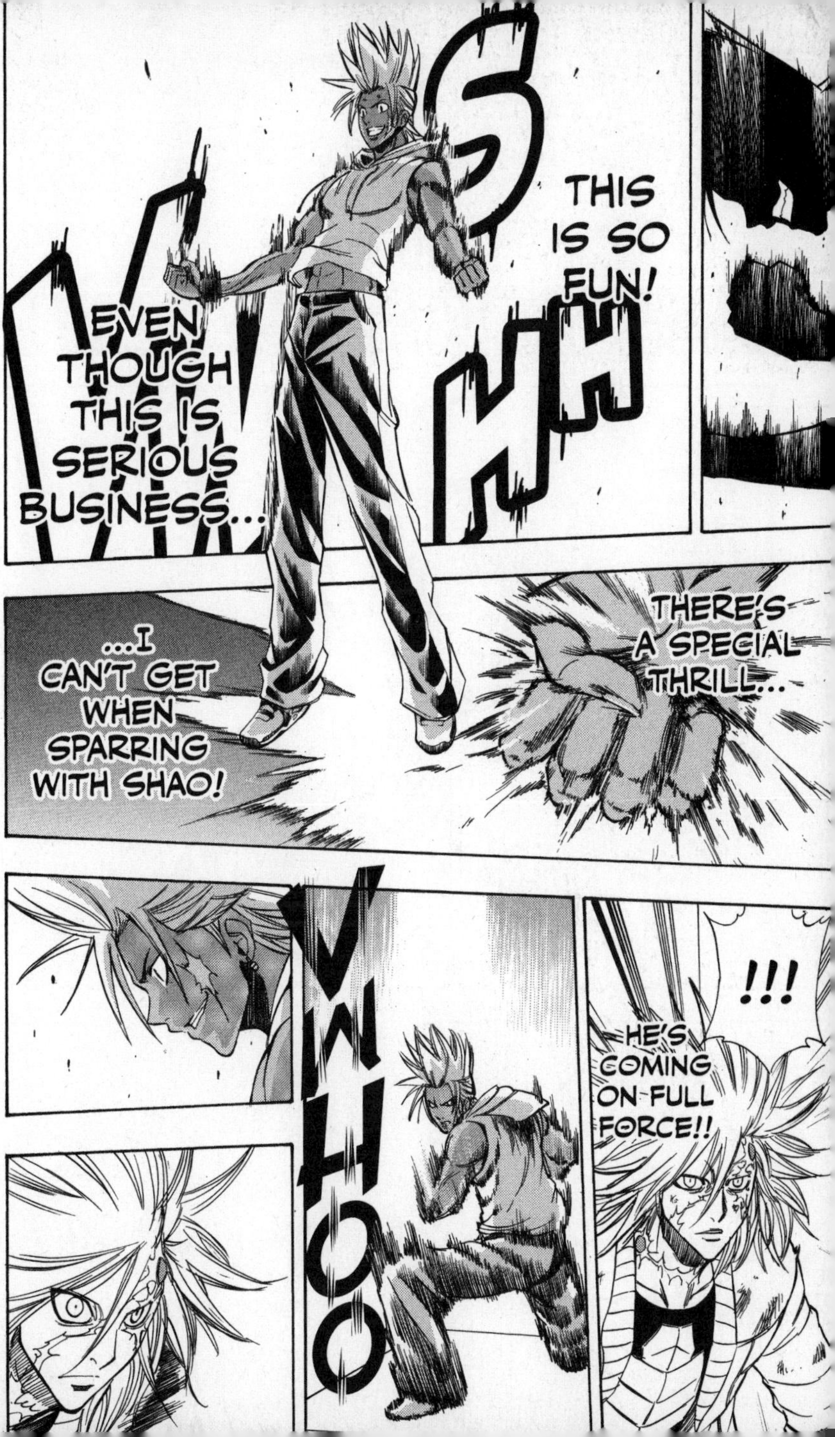
THIS IS SO FUN!
EVEN THOUGH THIS IS SERIOUS BUSINESS...
THERE'S A SPECIAL THRILL...
...I CAN'T GET WHEN SPARRING WITH SHAO!
!!!
HE'S COMING ON FULL FORCE!!

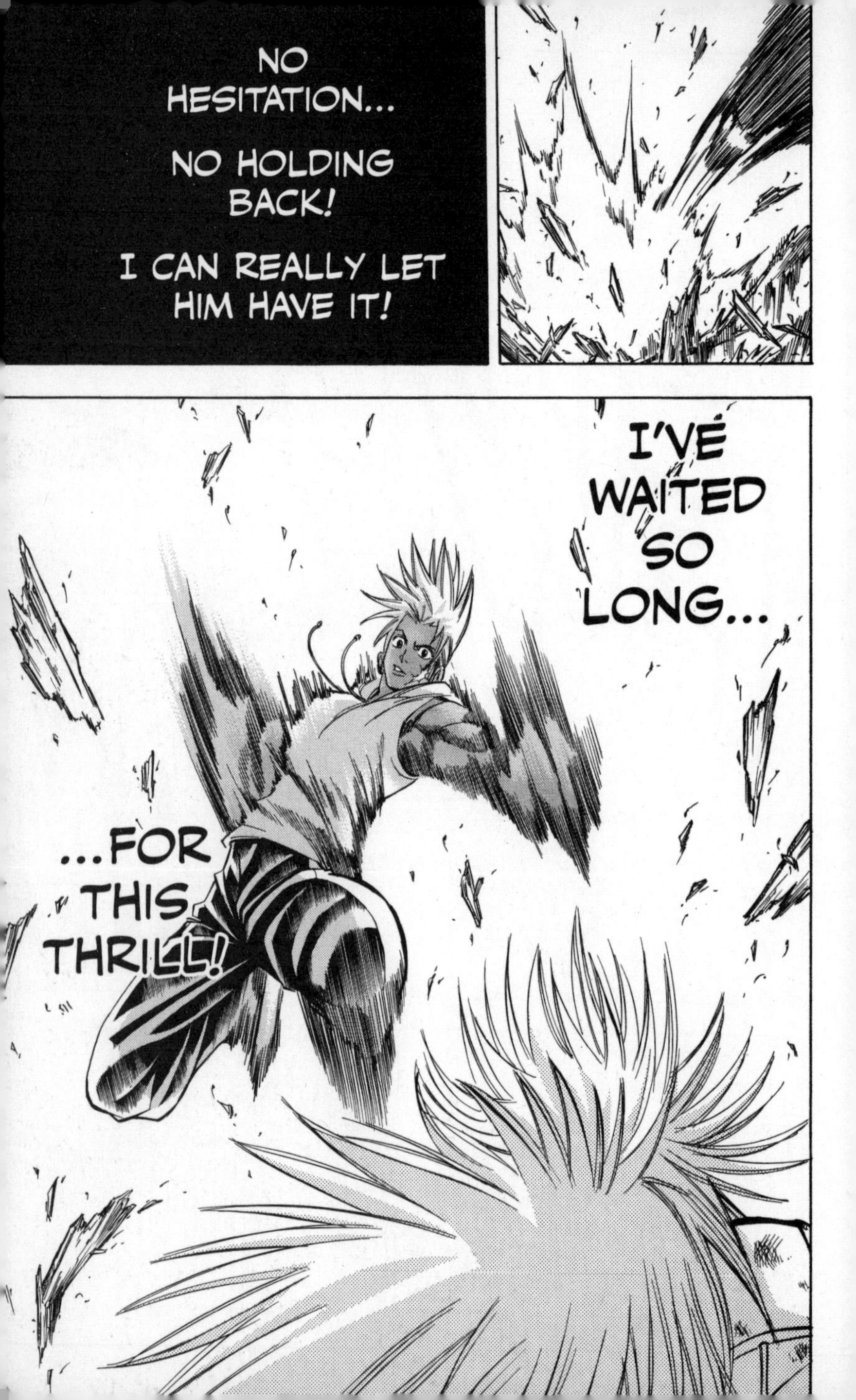
NO HESITATION...
NO HOLDING BACK!
I CAN REALLY LET HIM HAVE IT!
I'VE WAITED SO LONG...
...FOR THIS THRILL!

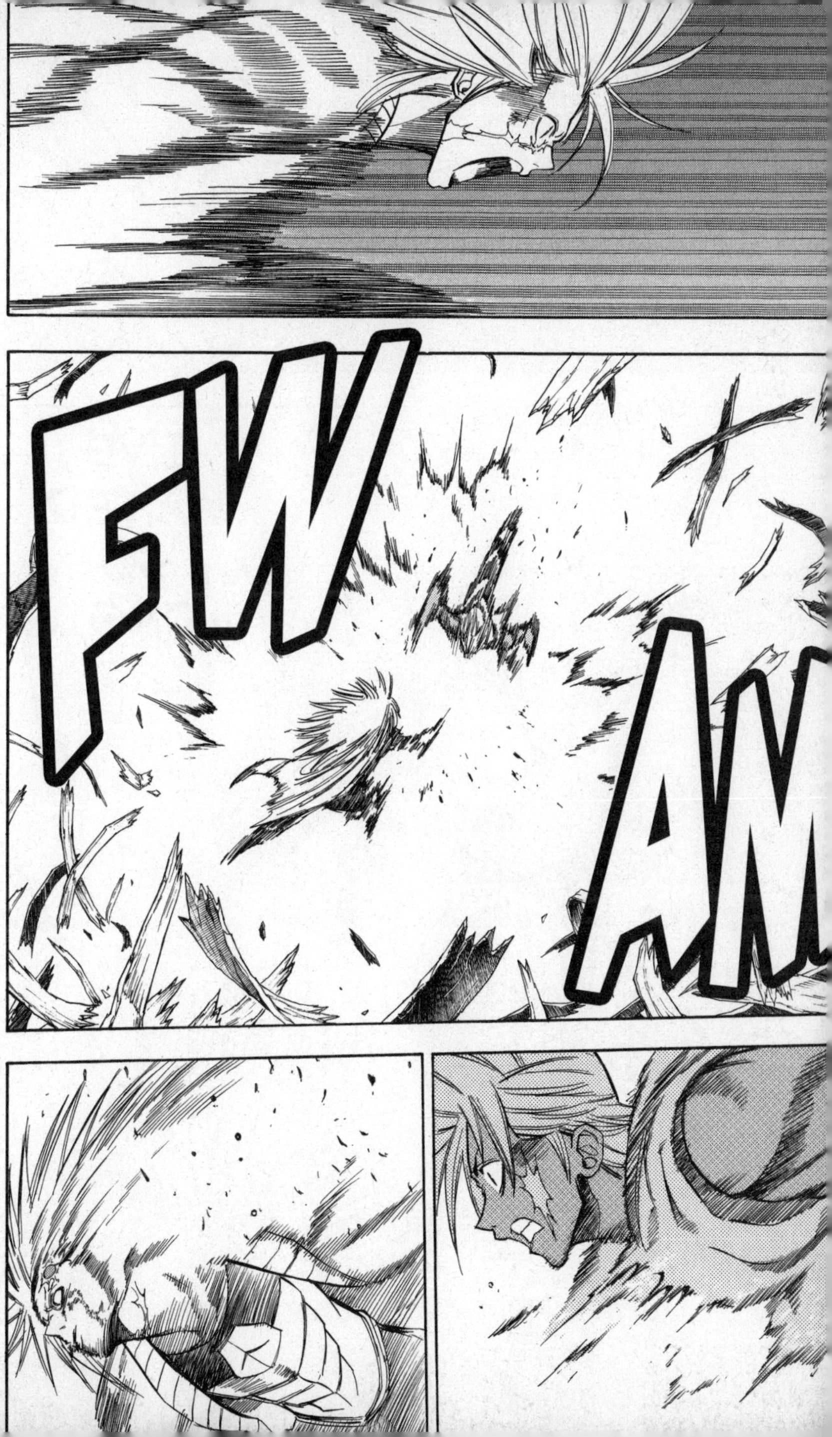
FW
AM

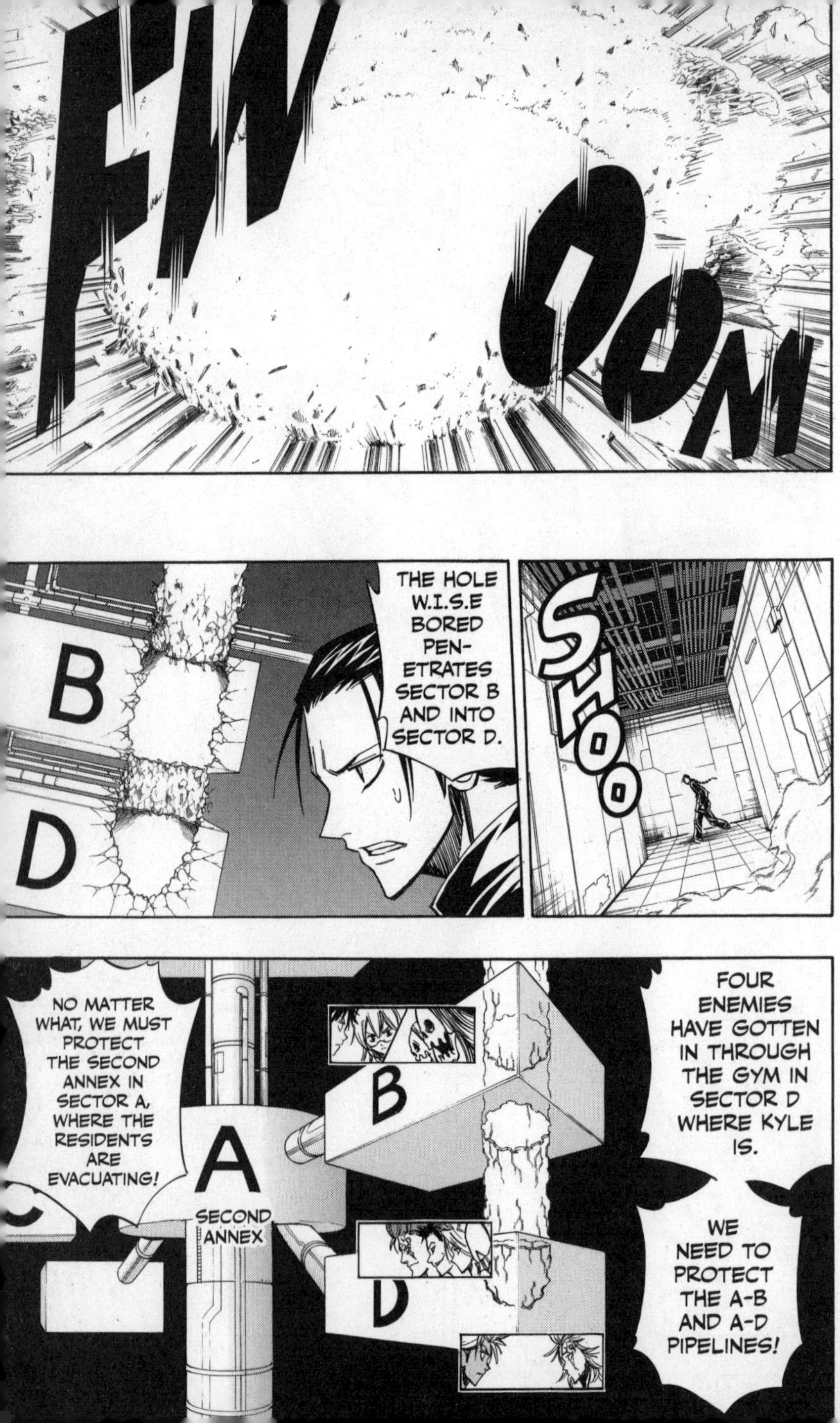
FWOOM
SHOOO
THE HOLE W.I.S.E BORED PEN-ETRATES SECTOR B AND INTO SECTOR D.
B
D
FOUR ENEMIES HAVE GOTTEN IN THROUGH THE GYM IN SECTOR D WHERE KYLE IS.
WE NEED TO PROTECT THE A-B AND A-D PIPELINES!
NO MATTER WHAT, WE MUST PROTECT THE SECOND ANNEX IN SECTOR A, WHERE THE RESIDENTS ARE EVACUATING!
B
A
SECOND ANNEX
D

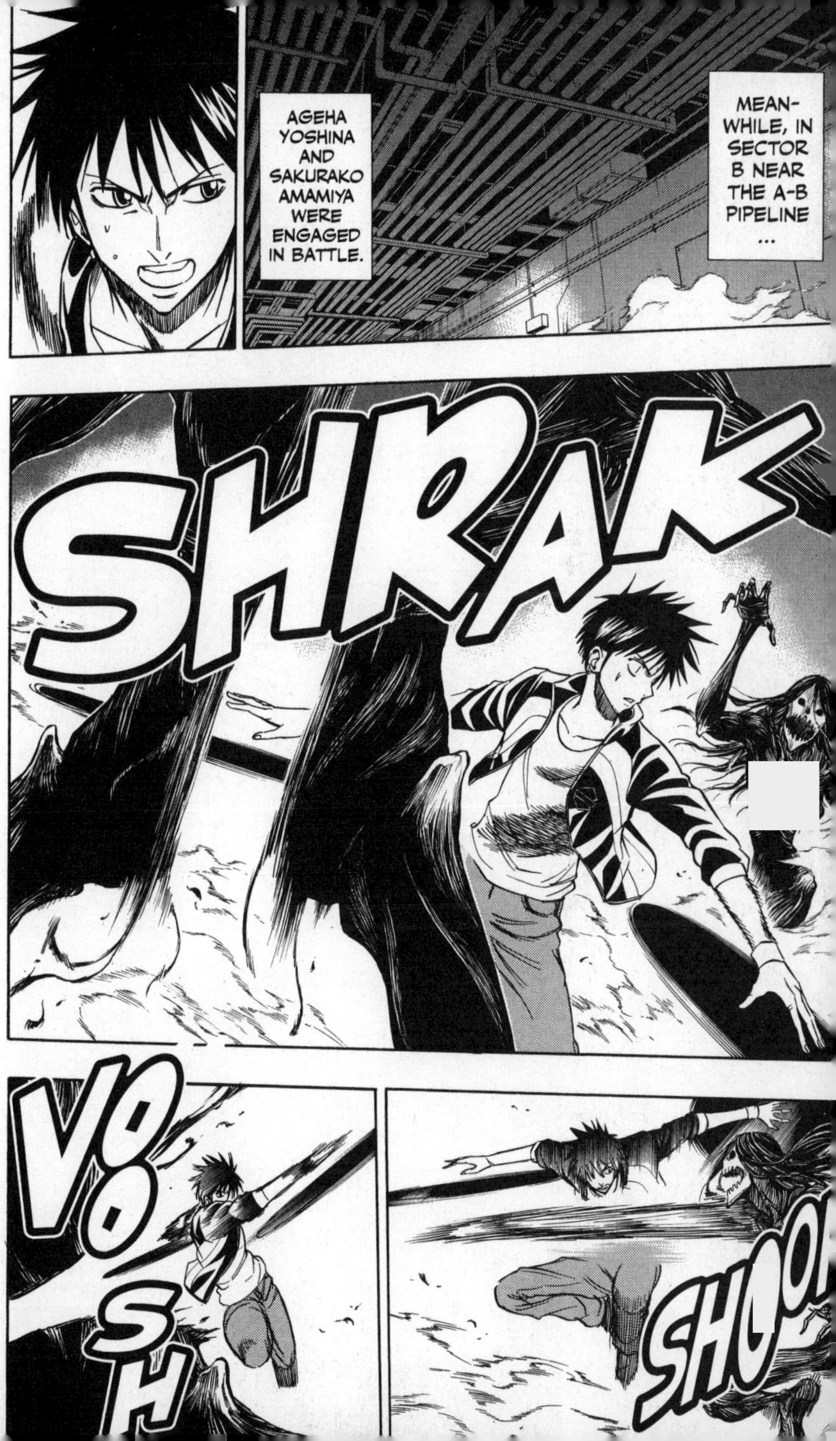
MEAN-WHILE, IN SECTOR B NEAR THE A-B PIPELINE ...
AGEHA YOSHINA AND SAKURAKO AMAMIYA WERE ENGAGED IN BATTLE.
SHRAK
SHOO
VOOSH

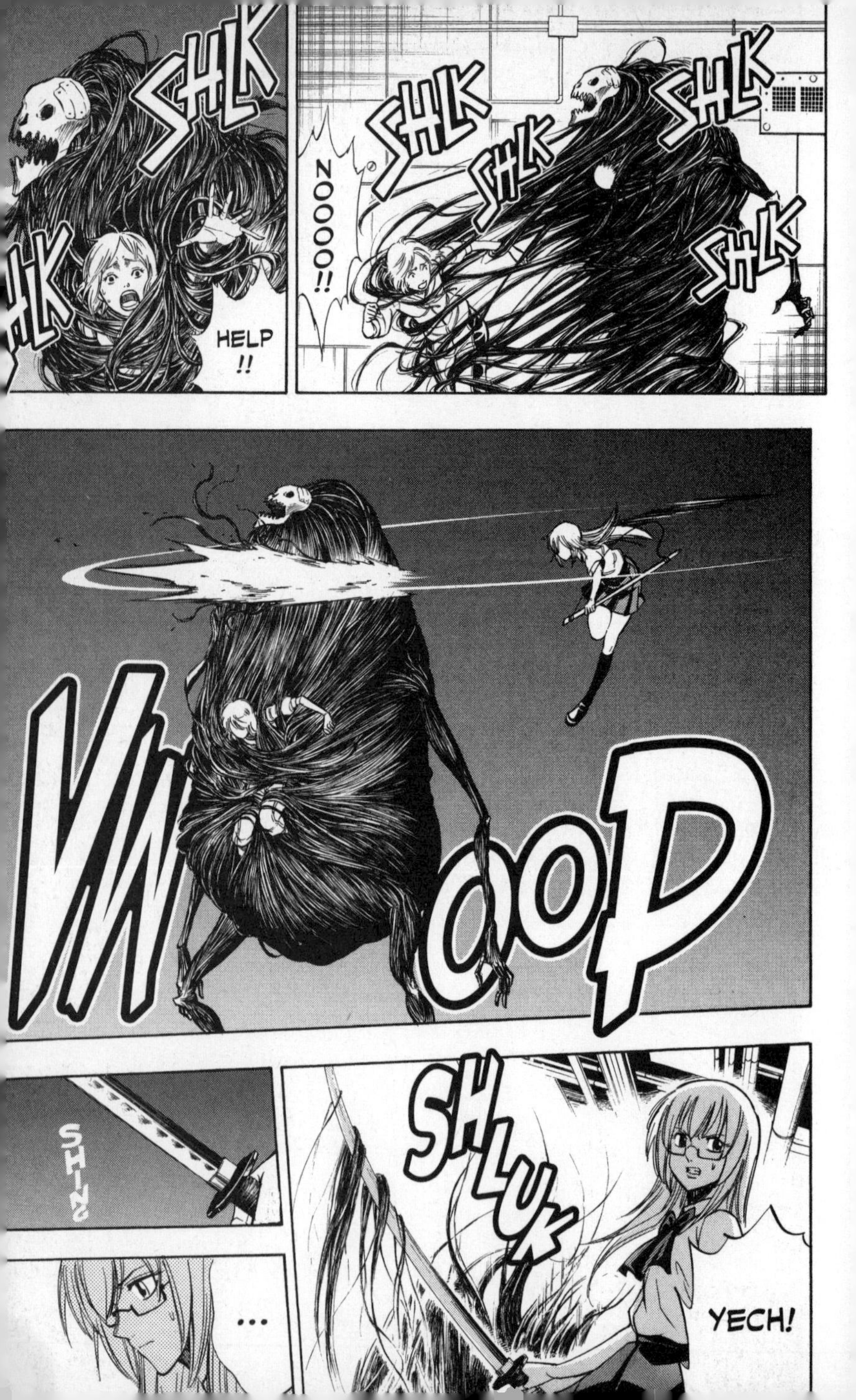
SHLK
SHLK
SHLK
SHLK
NOOOOO!!
SHLK
SHLK
HELP!!
WOOP
SHLUK
YECH!
SHING
...

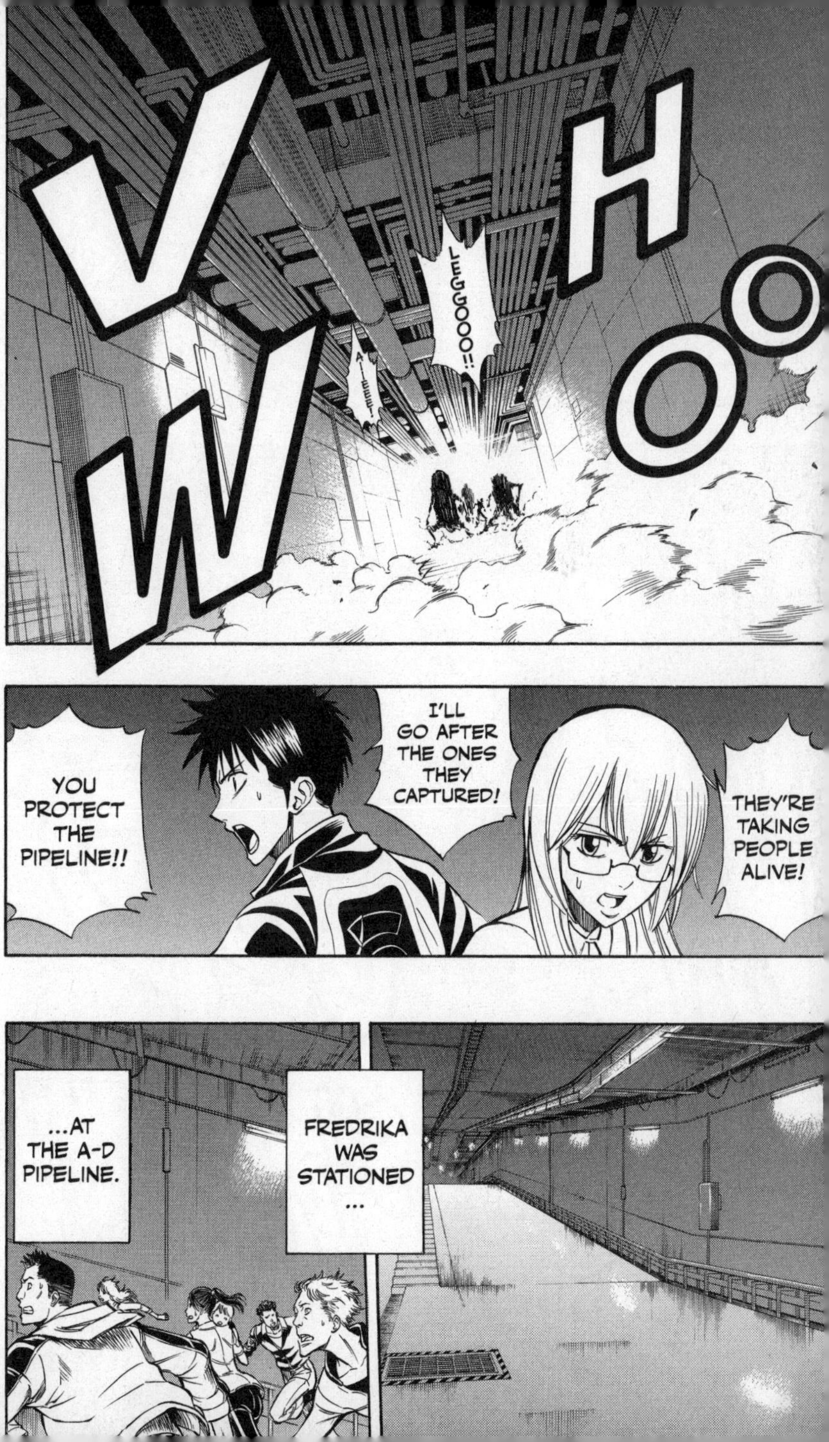
VWHOOO
LEGGOOO!!
AIIEEE!
THEY'RE TAKING PEOPLE ALIVE!
I'LL GO AFTER THE ONES THEY CAPTURED!
YOU PROTECT THE PIPELINE!!
FREDRIKA WAS STATIONED ...
...AT THE A-D PIPELINE.

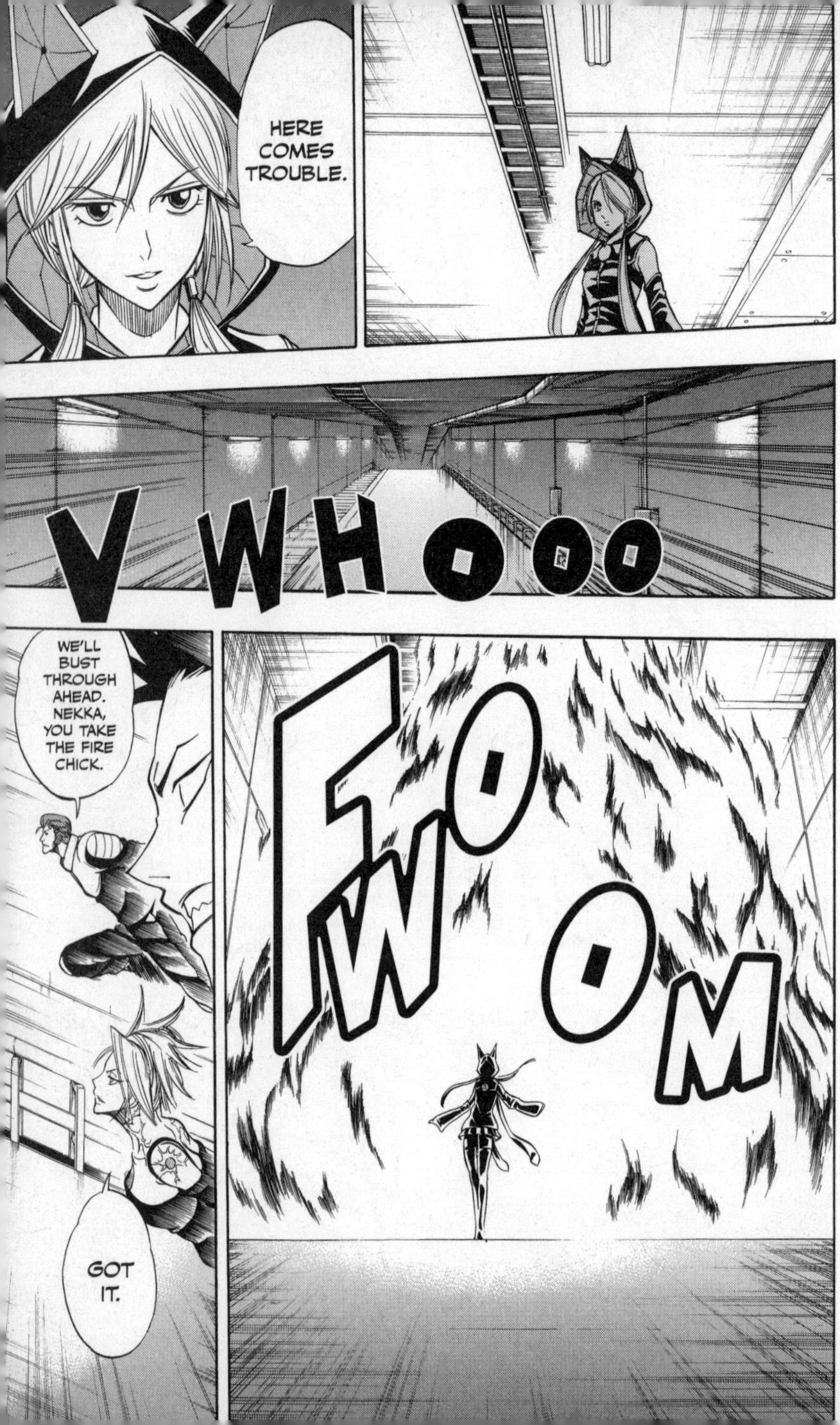
HERE COMES TROUBLE.
VWHOOO
FWOOM
WE'LL BUST THROUGH AHEAD. NEKKA, YOU TAKE THE FIRE CHICK.
GOT IT.

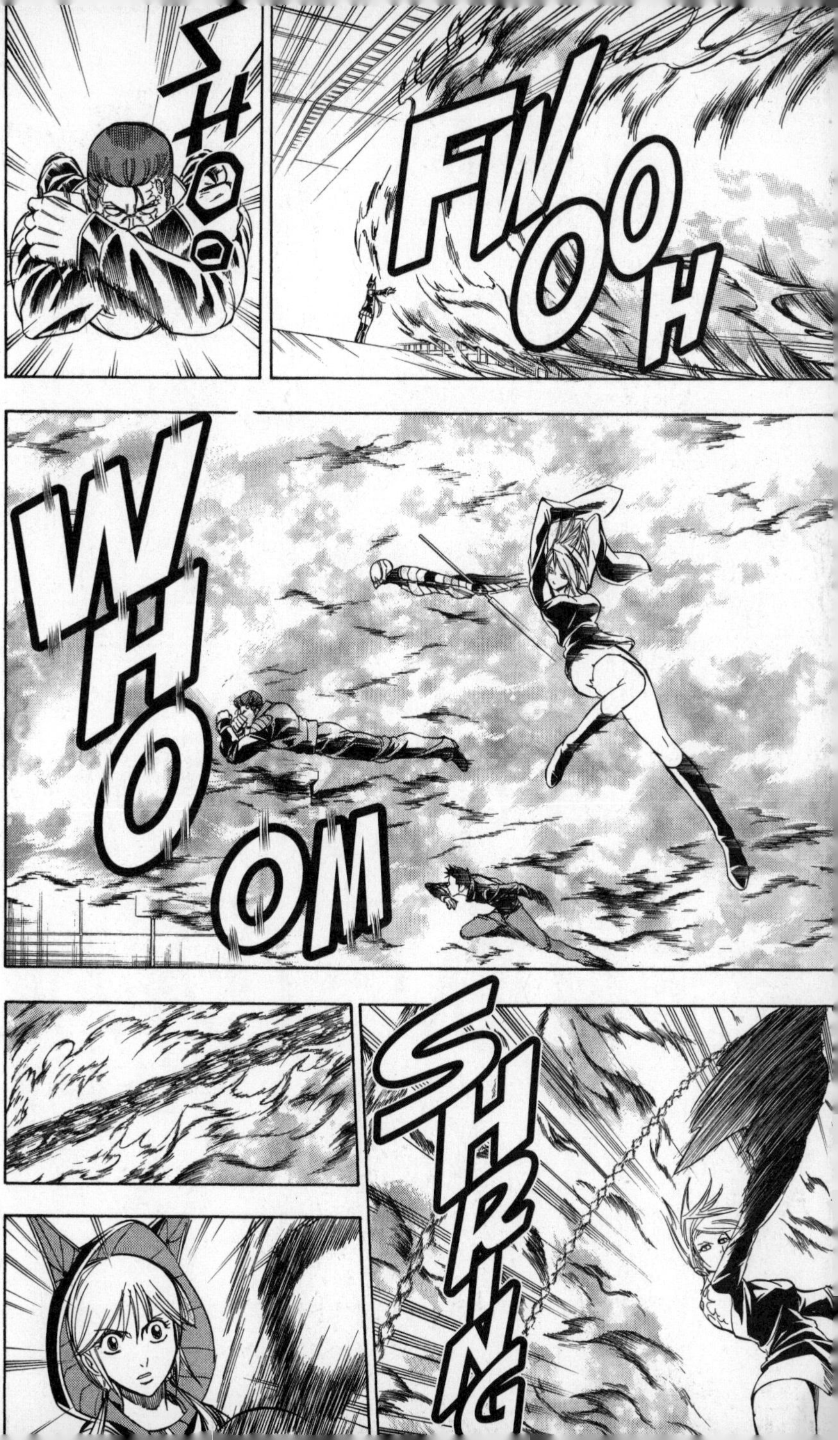
FWOOOH
SHOOO
WHOOOM
SHRING

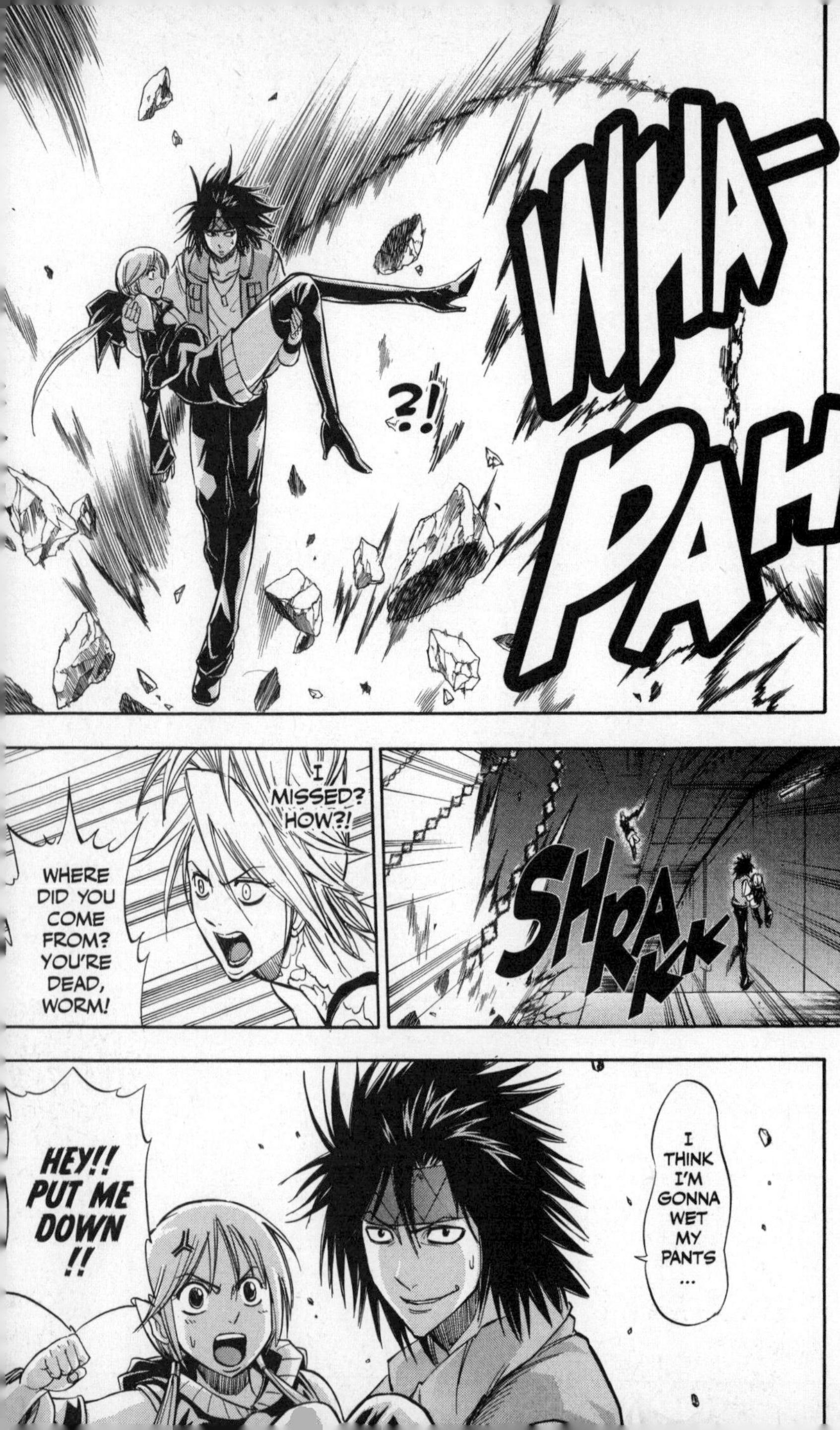
WHA-PAH
?!
SHRAKKK
I MISSED? HOW?!
WHERE DID YOU COME FROM? YOU'RE DEAD, WORM!
I THINK I'M GONNA WET MY PANTS...
HEY!! PUT ME DOWN!!

Mutters and mumblings...

I'VE BEEN DOING A LOT OF IMPULSE BUYING OF GAMES, MOVIES, AND DVDS.

THE GAMES ARE STARTING TO PILE UP.

GOTTA FOCUS ON WORK...BUT I'M LOOKING FORWARD TO PLAYING ZOMBIELAND AND GOONIES.

PSYREN

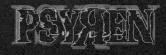

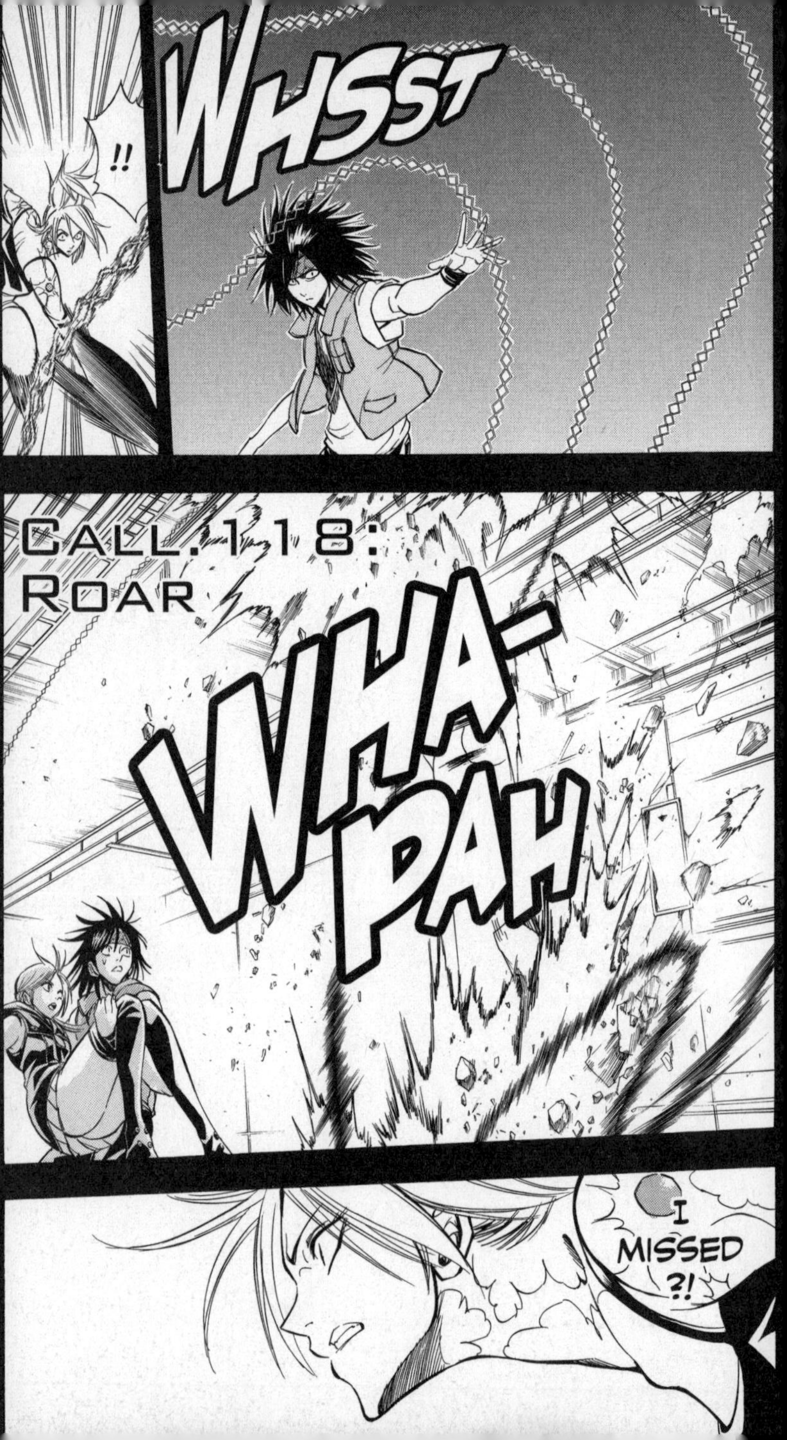
WHSST
!!
CALL. 118:
ROAR
WHA-PAH
I MISSED ?!

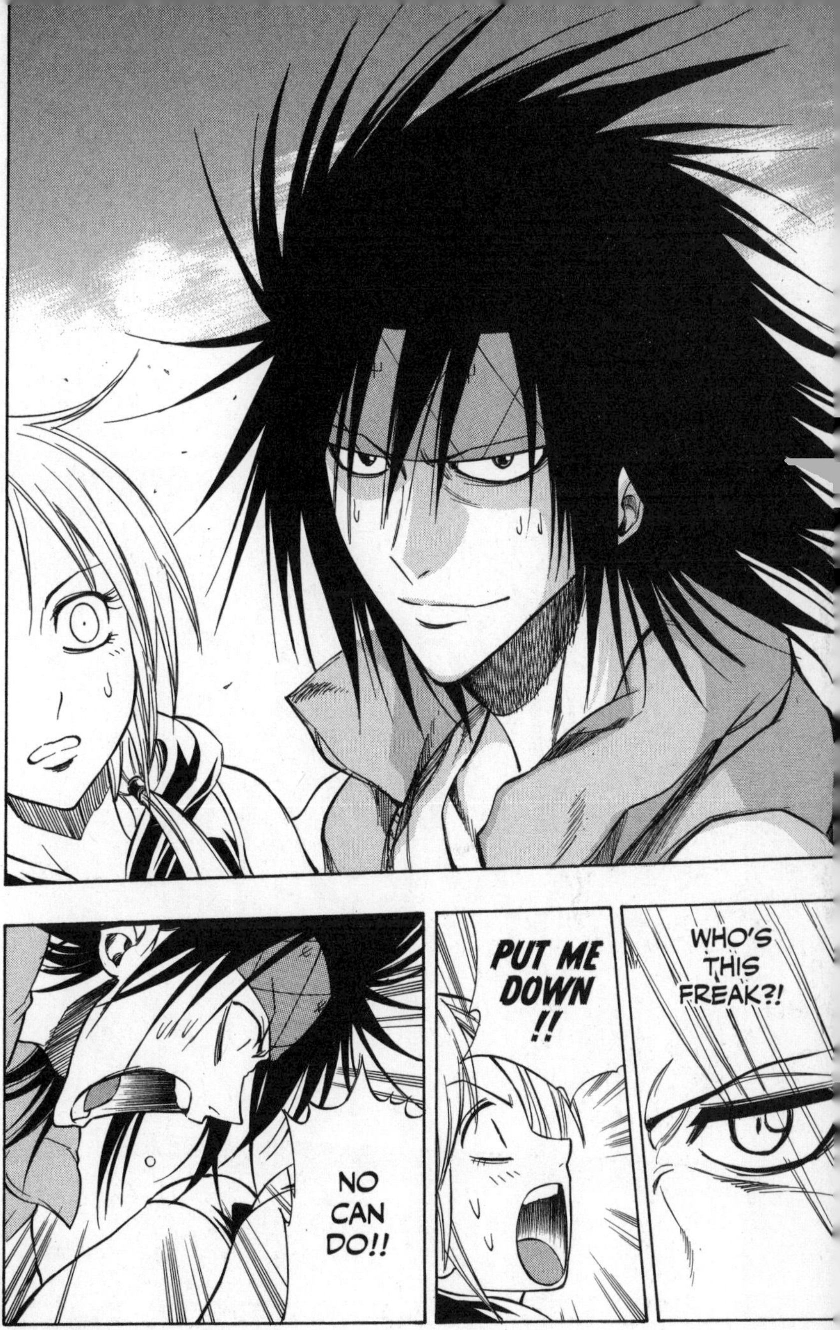
WHO'S THIS FREAK?!
PUT ME DOWN!!
NO CAN DO!!

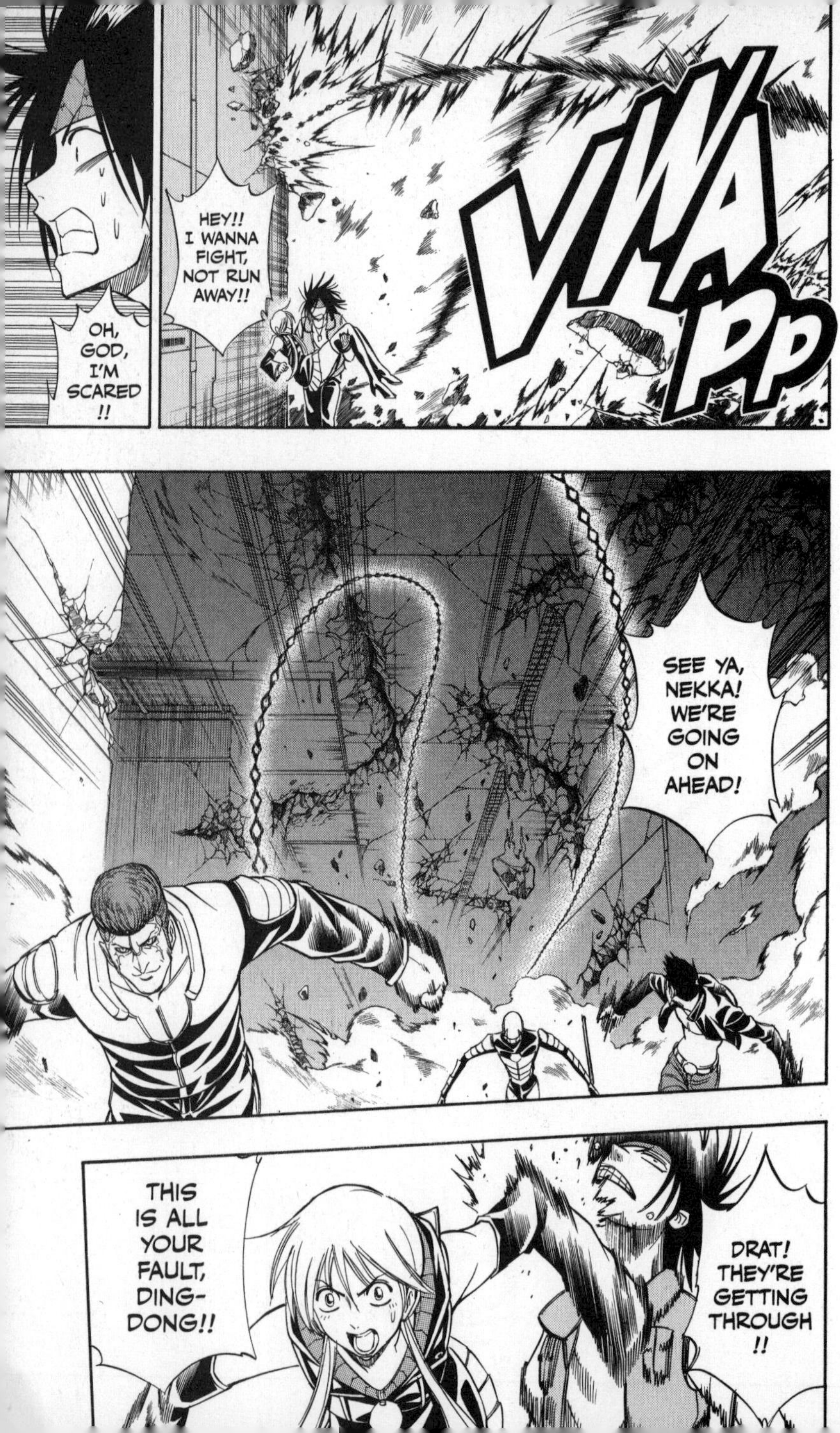
VWAPP
HEY!! I WANNA FIGHT, NOT RUN AWAY!!
OH, GOD, I'M SCARED!!
SEE YA, NEKKA! WE'RE GOING ON AHEAD!
DRAT! THEY'RE GETTING THROUGH!!
THIS IS ALL YOUR FAULT, DING-DONG!!

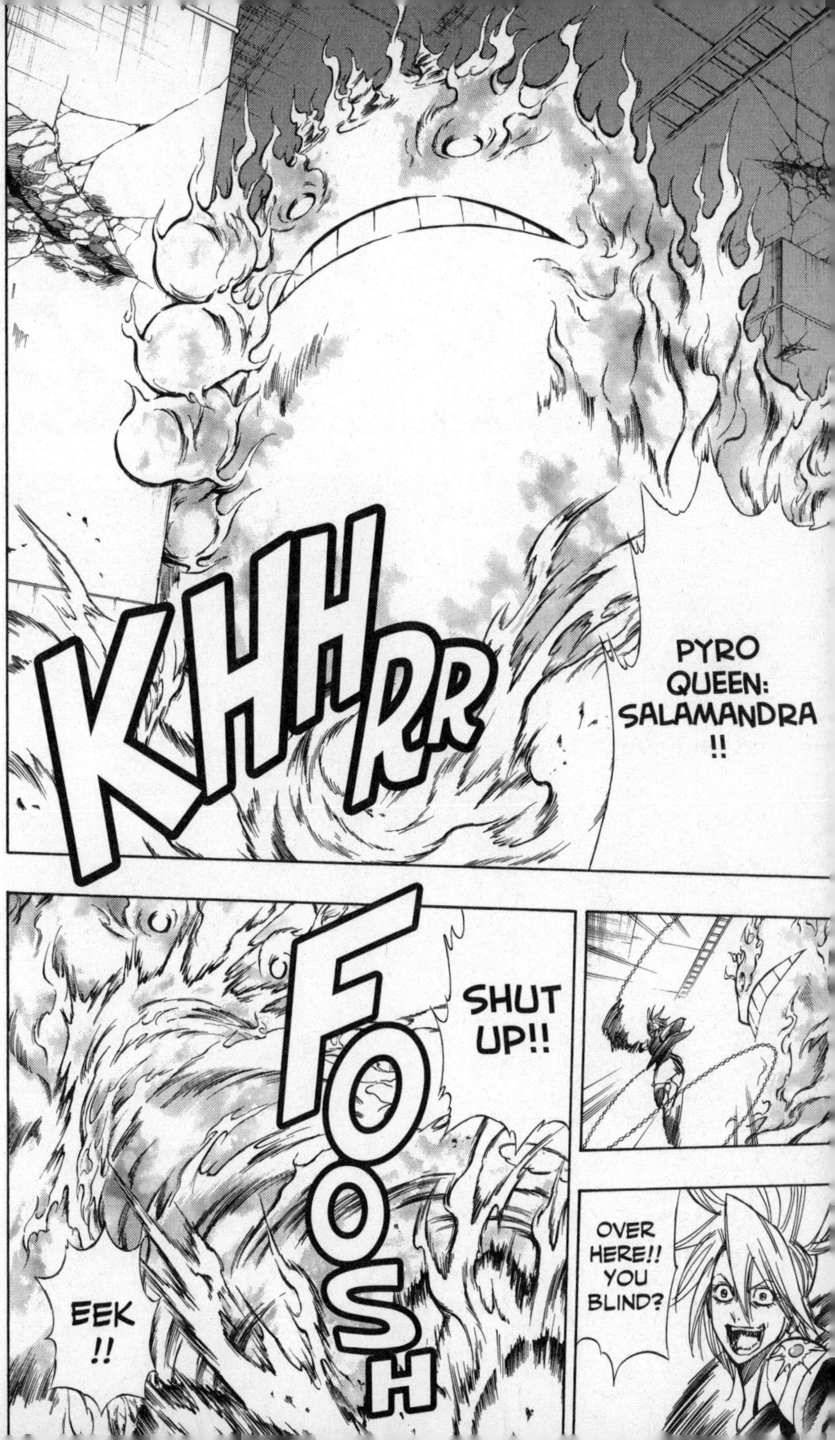
PYRO QUEEN: SALAMANDRA!!
KHHRR
OVER HERE!! YOU BLIND?
SHUT UP!!
FOOSH
EEK!!

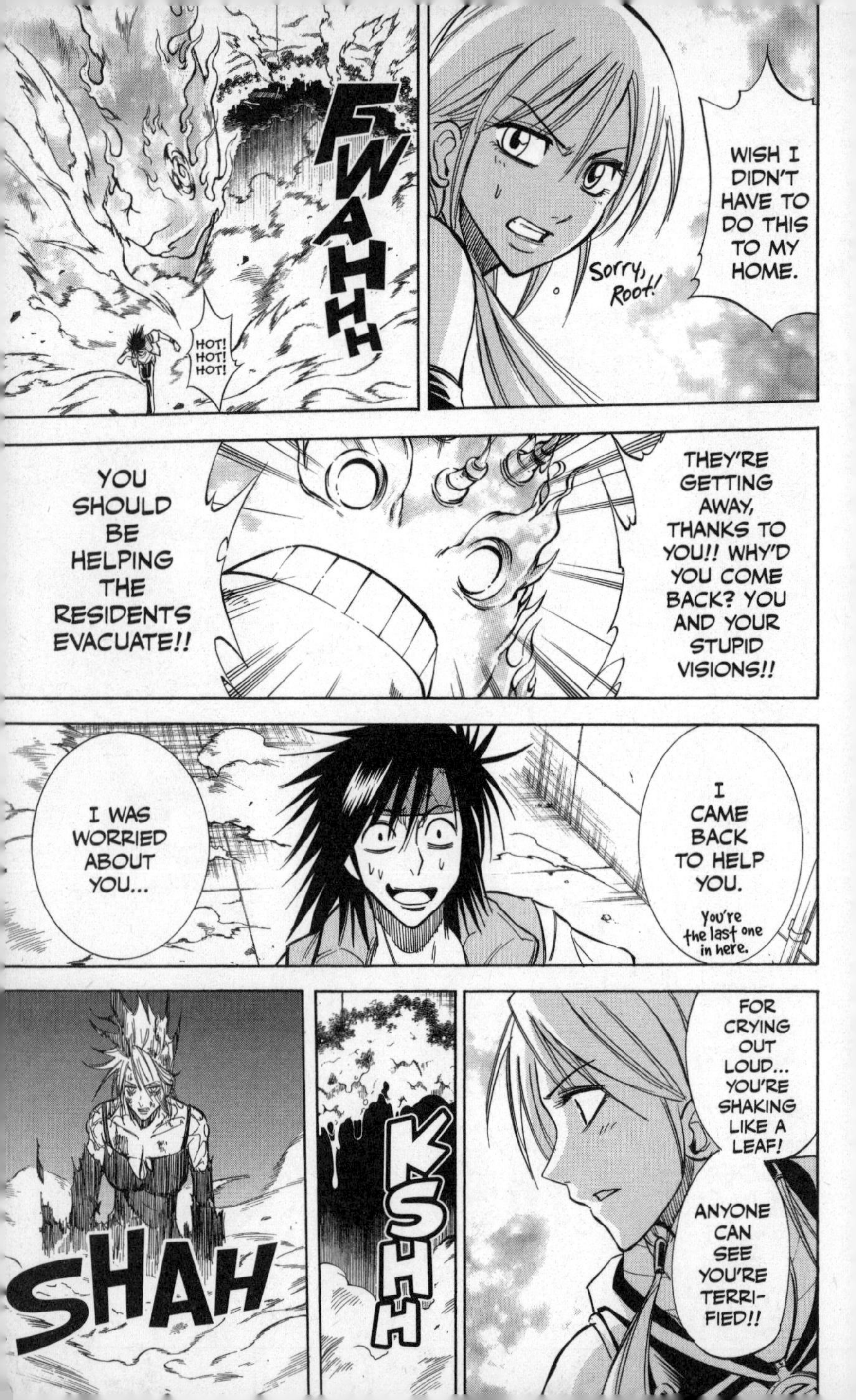
WISH I DIDN'T HAVE TO DO THIS TO MY HOME.
Sorry, Root!
FWAHHH
HOT! HOT! HOT!
THEY'RE GETTING AWAY, THANKS TO YOU!! WHY'D YOU COME BACK? YOU AND YOUR STUPID VISIONS!!
YOU SHOULD BE HELPING THE RESIDENTS EVACUATE!!
I CAME BACK TO HELP YOU.
You're the last one in here.
I WAS WORRIED ABOUT YOU...
FOR CRYING OUT LOUD... YOU'RE SHAKING LIKE A LEAF!
ANYONE CAN SEE YOU'RE TERRIFIED!!
KSHHH
SHAH

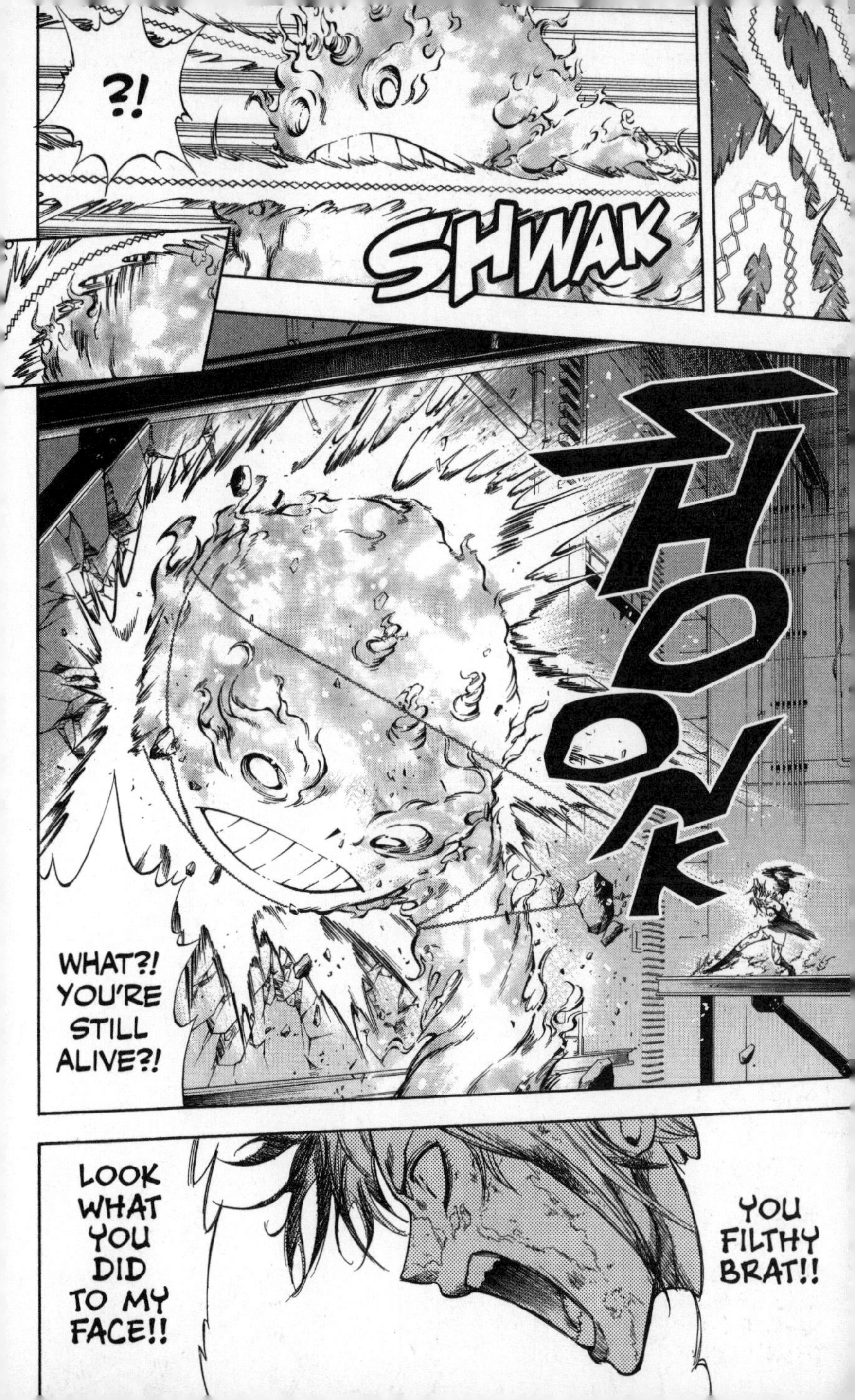
?!
SHWAK
THOOK
WHAT?! YOU'RE STILL ALIVE?!
YOU FILTHY BRAT!!
LOOK WHAT YOU DID TO MY FACE!!

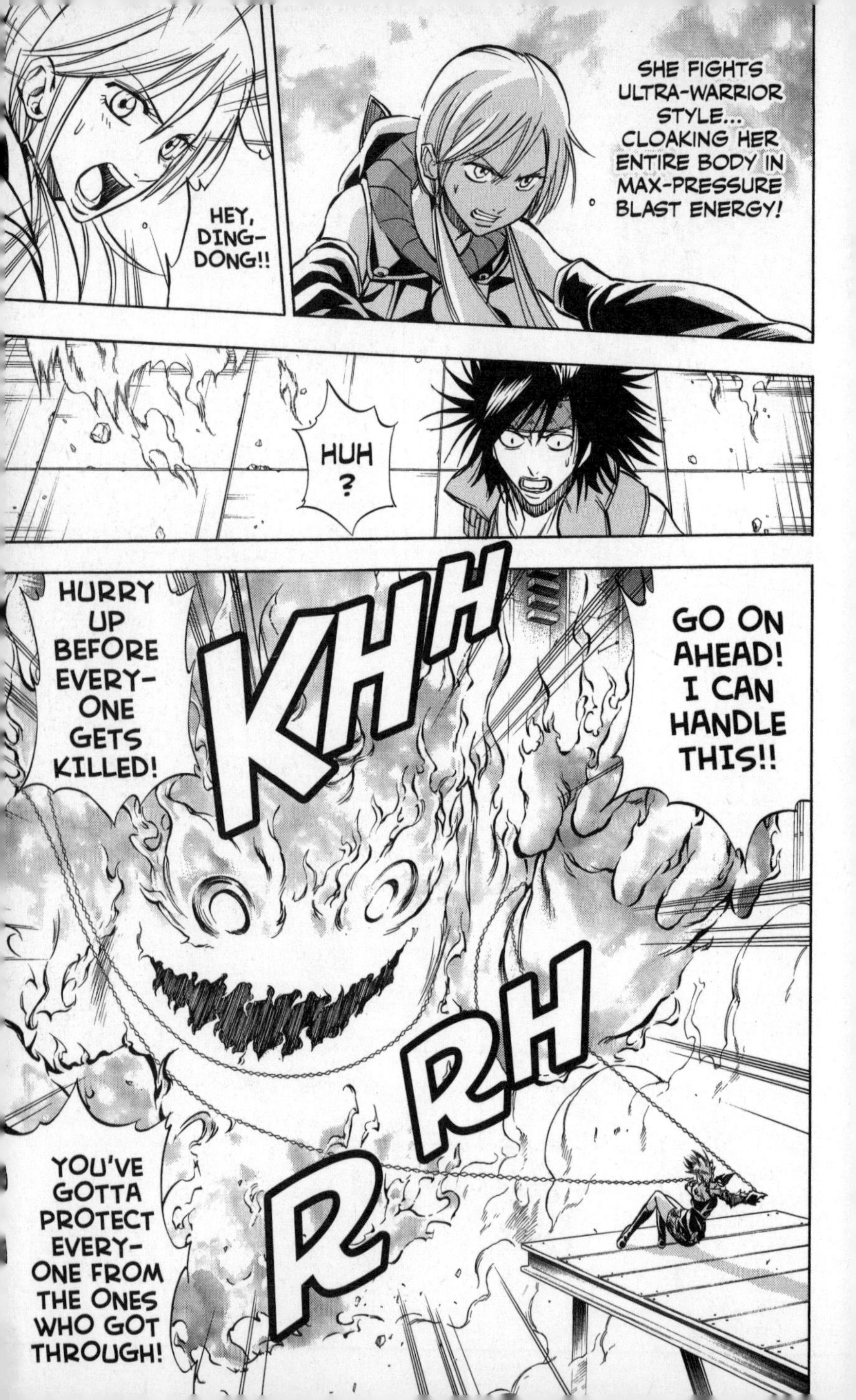
SHE FIGHTS ULTRA-WARRIOR STYLE... CLOAKING HER ENTIRE BODY IN MAX-PRESSURE BLAST ENERGY!
HEY, DING-DONG!!
HUH ?
GO ON AHEAD! I CAN HANDLE THIS!!
KHH
RRH
HURRY UP BEFORE EVERY-ONE GETS KILLED!
YOU'VE GOTTA PROTECT EVERY-ONE FROM THE ONES WHO GOT THROUGH!

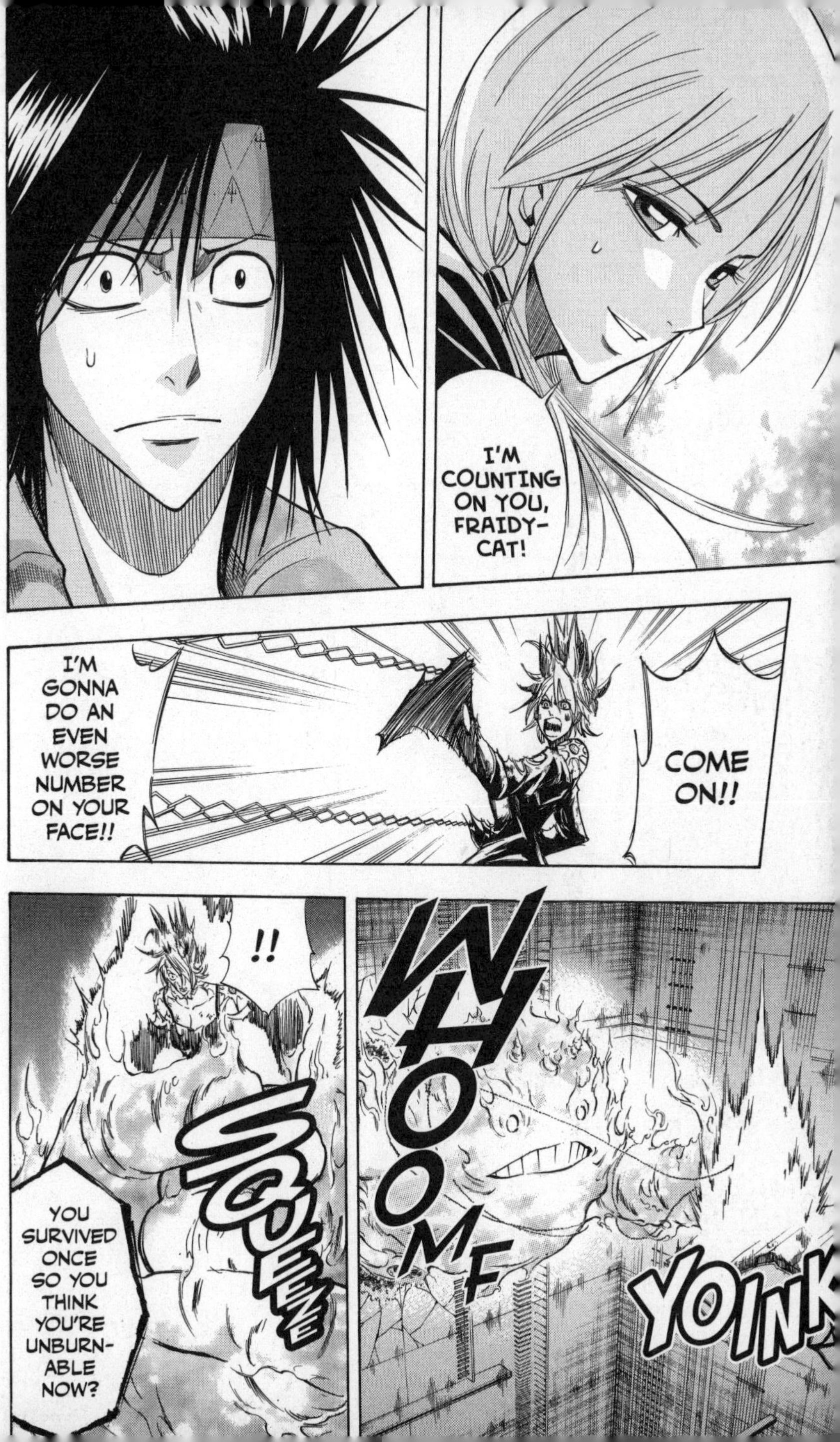
I'M COUNTING ON YOU, FRAIDY-CAT!
COME ON!!
I'M GONNA DO AN EVEN WORSE NUMBER ON YOUR FACE!!
WHOOMF
YOINK
!!
SQUEEZE
YOU SURVIVED ONCE SO YOU THINK YOU'RE UNBURN-ABLE NOW?

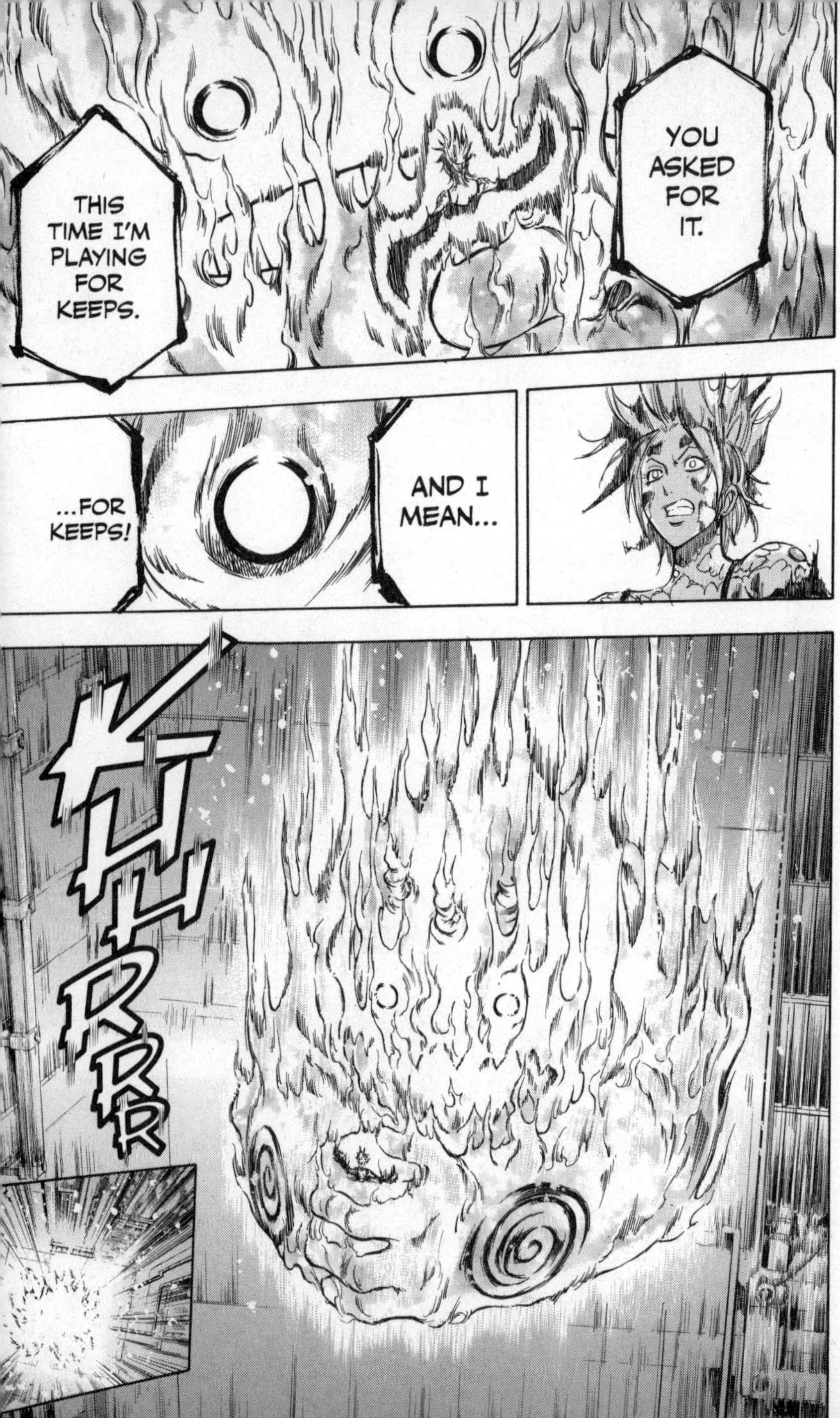
YOU ASKED FOR IT.
THIS TIME I'M PLAYING FOR KEEPS.
AND I MEAN...
...FOR KEEPS!
WHIRRR

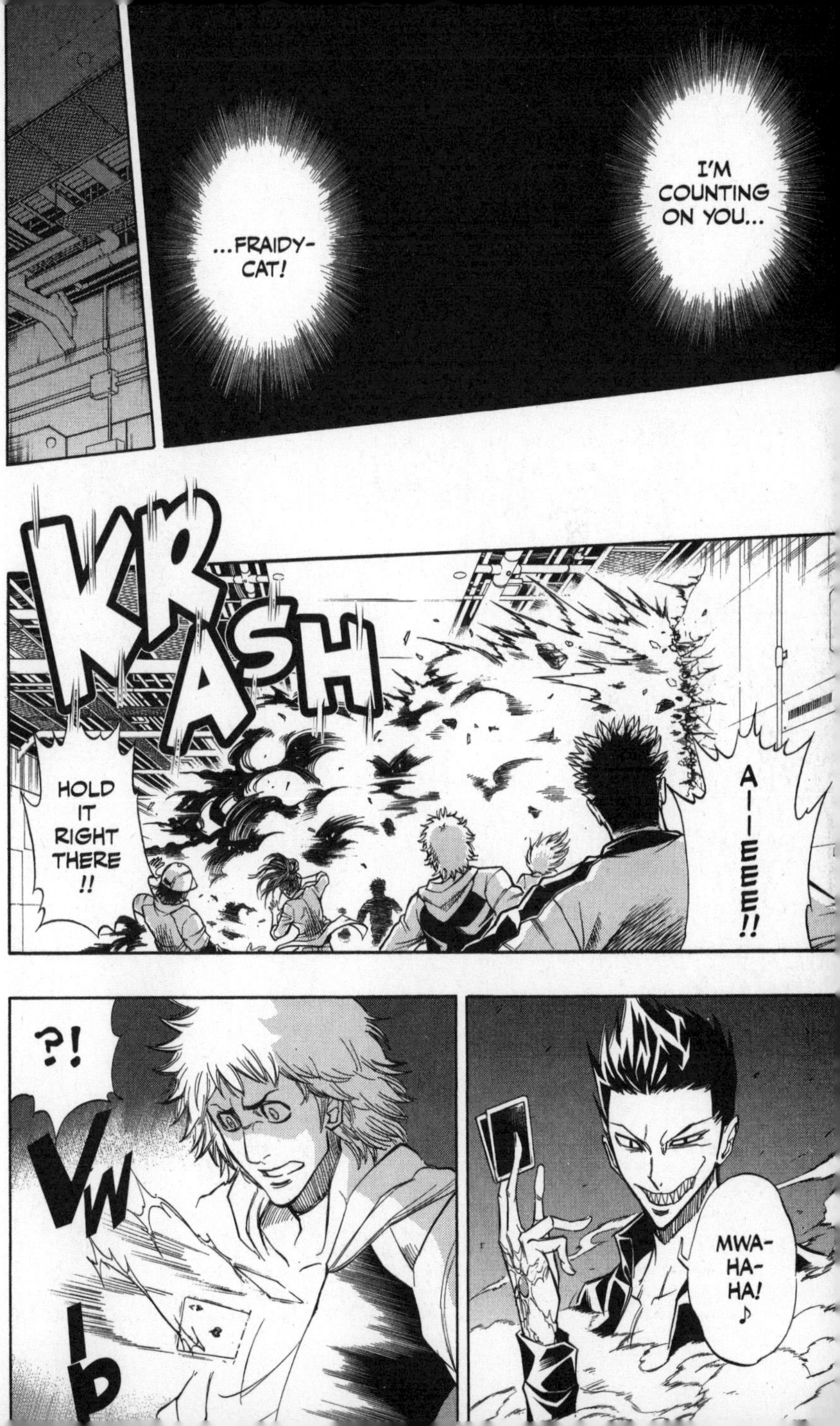
I'M COUNTING ON YOU...
...FRAIDY-CAT!
KRASH
AIIEEE!!
HOLD IT RIGHT THERE!!
MWA-HA-HA! ♪
?!
VWIP

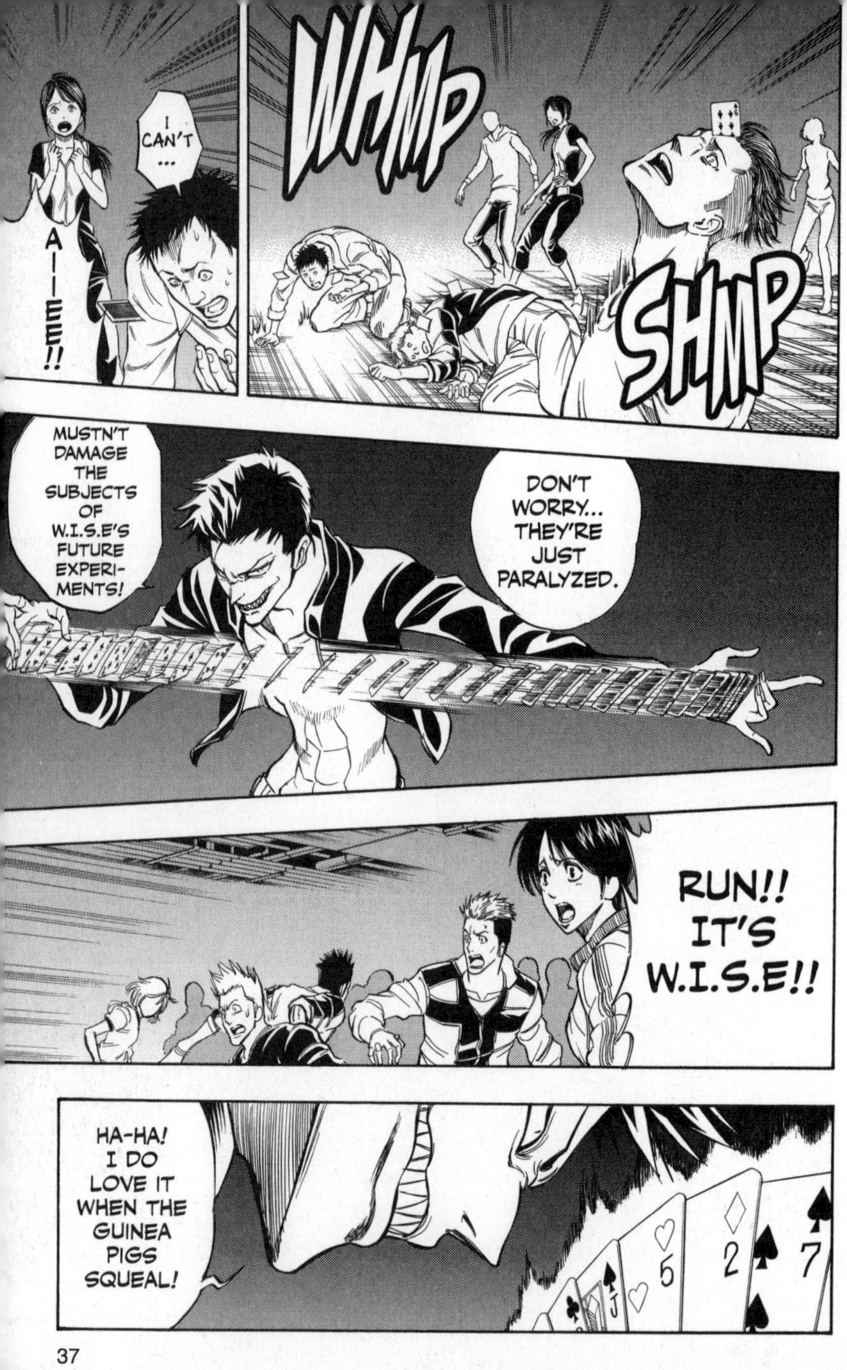
WHMP
SHMP
I CAN'T ...
AIIEEE!!
DON'T WORRY... THEY'RE JUST PARALYZED.
MUSTN'T DAMAGE THE SUBJECTS OF W.I.S.E'S FUTURE EXPERIMENTS!
RUN!! IT'S W.I.S.E!!
HA-HA! I DO LOVE IT WHEN THE GUINEA PIGS SQUEAL!

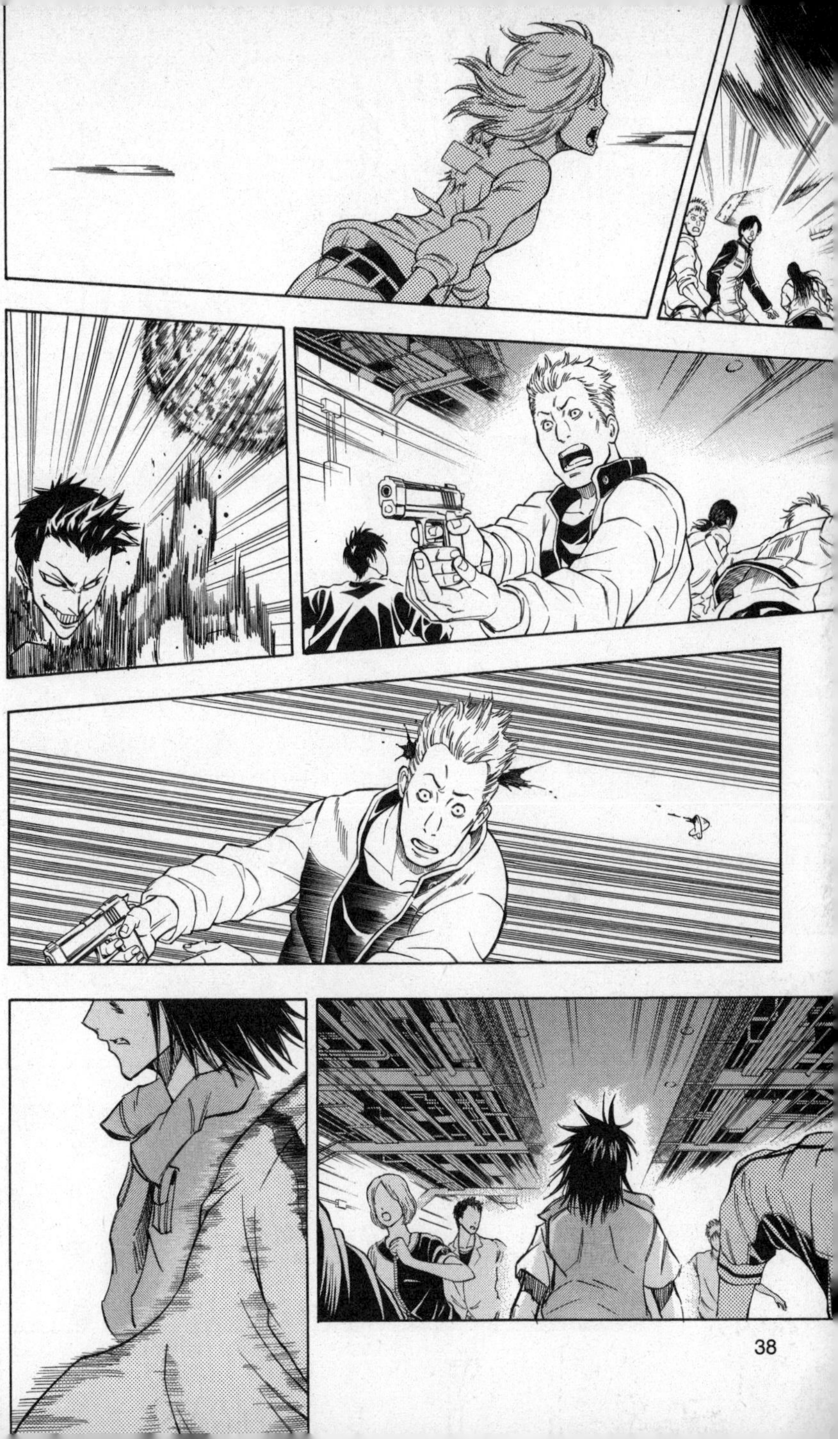

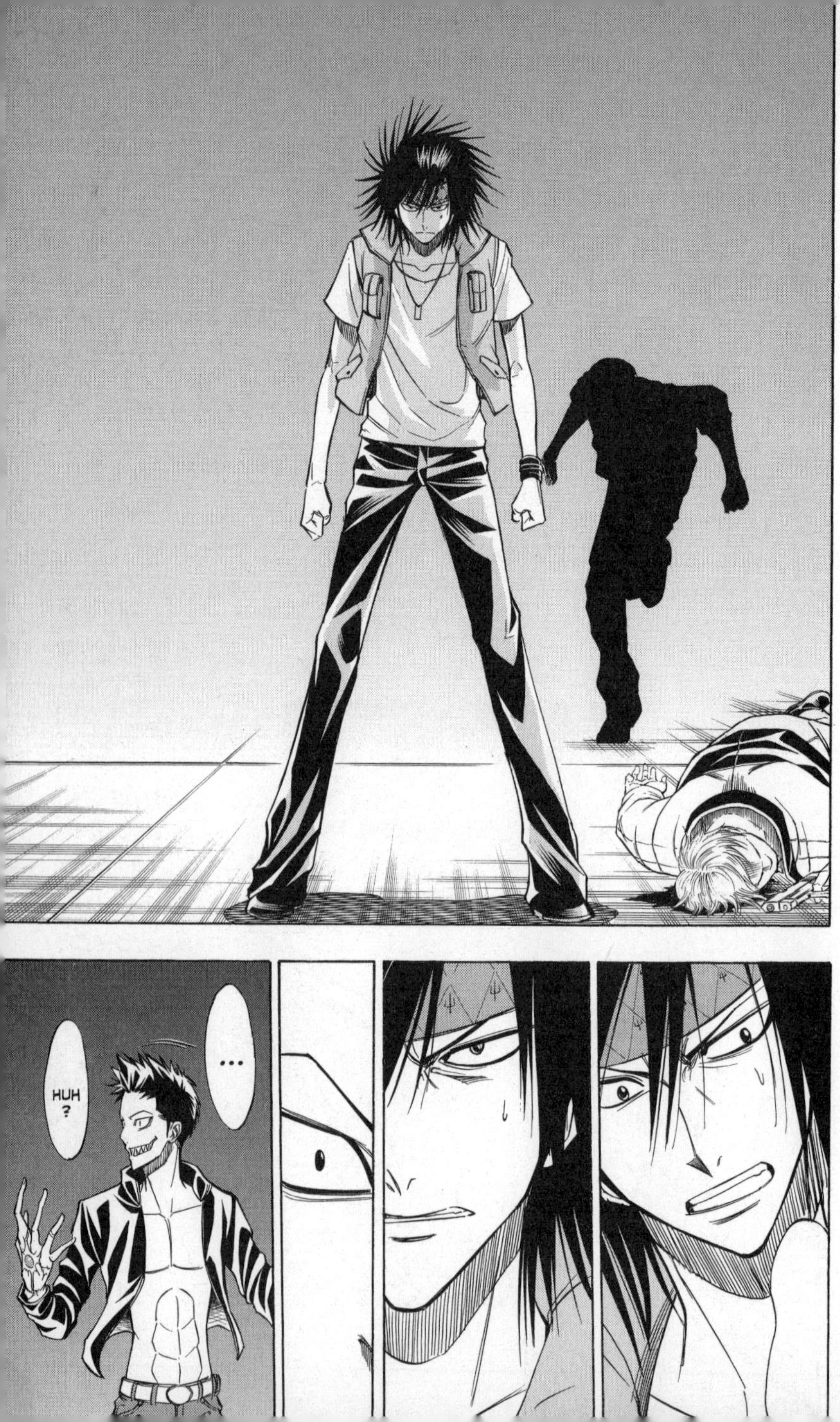
...
HUH?

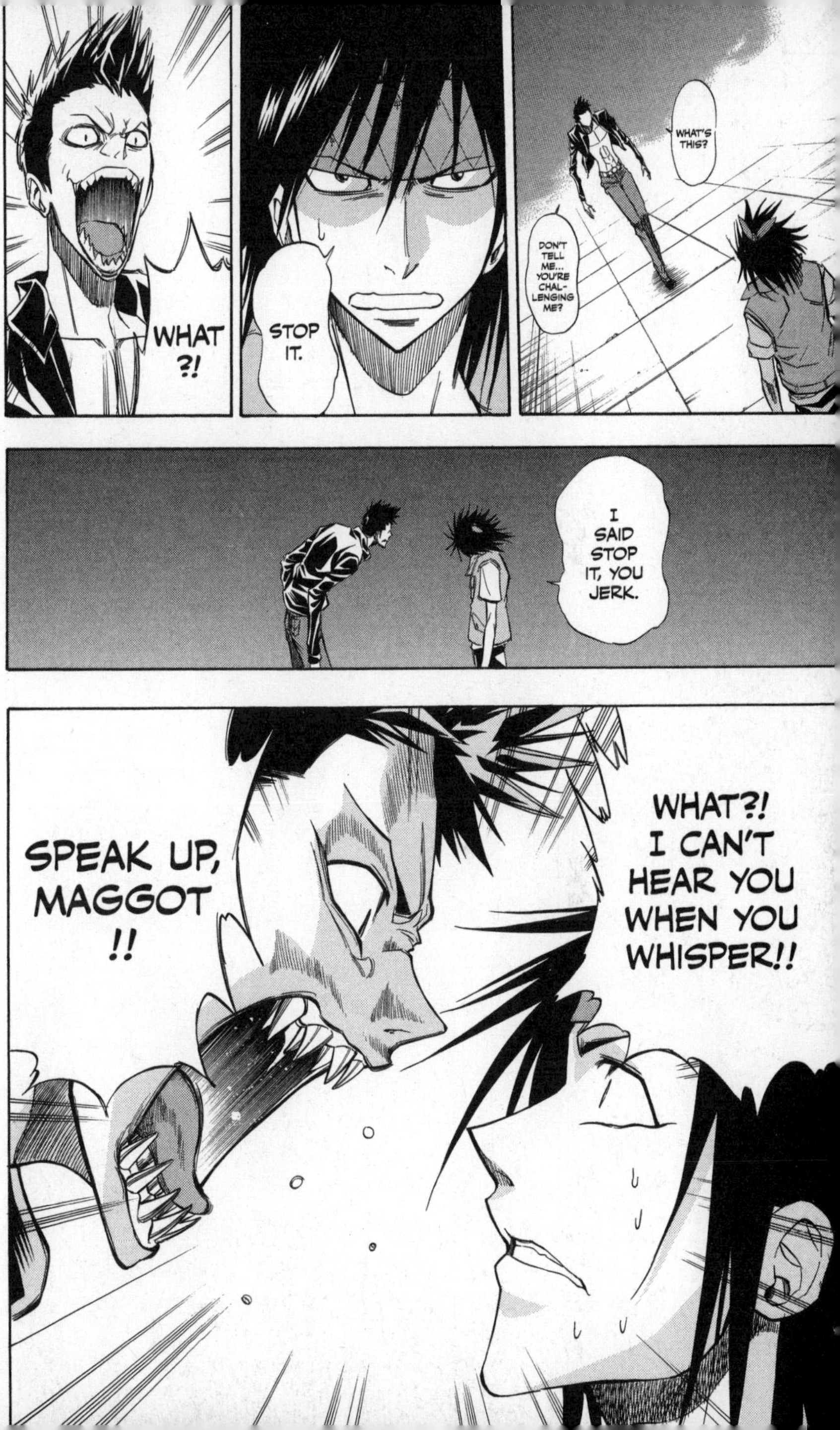
WHAT'S THIS?
DON'T TELL ME... YOU'RE CHAL-LENGING ME?
STOP IT.
WHAT ?!
I SAID STOP IT, YOU JERK.
WHAT?! I CAN'T HEAR YOU WHEN YOU WHISPER!!
SPEAK UP, MAGGOT !!

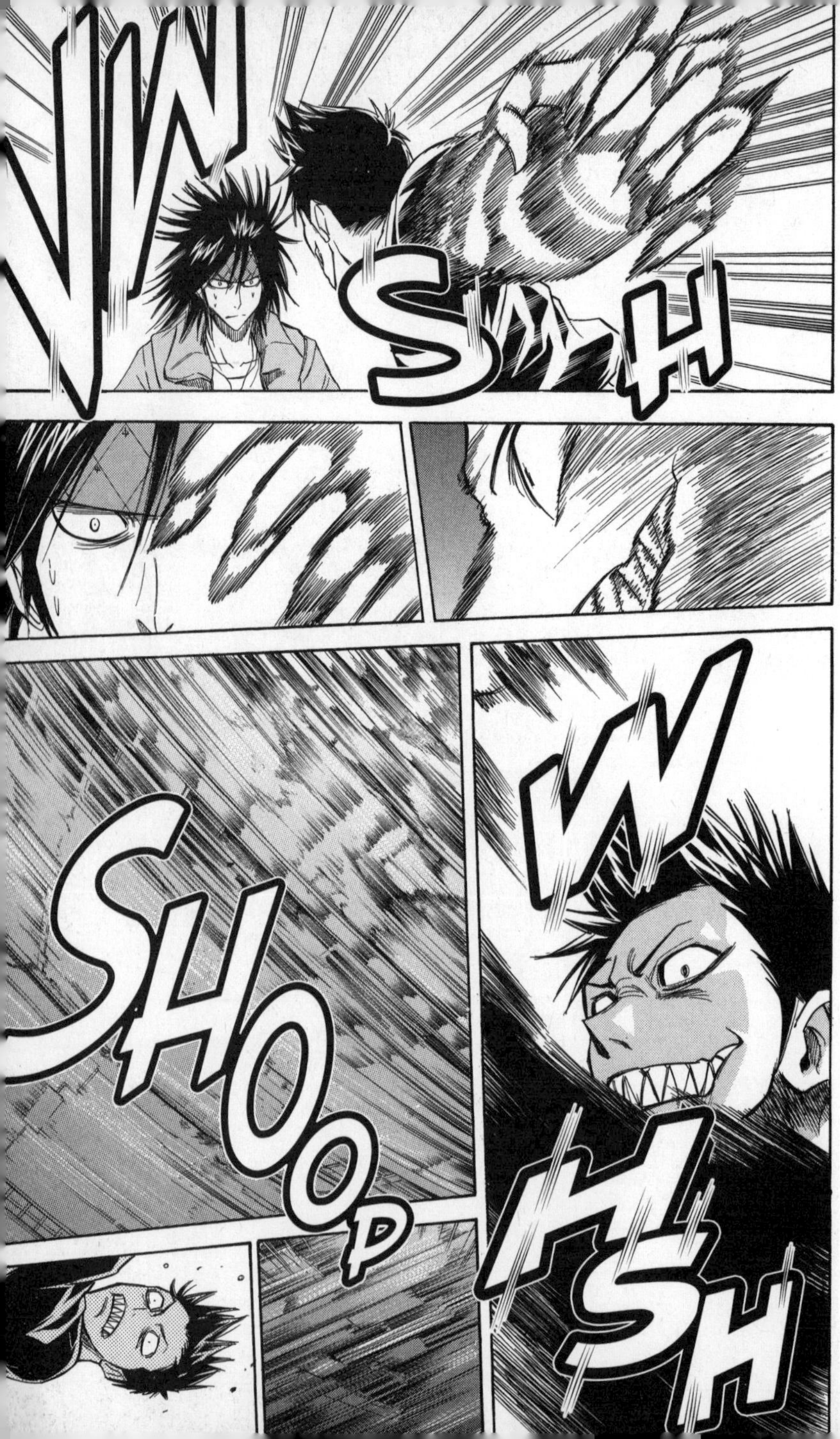
VWSH
VWHSH
SHOOOP

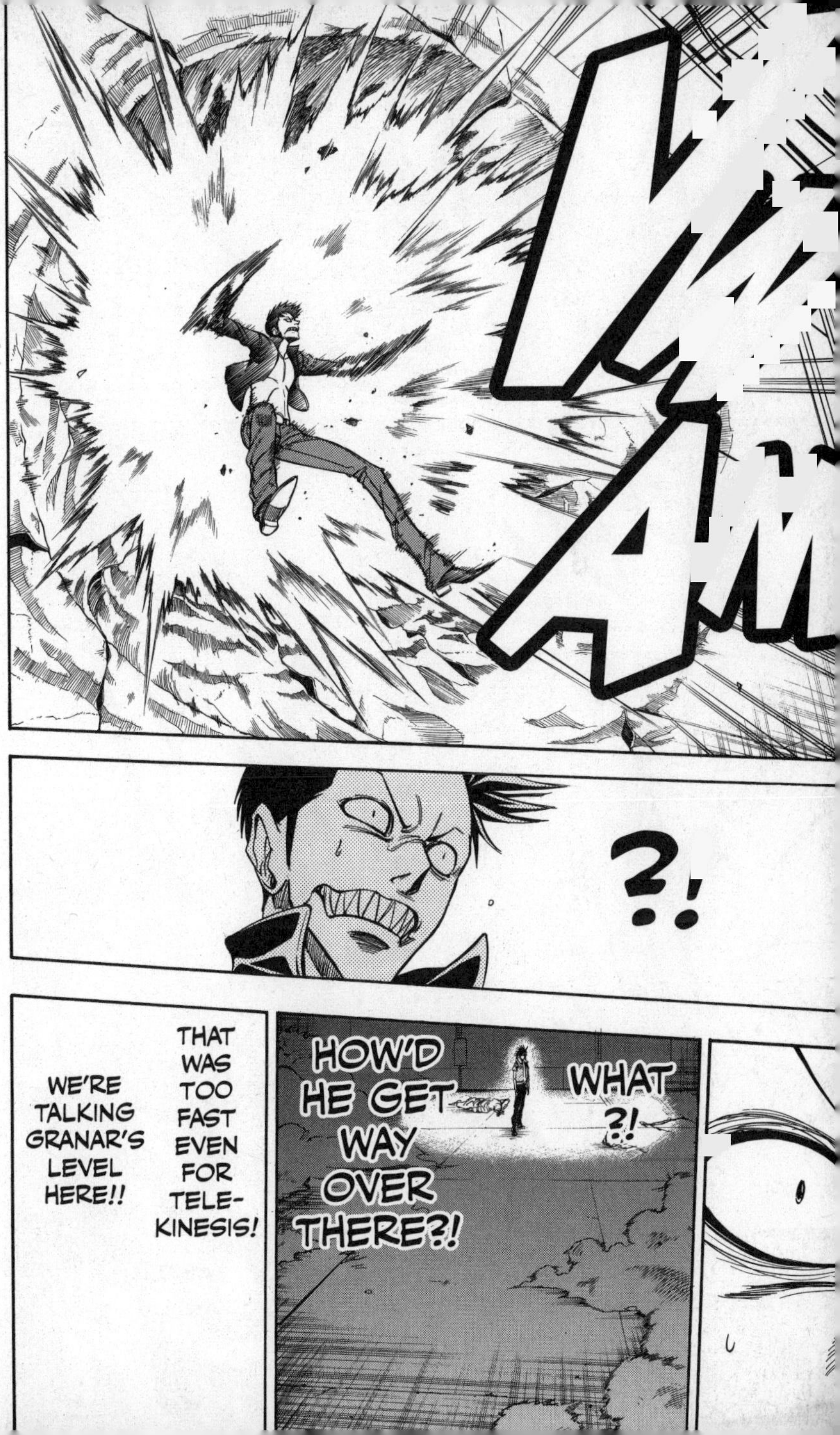
?!
WHAT?!
HOW'D HE GET WAY OVER THERE?!
THAT WAS TOO FAST EVEN FOR TELE-KINESIS!
WE'RE TALKING GRANAR'S LEVEL HERE!!

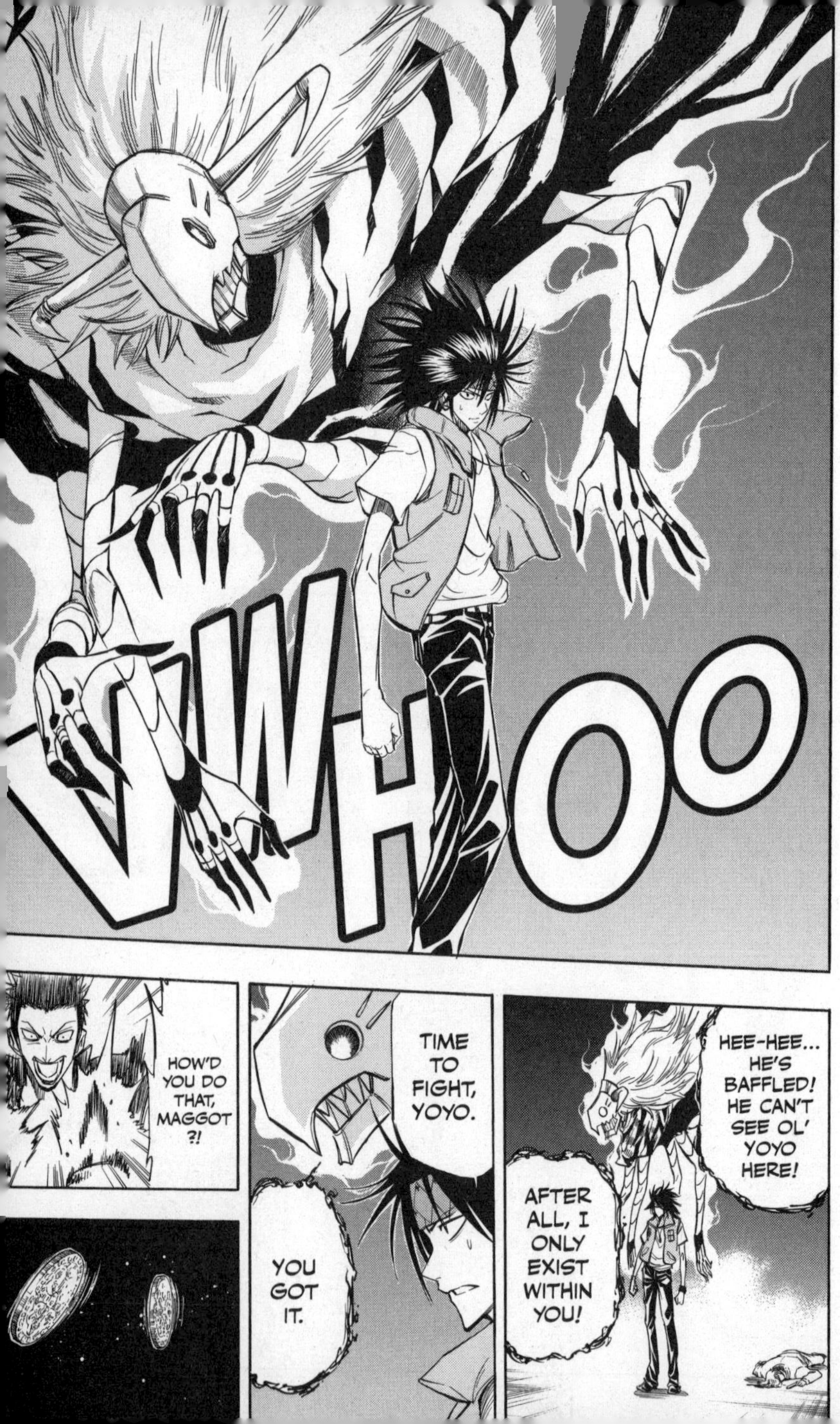
VWHOO
HEE-HEE... HE'S BAFFLED! HE CAN'T SEE OL' YOYO HERE!
AFTER ALL, I ONLY EXIST WITHIN YOU!
TIME TO FIGHT, YOYO.
YOU GOT IT.
HOW'D YOU DO THAT, MAGGOT?!

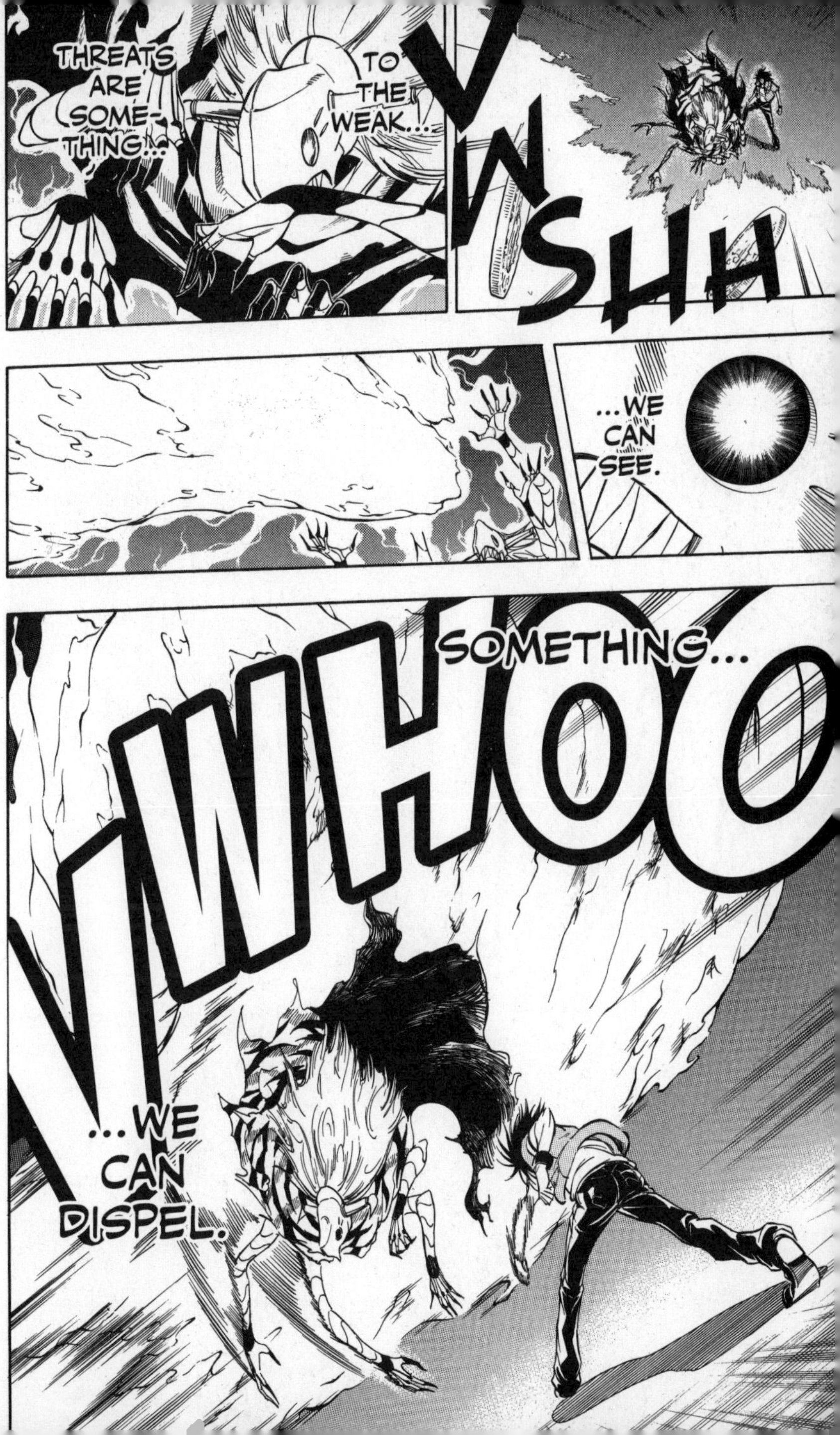
VWSHH
TO THE WEAK...
THREATS ARE SOMETHING...
...WE CAN SEE.
SOMETHING...
VWHOO
...WE CAN DISPEL.

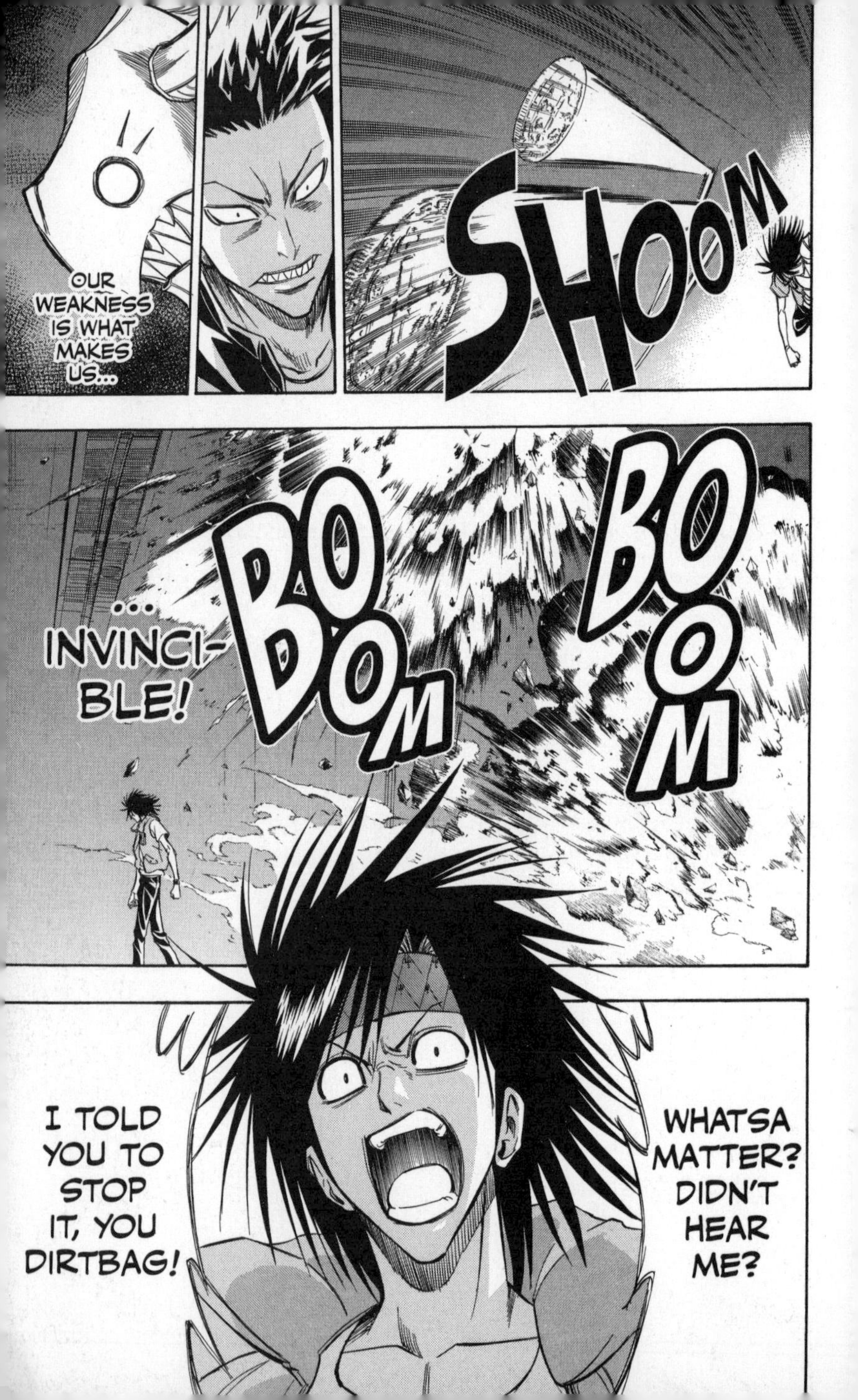
SHOOM
OUR WEAKNESS IS WHAT MAKES US...
BOOM
BOOM
...INVINCI-BLE!
WHATSA MATTER? DIDN'T HEAR ME?
I TOLD YOU TO STOP IT, YOU DIRTBAG!

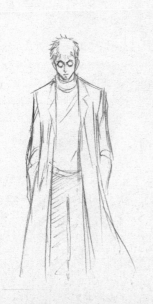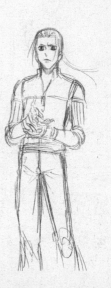

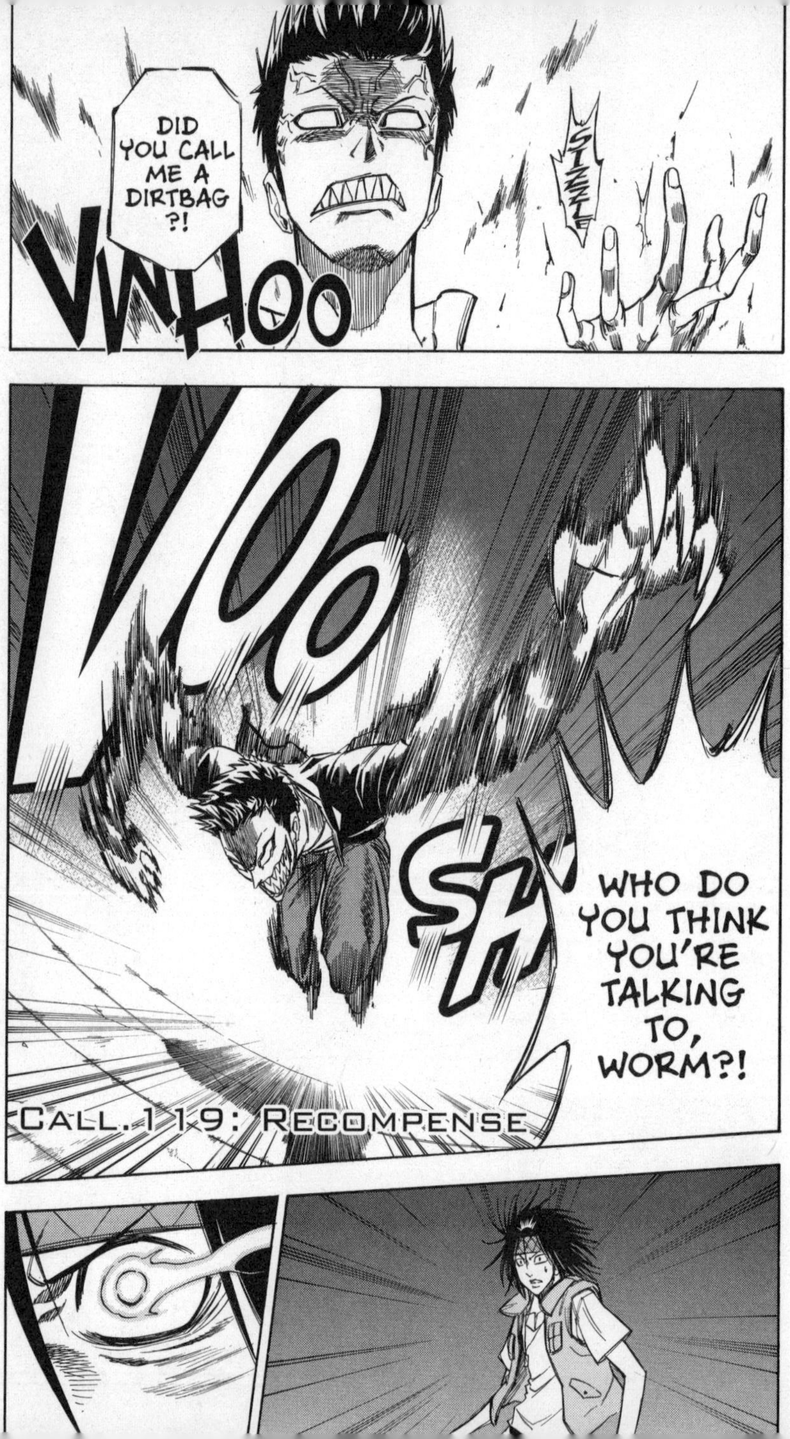
SIZZLE
DID YOU CALL ME A DIRTBAG?!
VWHOO
WHO DO YOU THINK YOU'RE TALKING TO, WORM?!
CALL.119: RECOMPENSE

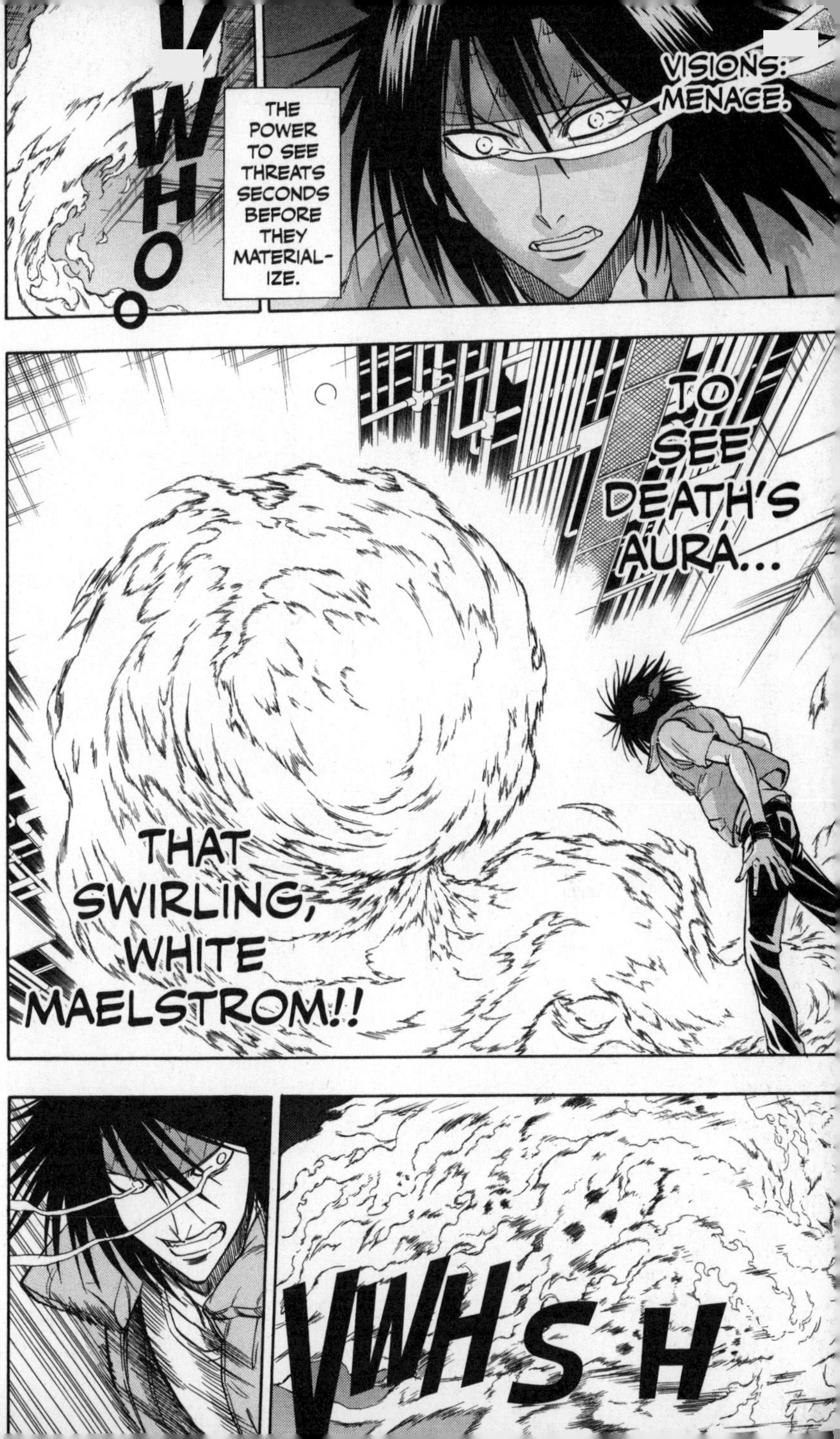
VISIONS: MENACE.
THE POWER TO SEE THREATS SECONDS BEFORE THEY MATERIAL-IZE.
WHOOO
TO SEE DEATH'S AURA...
THAT SWIRLING, WHITE MAELSTROM!!
VWHSH

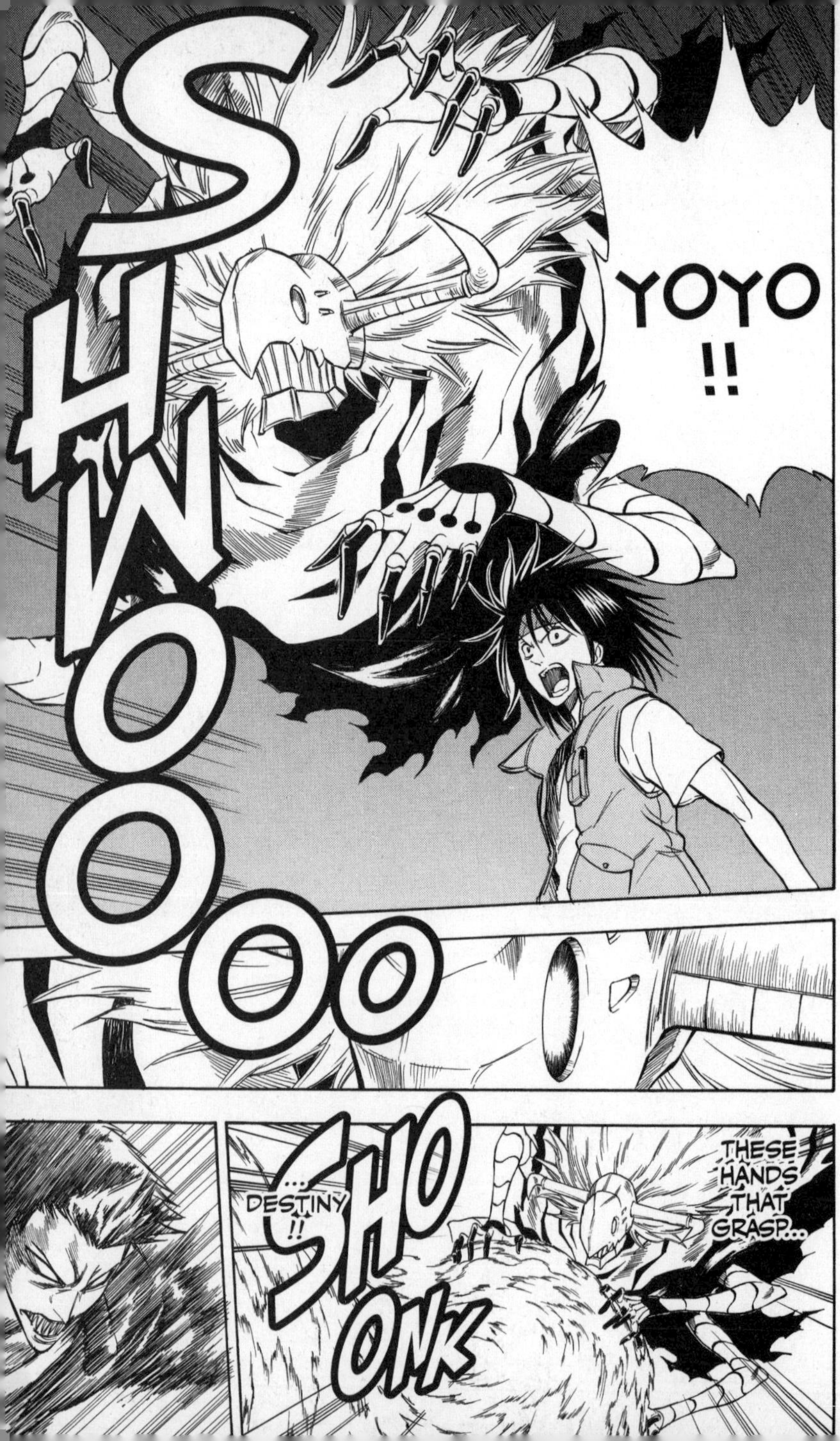
YOYO
!!
SHWOOOOO
THESE HANDS THAT GRASP...
SHOONK
...DESTINY!!

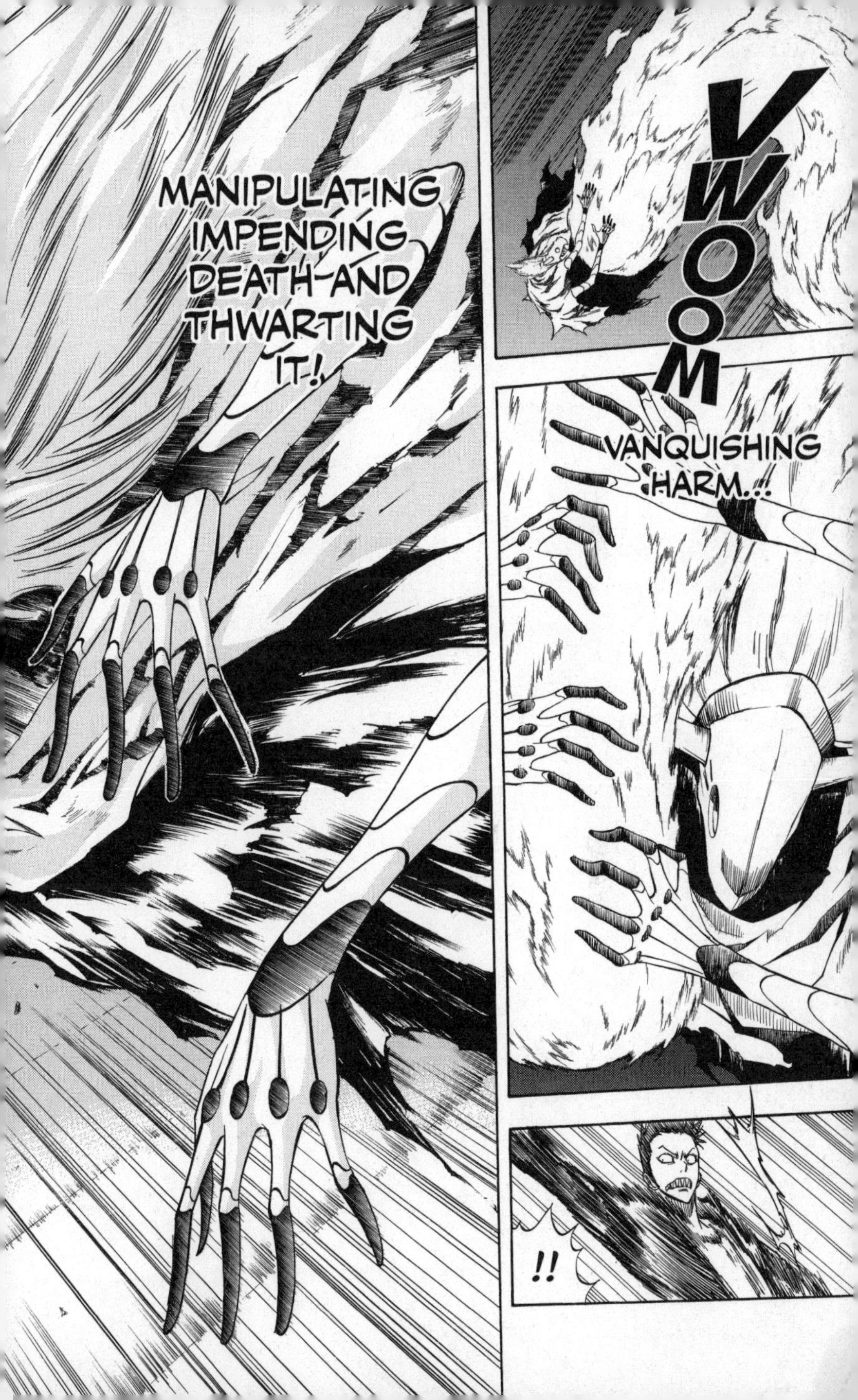
VWOOM
VANQUISHING HARM...
!!
MANIPULATING IMPENDING DEATH AND THWARTING IT!

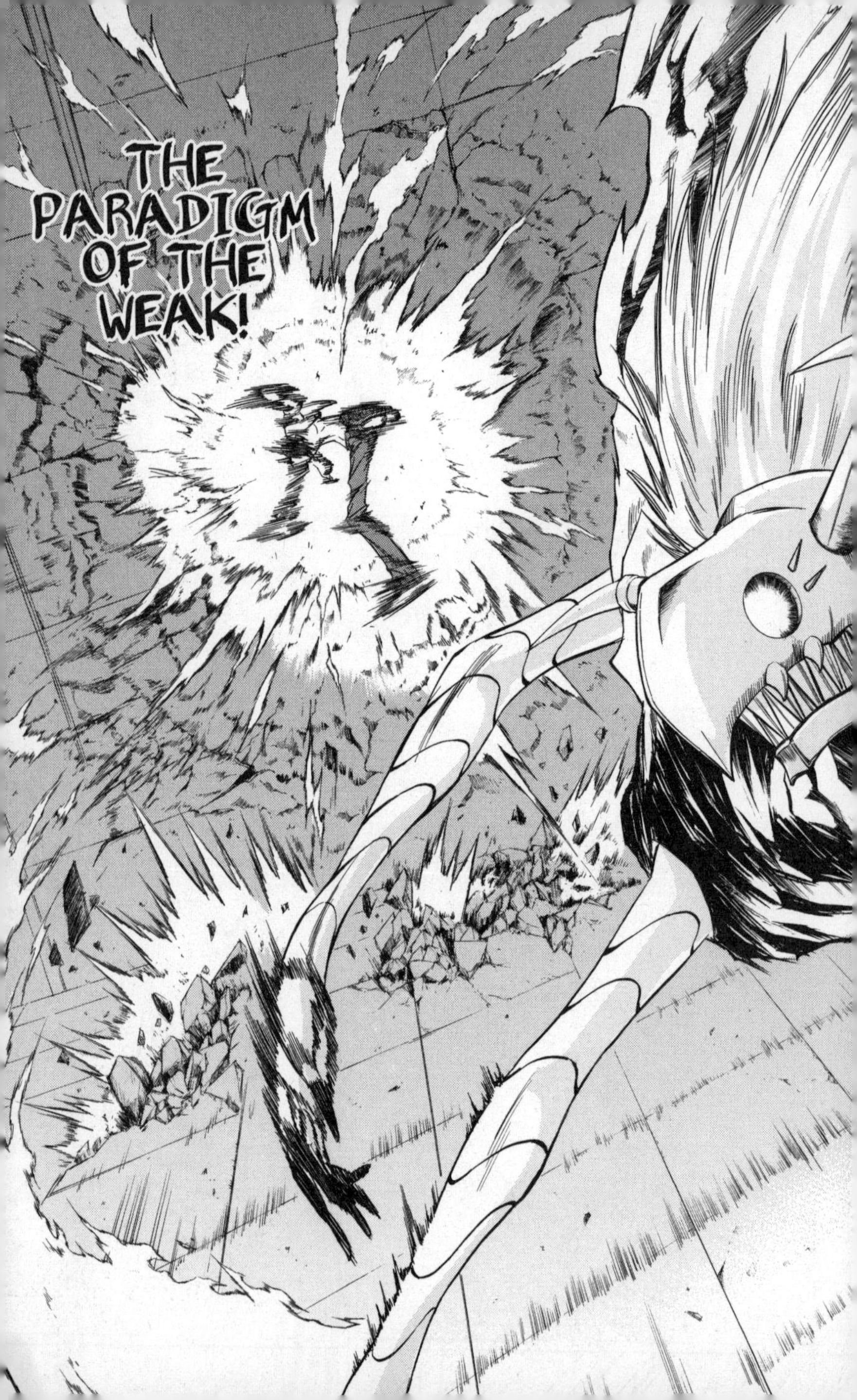
THE PARADIGM OF THE WEAK!

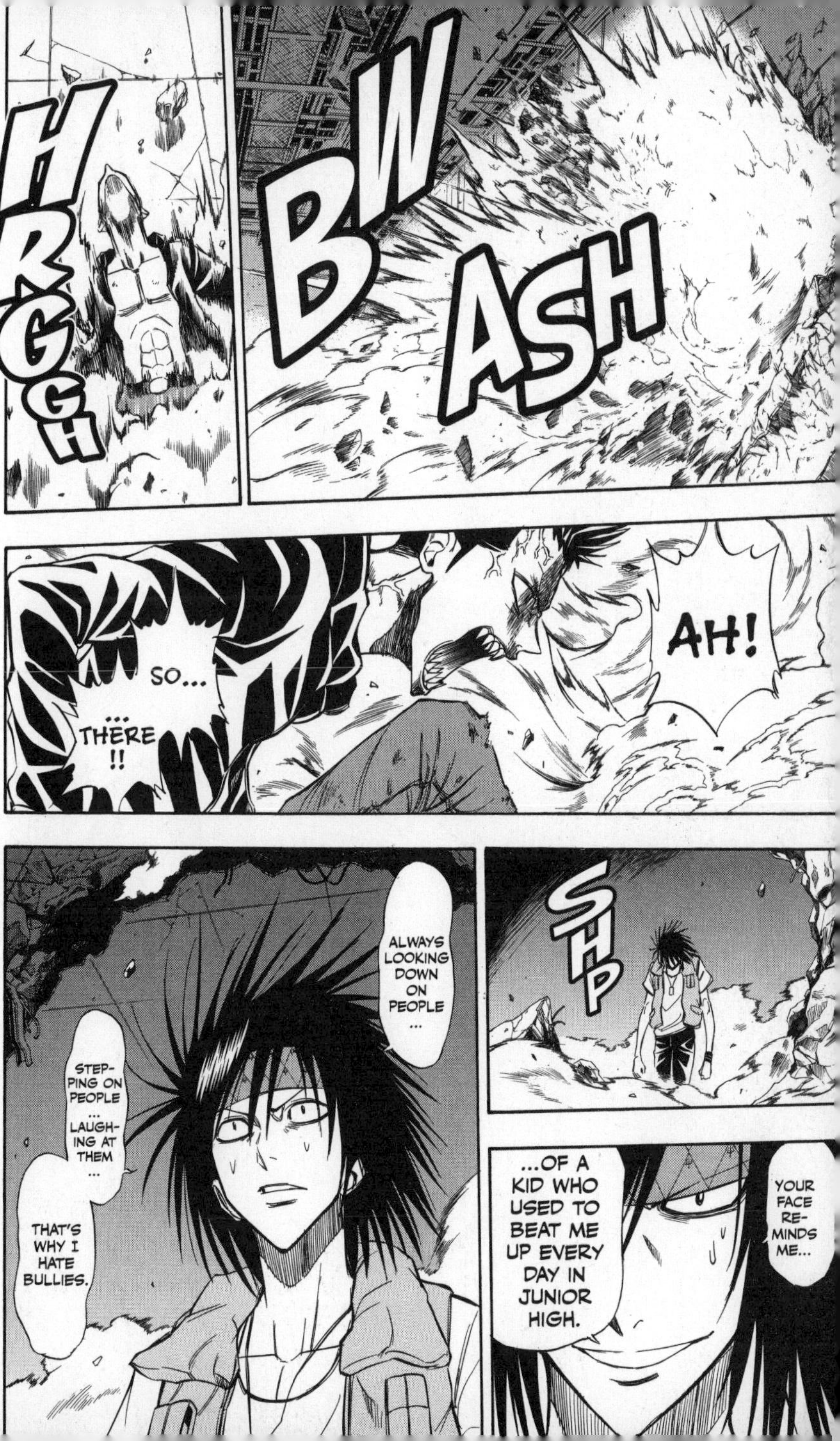
BWASH
HRGGH
AH!
SO...
...THERE!!
SHP
YOUR FACE REMINDS ME...
...OF A KID WHO USED TO BEAT ME UP EVERY DAY IN JUNIOR HIGH.
ALWAYS LOOKING DOWN ON PEOPLE...
STEPPING ON PEOPLE... LAUGHING AT THEM...
THAT'S WHY I HATE BULLIES.

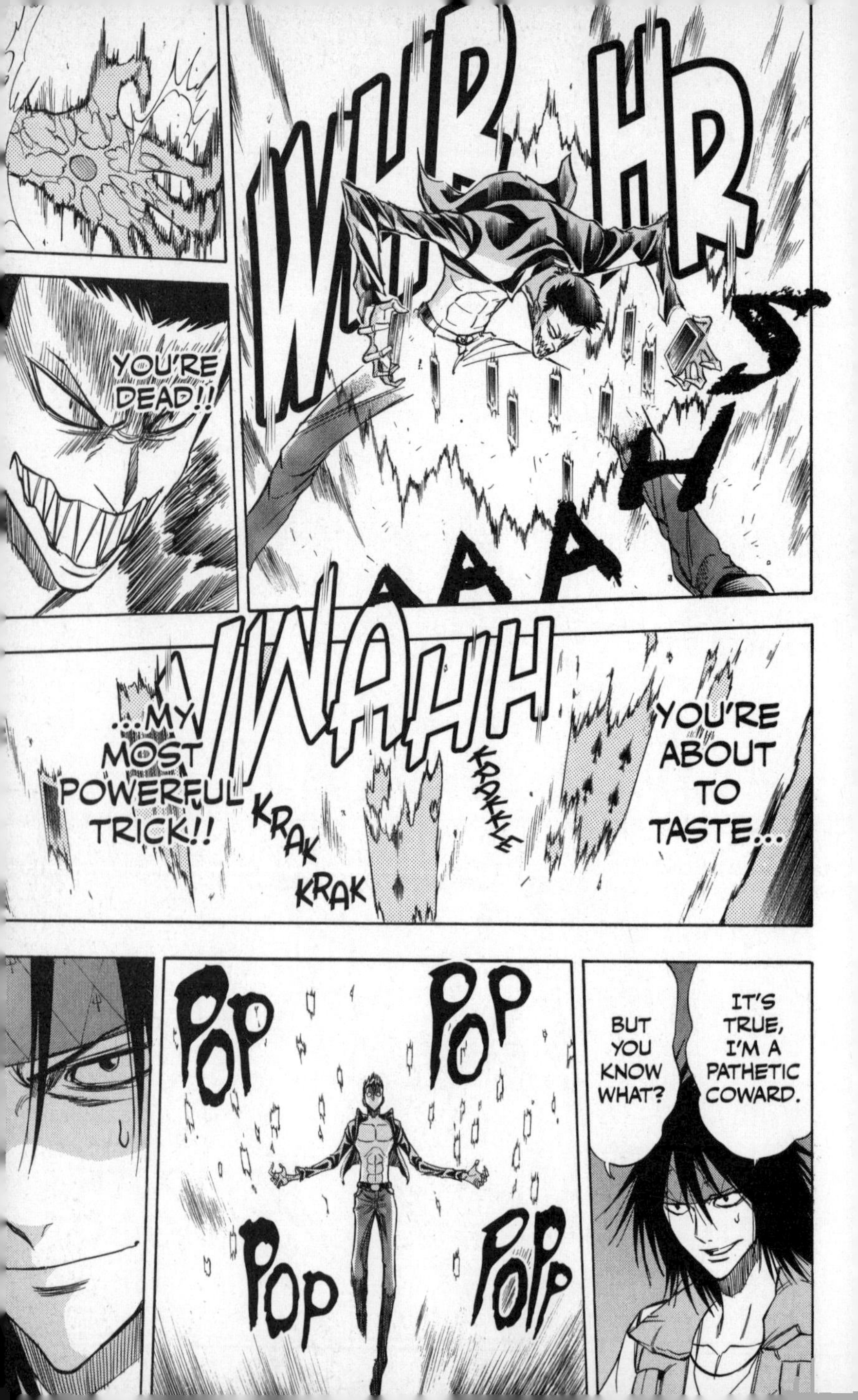
WHR WHR
AAA
YOU'RE DEAD!!
YOU'RE ABOUT TO TASTE...
WAHH
KRAKKLE
KRAK KRAK
...MY MOST POWERFUL TRICK!!
IT'S TRUE, I'M A PATHETIC COWARD.
BUT YOU KNOW WHAT?
POP POP
POP POPP

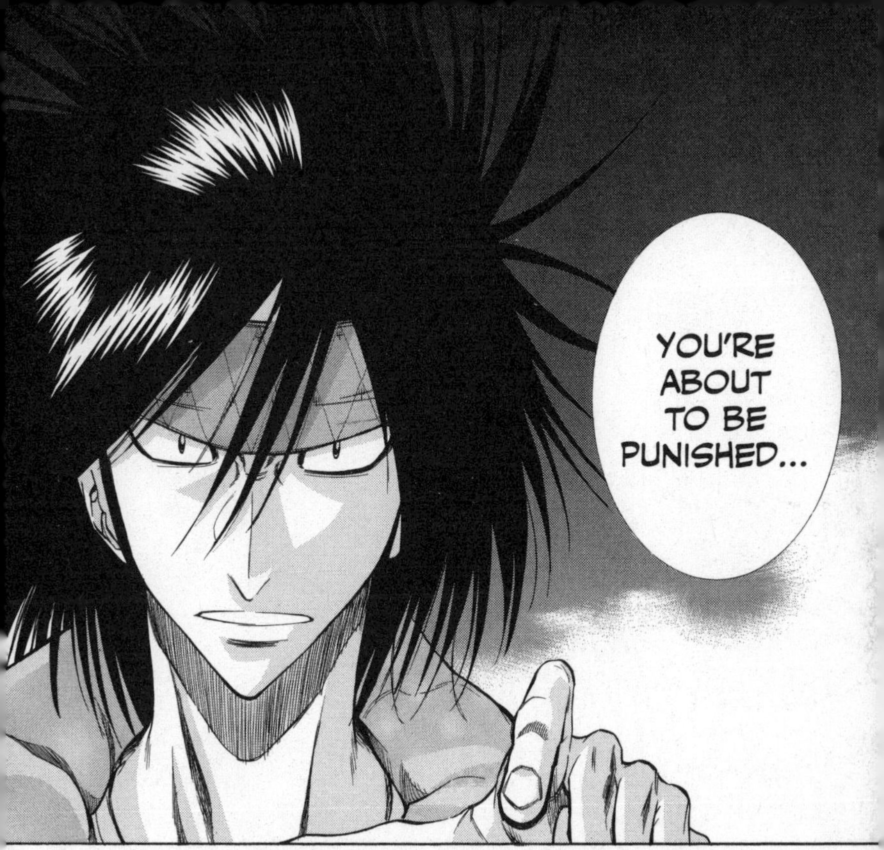
YOU'RE ABOUT TO BE PUNISHED...
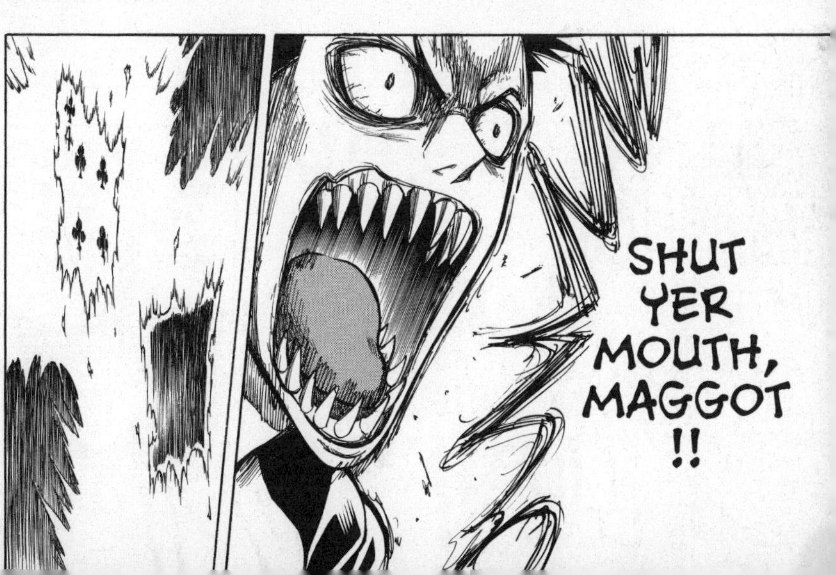
SHUT YER MOUTH, MAGGOT !!

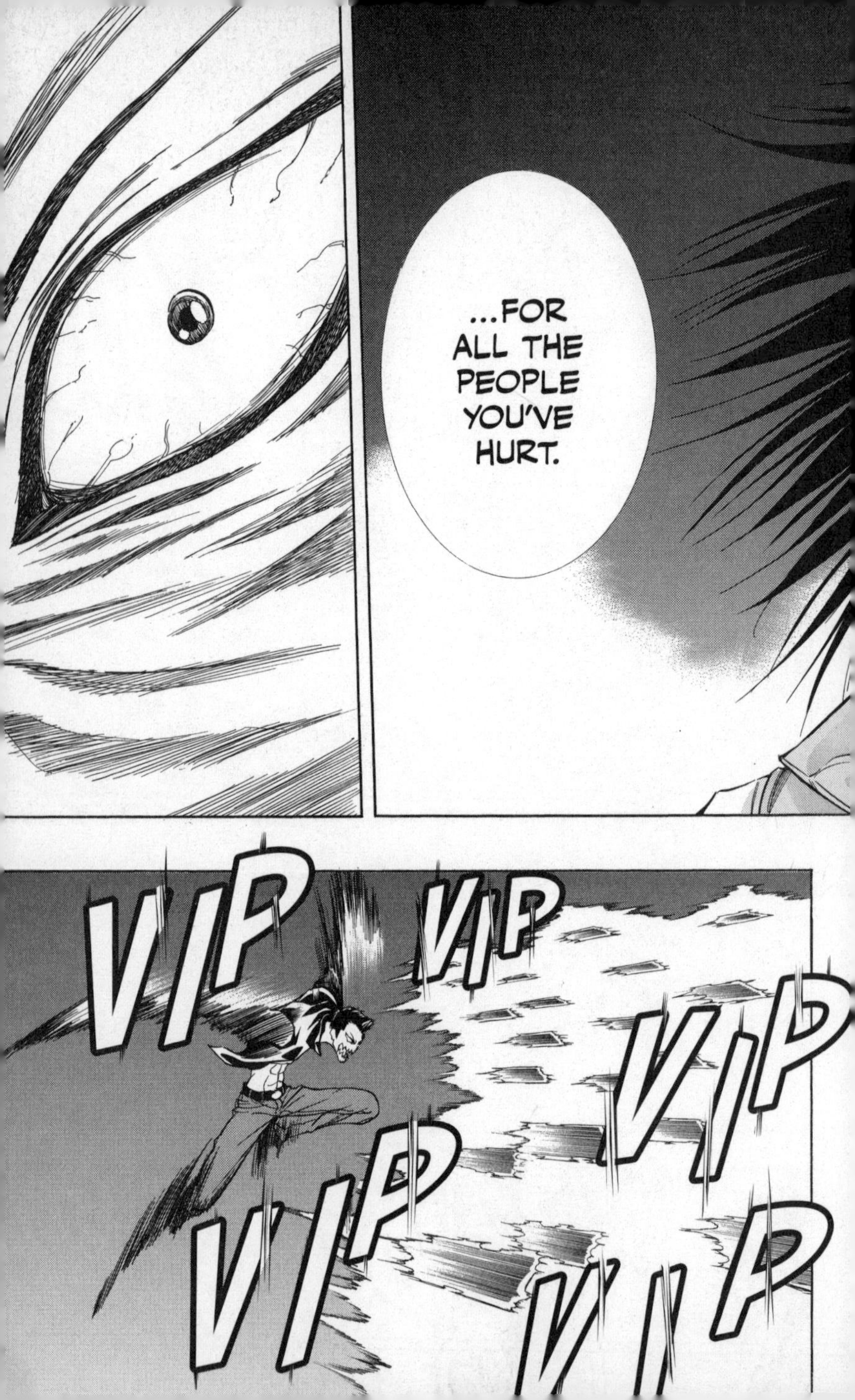
...FOR ALL THE PEOPLE YOU'VE HURT.
VIP
VIP
VIP
VIP
VIP
VIP

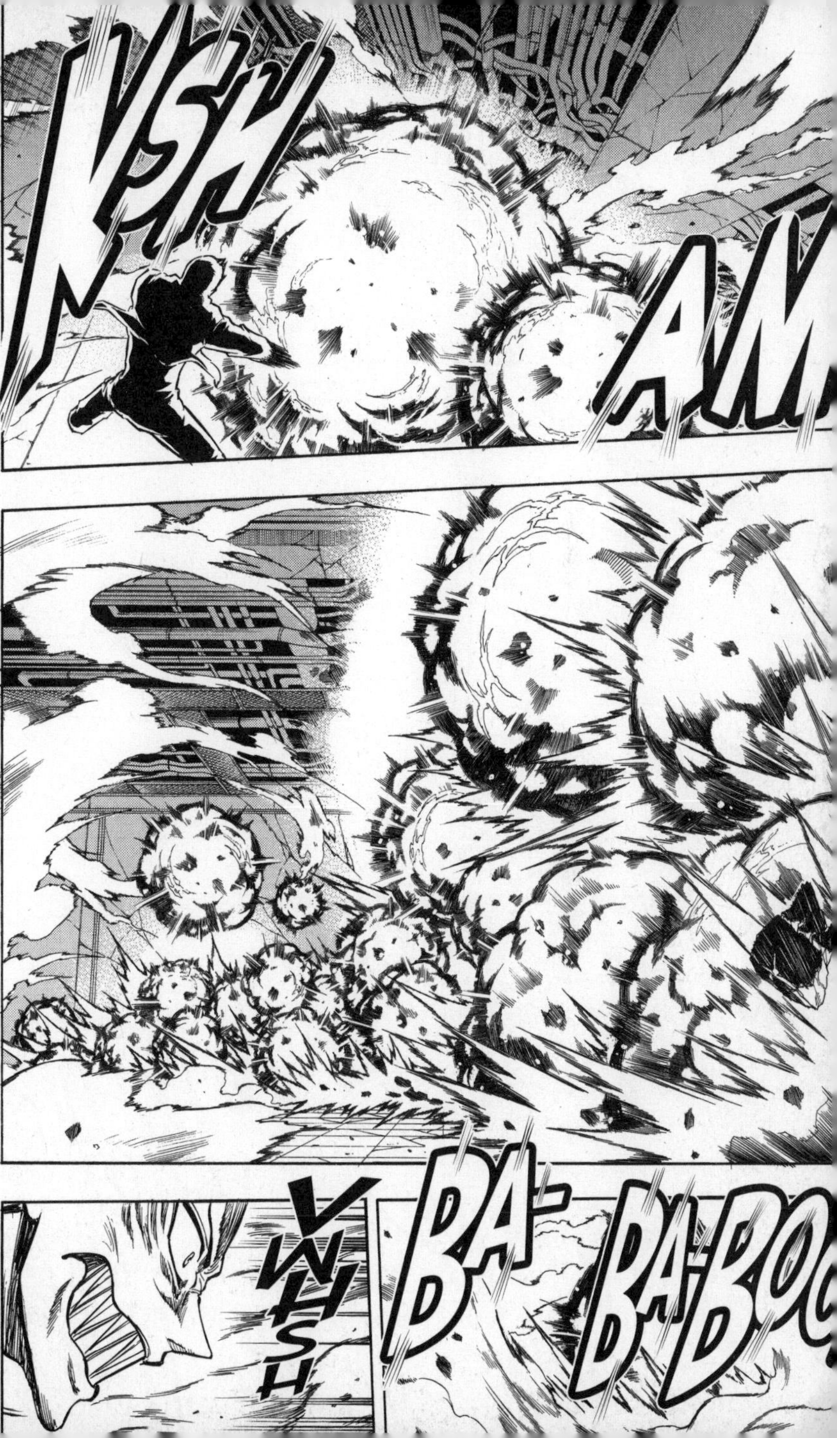
AM
VSH
BA-
BA-BOO
VWHSH

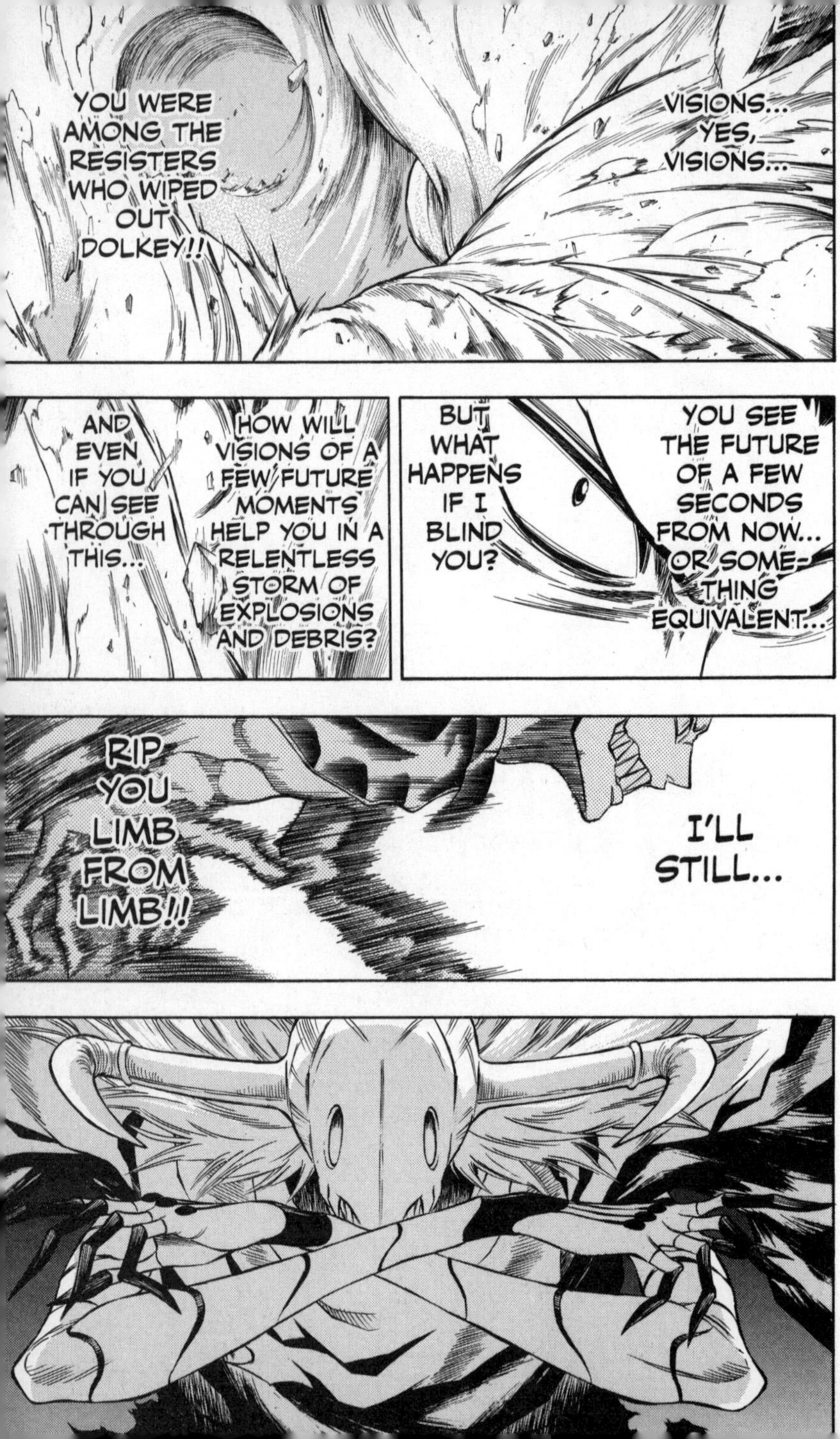
VISIONS... YES, VISIONS...
YOU WERE AMONG THE RESISTERS WHO WIPED OUT DOLKEY!!
YOU SEE THE FUTURE OF A FEW SECONDS FROM NOW... OR SOMETHING EQUIVALENT...
BUT WHAT HAPPENS IF I BLIND YOU?
HOW WILL VISIONS OF A FEW FUTURE MOMENTS HELP YOU IN A RELENTLESS STORM OF EXPLOSIONS AND DEBRIS?
AND EVEN IF YOU CAN SEE THROUGH THIS...
I'LL STILL...
RIP YOU LIMB FROM LIMB!!

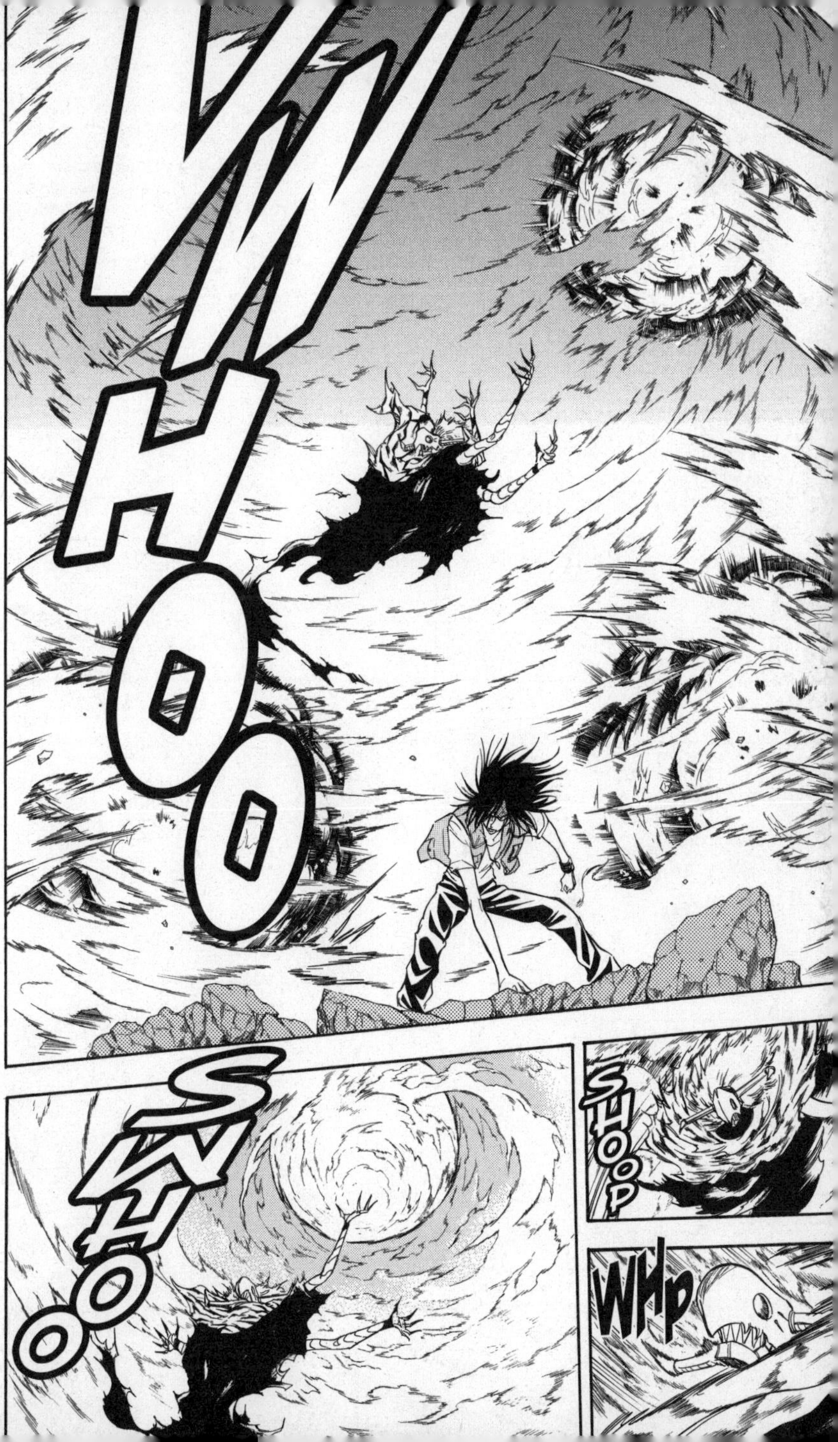
WHOO
SHOOP
WHP
SWHOOO

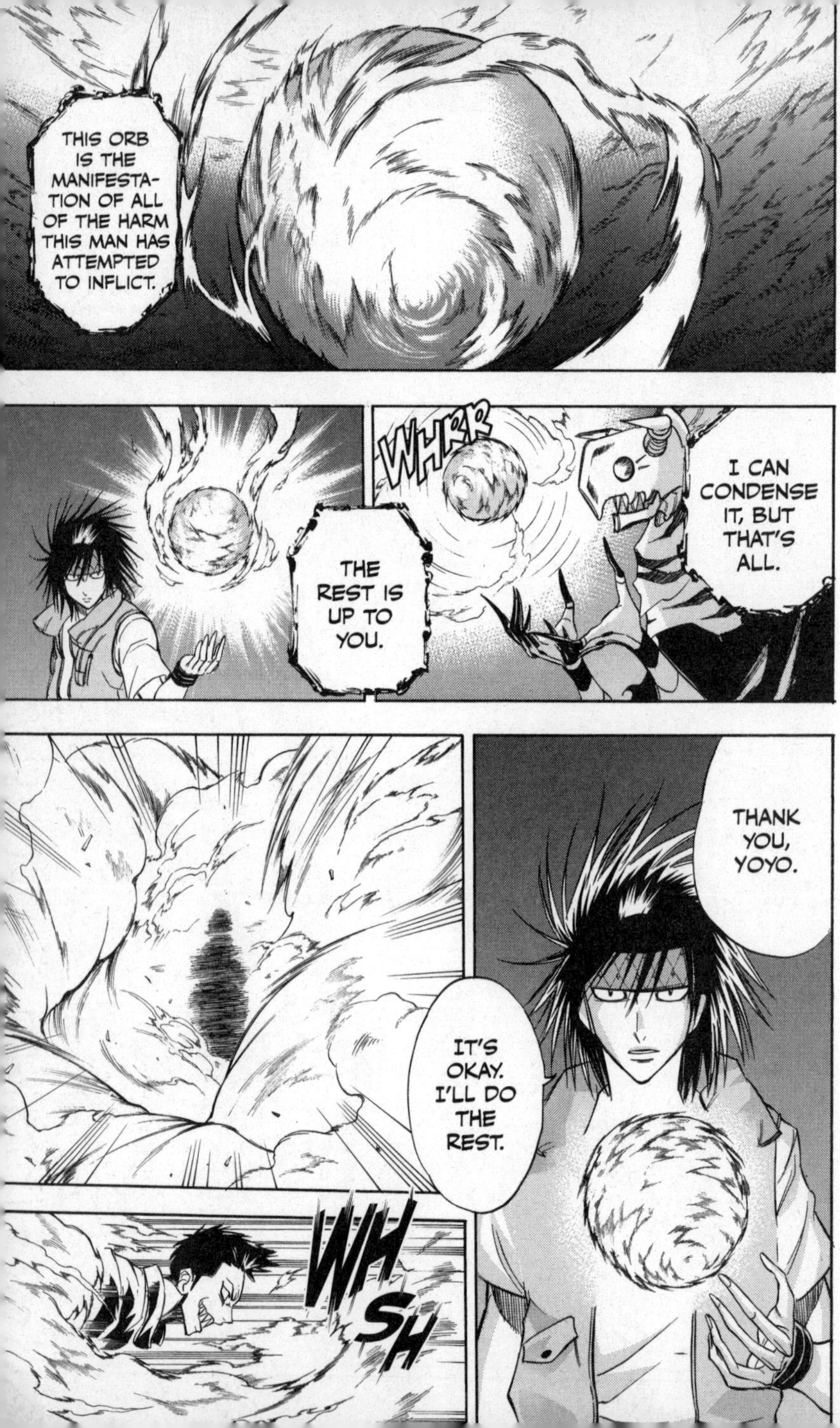
THIS ORB IS THE MANIFESTATION OF ALL OF THE HARM THIS MAN HAS ATTEMPTED TO INFLICT.
WHRR
I CAN CONDENSE IT, BUT THAT'S ALL.
THE REST IS UP TO YOU.
THANK YOU, YOYO.
IT'S OKAY. I'LL DO THE REST.
WHSH

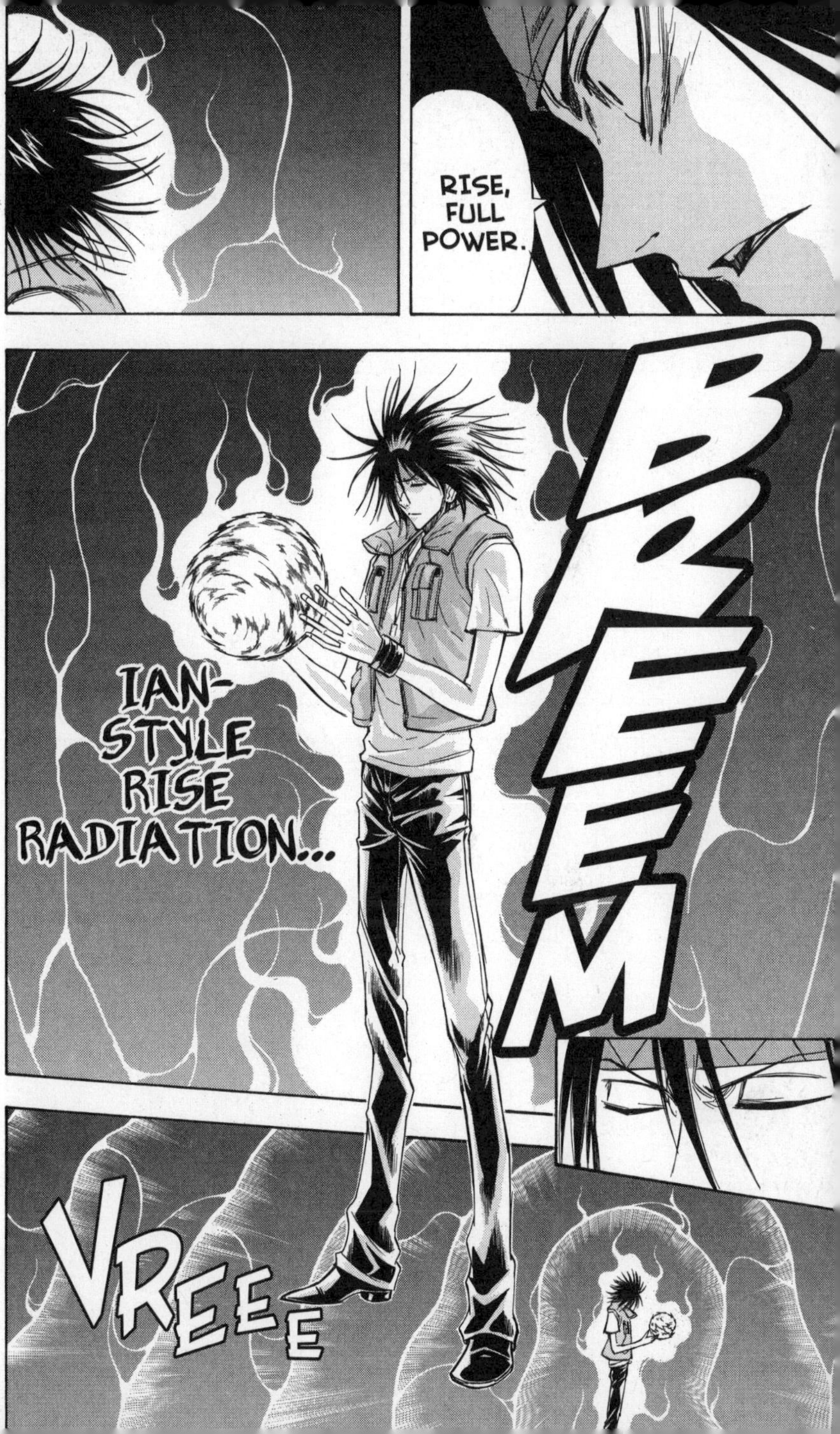
RISE, FULL POWER.
BREEEM
IAN-STYLE RISE RADIATION...
VREEEE

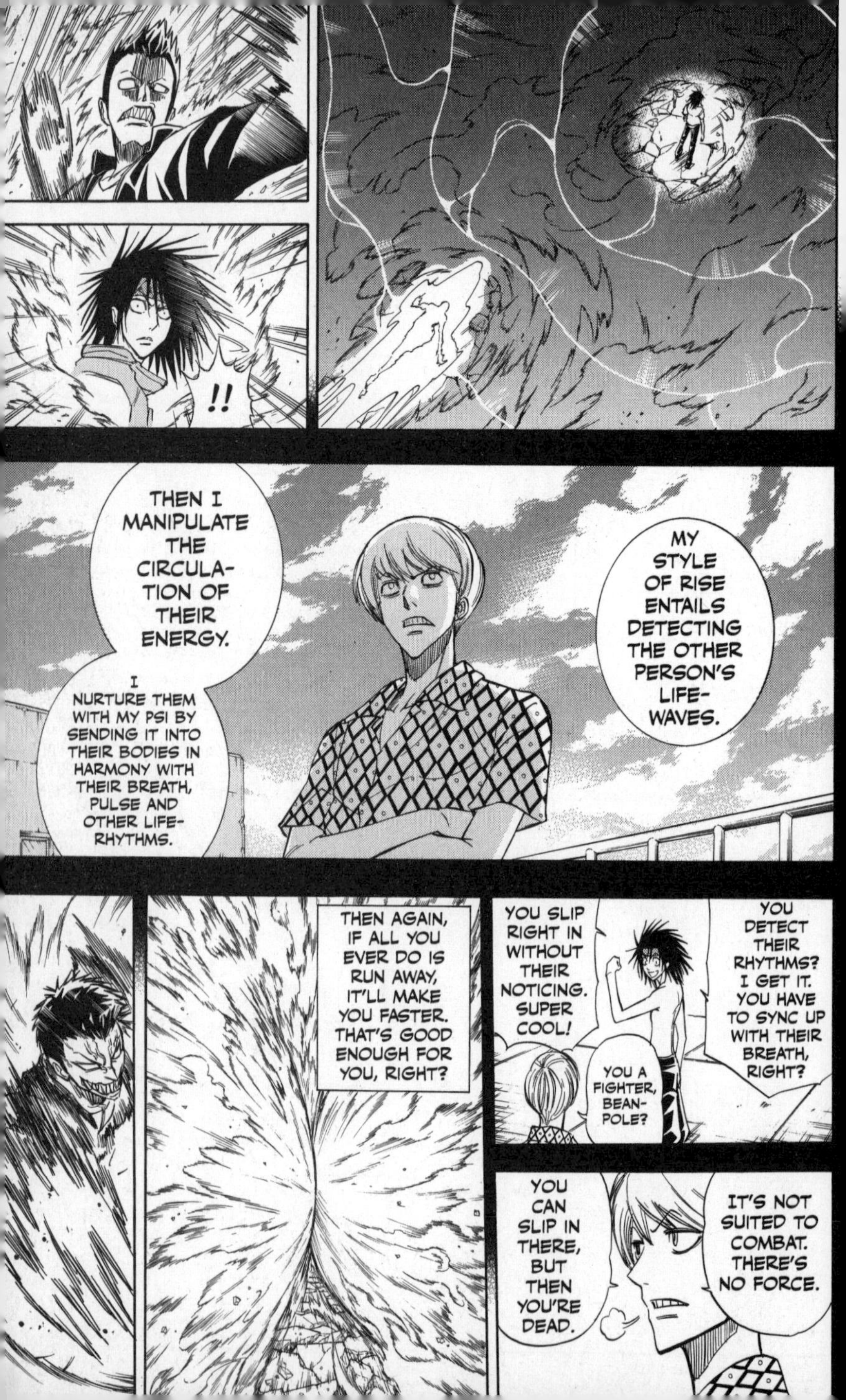
!!
MY STYLE OF RISE ENTAILS DETECTING THE OTHER PERSON'S LIFE-WAVES.
THEN I MANIPULATE THE CIRCULATION OF THEIR ENERGY.
I NURTURE THEM WITH MY PSI BY SENDING IT INTO THEIR BODIES IN HARMONY WITH THEIR BREATH, PULSE AND OTHER LIFE-RHYTHMS.
YOU DETECT THEIR RHYTHMS? I GET IT. YOU HAVE TO SYNC UP WITH THEIR BREATH, RIGHT?
YOU SLIP RIGHT IN WITHOUT THEIR NOTICING. SUPER COOL!
YOU A FIGHTER, BEAN-POLE?
IT'S NOT SUITED TO COMBAT. THERE'S NO FORCE.
YOU CAN SLIP IN THERE, BUT THEN YOU'RE DEAD.
THEN AGAIN, IF ALL YOU EVER DO IS RUN AWAY, IT'LL MAKE YOU FASTER. THAT'S GOOD ENOUGH FOR YOU, RIGHT?

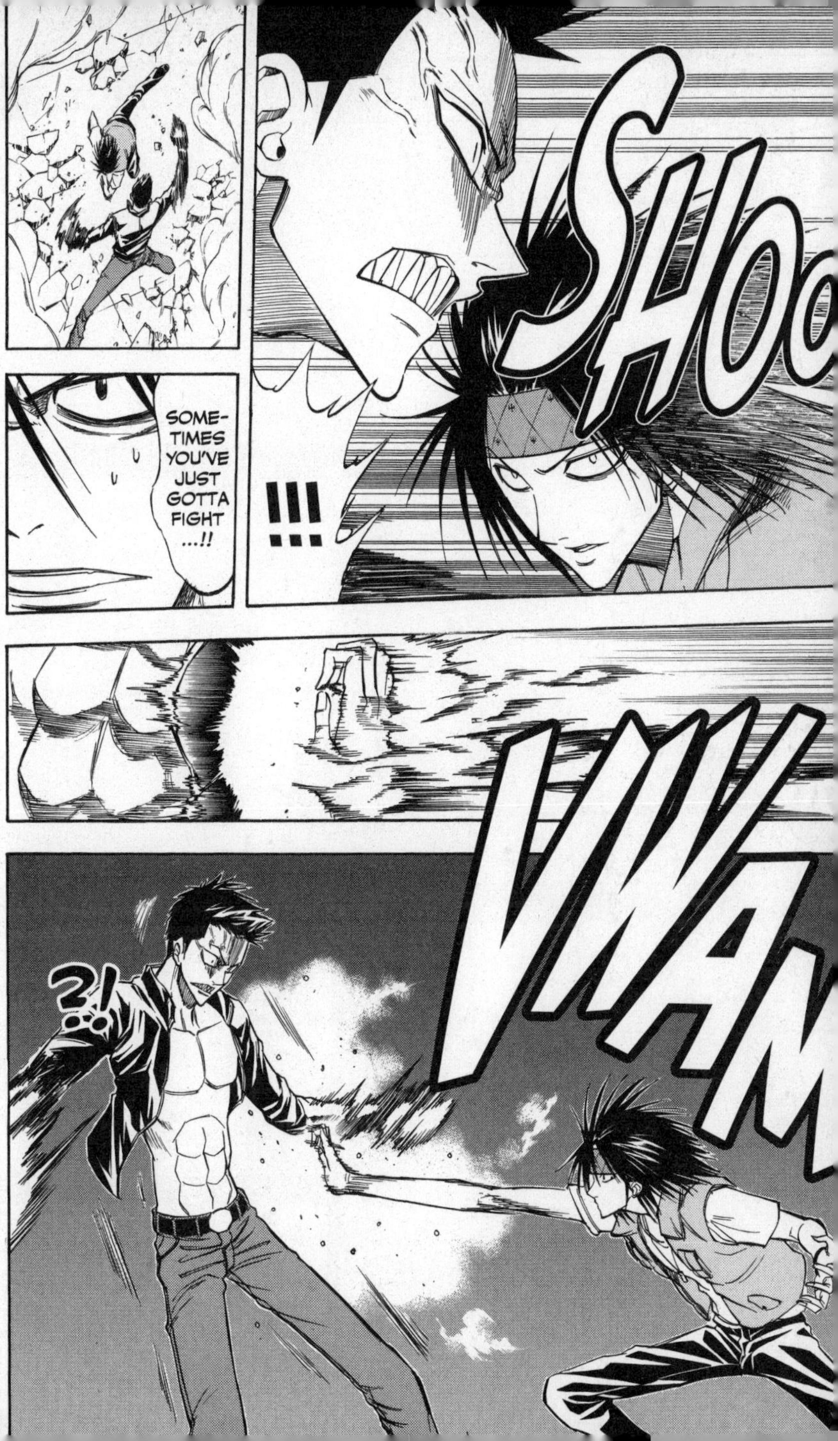

SHOO
!!!
SOME-TIMES YOU'VE JUST GOTTA FIGHT ...!!
VWAM
?!

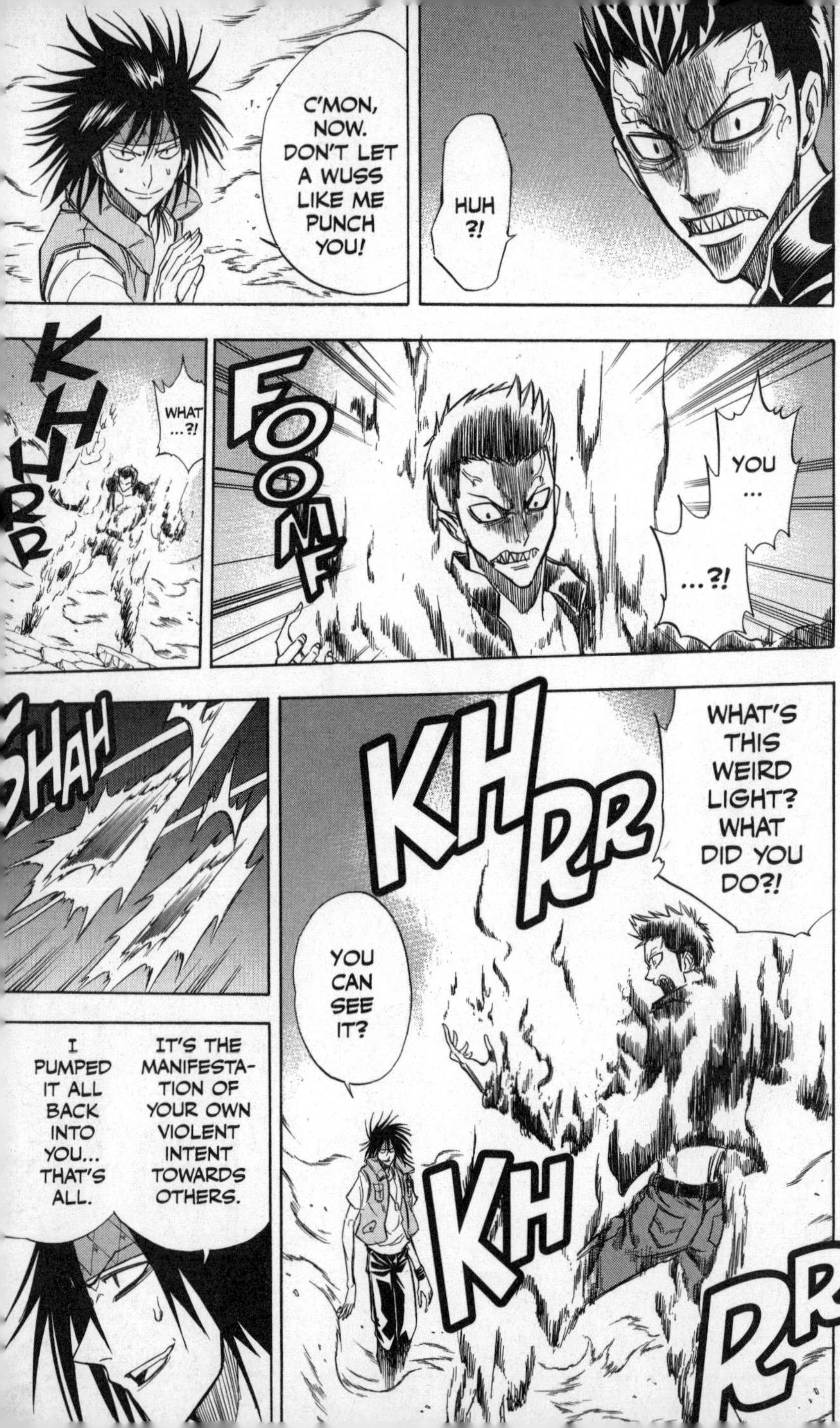
HUH ?!
C'MON, NOW. DON'T LET A WUSS LIKE ME PUNCH YOU!
YOU ...
...?!
FOOMF
KHRR
WHAT ...?!
WHAT'S THIS WEIRD LIGHT? WHAT DID YOU DO?!
KHRR
YOU CAN SEE IT?
KHRR
SHAH
IT'S THE MANIFESTATION OF YOUR OWN VIOLENT INTENT TOWARDS OTHERS.
I PUMPED IT ALL BACK INTO YOU... THAT'S ALL.

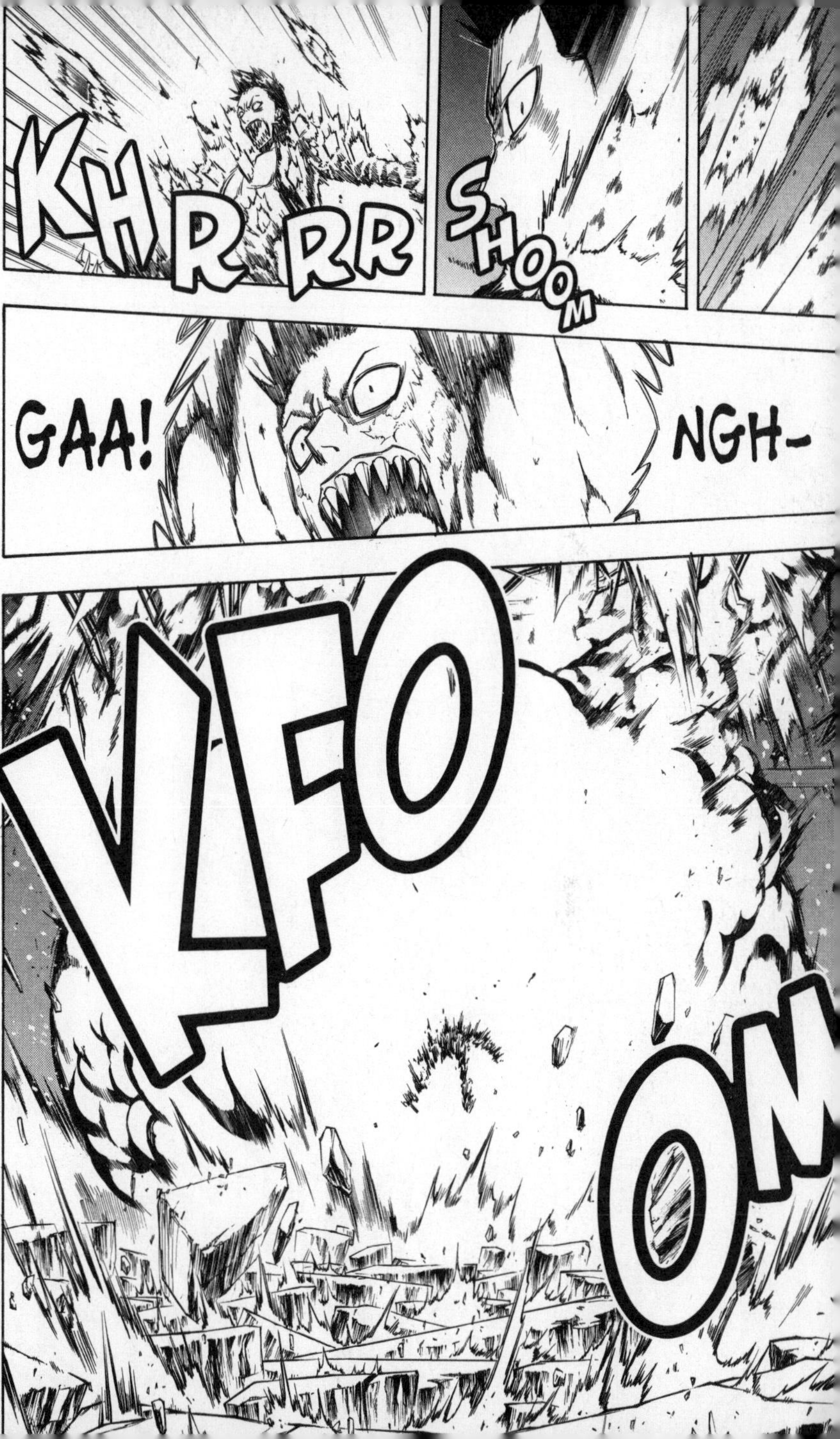

SHOOM
KHRRRR
NGH-
GAA!
KFOOM

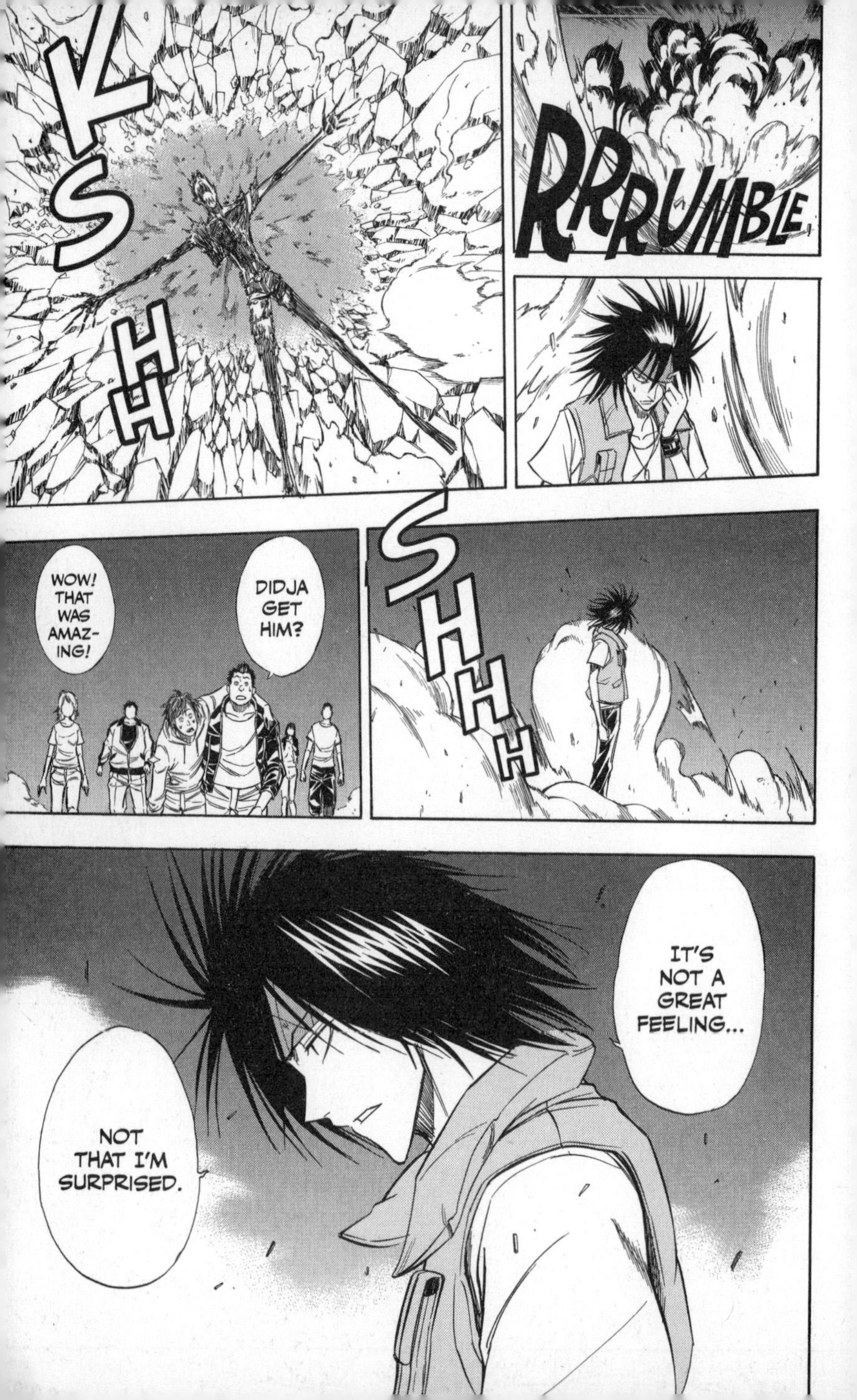
RRRUMBLE
KSHHH
SHHHH
DIDJA GET HIM?
WOW! THAT WAS AMAZ-ING!
IT'S NOT A GREAT FEELING...
NOT THAT I'M SURPRISED.

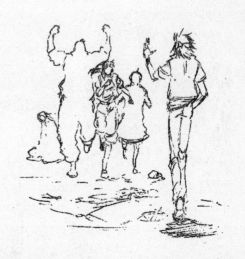

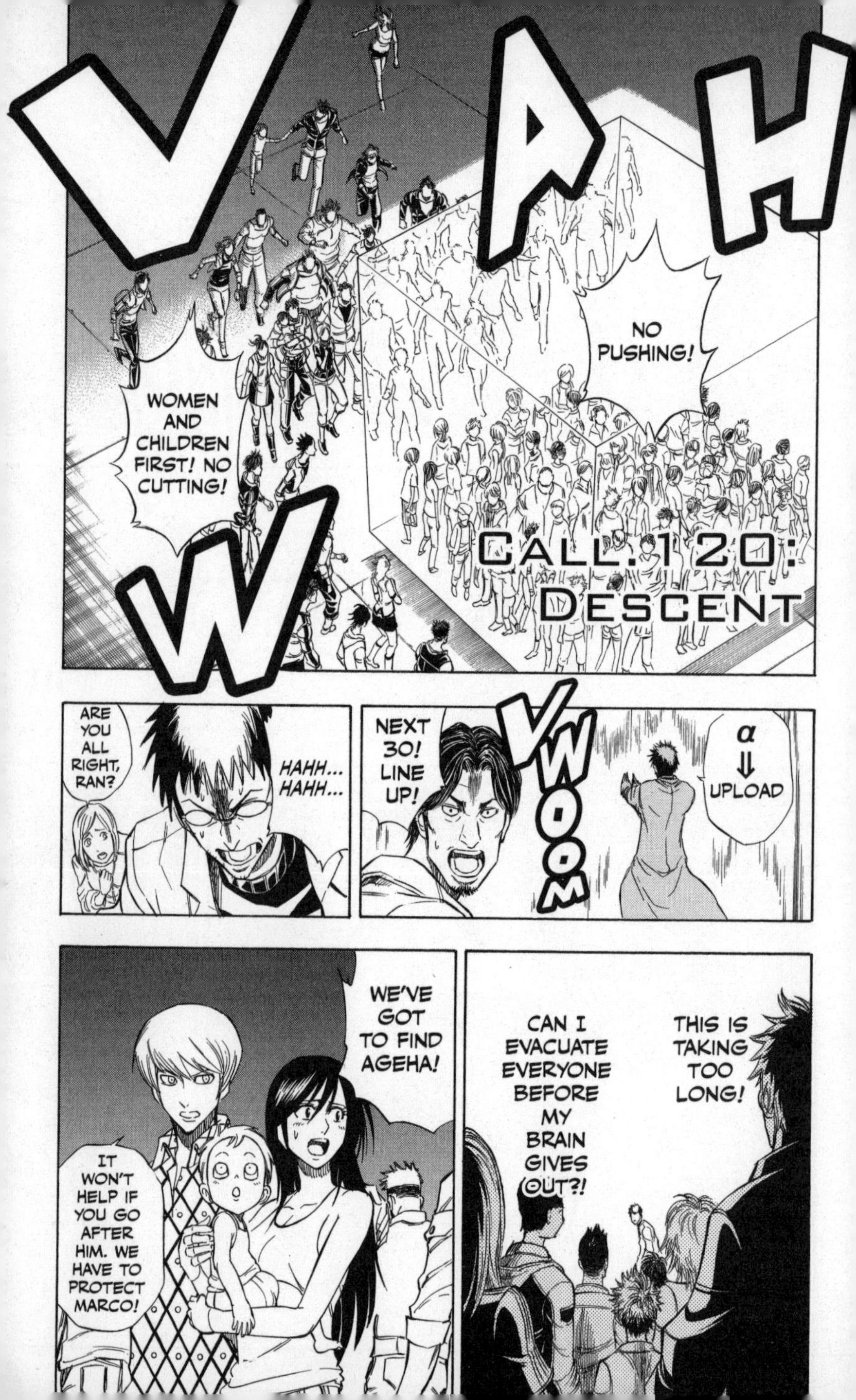
NO PUSHING!
WOMEN AND CHILDREN FIRST! NO CUTTING!
CALL.120: DESCENT
α ⇓ UPLOAD
VWOOM
NEXT 30! LINE UP!
HAHH... HAHH...
ARE YOU ALL RIGHT, RAN?
THIS IS TAKING TOO LONG!
CAN I EVACUATE EVERYONE BEFORE MY BRAIN GIVES OUT?!
WE'VE GOT TO FIND AGEHA!
IT WON'T HELP IF YOU GO AFTER HIM. WE HAVE TO PROTECT MARCO!

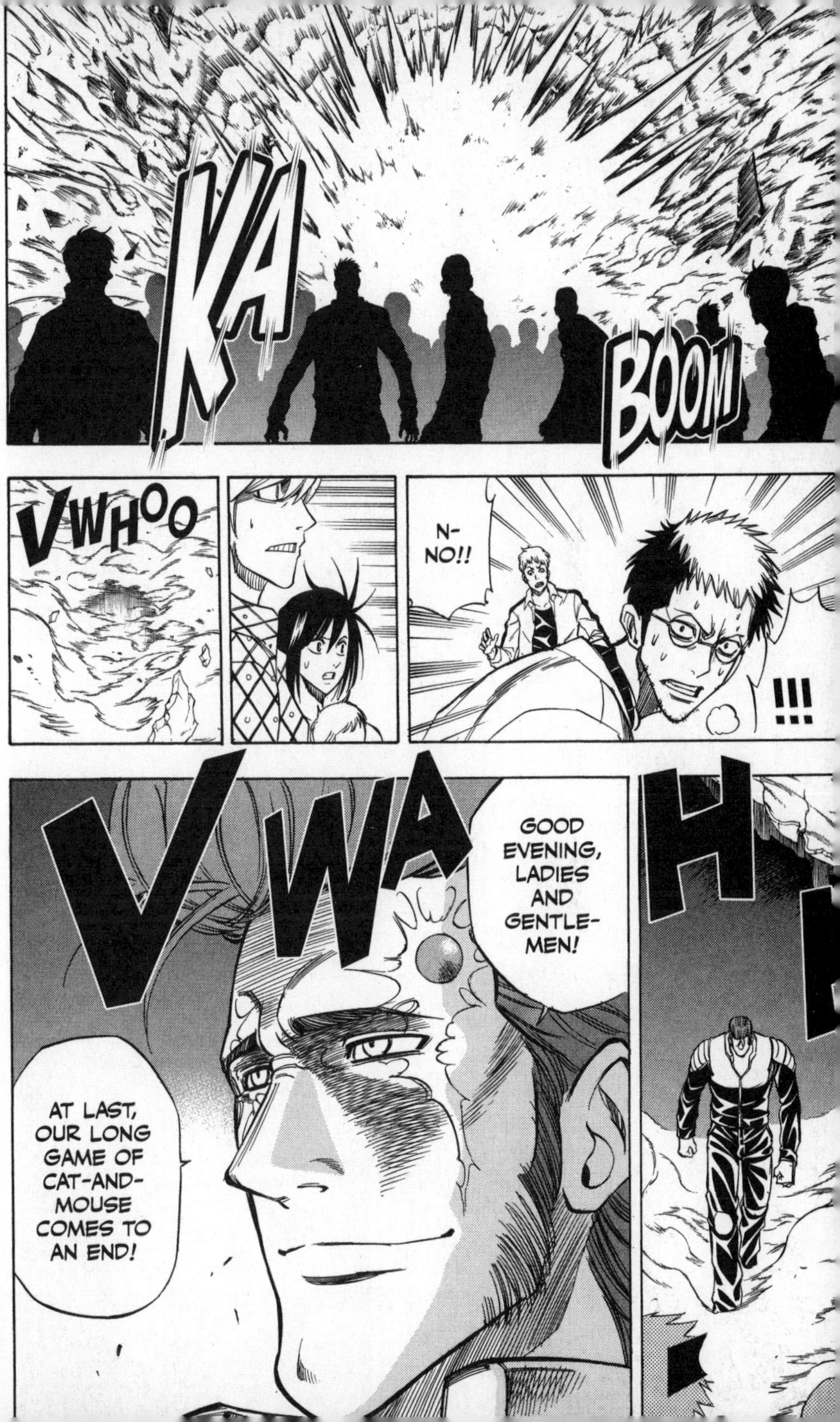

KA
BOOM
N-NO!!
!!!
VWHOO
H
VWA
GOOD EVENING, LADIES AND GENTLE-MEN!
AT LAST, OUR LONG GAME OF CAT-AND-MOUSE COMES TO AN END!

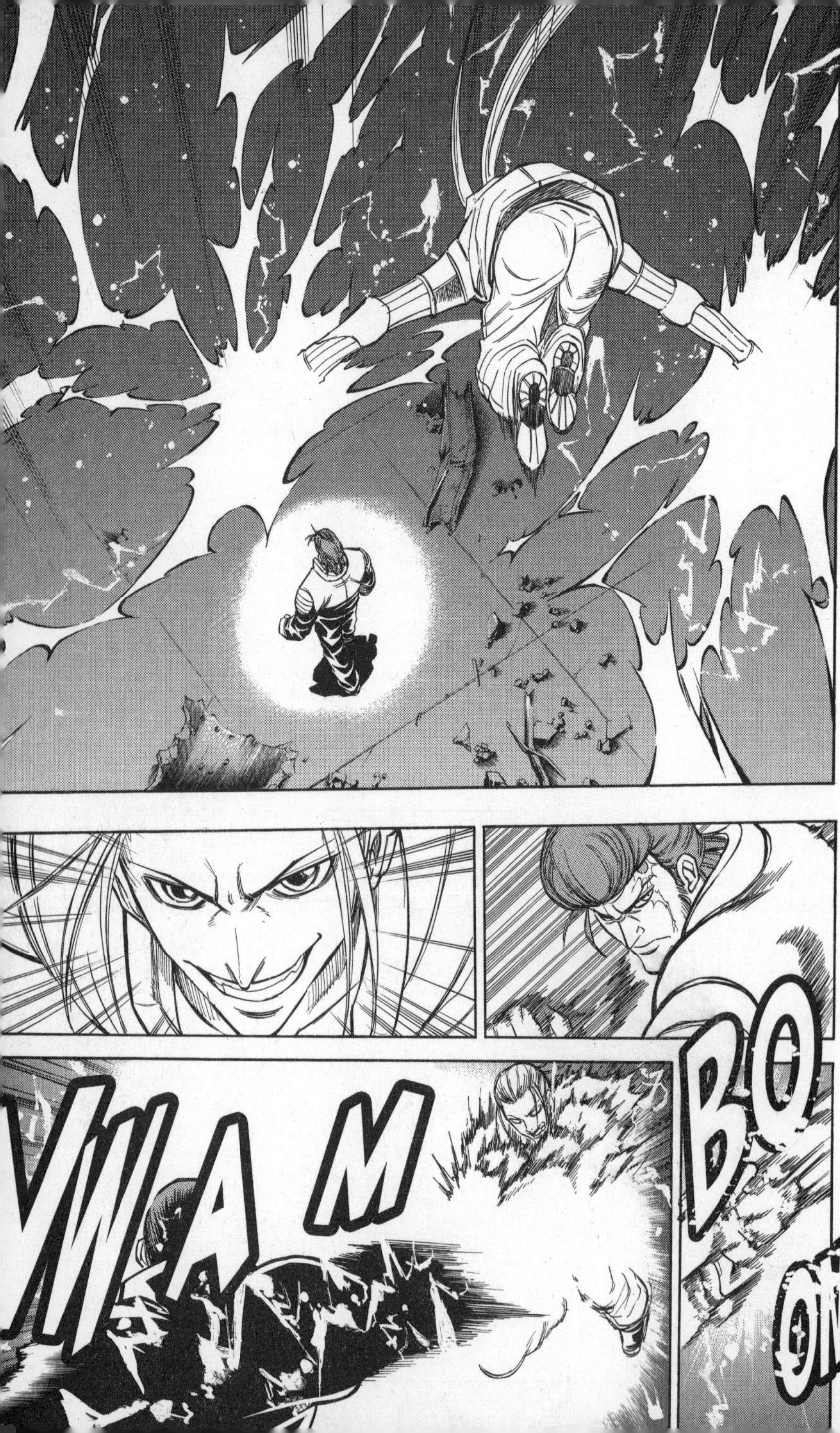
BOOM
WHAM

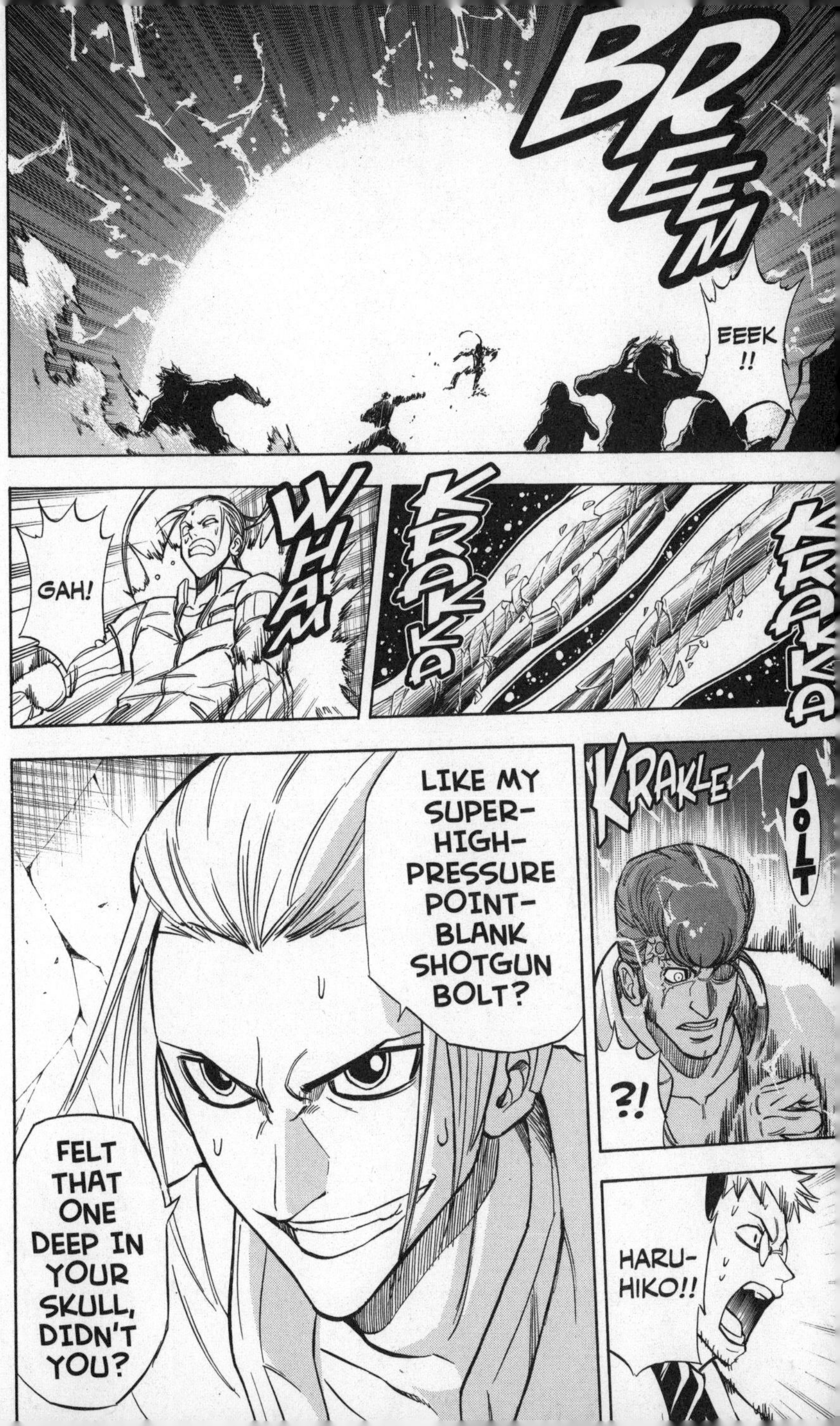
BREEEM
EEEK !!
KRAKA
KRAKA
WHAM
GAH!
KRAKLE
JOLT
?!
HARU-HIKO!!
LIKE MY SUPER-HIGH-PRESSURE POINT-BLANK SHOTGUN BOLT?
FELT THAT ONE DEEP IN YOUR SKULL, DIDN'T YOU?

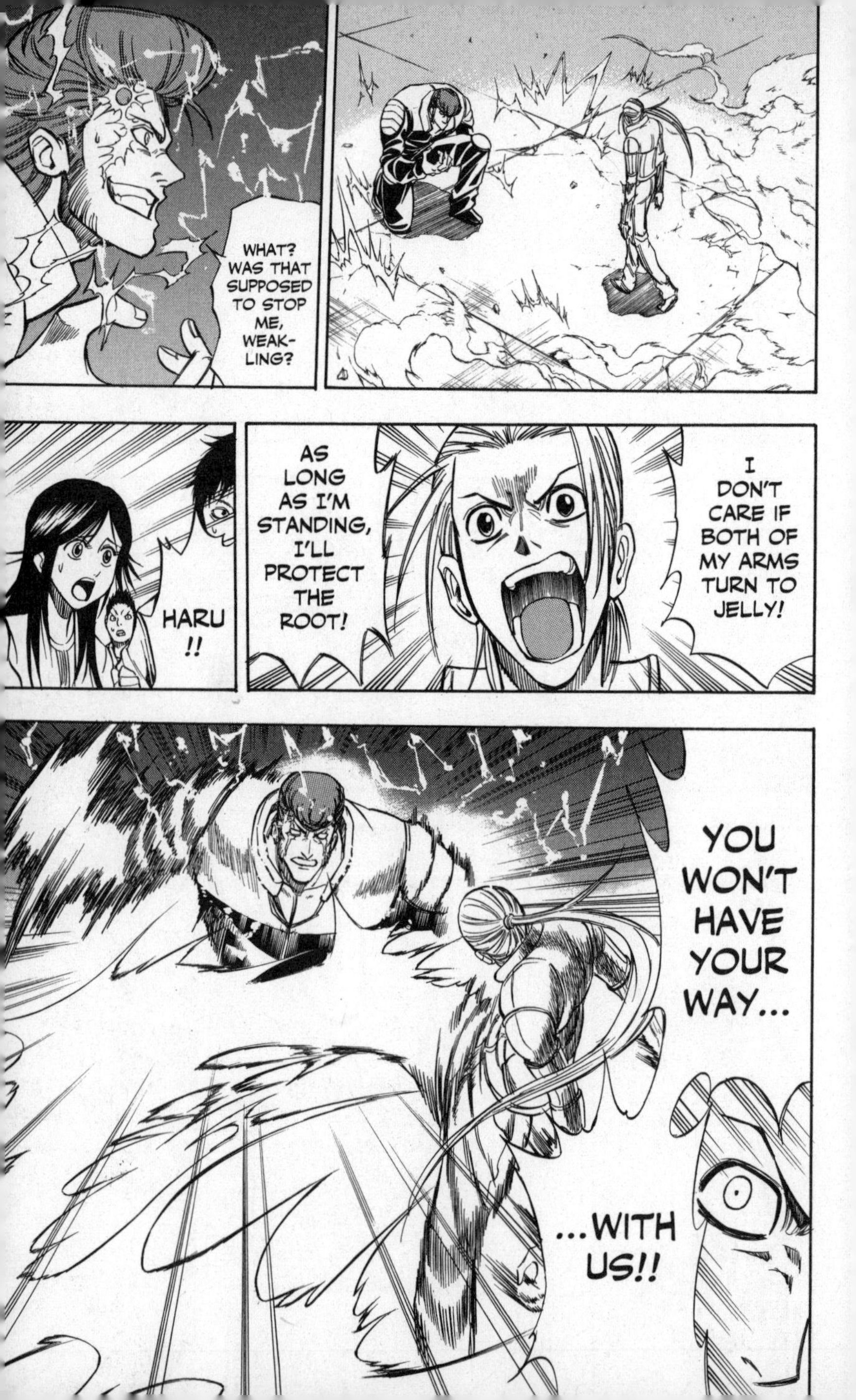
WHAT? WAS THAT SUPPOSED TO STOP ME, WEAK-LING?
I DON'T CARE IF BOTH OF MY ARMS TURN TO JELLY!
AS LONG AS I'M STANDING, I'LL PROTECT THE ROOT!
HARU !!
YOU WON'T HAVE YOUR WAY...
...WITH US!!

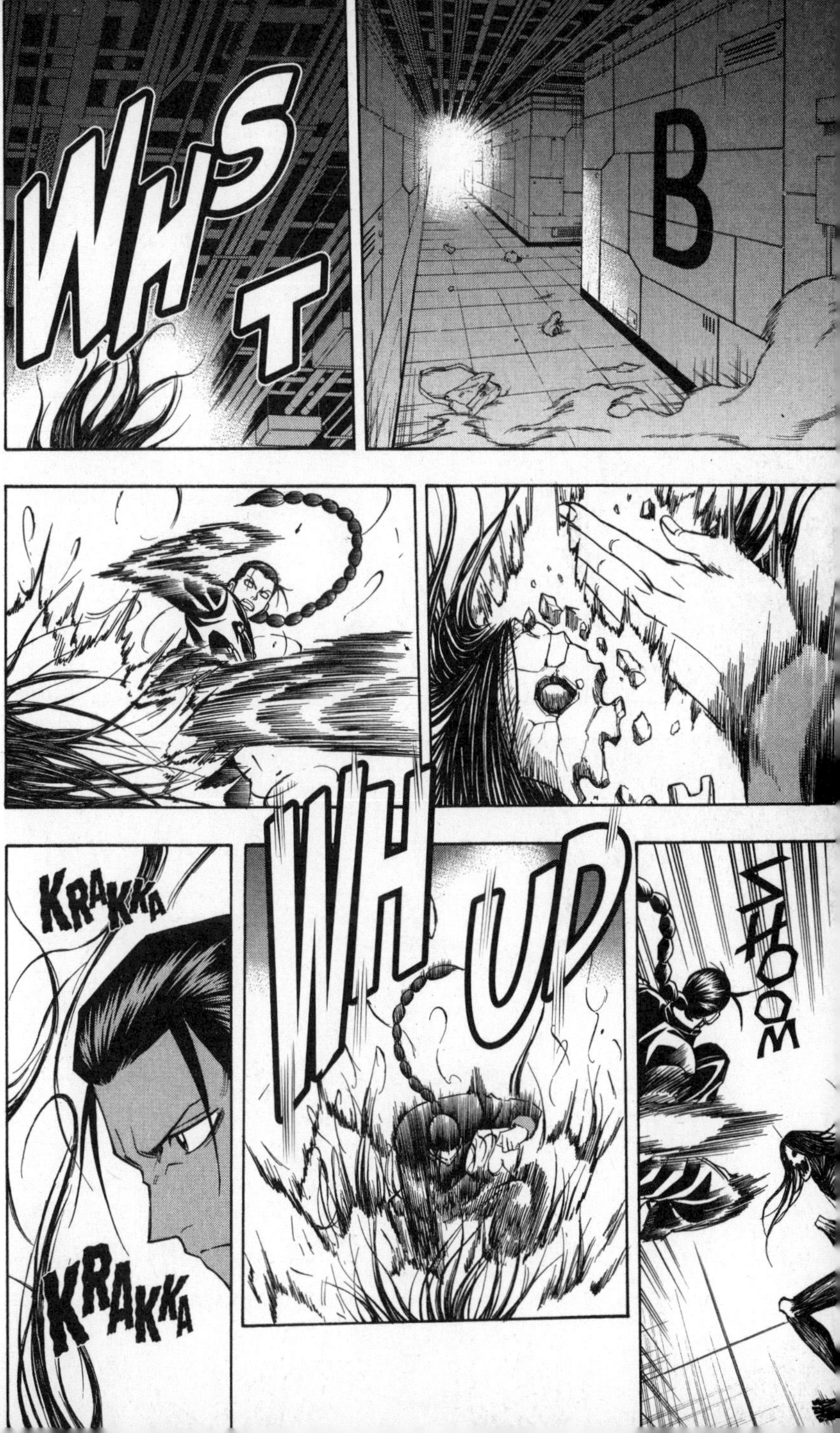
B
WHST
SHOOM
WHUD
KRAKKA
KRAKKA

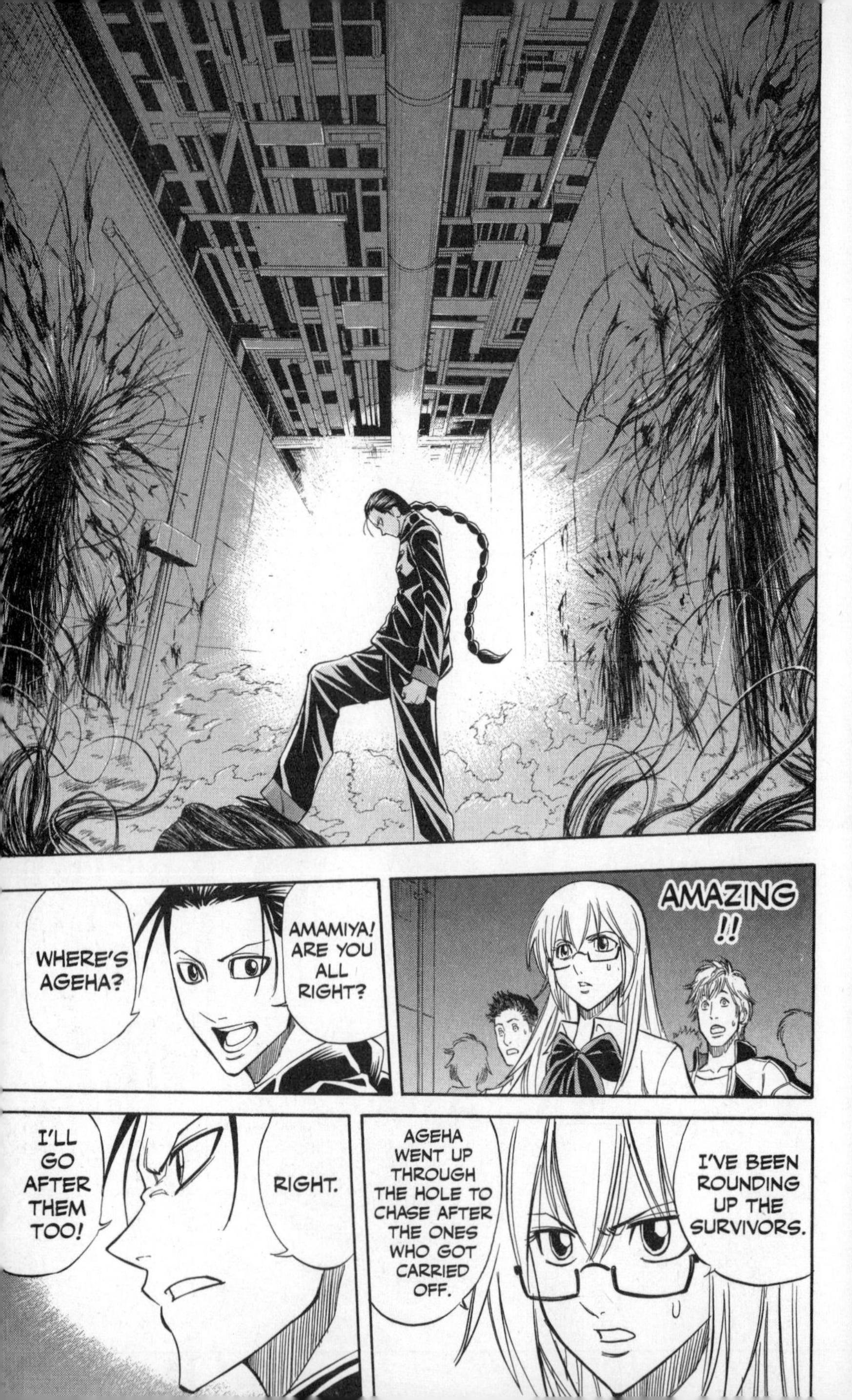
AMAZING!!
AMAMIYA! ARE YOU ALL RIGHT?
WHERE'S AGEHA?
I'VE BEEN ROUNDING UP THE SURVIVORS.
AGEHA WENT UP THROUGH THE HOLE TO CHASE AFTER THE ONES WHO GOT CARRIED OFF.
RIGHT.
I'LL GO AFTER THEM TOO!

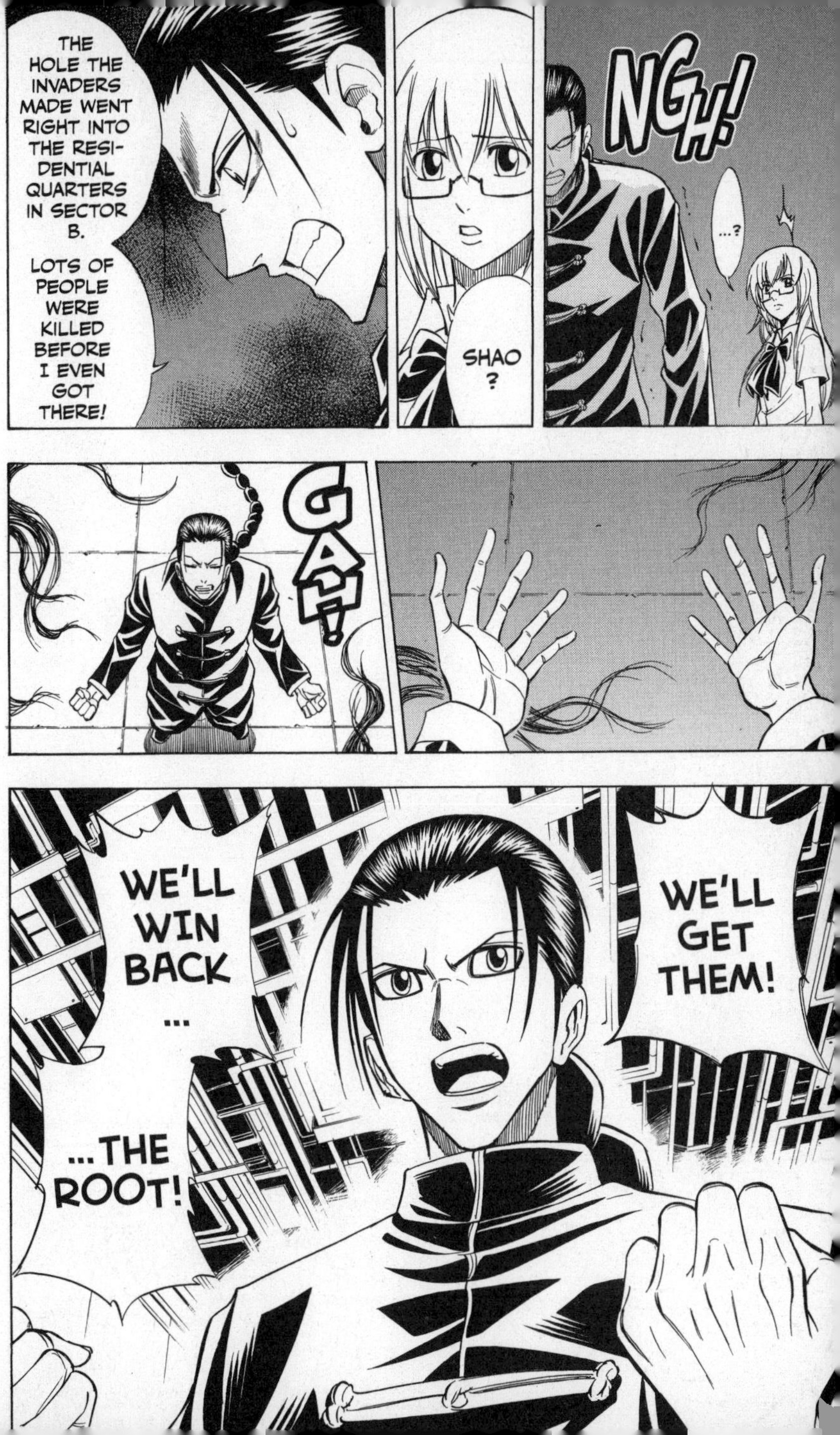
NGH!
...?
SHAO?
THE HOLE THE INVADERS MADE WENT RIGHT INTO THE RESI-DENTIAL QUARTERS IN SECTOR B.
LOTS OF PEOPLE WERE KILLED BEFORE I EVEN GOT THERE!
GAH!
WE'LL GET THEM!
WE'LL WIN BACK...
...THE ROOT!

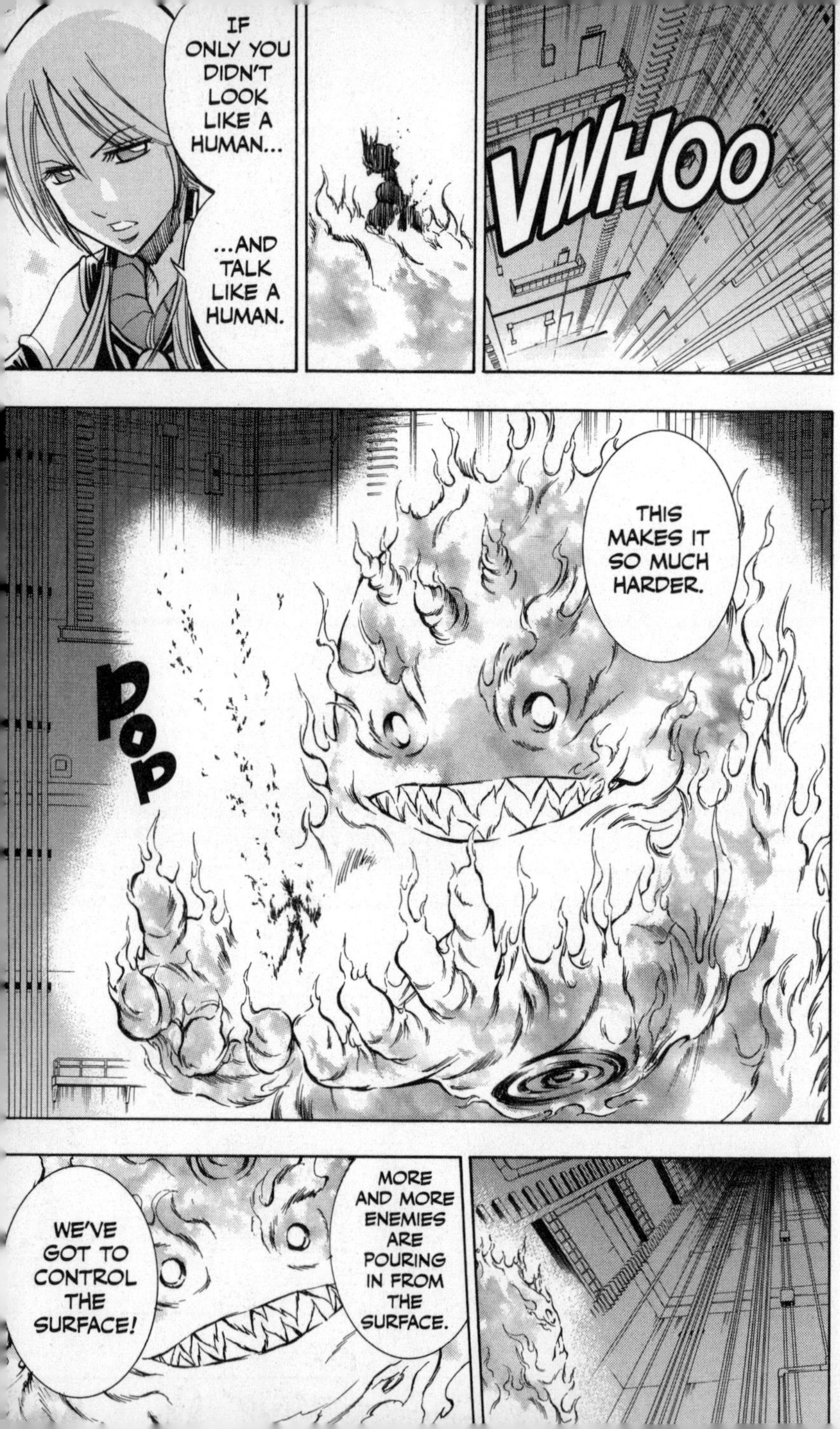
VWHOO
IF ONLY YOU DIDN'T LOOK LIKE A HUMAN...
...AND TALK LIKE A HUMAN.
THIS MAKES IT SO MUCH HARDER.
POP
MORE AND MORE ENEMIES ARE POURING IN FROM THE SURFACE.
WE'VE GOT TO CONTROL THE SURFACE!

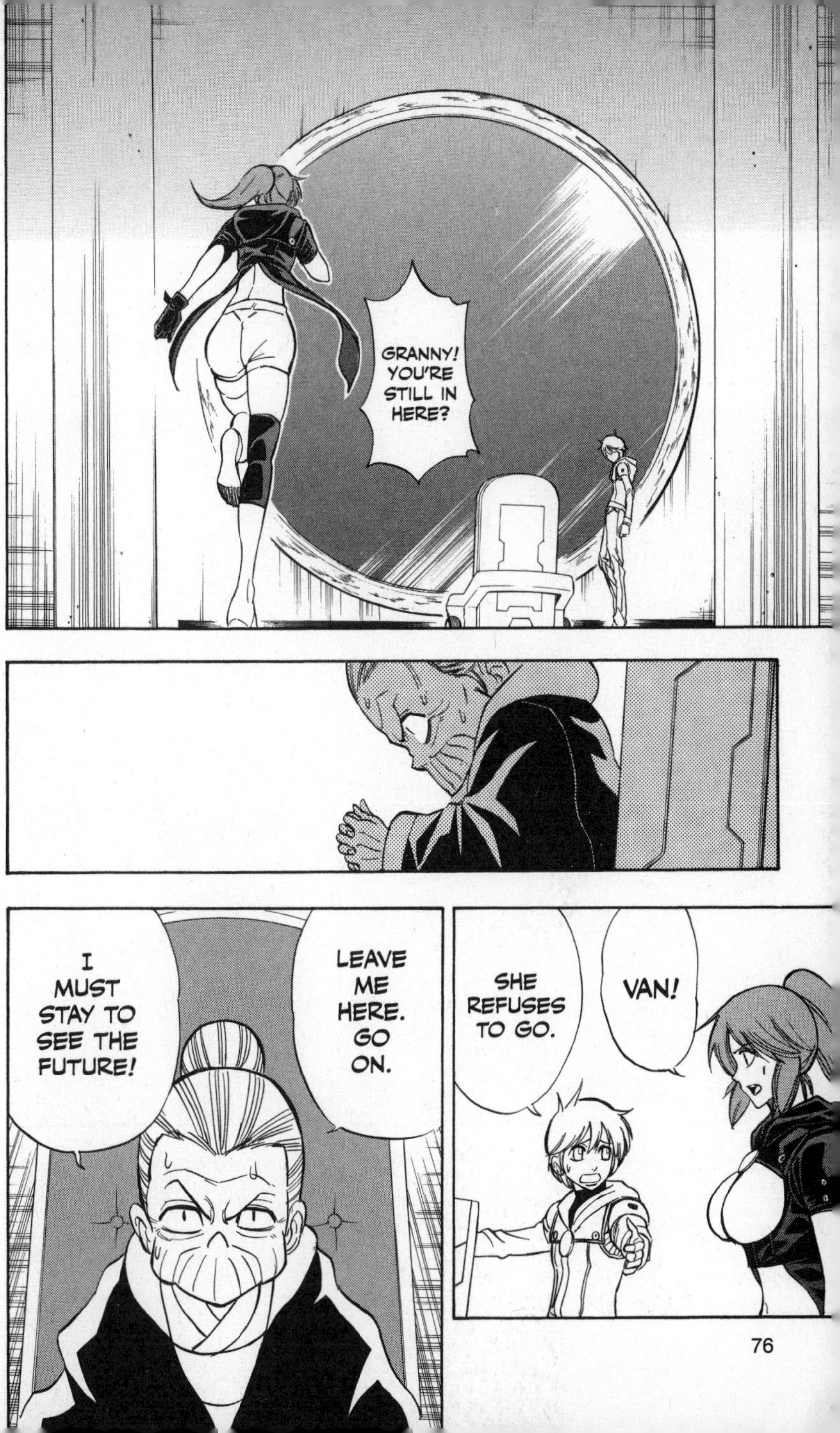
GRANNY! YOU'RE STILL IN HERE?
VAN!
SHE REFUSES TO GO.
LEAVE ME HERE. GO ON.
I MUST STAY TO SEE THE FUTURE!

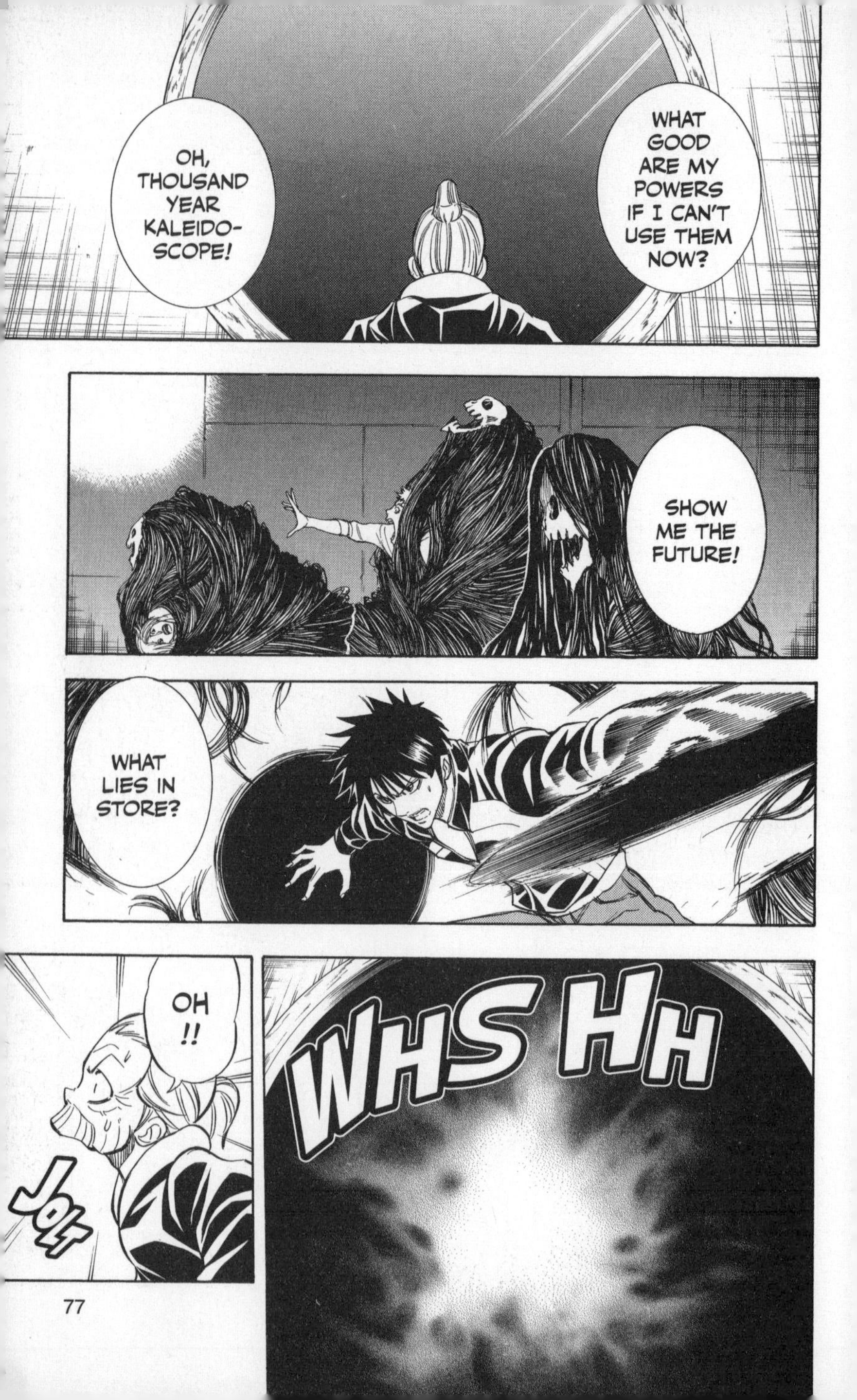
WHAT GOOD ARE MY POWERS IF I CAN'T USE THEM NOW?
OH, THOUSAND YEAR KALEIDO-SCOPE!
SHOW ME THE FUTURE!
WHAT LIES IN STORE?
WHSHH
OH !!
JOLT

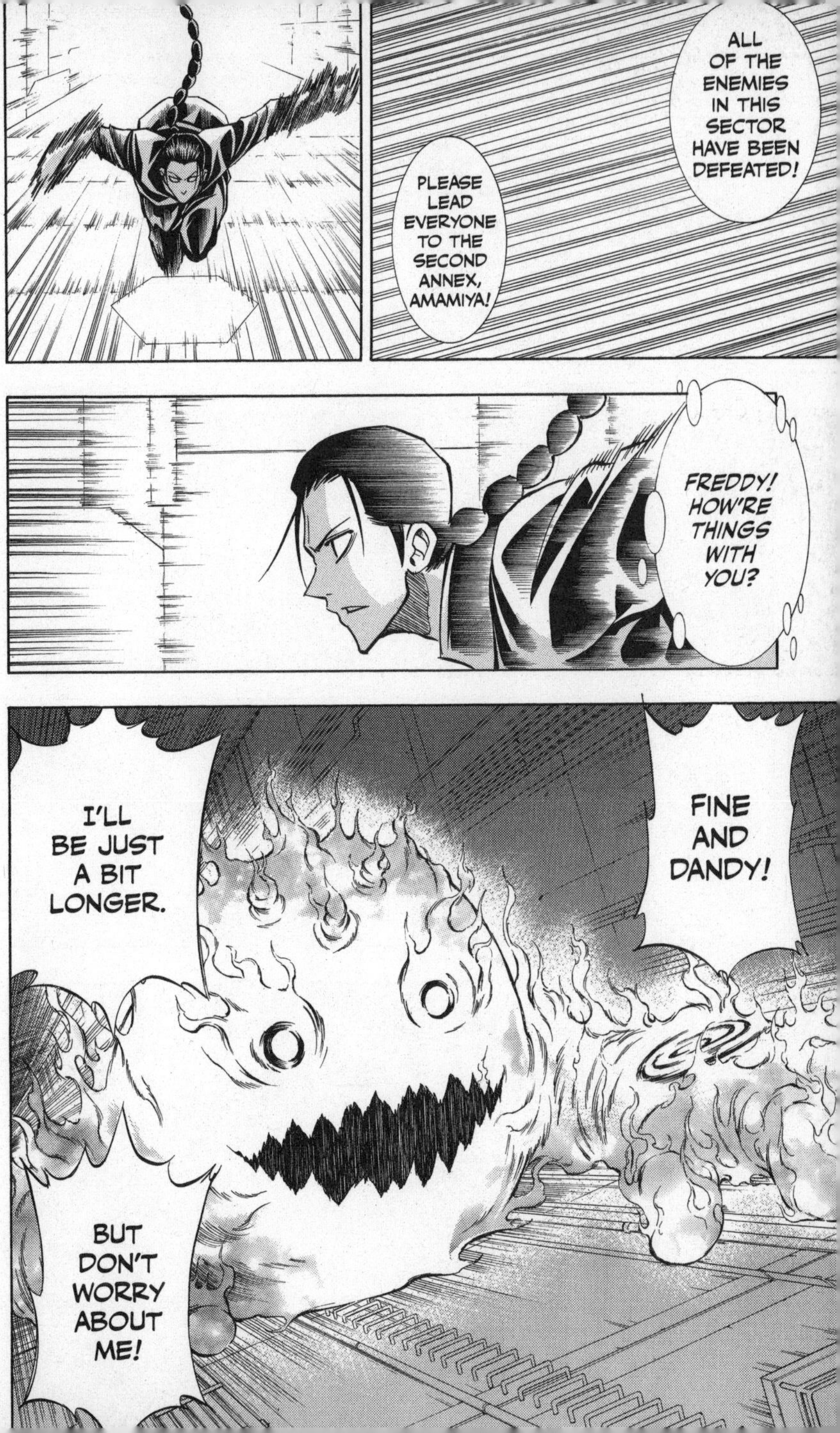
ALL OF THE ENEMIES IN THIS SECTOR HAVE BEEN DEFEATED!
PLEASE LEAD EVERYONE TO THE SECOND ANNEX, AMAMIYA!
FREDDY! HOW'RE THINGS WITH YOU?
FINE AND DANDY!
I'LL BE JUST A BIT LONGER.
BUT DON'T WORRY ABOUT ME!

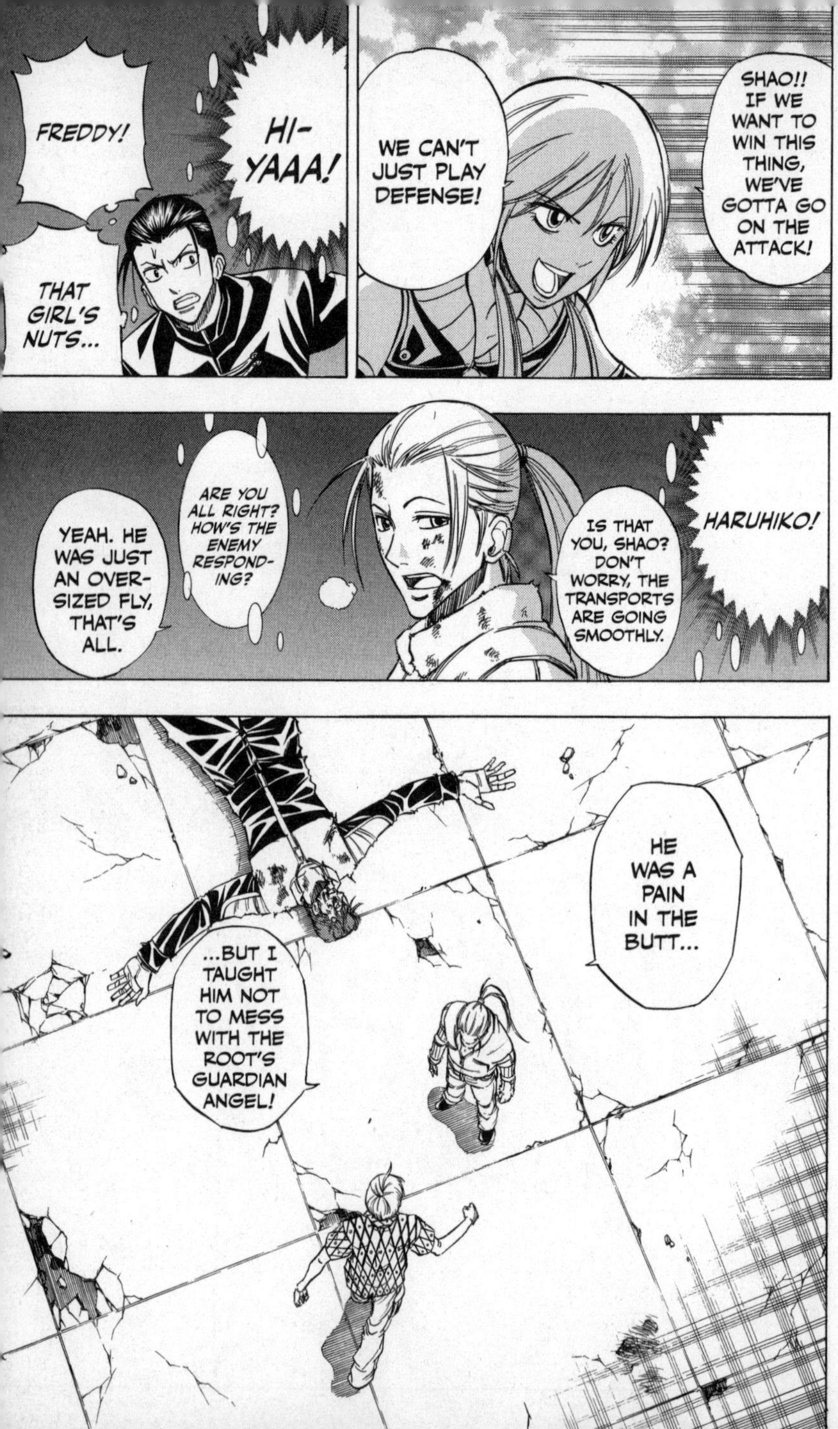
SHAO!! IF WE WANT TO WIN THIS THING, WE'VE GOTTA GO ON THE ATTACK!
WE CAN'T JUST PLAY DEFENSE!
HI-YAAA!
FREDDY!
THAT GIRL'S NUTS...
HARUHIKO!
IS THAT YOU, SHAO? DON'T WORRY, THE TRANSPORTS ARE GOING SMOOTHLY.
ARE YOU ALL RIGHT? HOW'S THE ENEMY RESPOND-ING?
YEAH. HE WAS JUST AN OVER-SIZED FLY, THAT'S ALL.
HE WAS A PAIN IN THE BUTT...
...BUT I TAUGHT HIM NOT TO MESS WITH THE ROOT'S GUARDIAN ANGEL!

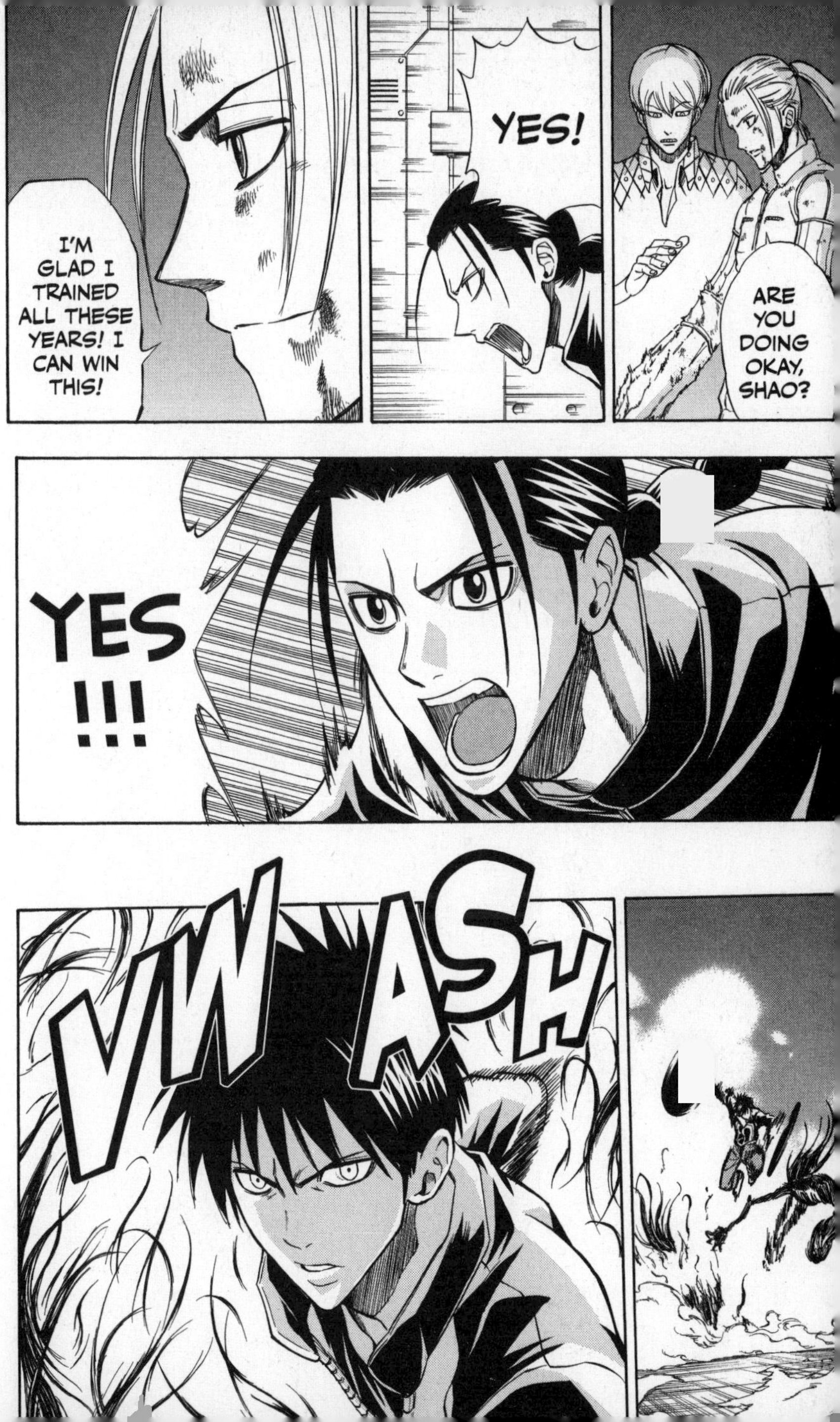
ARE YOU DOING OKAY, SHAO?
YES!
I'M GLAD I TRAINED ALL THESE YEARS! I CAN WIN THIS!
YES !!!
VWASH

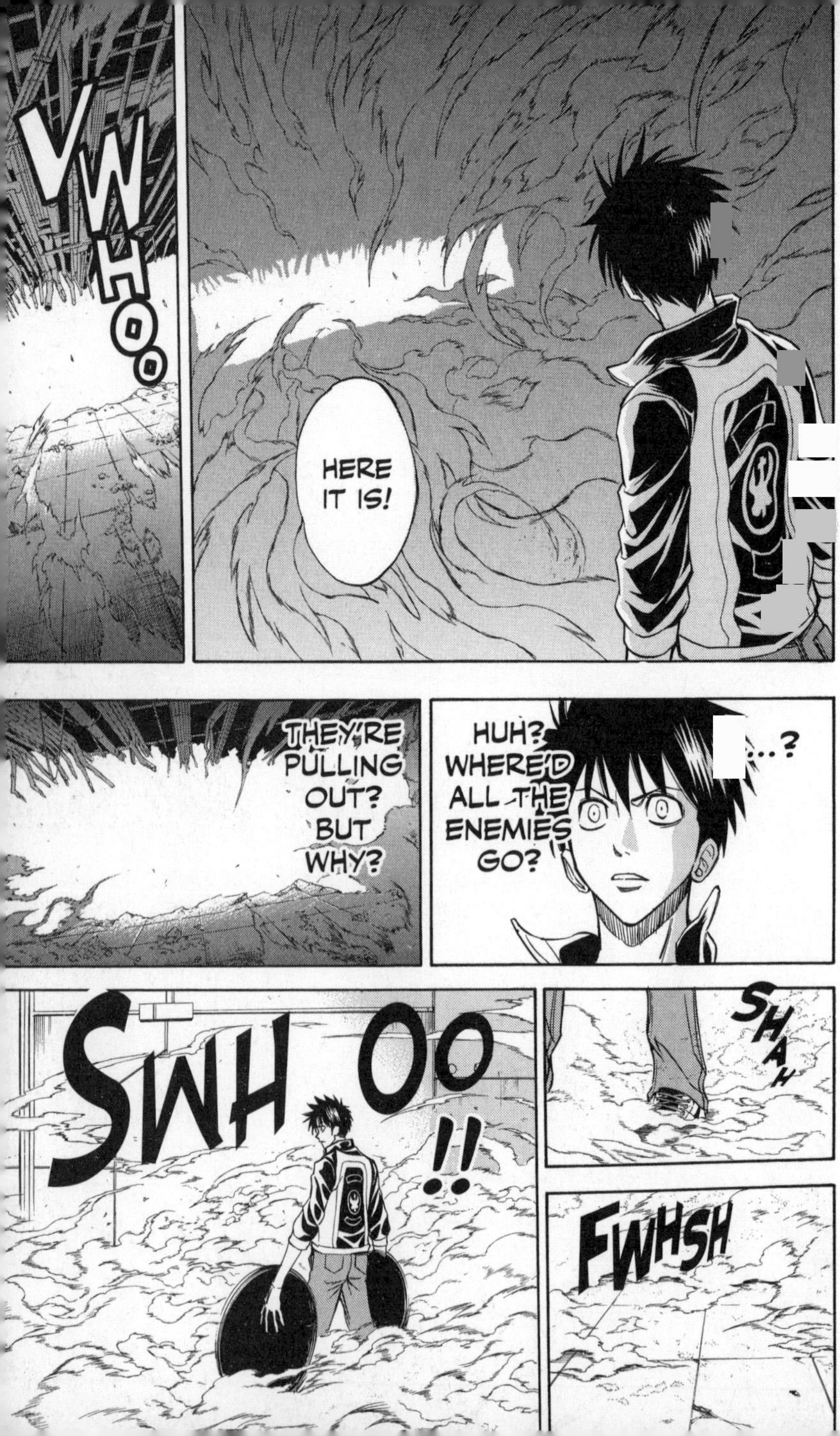
HERE IT IS!
VWHOOO
...?
HUH? WHERE'D ALL THE ENEMIES GO?
THEY'RE PULLING OUT? BUT WHY?
SHAH
FWHSH
SWHOO!!

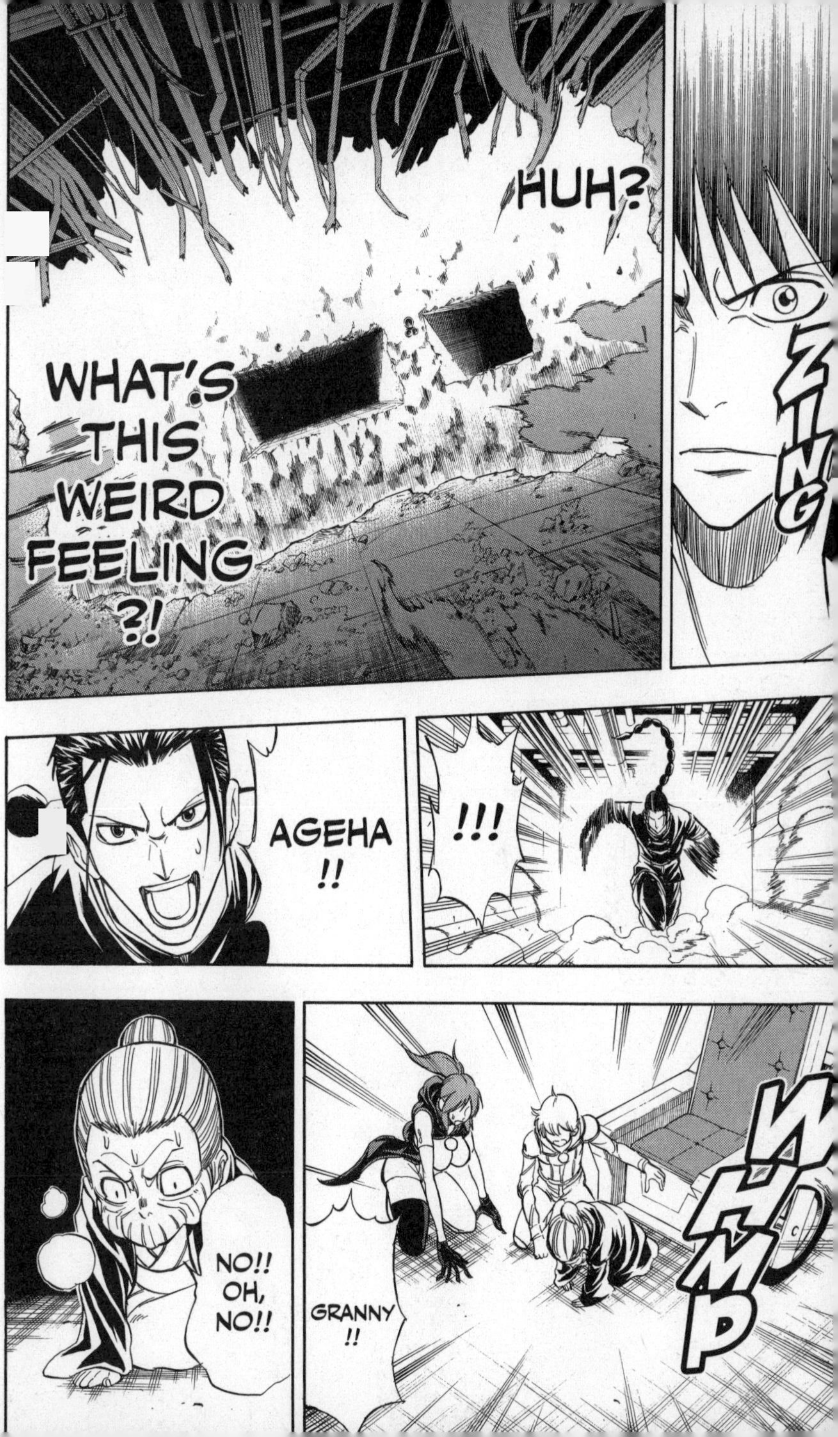
ZING
HUH?
WHAT'S THIS WEIRD FEELING ?!
!!!
AGEHA !!
WHUMP
GRANNY !!
NO!! OH, NO!!

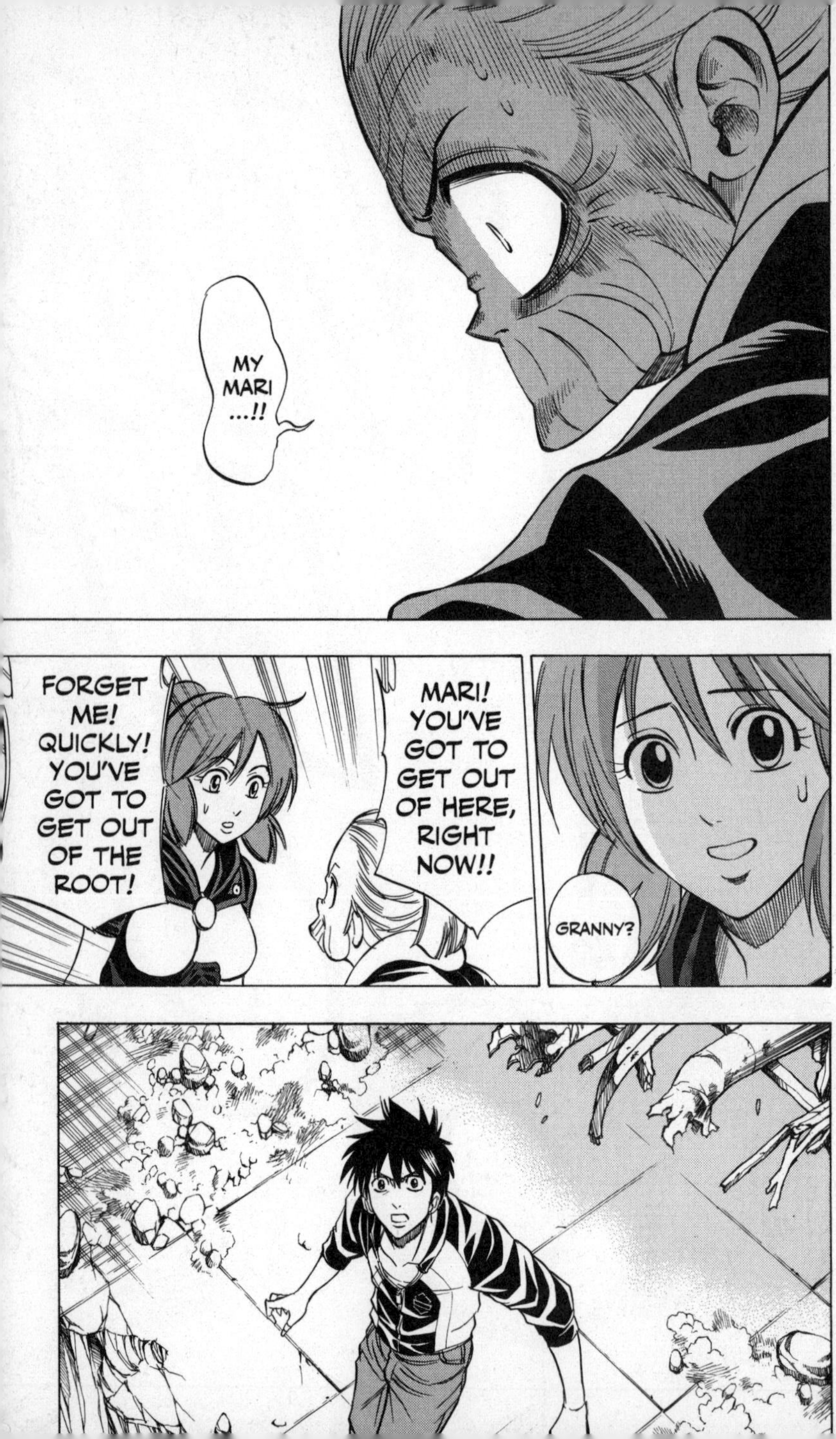
MY MARI ...!!
GRANNY?
MARI! YOU'VE GOT TO GET OUT OF HERE, RIGHT NOW!!
FORGET ME! QUICKLY! YOU'VE GOT TO GET OUT OF THE ROOT!

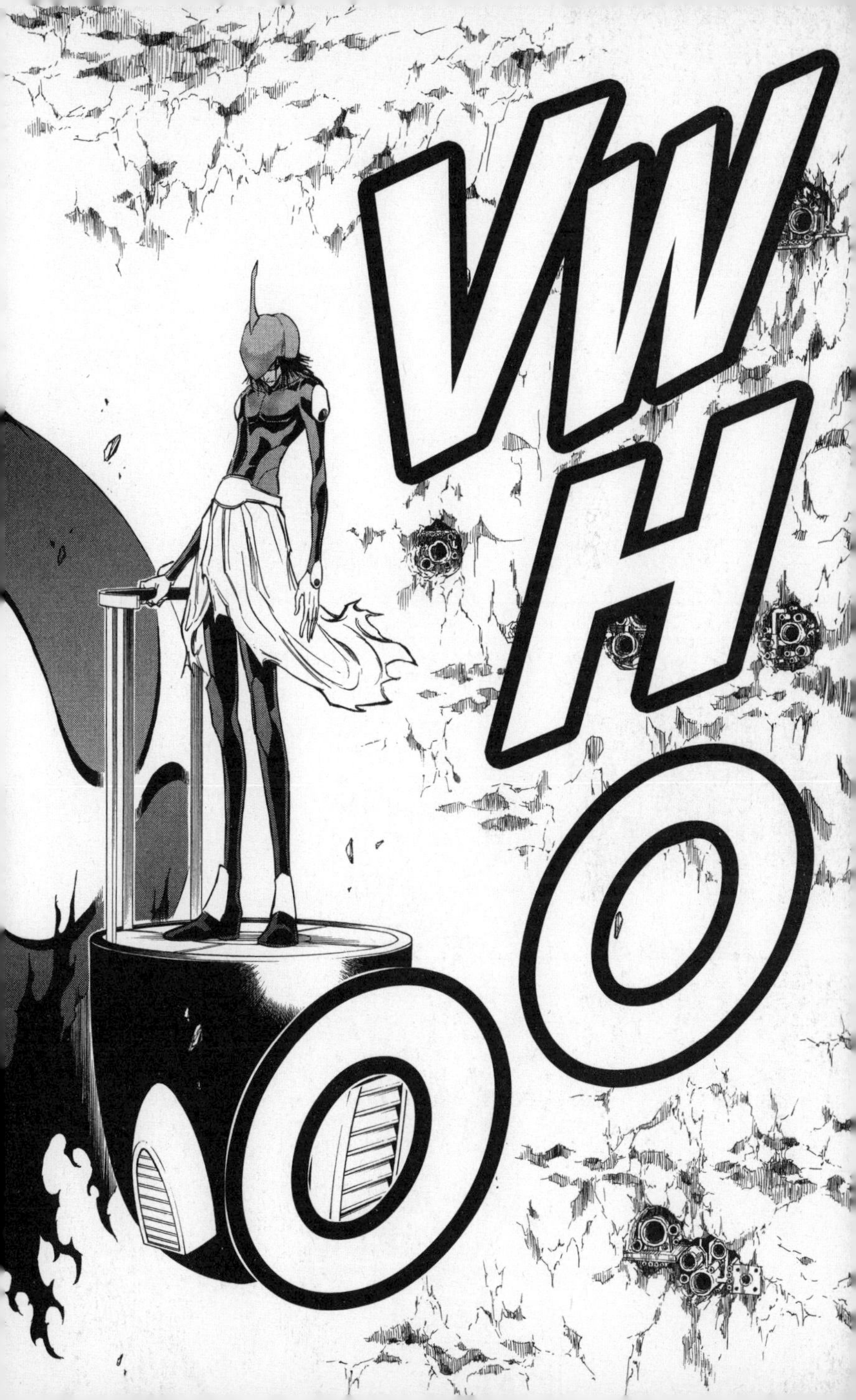
VWHOO

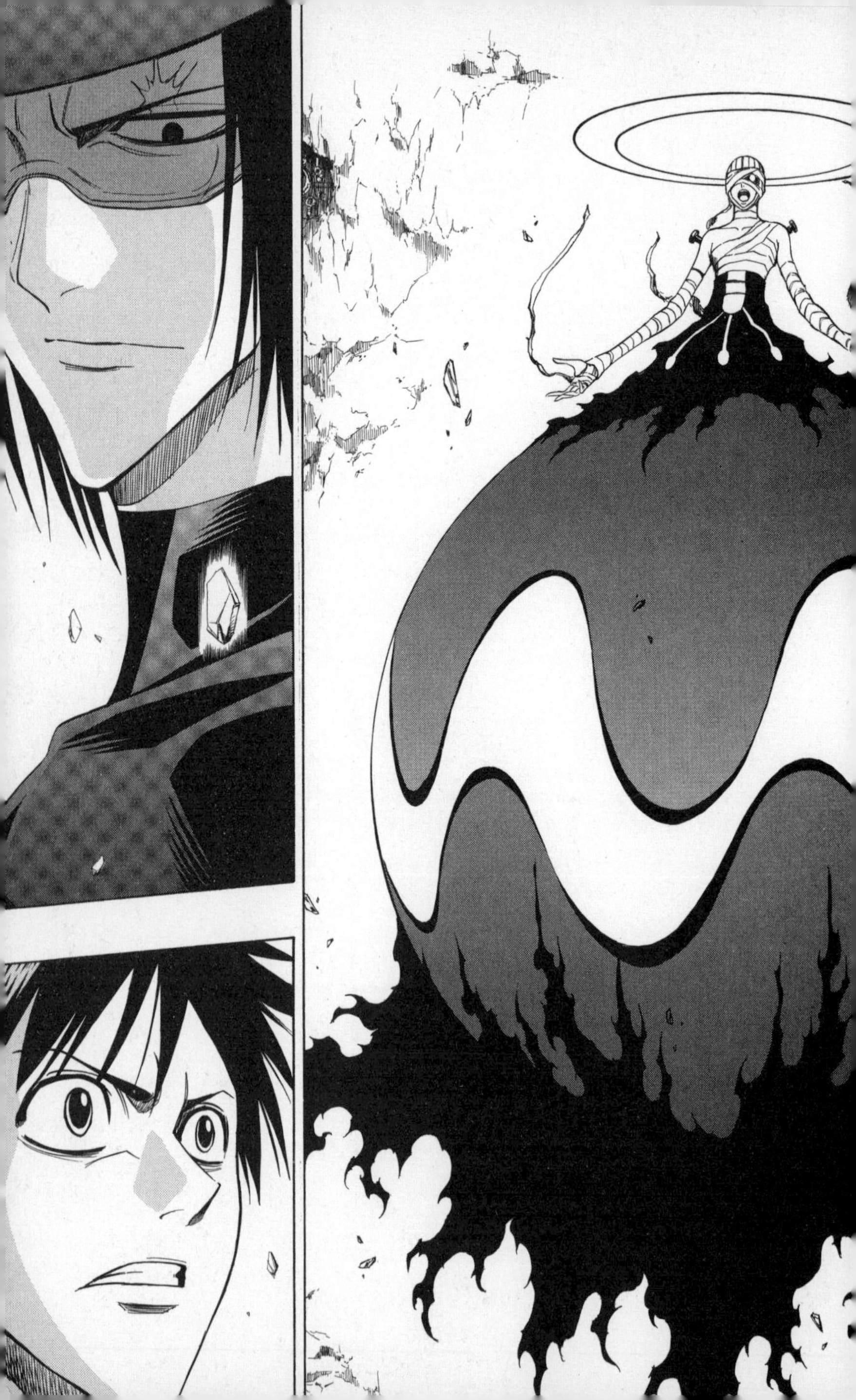

Mutters and mumblings...

I WON'T SAY BATTLE SCENES ARE FUN TO DRAW,
BUT I LIKE SITUATIONS IN WHICH VARIOUS CHARACTERS
ARE STRUGGLING TO OVERCOME CHALLENGES IN
DIFFERENT PLACES. IT'S REALLY SATISFYING TO COME
UP WITH A TIGHT, FAST-PACED STORYBOARD THAT JUST
SHOWS THE KEY MOMENTS OF EACH SCENE.

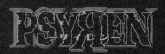

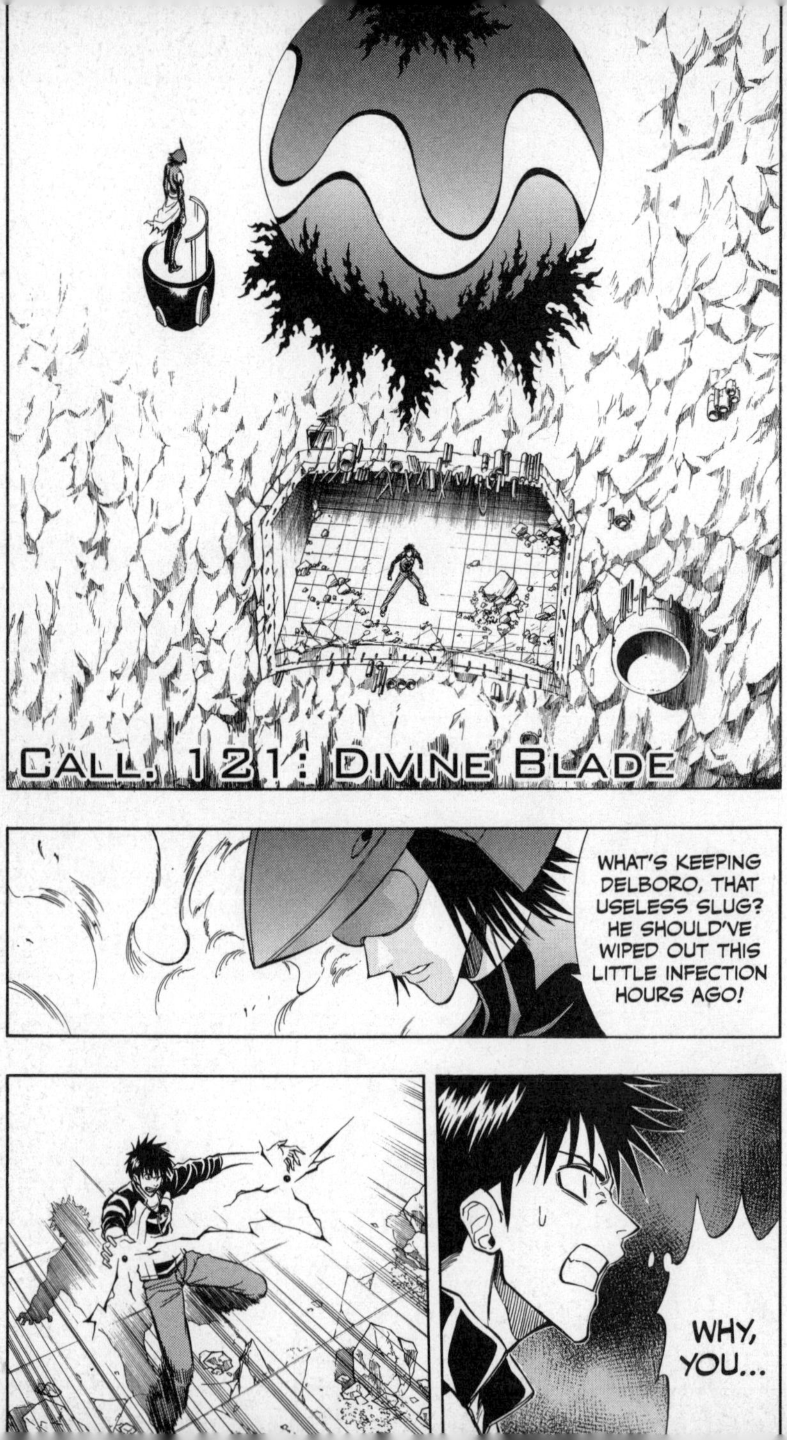
CALL. 121: DIVINE BLADE
WHAT'S KEEPING DELBORO, THAT USELESS SLUG? HE SHOULD'VE WIPED OUT THIS LITTLE INFECTION HOURS AGO!
WHY, YOU...

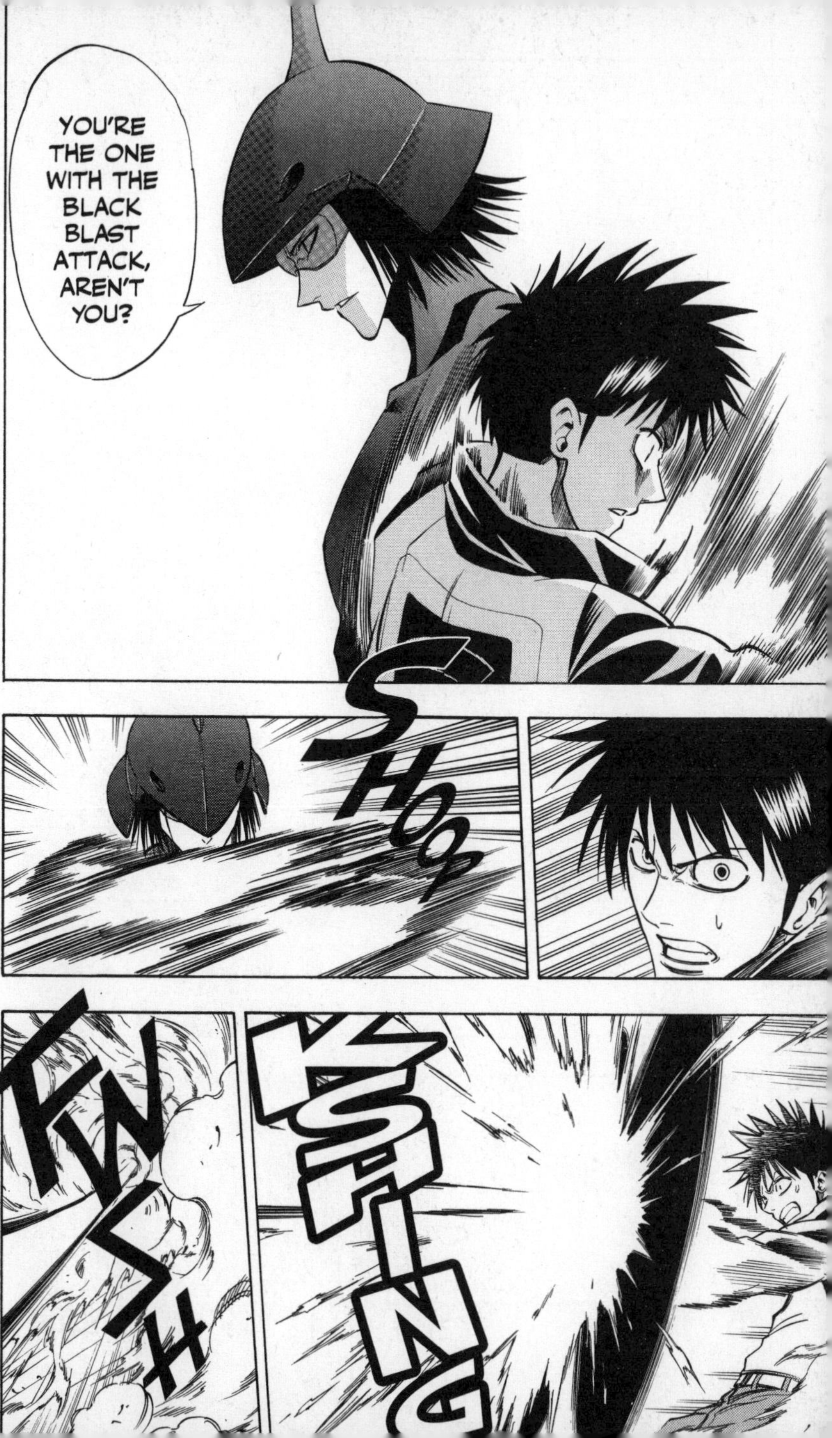
YOU'RE THE ONE WITH THE BLACK BLAST ATTACK, AREN'T YOU?
SHOOM
KSHING
FWSH

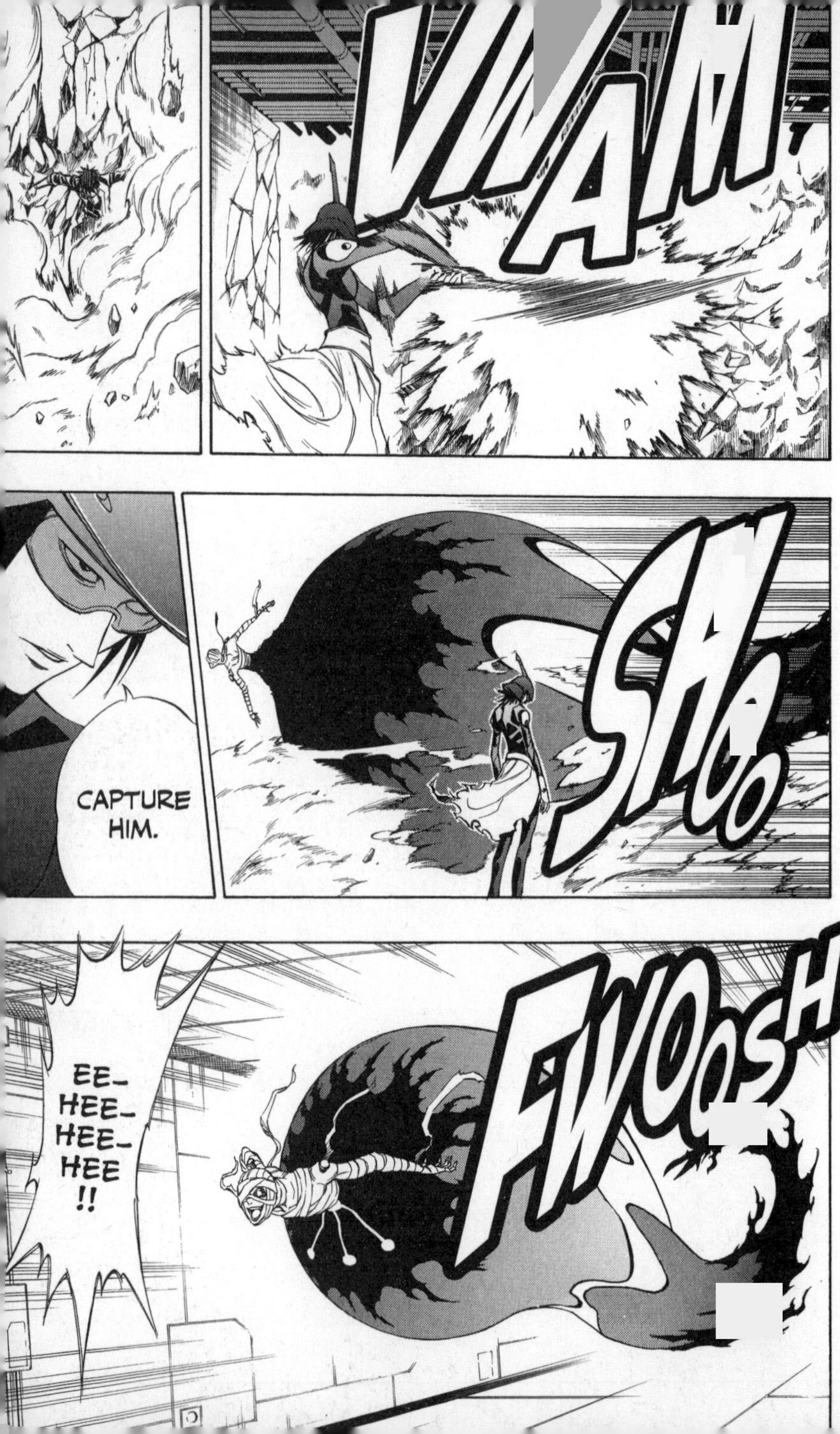
VVAM
SHOO
CAPTURE HIM.
FWOOSH
EE-HEE-HEE-HEE!!

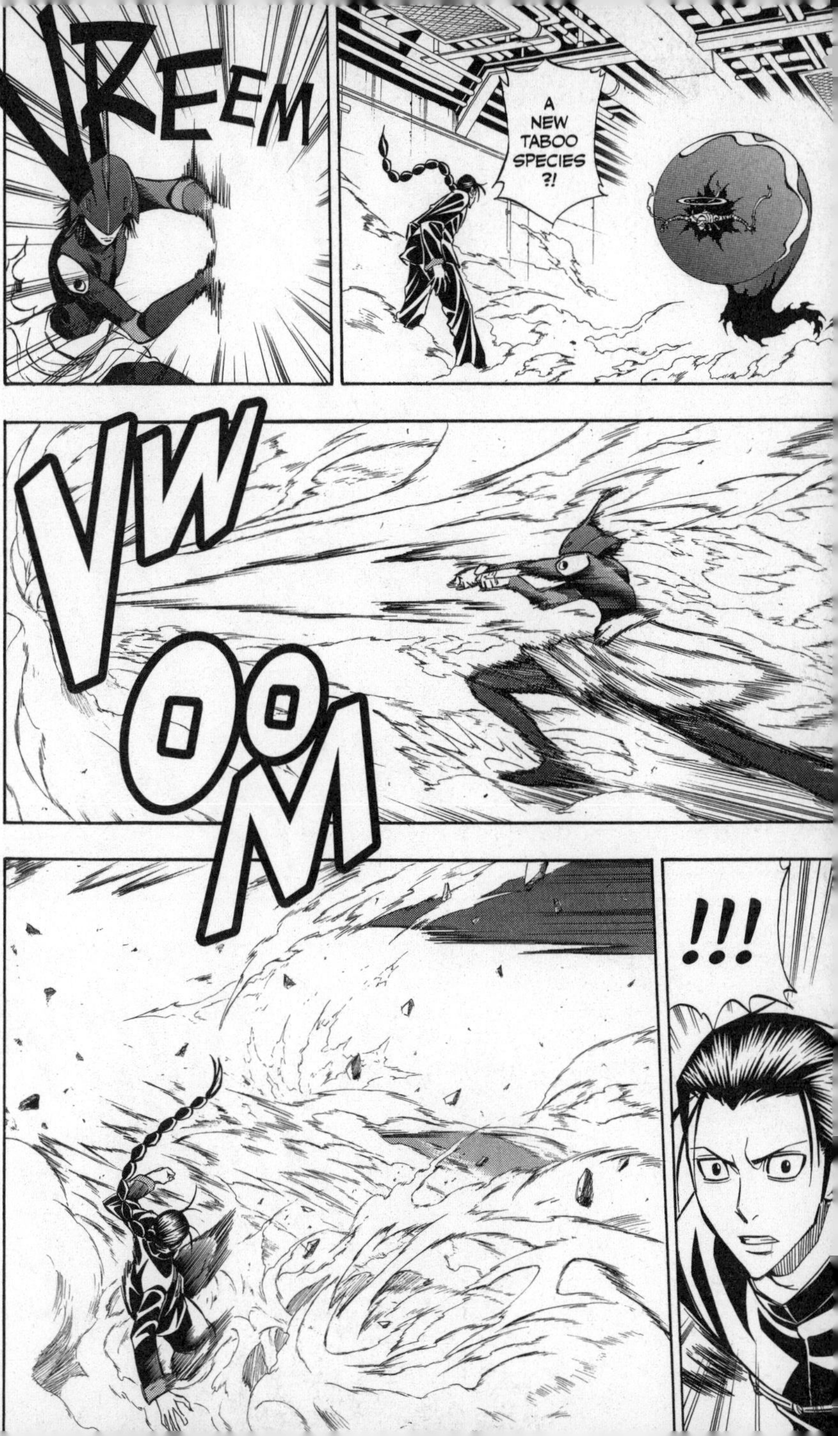
A NEW TABOO SPECIES ?!
VREEM
VWOOM
!!!

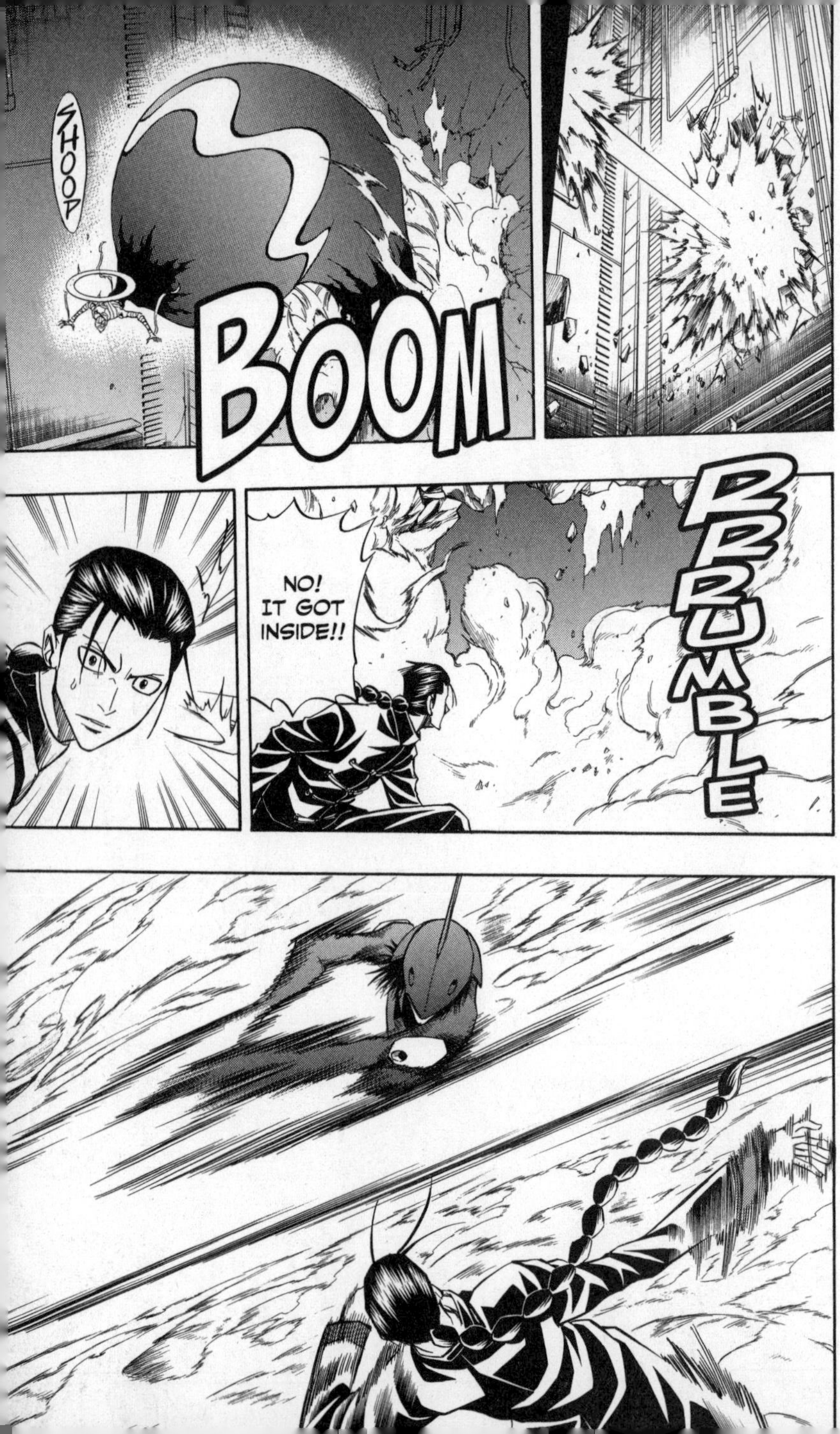
SHOOP
BOOM
RRRUMBLE
NO! IT GOT INSIDE!!

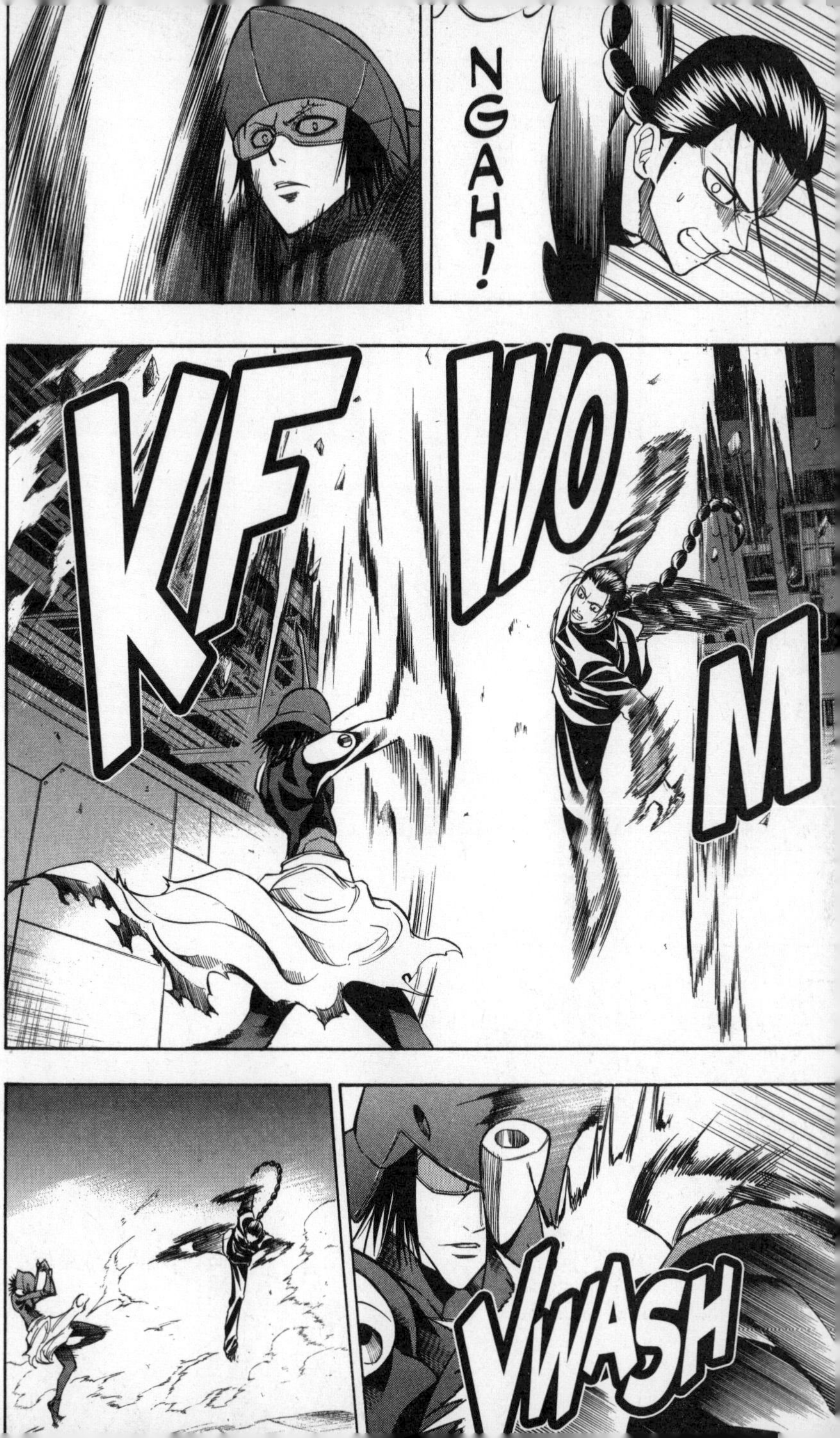
NGAH!
KFWOMM
VWASH

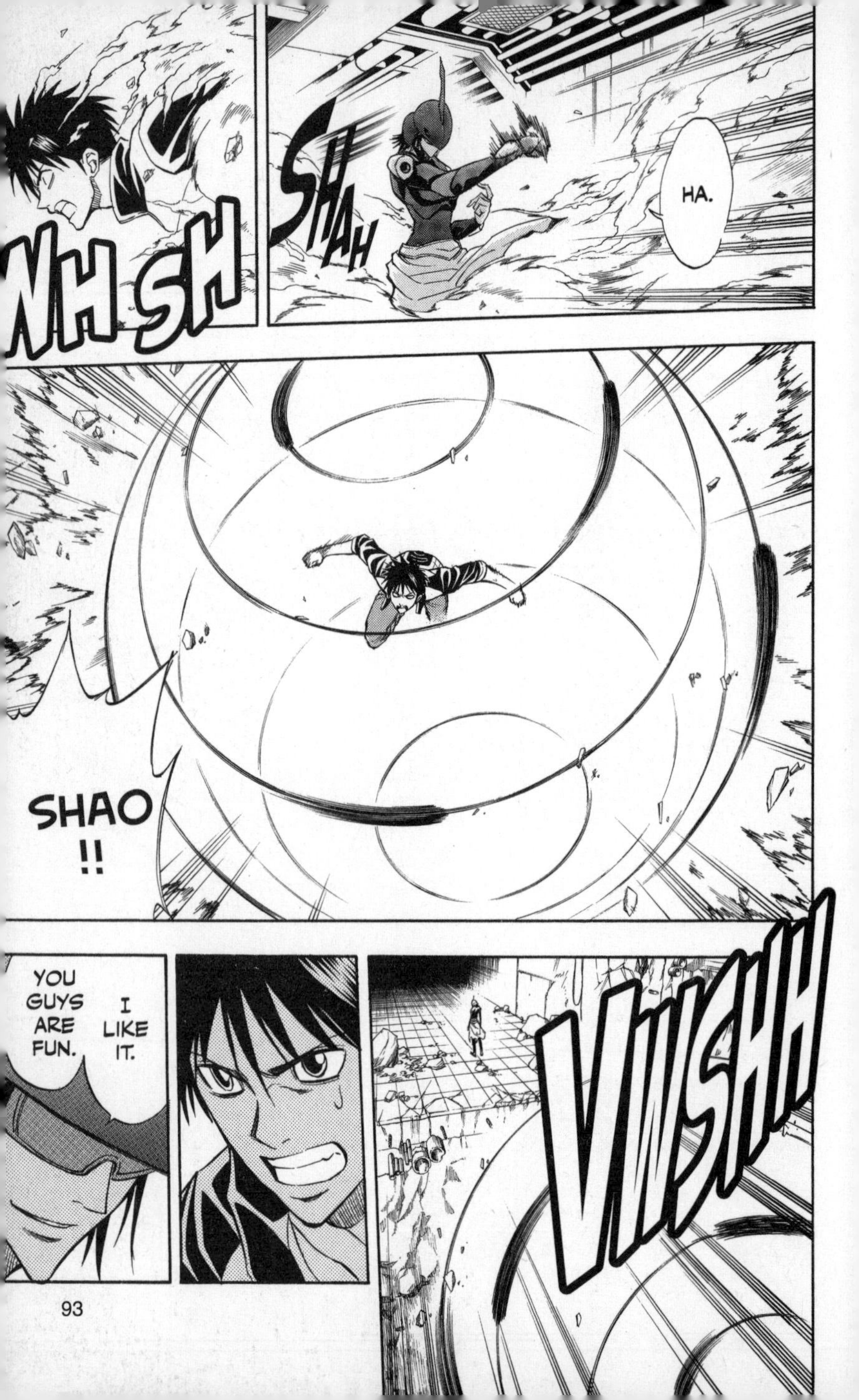
HA.
SHAH
NH SH
SHAO !!
VIISHH
I LIKE IT.
YOU GUYS ARE FUN.

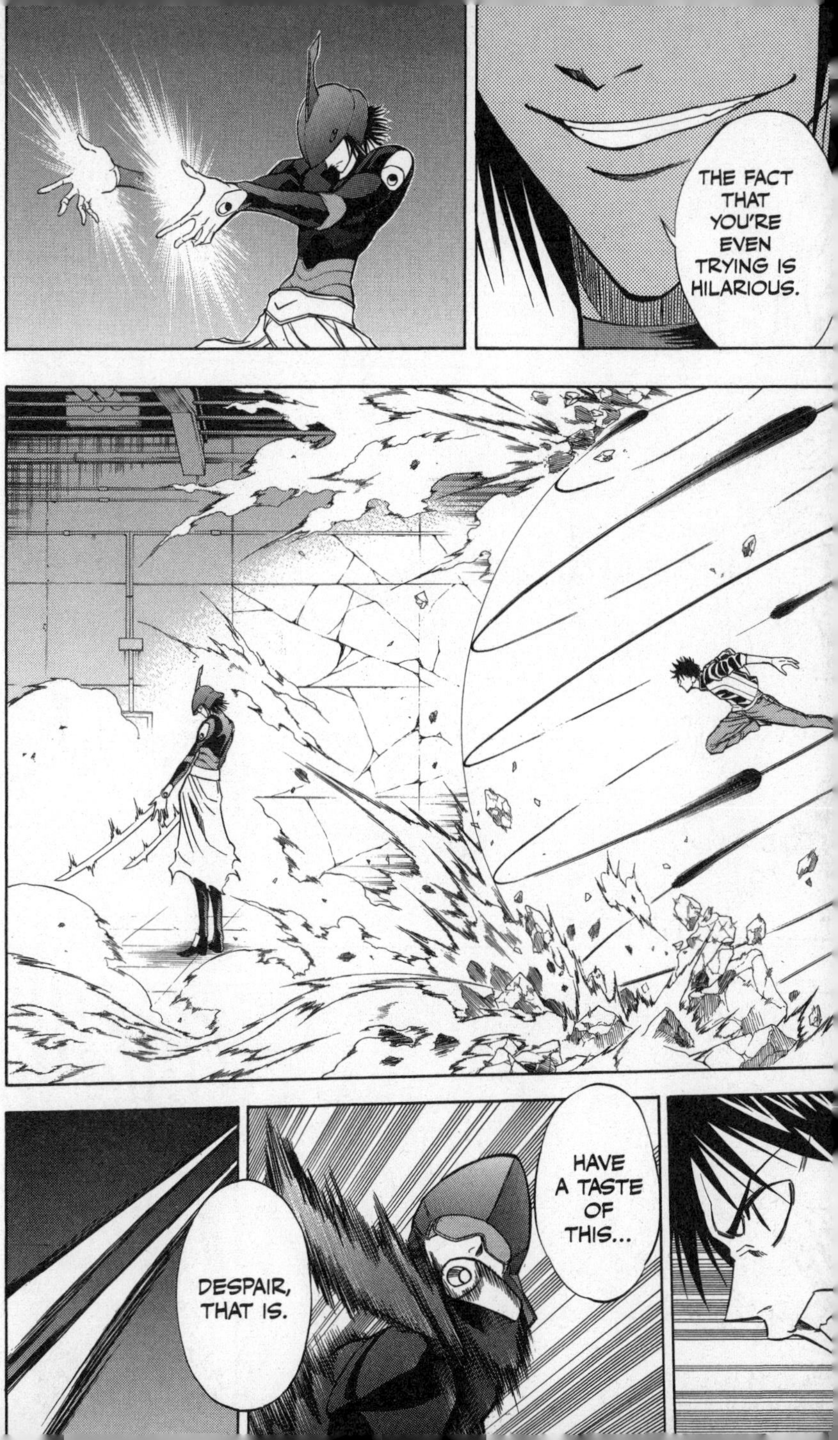
THE FACT THAT YOU'RE EVEN TRYING IS HILARIOUS.
HAVE A TASTE OF THIS...
DESPAIR, THAT IS.

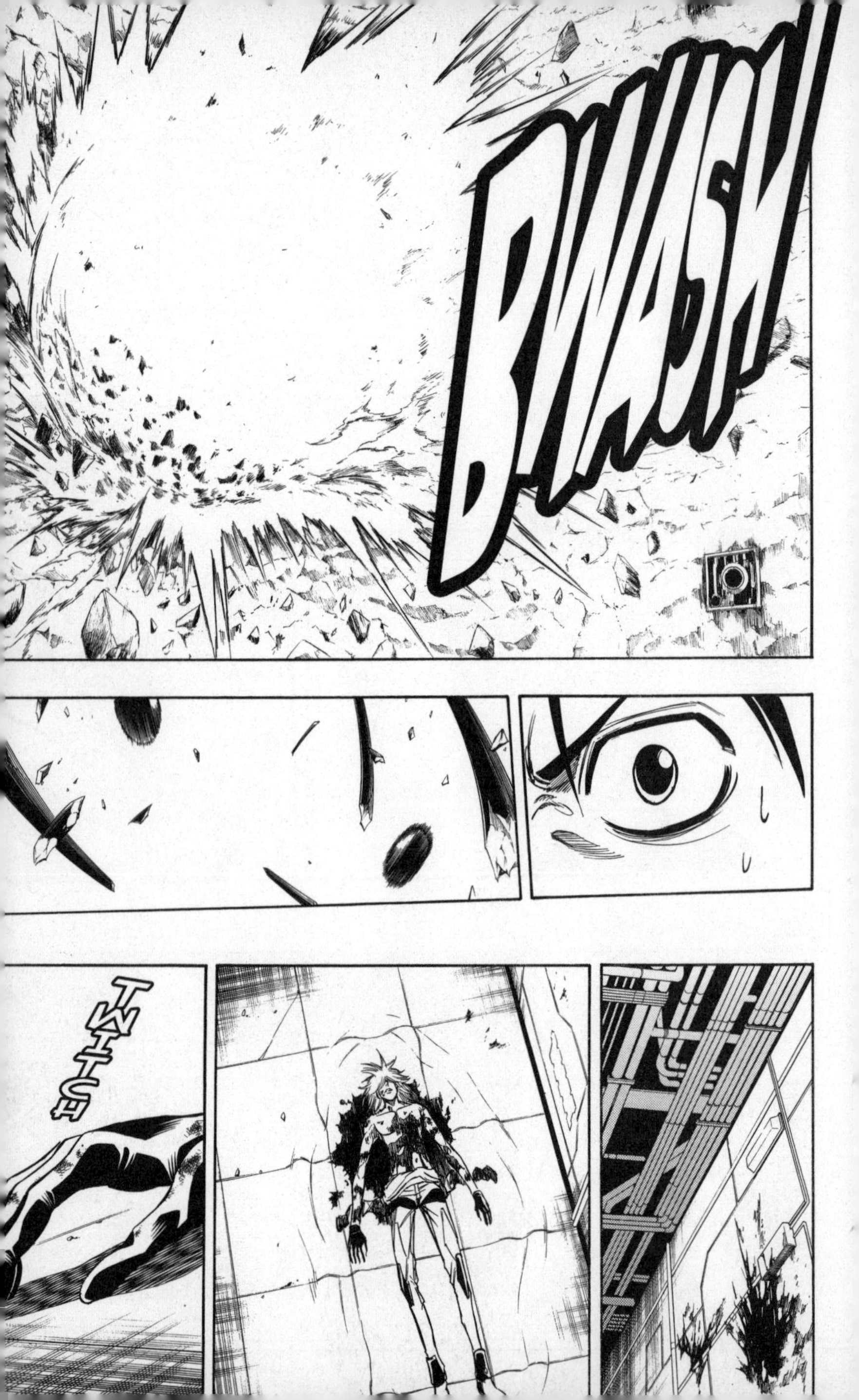
BWASH
TWITCH

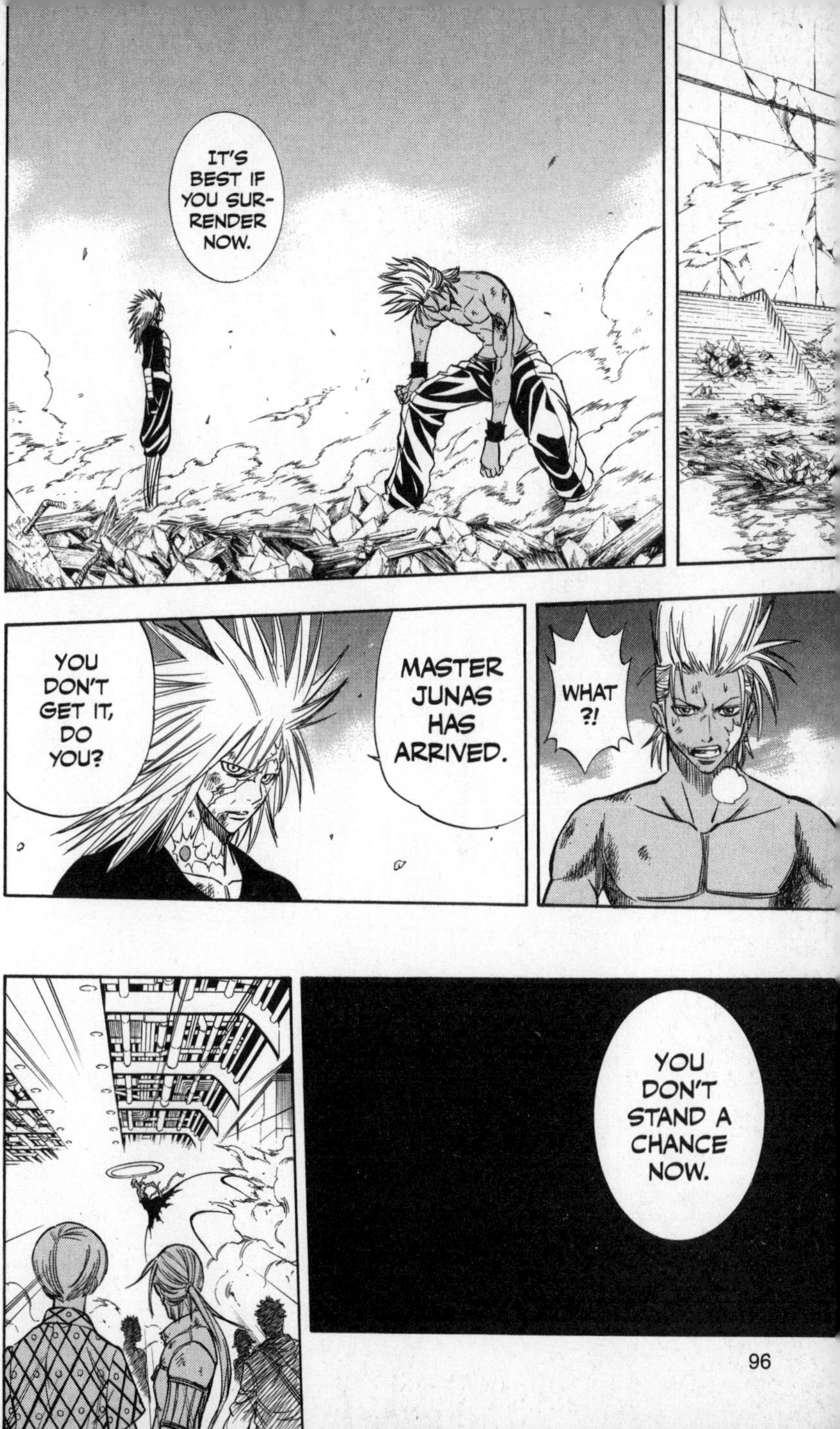
IT'S BEST IF YOU SUR-RENDER NOW.
WHAT?!
MASTER JUNAS HAS ARRIVED.
YOU DON'T GET IT, DO YOU?
YOU DON'T STAND A CHANCE NOW.

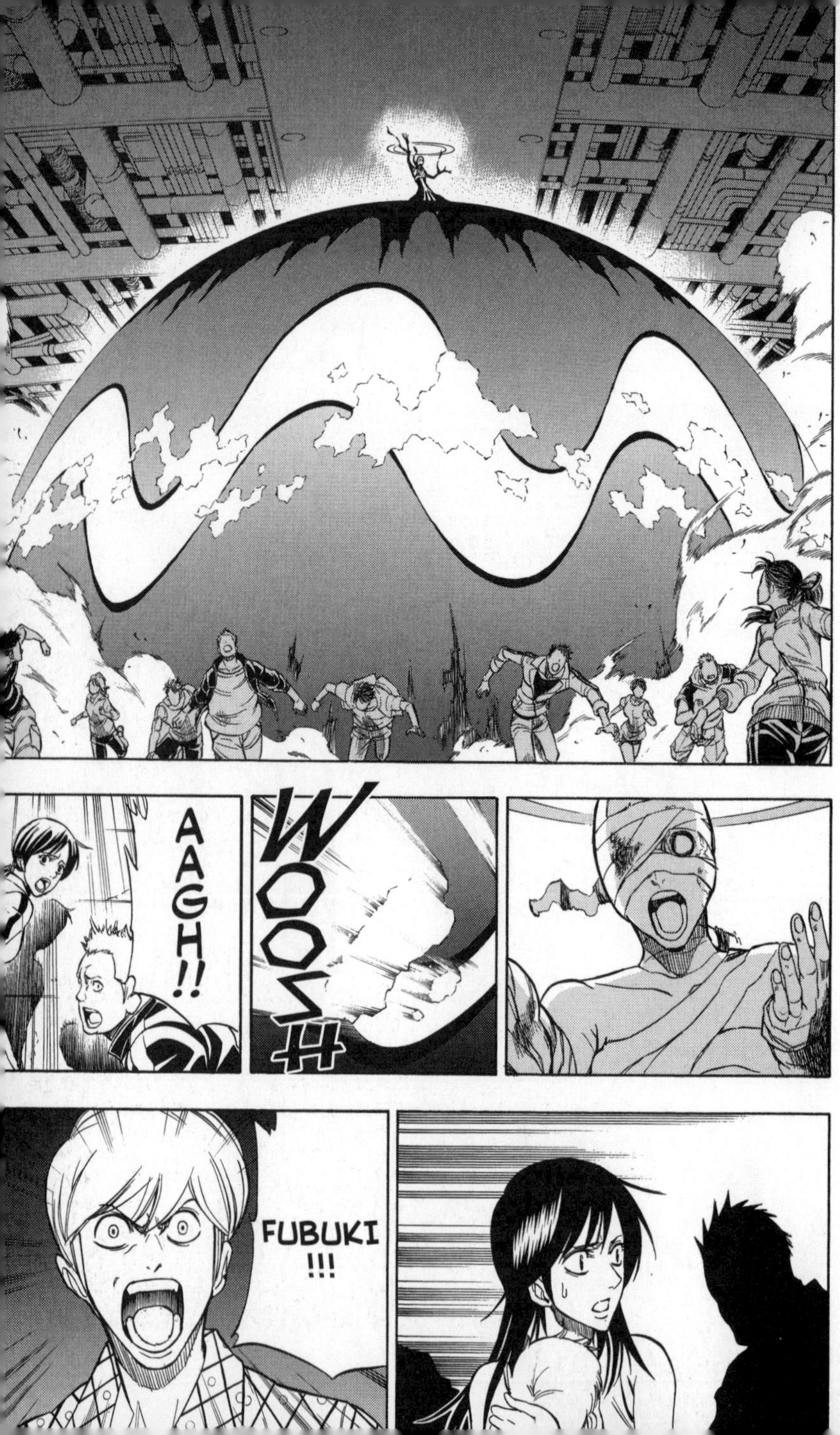
WOOSH
AAGH!!
FUBUKI!!!

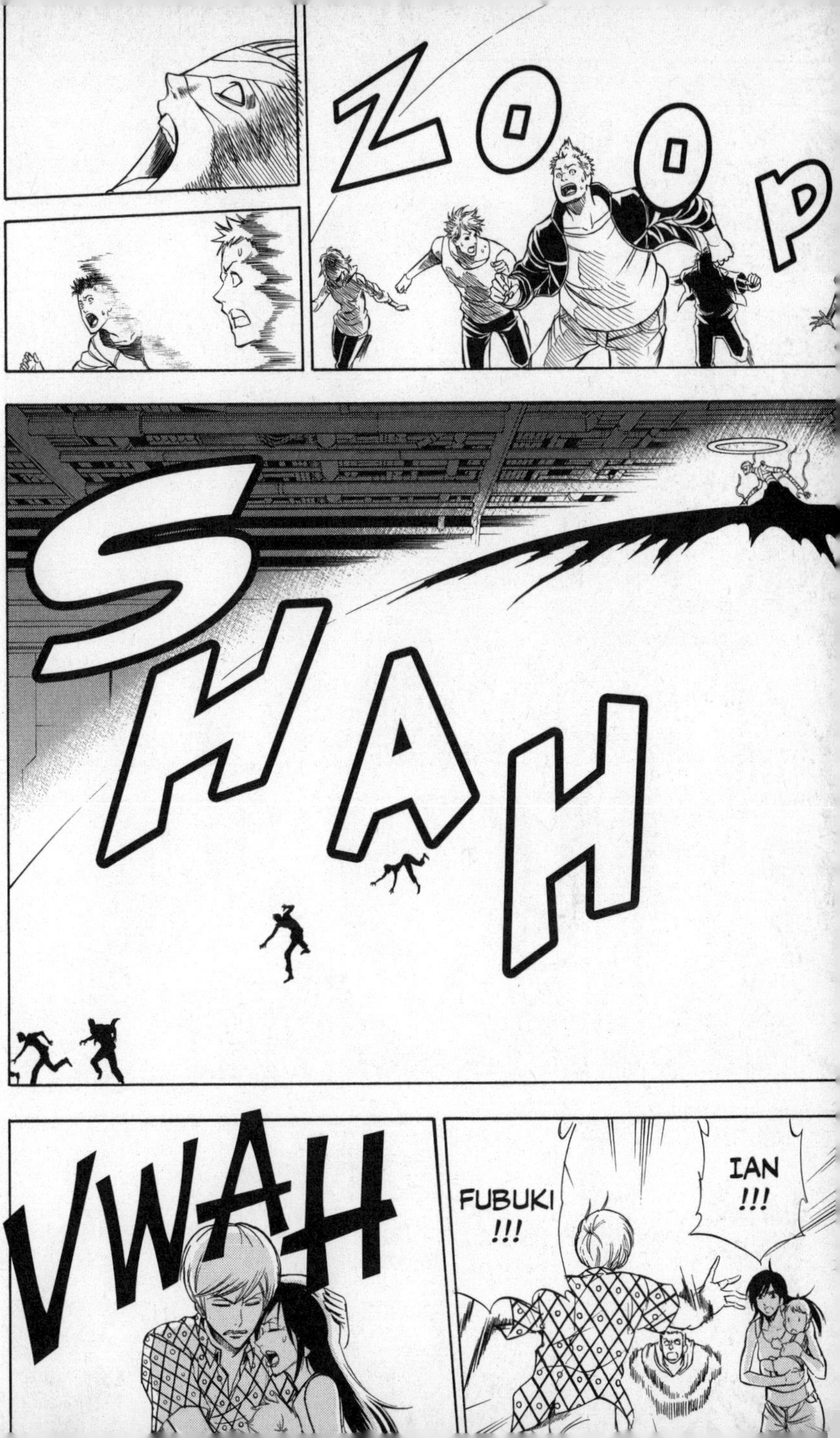
ZOOP
SHAH
IAN !!!
FUBUKI !!!
VWAH

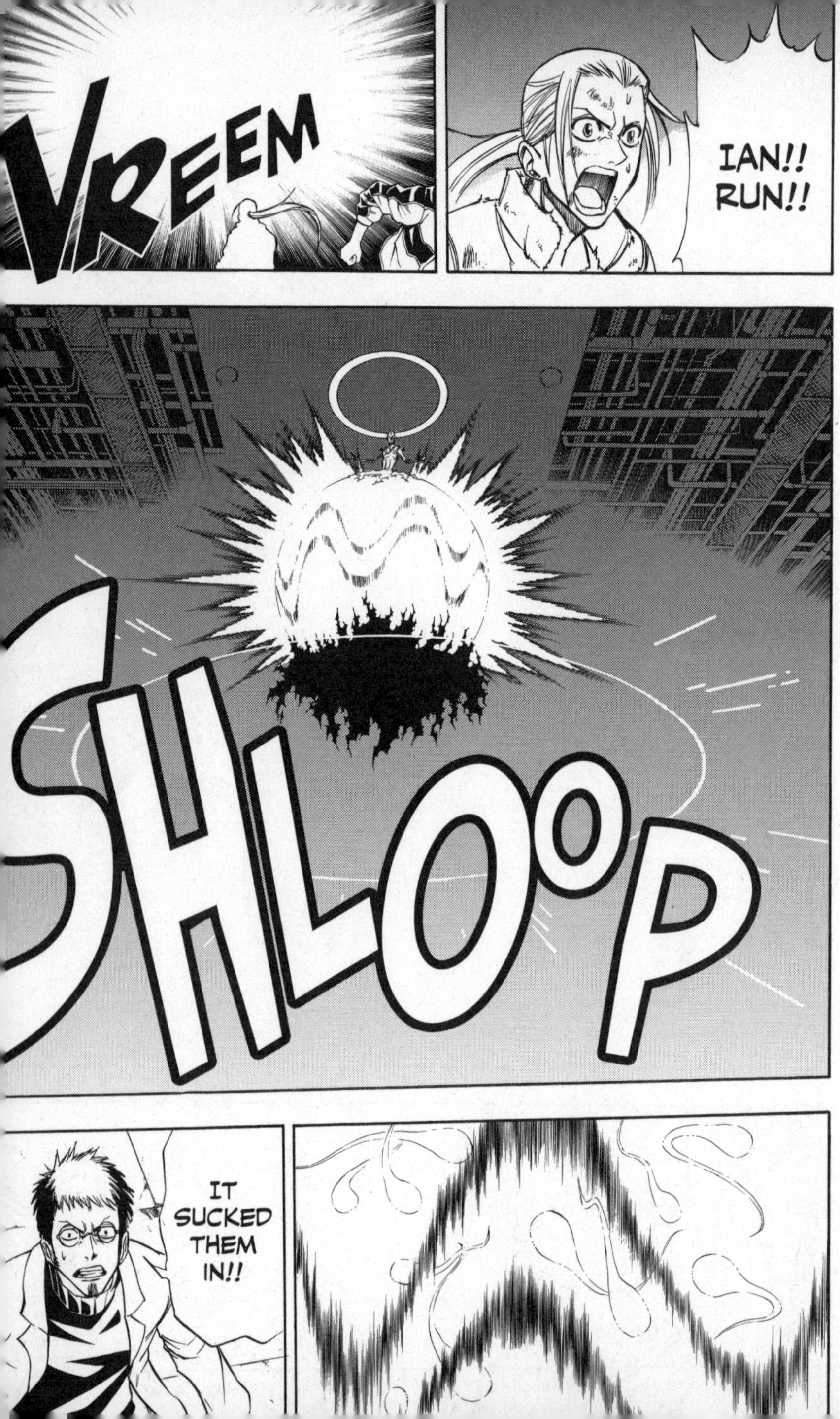
IAN!! RUN!!
VREEM
SHLOOP
IT SUCKED THEM IN!!

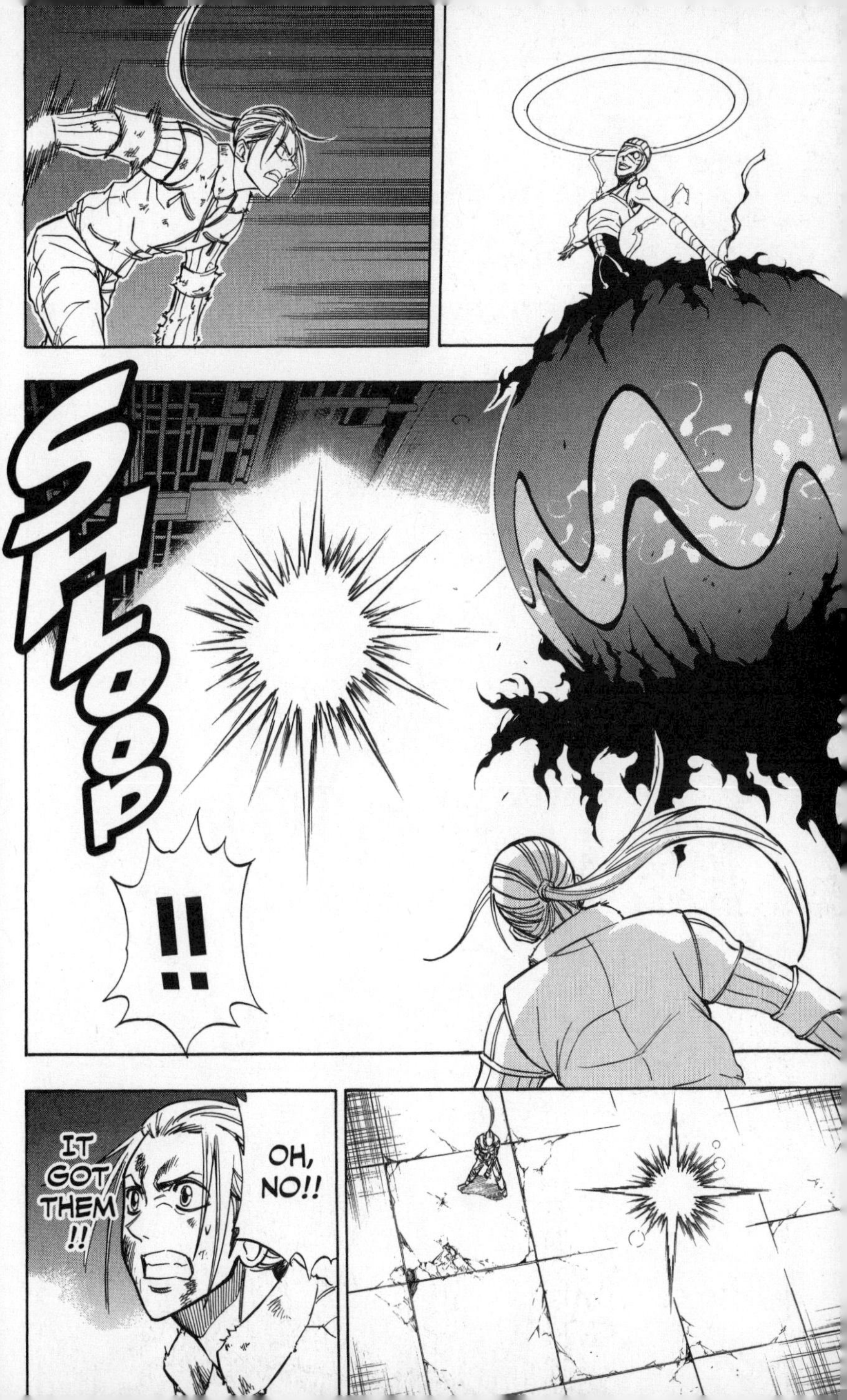
SHLOOP
!!
OH, NO!!
IT GOT THEM!!

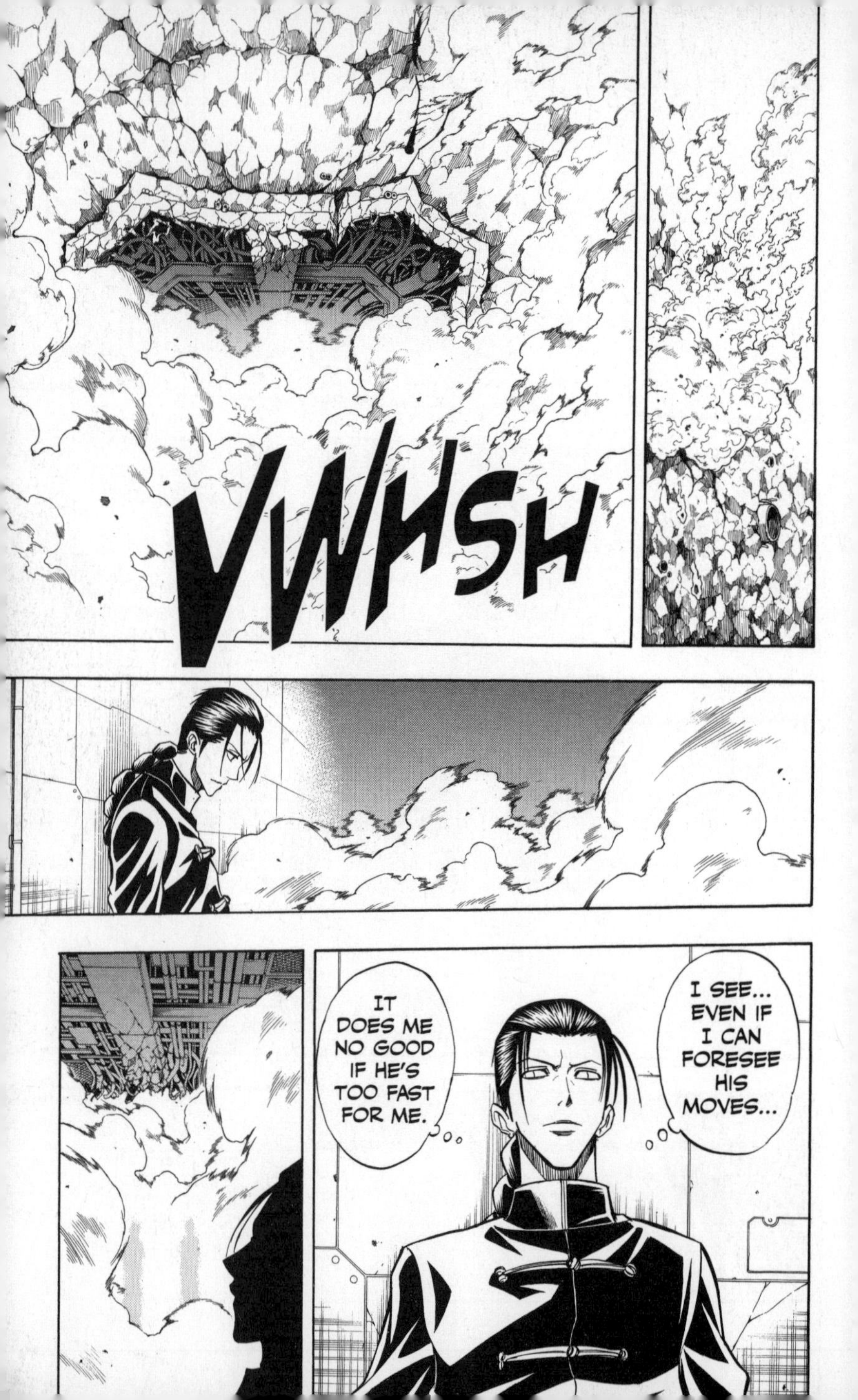
VWHSH
I SEE... EVEN IF I CAN FORESEE HIS MOVES...
IT DOES ME NO GOOD IF HE'S TOO FAST FOR ME.

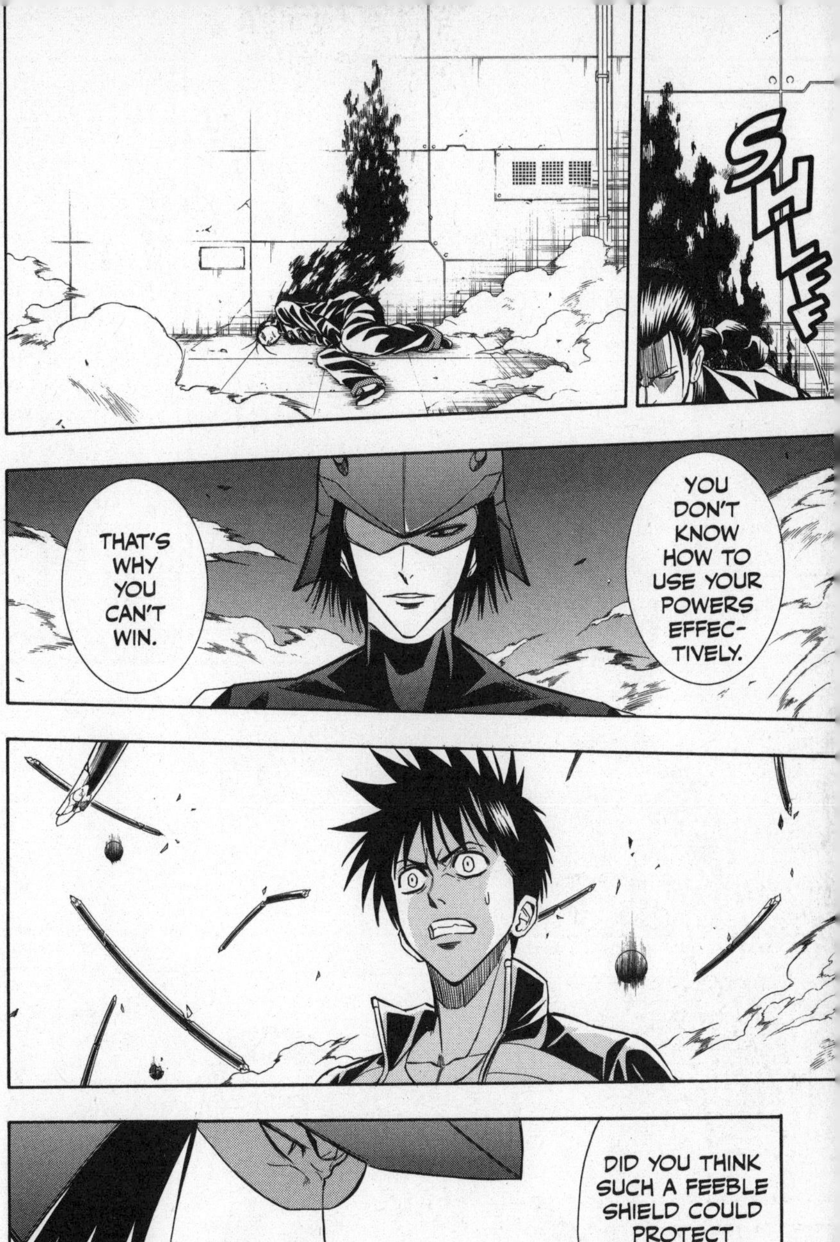
SHLFF
YOU DON'T KNOW HOW TO USE YOUR POWERS EFFEC- TIVELY.
THAT'S WHY YOU CAN'T WIN.
DID YOU THINK SUCH A FEEBLE SHIELD COULD PROTECT YOU FROM MY DIVINE BLADE?

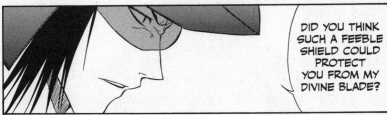

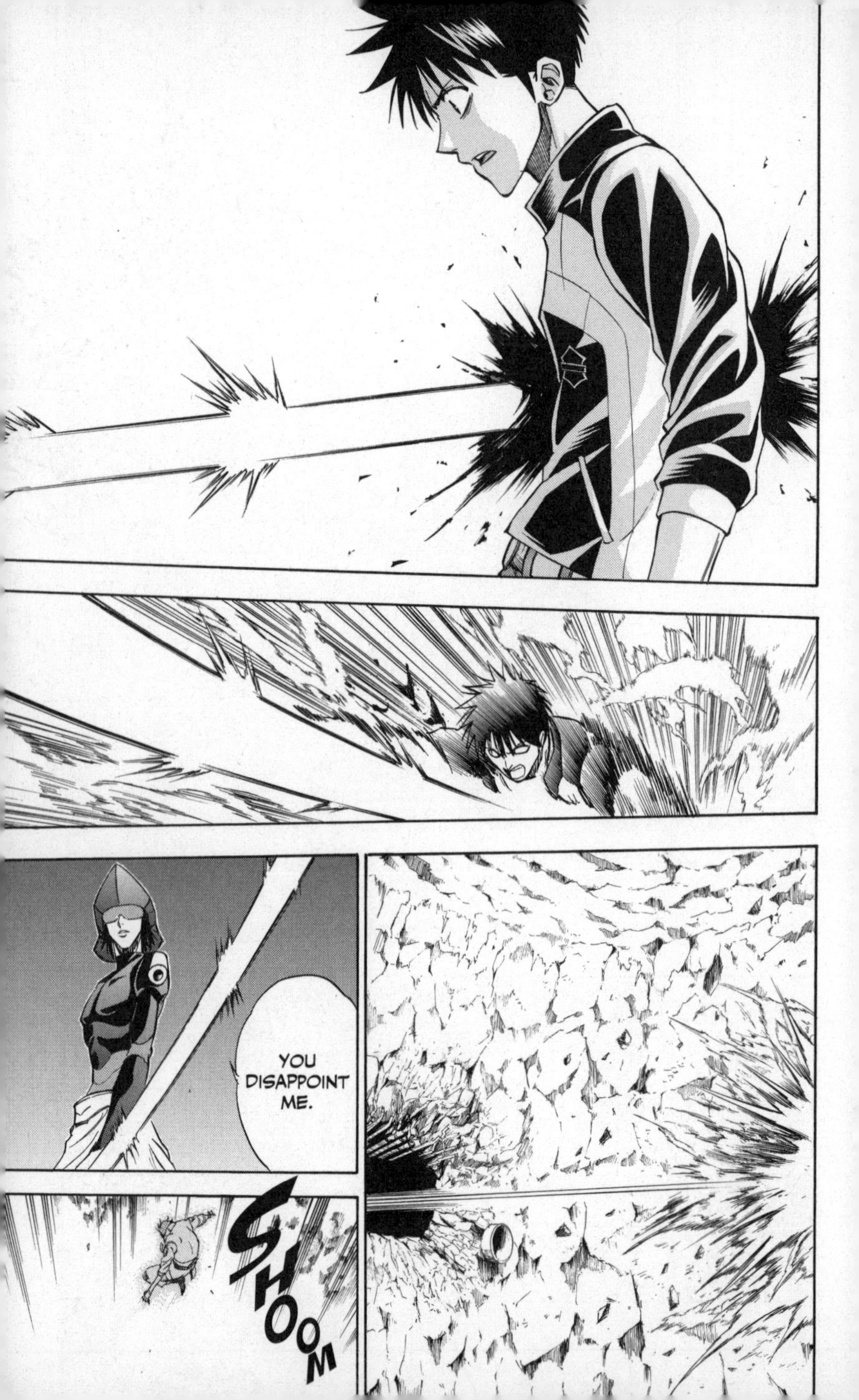
YOU DISAPPOINT ME.
SHOOM

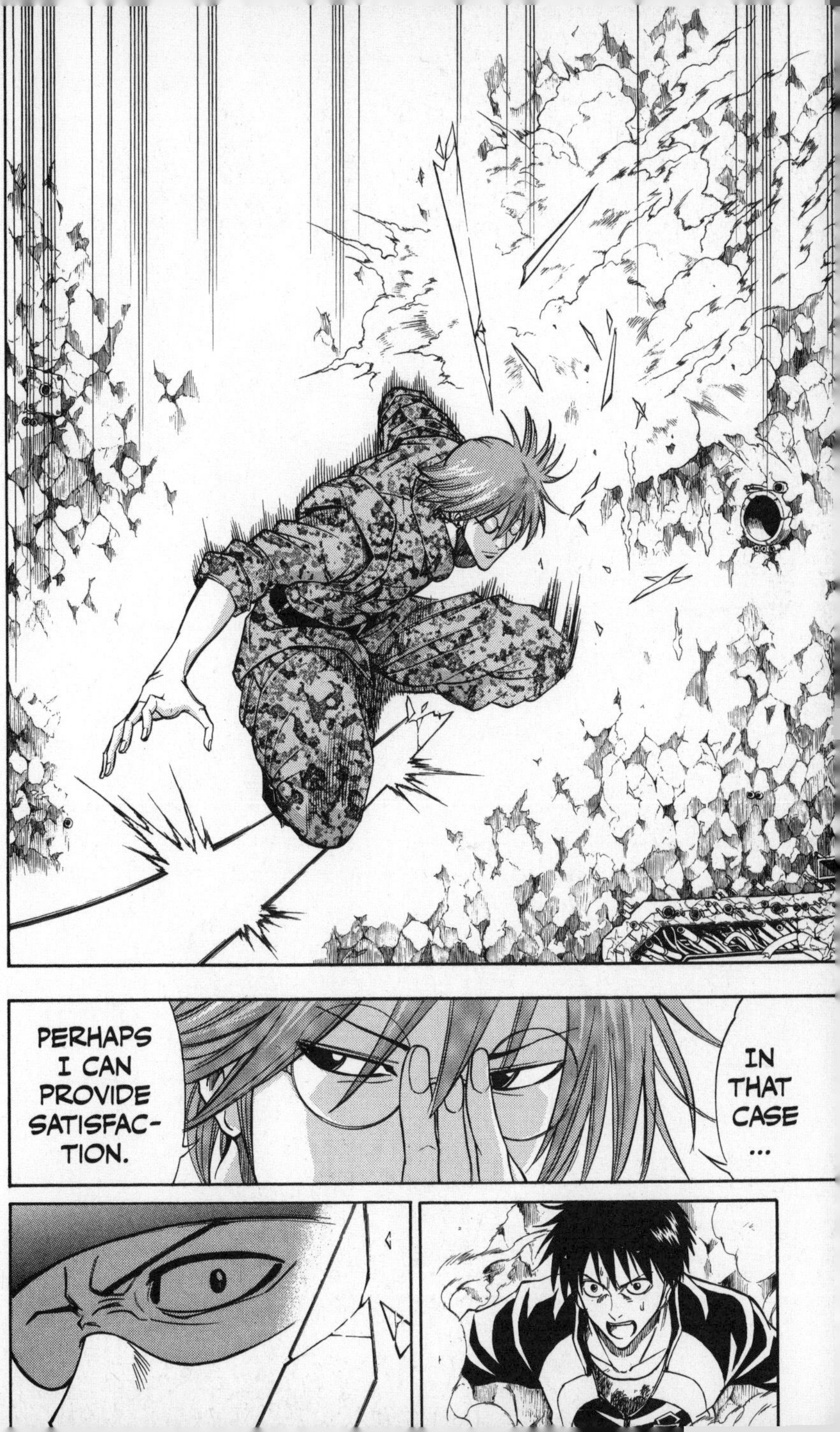
IN THAT CASE ...
PERHAPS I CAN PROVIDE SATISFACTION.

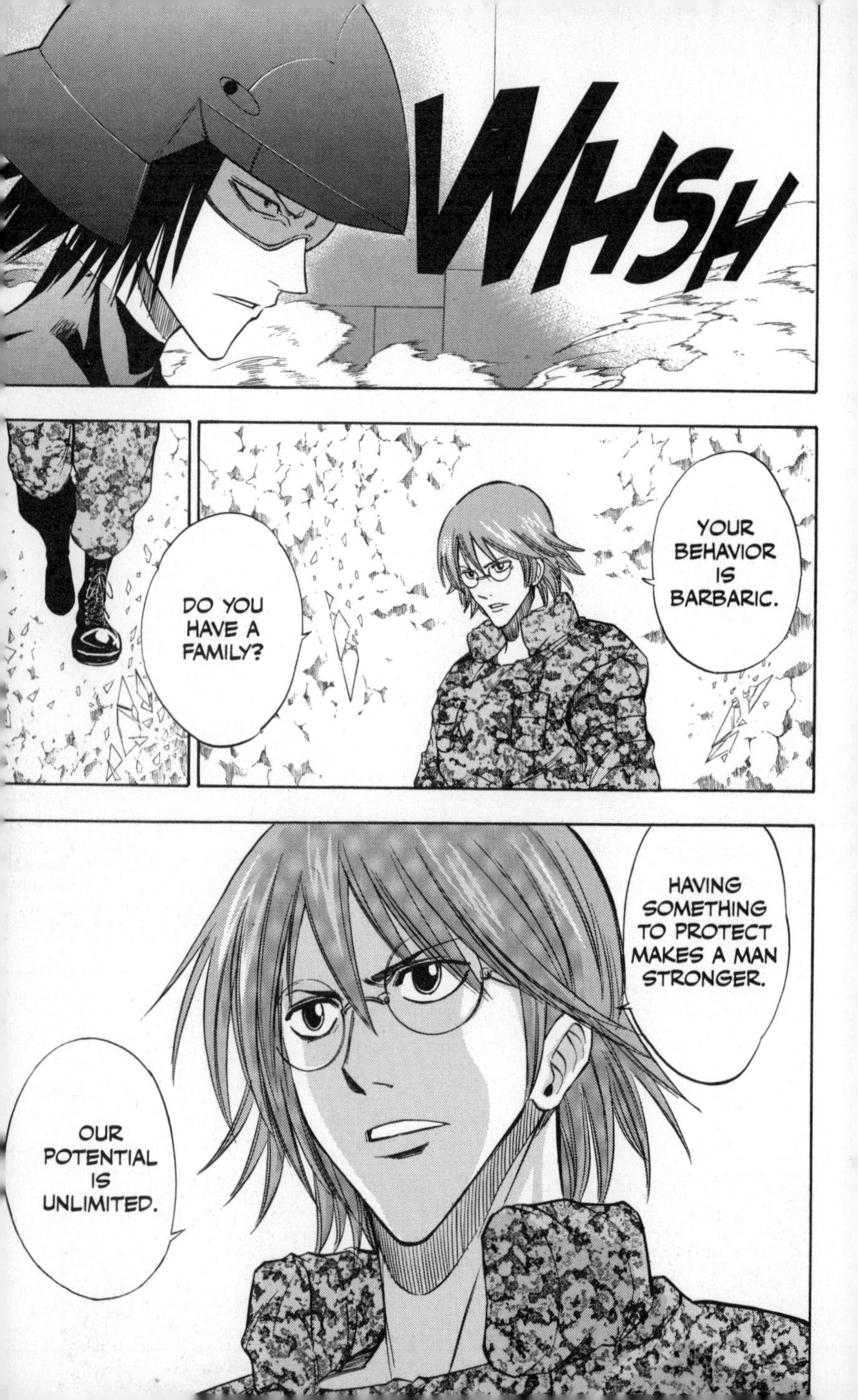
WHSH
YOUR BEHAVIOR IS BARBARIC.
DO YOU HAVE A FAMILY?
HAVING SOMETHING TO PROTECT MAKES A MAN STRONGER.
OUR POTENTIAL IS UNLIMITED.

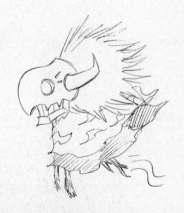

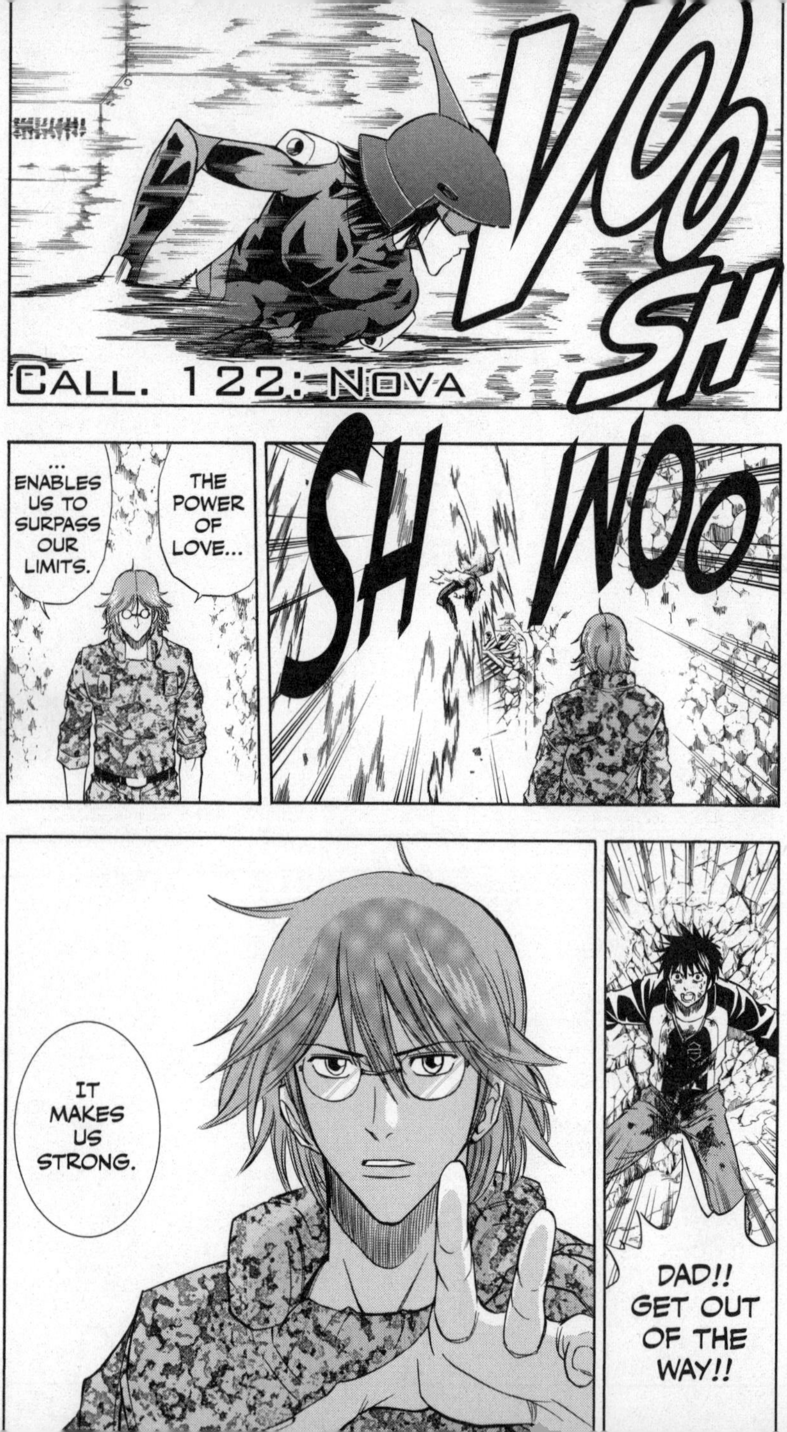
VOOSH
CALL. 122: NOVA
SH WOO
THE POWER OF LOVE...
... ENABLES US TO SURPASS OUR LIMITS.
DAD!! GET OUT OF THE WAY!!
IT MAKES US STRONG.

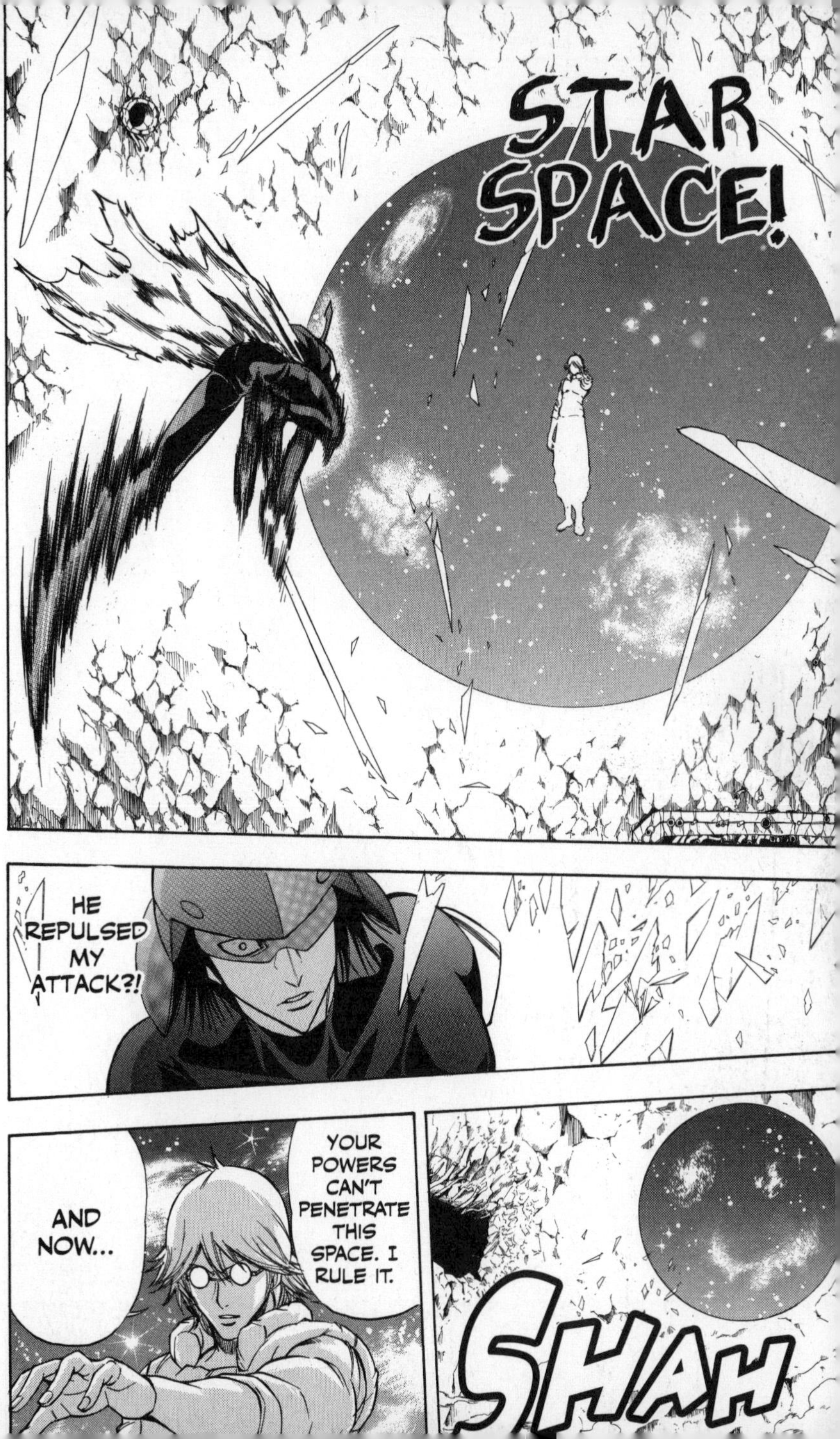
STAR SPACE!
HE REPULSED MY ATTACK?!
YOUR POWERS CAN'T PENETRATE THIS SPACE. I RULE IT.
AND NOW...
SHAH

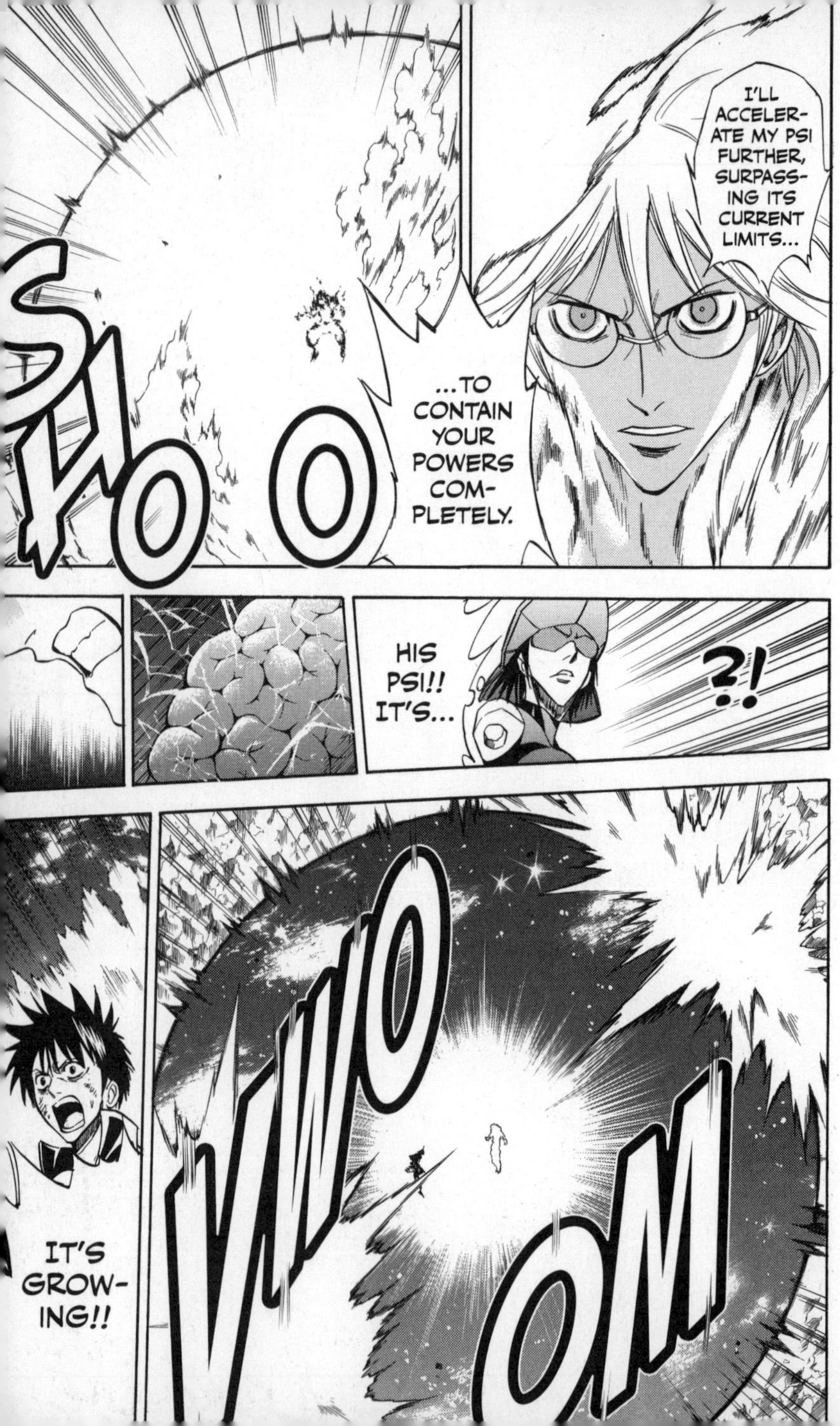
I'LL ACCELERATE MY PSI FURTHER, SURPASSING ITS CURRENT LIMITS...
...TO CONTAIN YOUR POWERS COMPLETELY.
SHOO
?!
HIS PSI!! IT'S...
VWOOM
IT'S GROWING!!

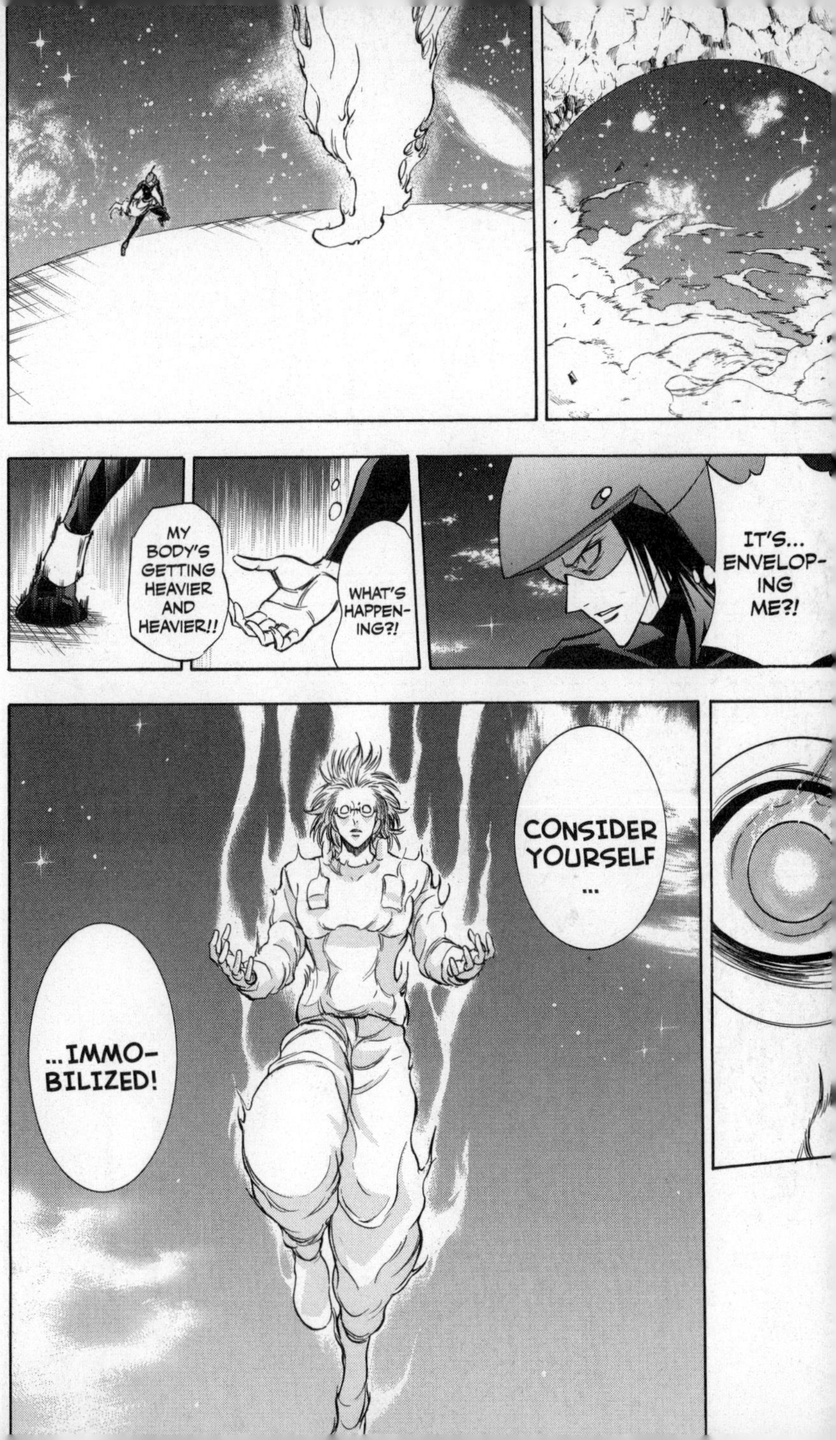
IT'S... ENVELOPING ME?!
WHAT'S HAPPENING?!
MY BODY'S GETTING HEAVIER AND HEAVIER!!
CONSIDER YOURSELF ...
...IMMOBILIZED!

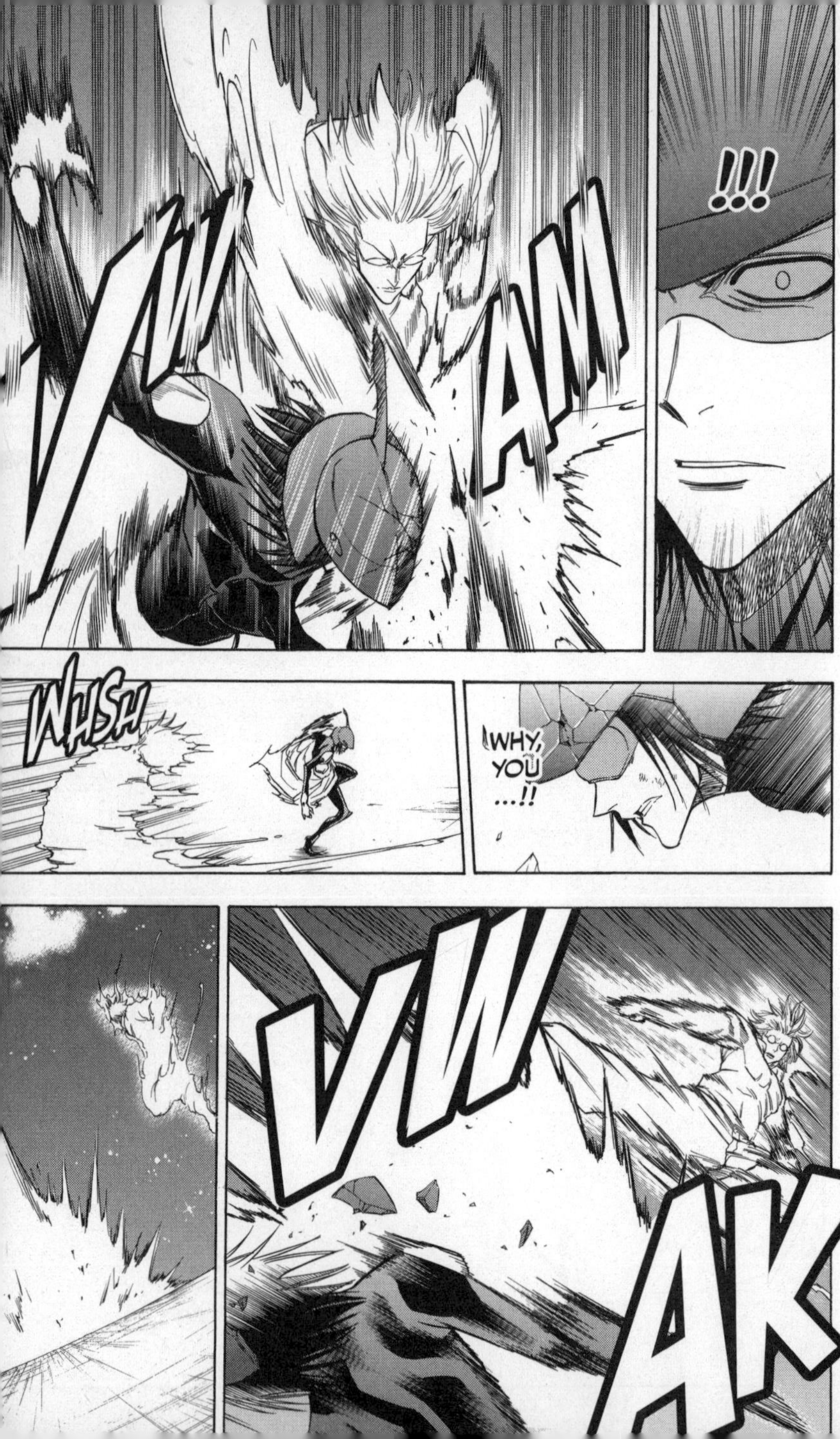
!!!
WAM
WHY, YOU ...!!
WHSH
WAK

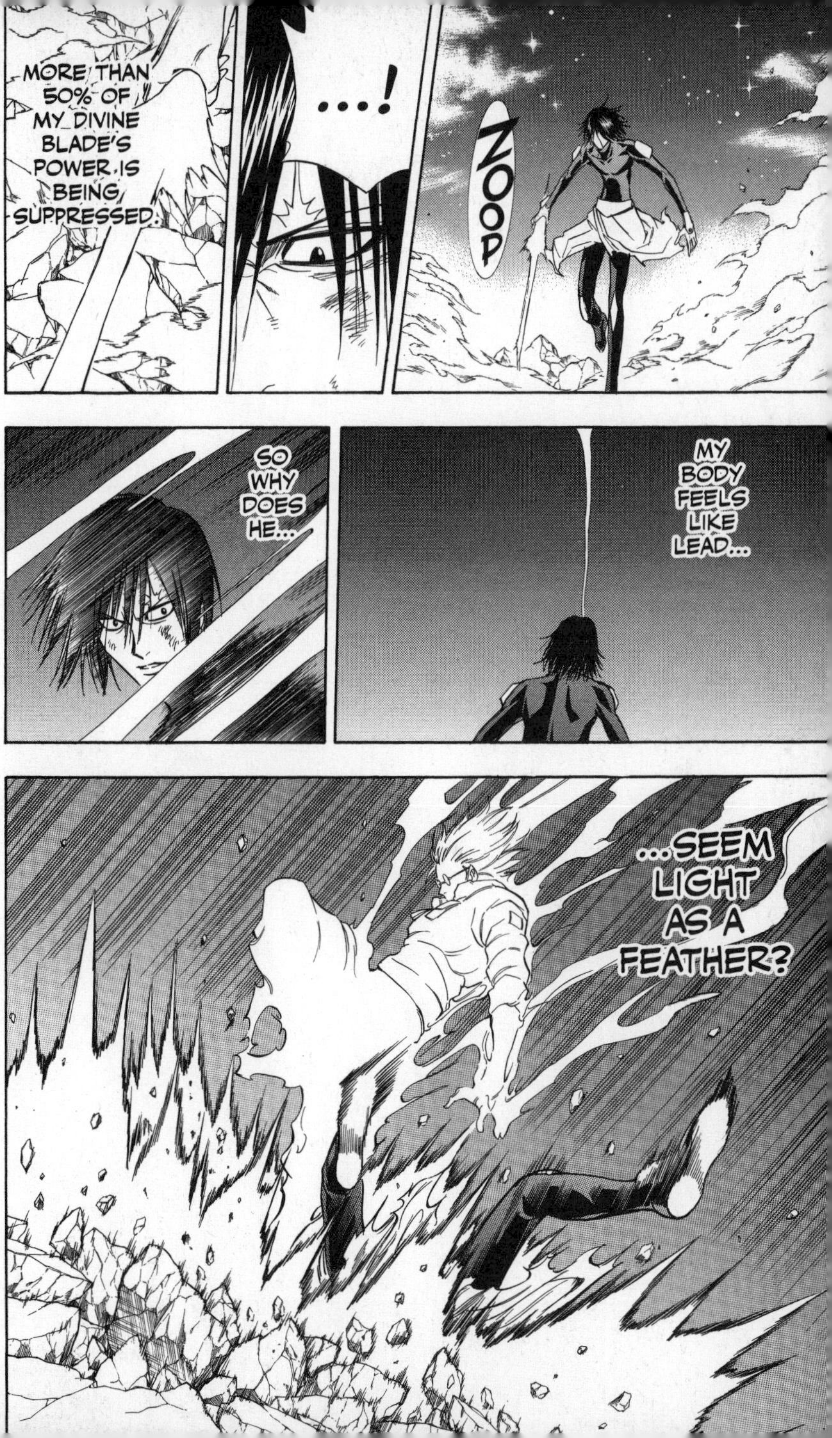
ZOOP
...!
MORE THAN 50% OF MY DIVINE BLADE'S POWER IS BEING SUPPRESSED.
MY BODY FEELS LIKE LEAD...
SO WHY DOES HE...
...SEEM LIGHT AS A FEATHER?

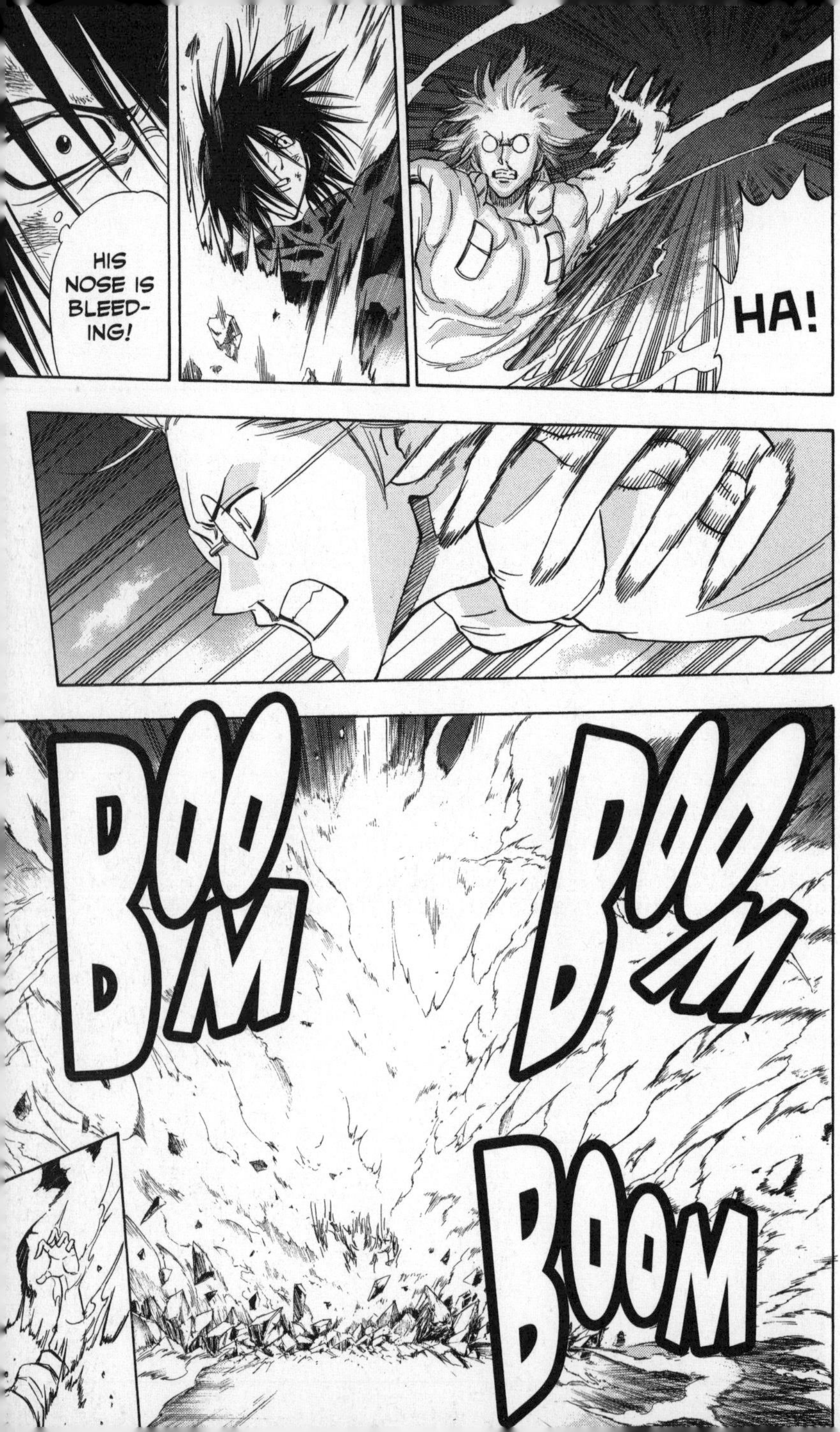
HA!
HIS NOSE IS BLEEDING!
BOOM
BOOM
BOOM

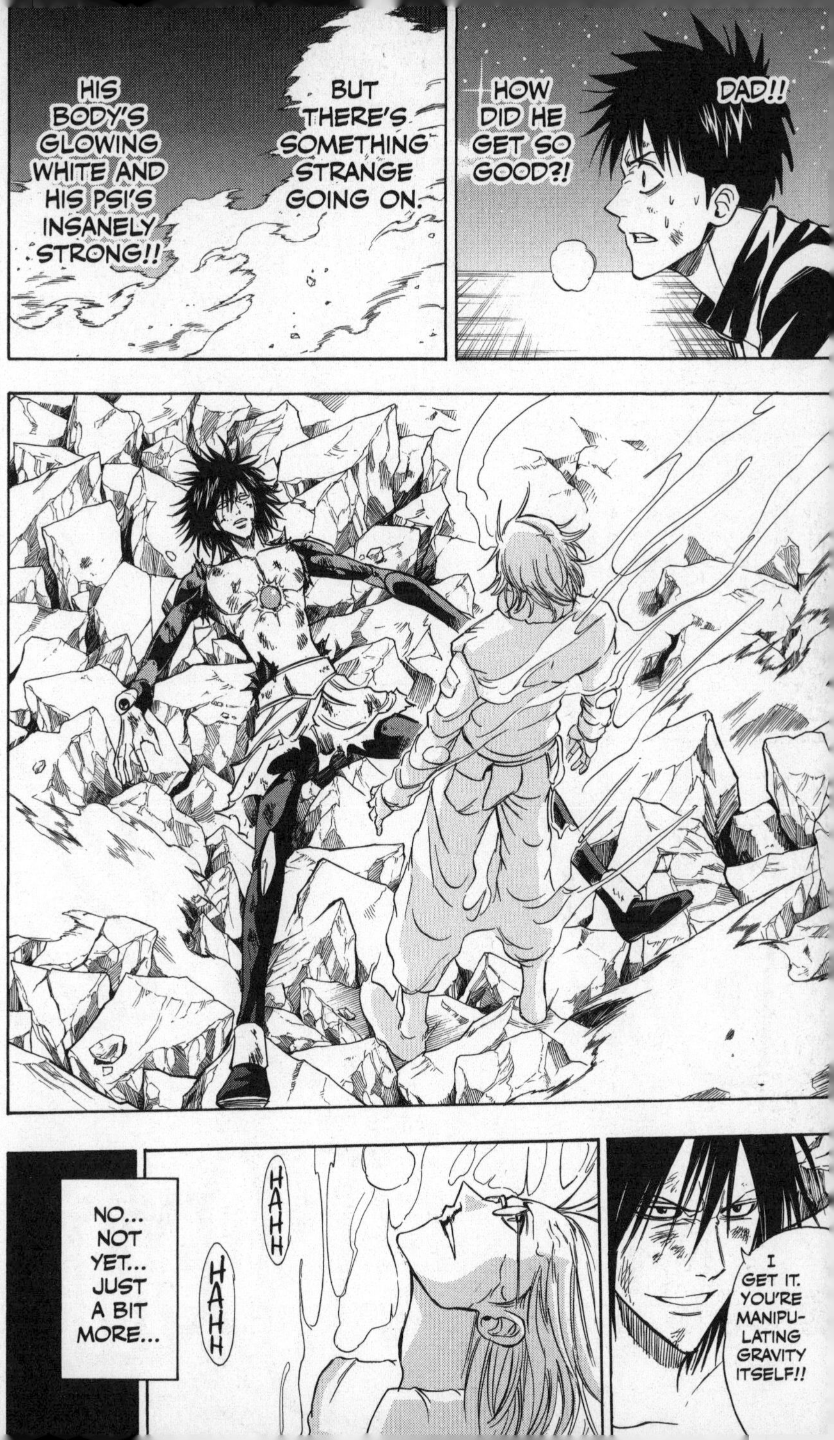
DAD!!
HOW DID HE GET SO GOOD?!
BUT THERE'S SOMETHING STRANGE GOING ON.
HIS BODY'S GLOWING WHITE AND HIS PSI'S INSANELY STRONG!!
I GET IT. YOU'RE MANIPU-LATING GRAVITY ITSELF!!
HAHH
HAHH
NO... NOT YET... JUST A BIT MORE...

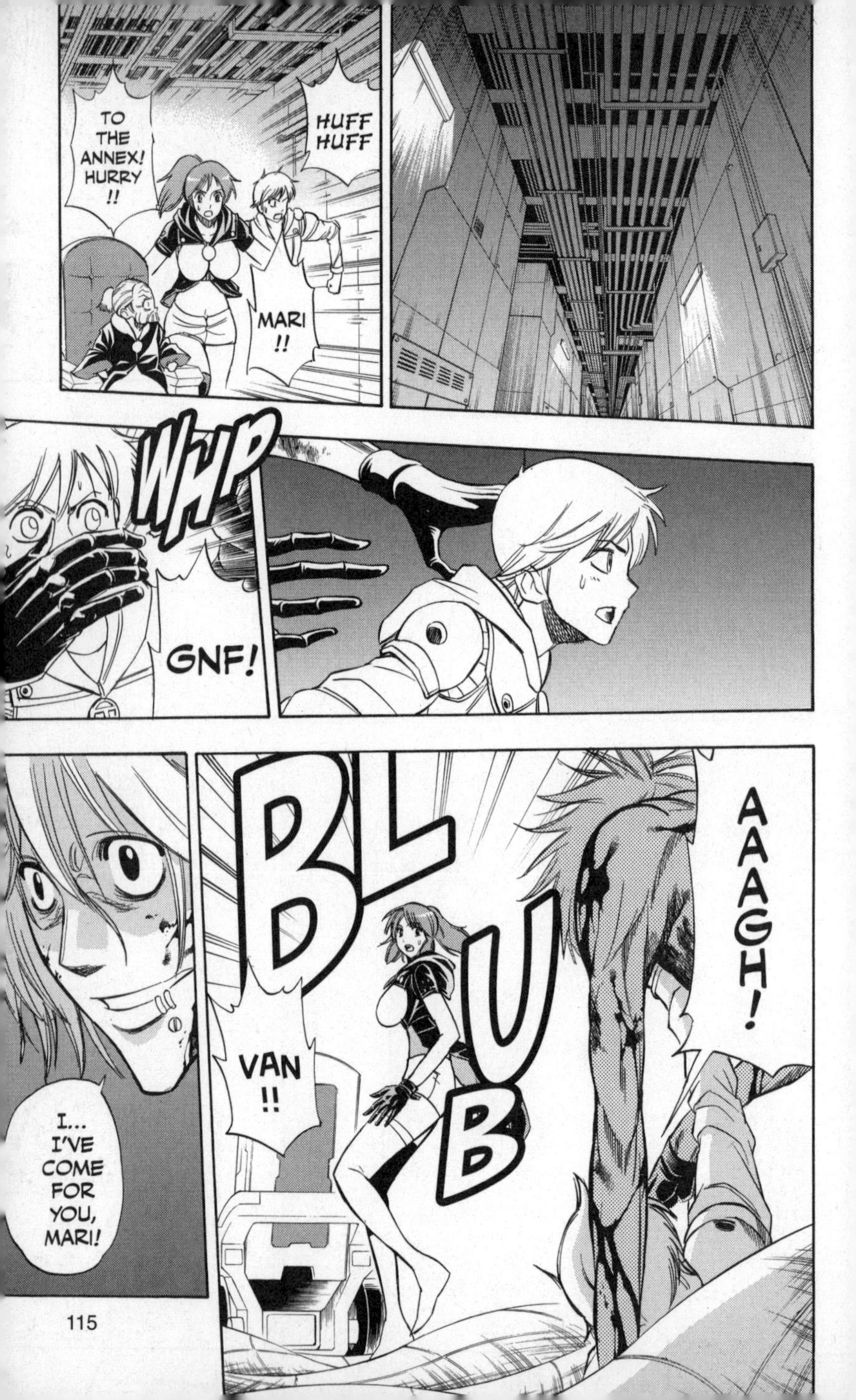
HUFF HUFF
TO THE ANNEX! HURRY !!
MARI !!
WHP
GNF!
AAAGH!
BLUB
VAN !!
I... I'VE COME FOR YOU, MARI!

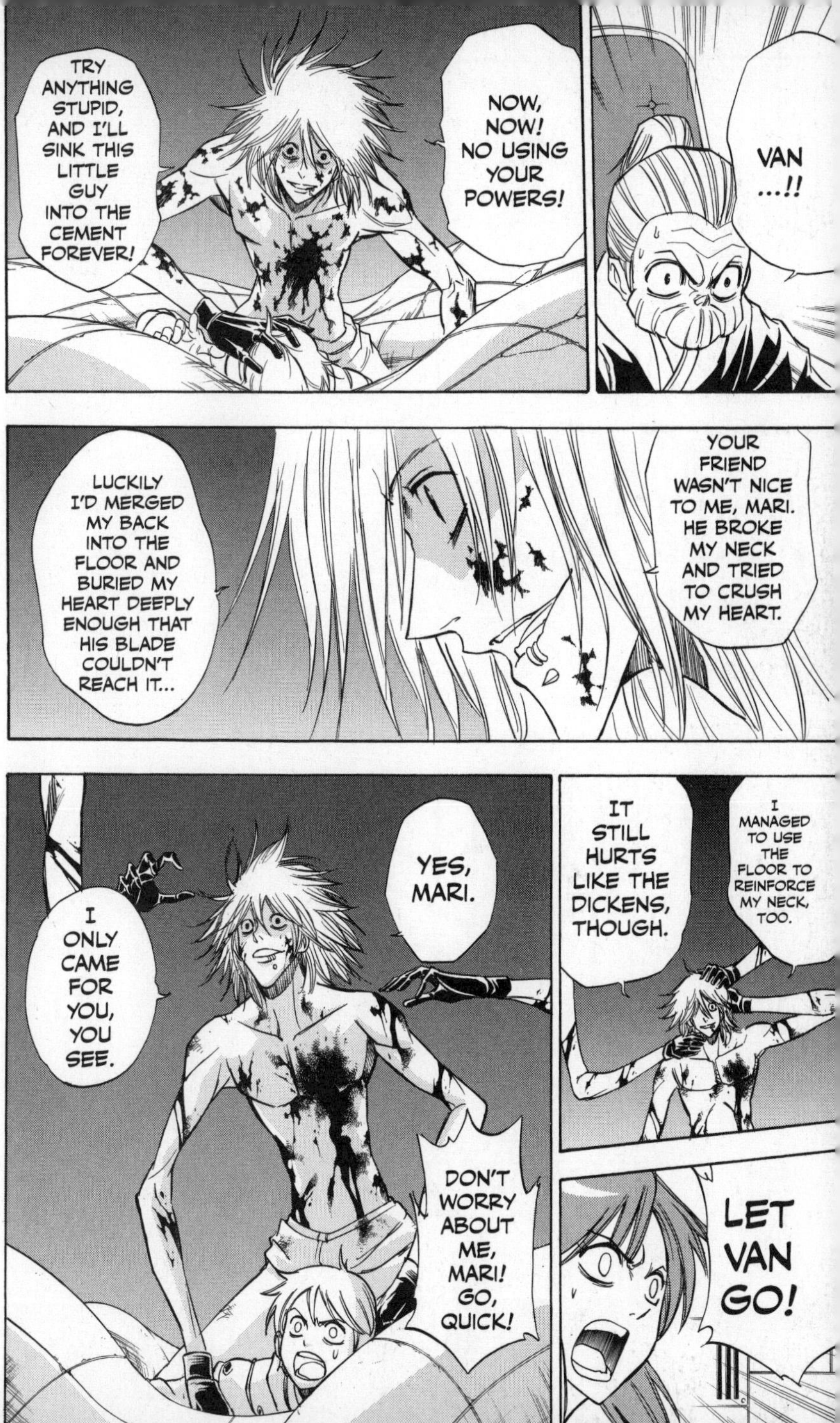
VAN ...!!
NOW, NOW! NO USING YOUR POWERS!
TRY ANYTHING STUPID, AND I'LL SINK THIS LITTLE GUY INTO THE CEMENT FOREVER!
YOUR FRIEND WASN'T NICE TO ME, MARI. HE BROKE MY NECK AND TRIED TO CRUSH MY HEART.
LUCKILY I'D MERGED MY BACK INTO THE FLOOR AND BURIED MY HEART DEEPLY ENOUGH THAT HIS BLADE COULDN'T REACH IT...
I MANAGED TO USE THE FLOOR TO REINFORCE MY NECK, TOO.
IT STILL HURTS LIKE THE DICKENS, THOUGH.
LET VAN GO!
YES, MARI.
I ONLY CAME FOR YOU, YOU SEE.
DON'T WORRY ABOUT ME, MARI! GO, QUICK!

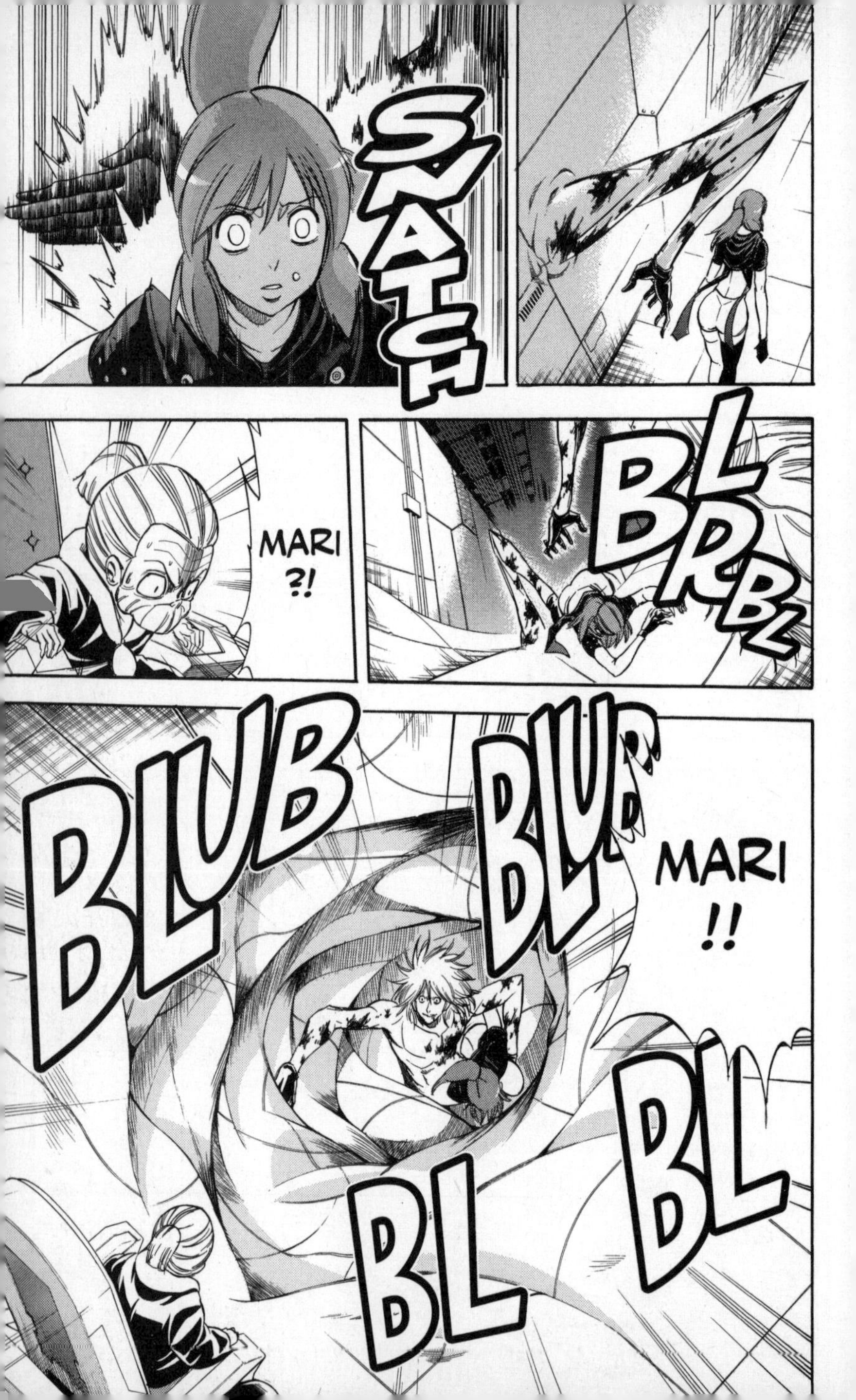
SNATCH
BLRRBL
MARI ?!
MARI !!
BLUB
BLUB
BL
BL

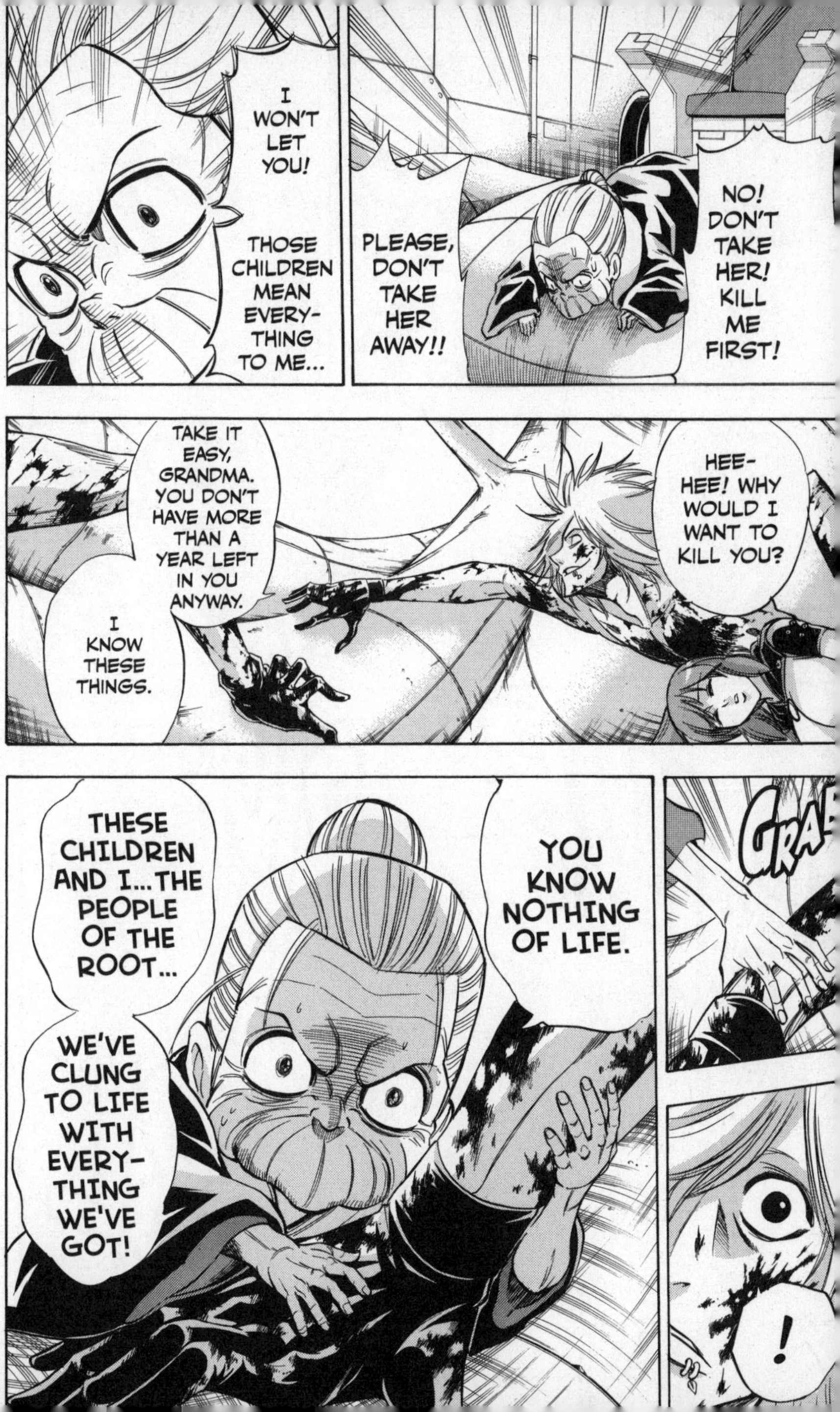
NO! DON'T TAKE HER! KILL ME FIRST!
PLEASE, DON'T TAKE HER AWAY!!
I WON'T LET YOU!
THOSE CHILDREN MEAN EVERYTHING TO ME...
HEE-HEE! WHY WOULD I WANT TO KILL YOU?
TAKE IT EASY, GRANDMA. YOU DON'T HAVE MORE THAN A YEAR LEFT IN YOU ANYWAY.
I KNOW THESE THINGS.
GRA
!
YOU KNOW NOTHING OF LIFE.
THESE CHILDREN AND I...THE PEOPLE OF THE ROOT...
WE'VE CLUNG TO LIFE WITH EVERYTHING WE'VE GOT!

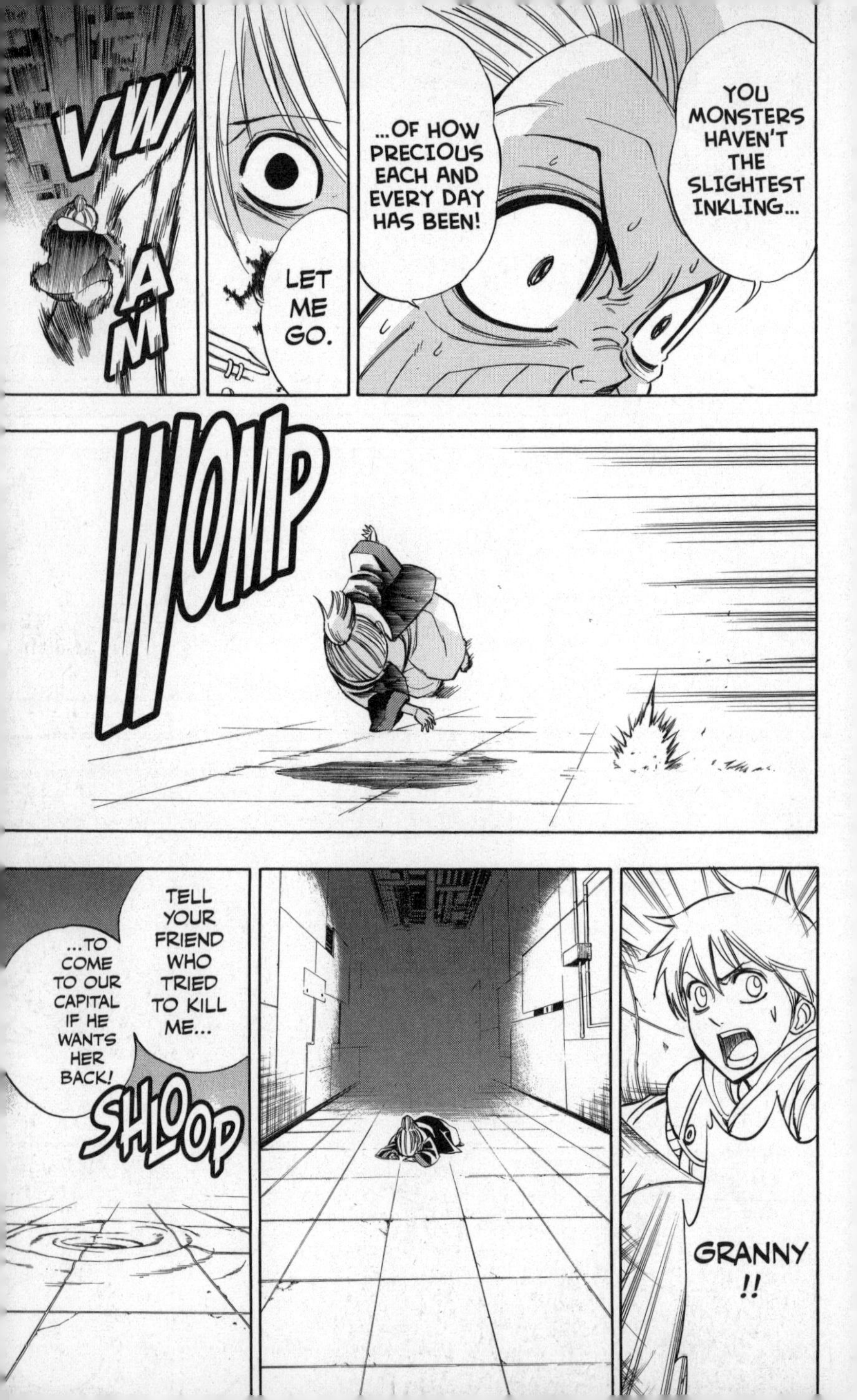
YOU MONSTERS HAVEN'T THE SLIGHTEST INKLING...
...OF HOW PRECIOUS EACH AND EVERY DAY HAS BEEN!
LET ME GO.
VWAM
WOMP
GRANNY !!
TELL YOUR FRIEND WHO TRIED TO KILL ME...
...TO COME TO OUR CAPITAL IF HE WANTS HER BACK!
SHLOOP

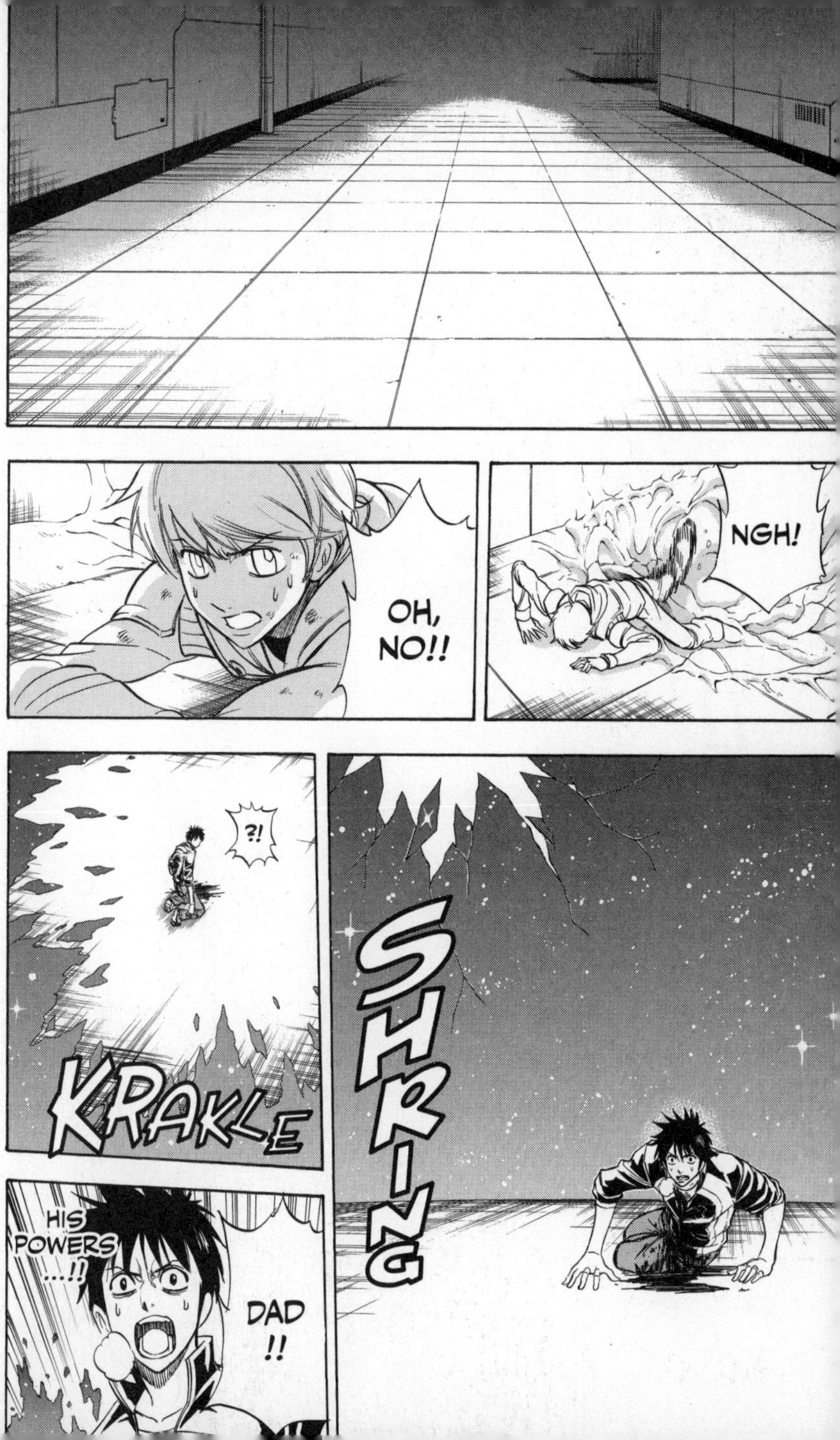
NGH!
OH, NO!!
SHRING
?!
KRAKLE
DAD !!
HIS POWERS ...!!

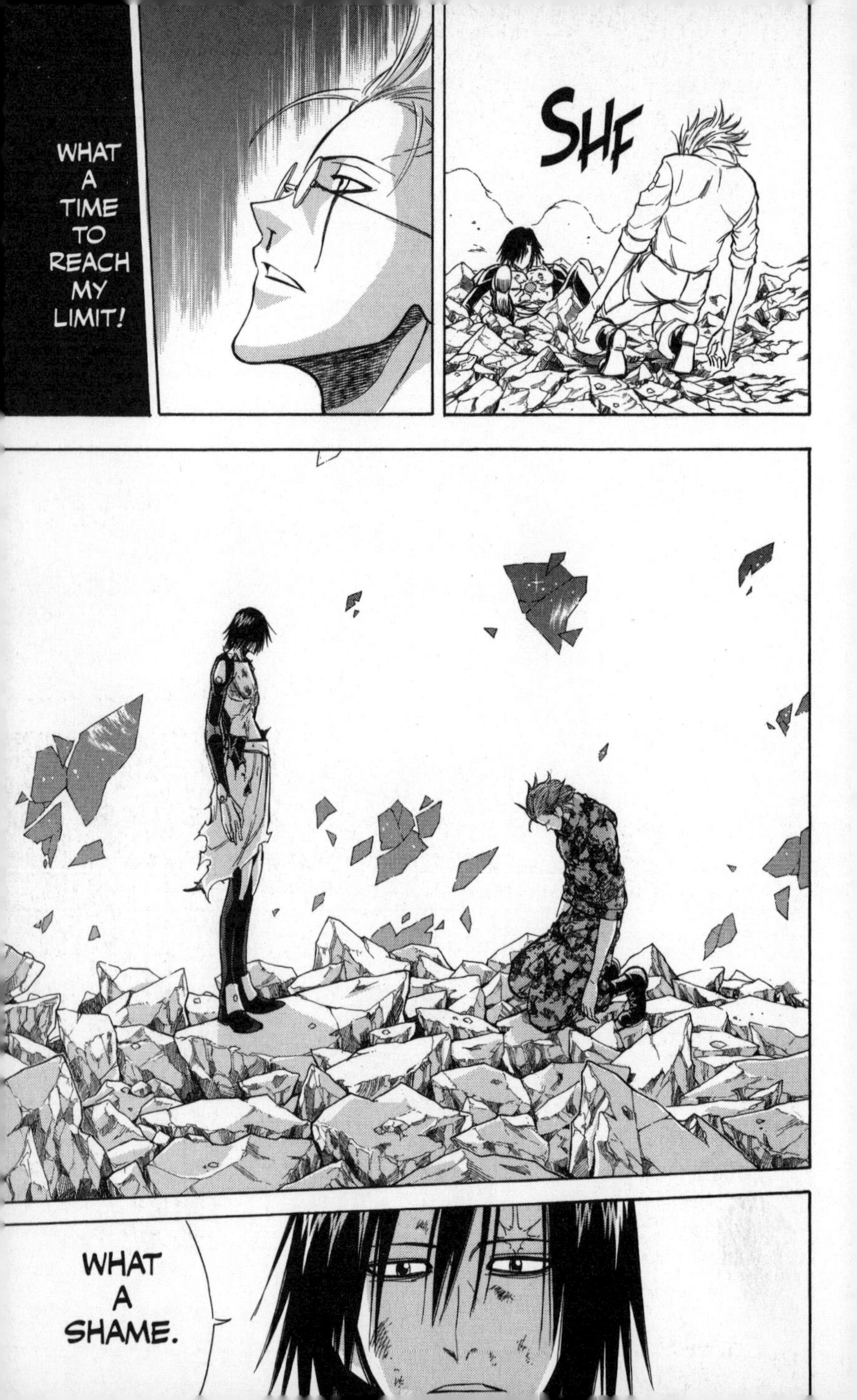
SHF
WHAT A TIME TO REACH MY LIMIT!
WHAT A SHAME.

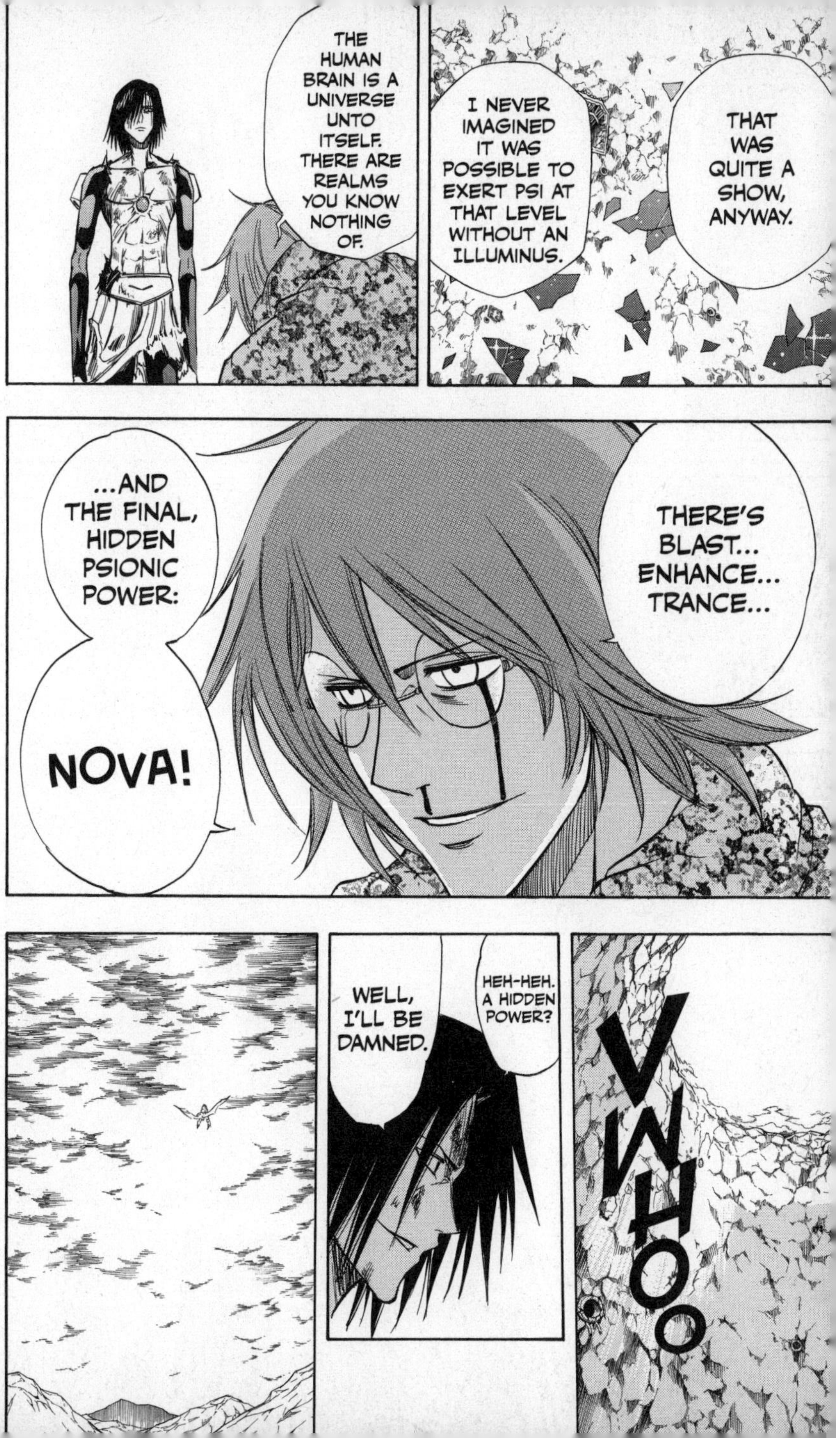
THAT WAS QUITE A SHOW, ANYWAY.
I NEVER IMAGINED IT WAS POSSIBLE TO EXERT PSI AT THAT LEVEL WITHOUT AN ILLUMINUS.
THE HUMAN BRAIN IS A UNIVERSE UNTO ITSELF. THERE ARE REALMS YOU KNOW NOTHING OF.
THERE'S BLAST... ENHANCE... TRANCE...
...AND THE FINAL, HIDDEN PSIONIC POWER:
NOVA!
VWHOO
HEH-HEH. A HIDDEN POWER?
WELL, I'LL BE DAMNED.

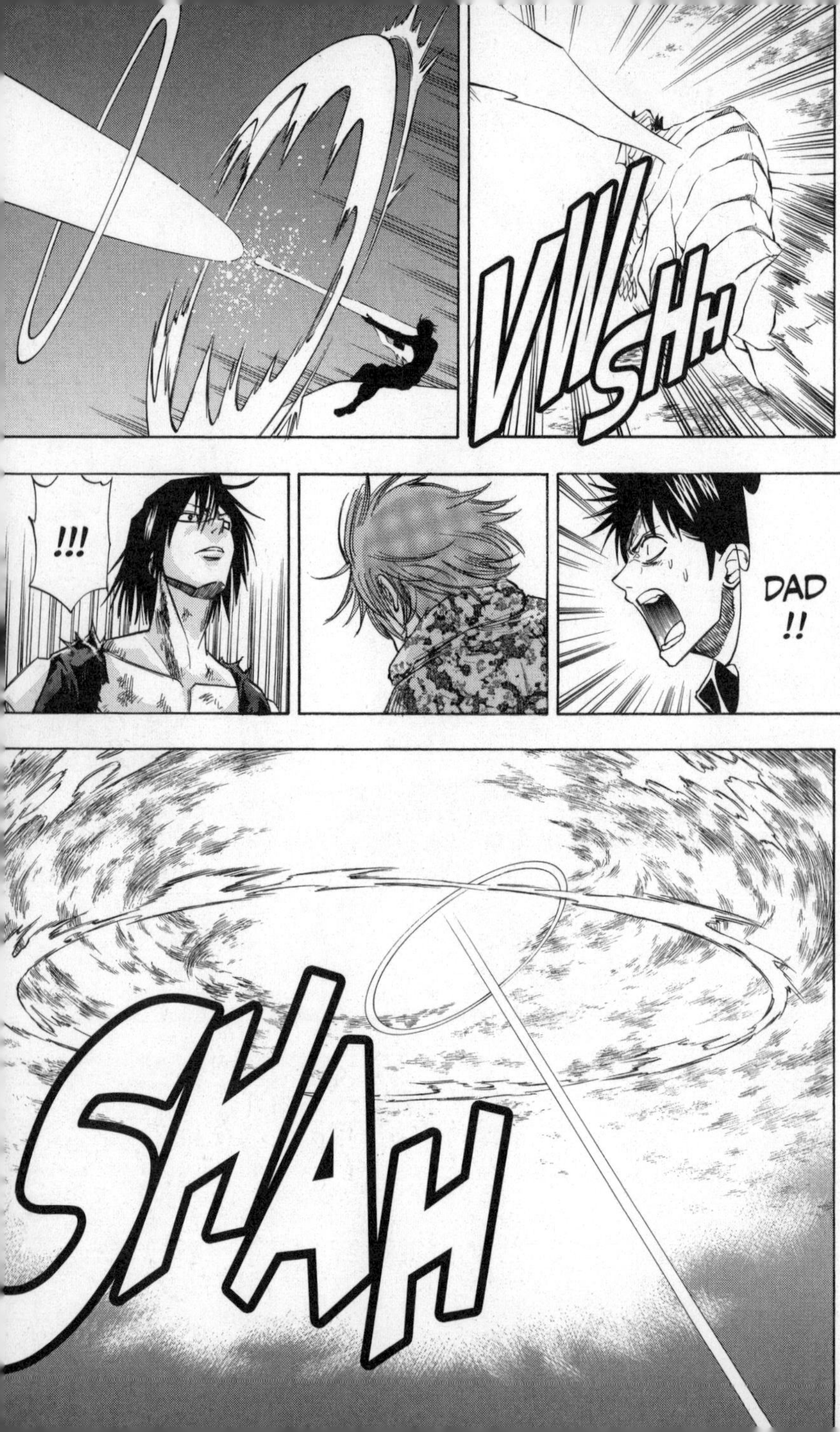
VWSHH
DAD !!
!!!
SHAH

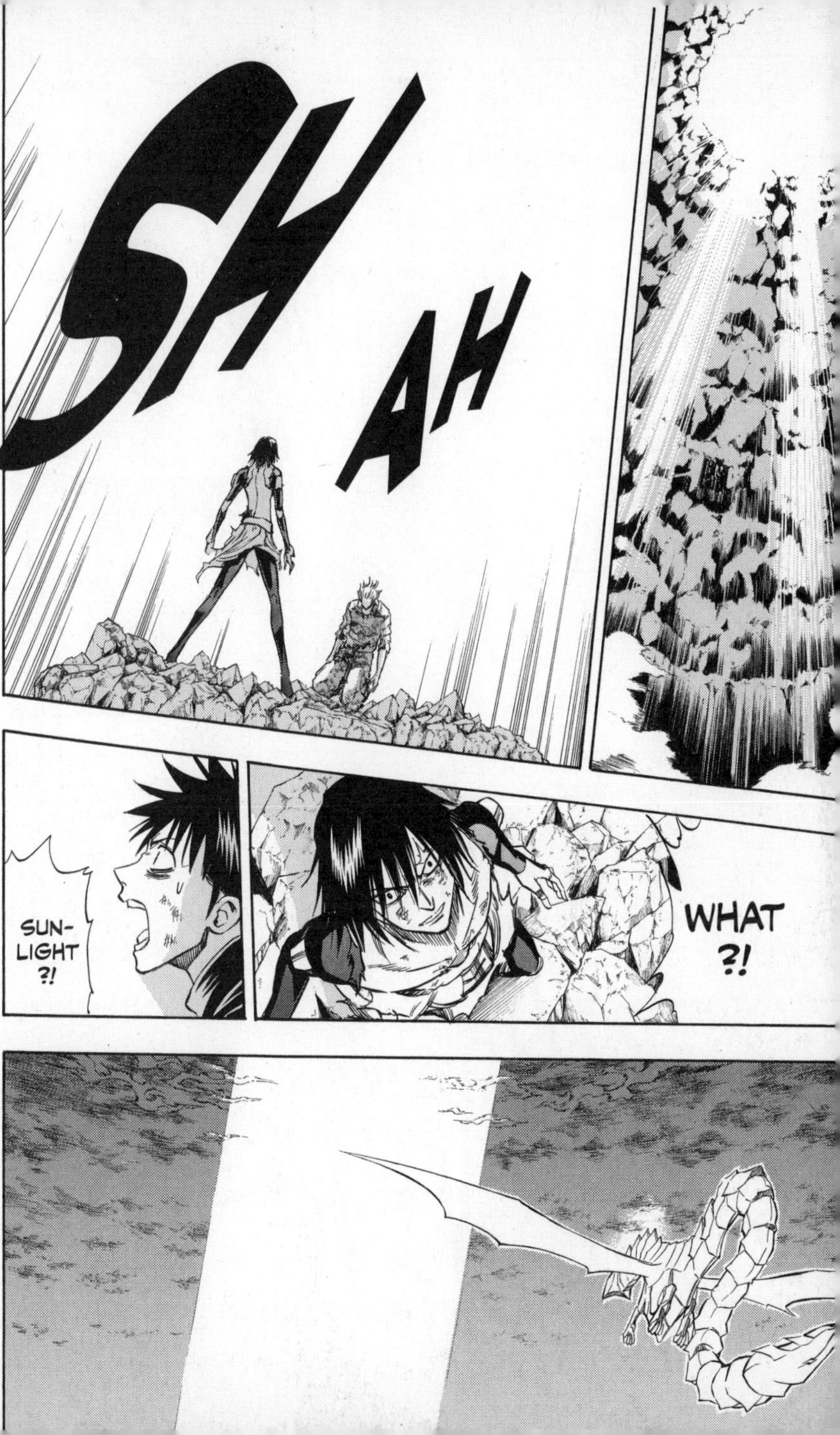
SHAH
WHAT ?!
SUN-LIGHT ?!

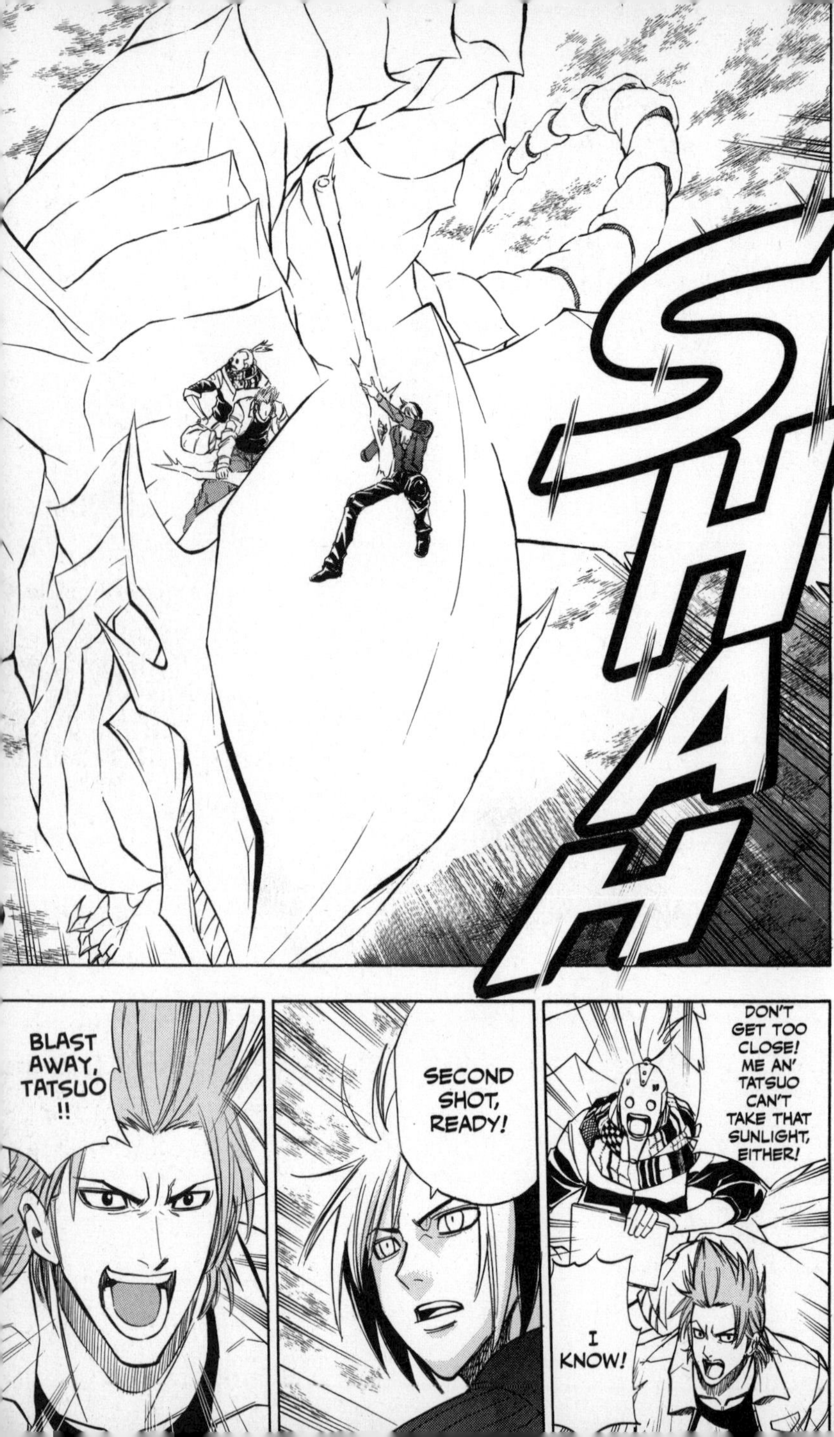
SHAAH
DON'T GET TOO CLOSE! ME AN' TATSUO CAN'T TAKE THAT SUNLIGHT, EITHER!
I KNOW!
SECOND SHOT, READY!
BLAST AWAY, TATSUO !!

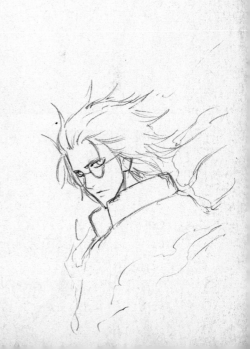

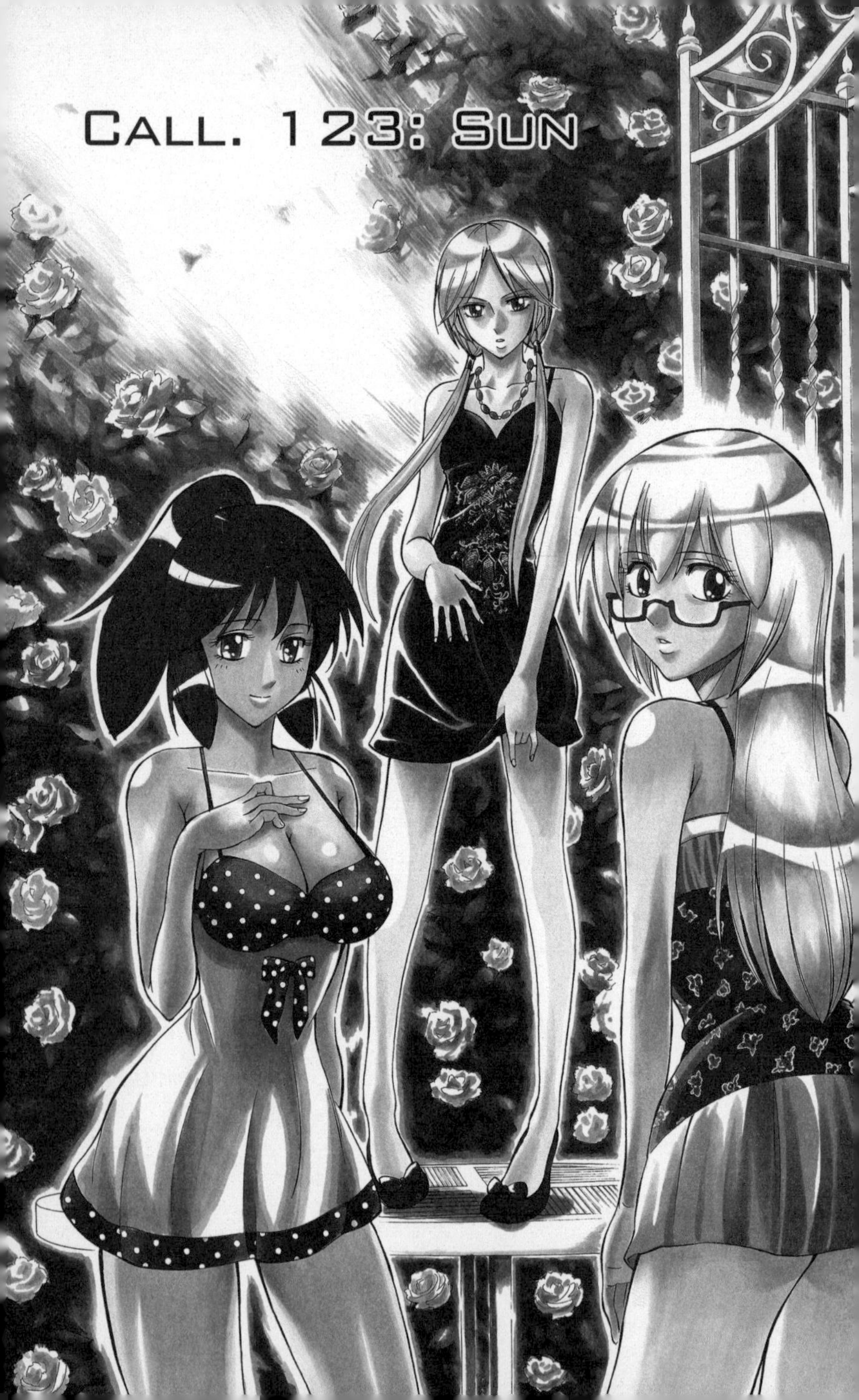
CALL. 123: SUN

PSYREN

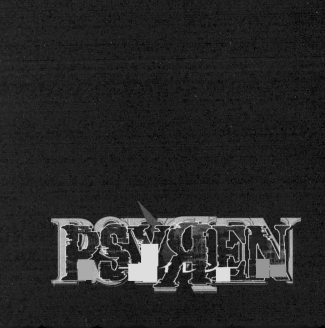

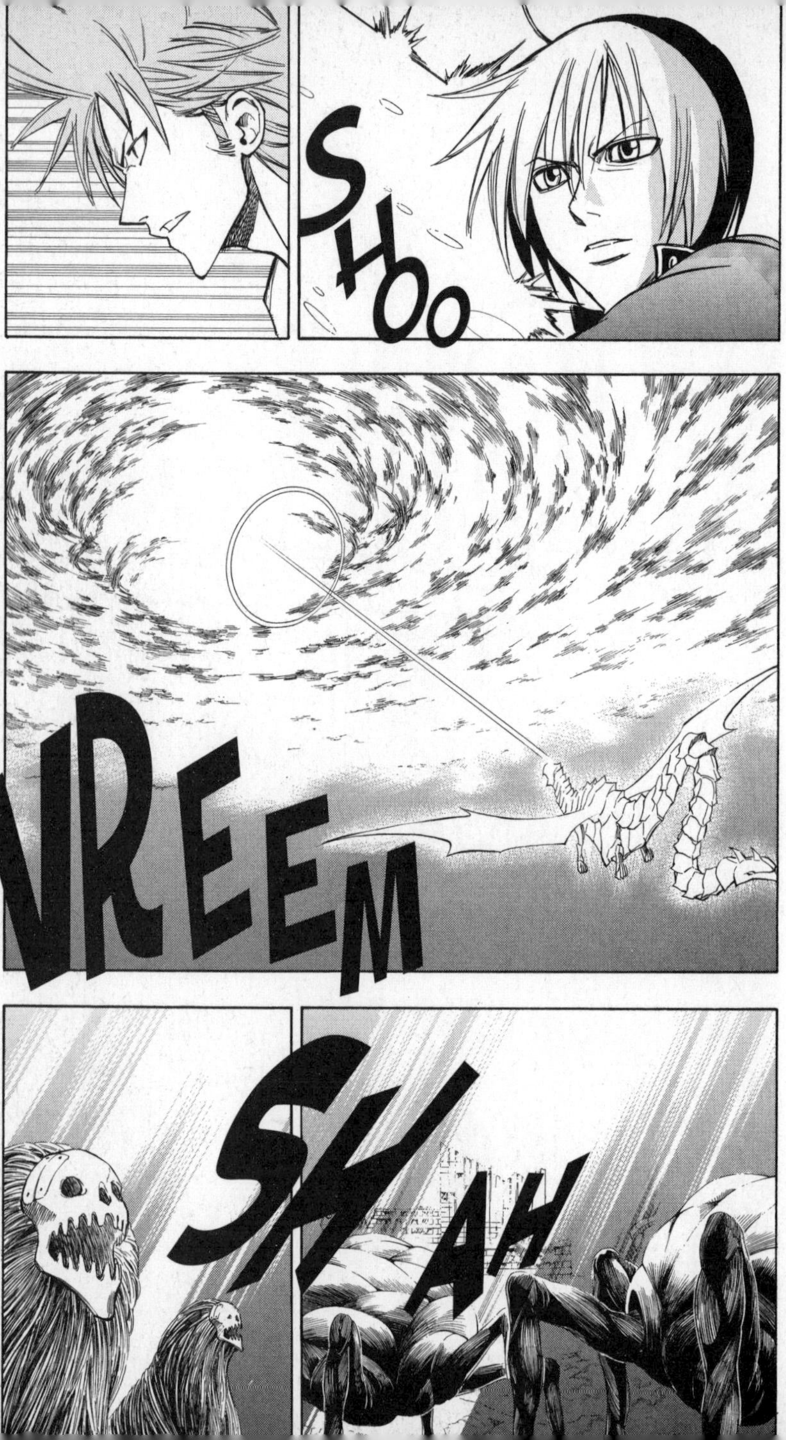
SHOO
VREEM
SHAH

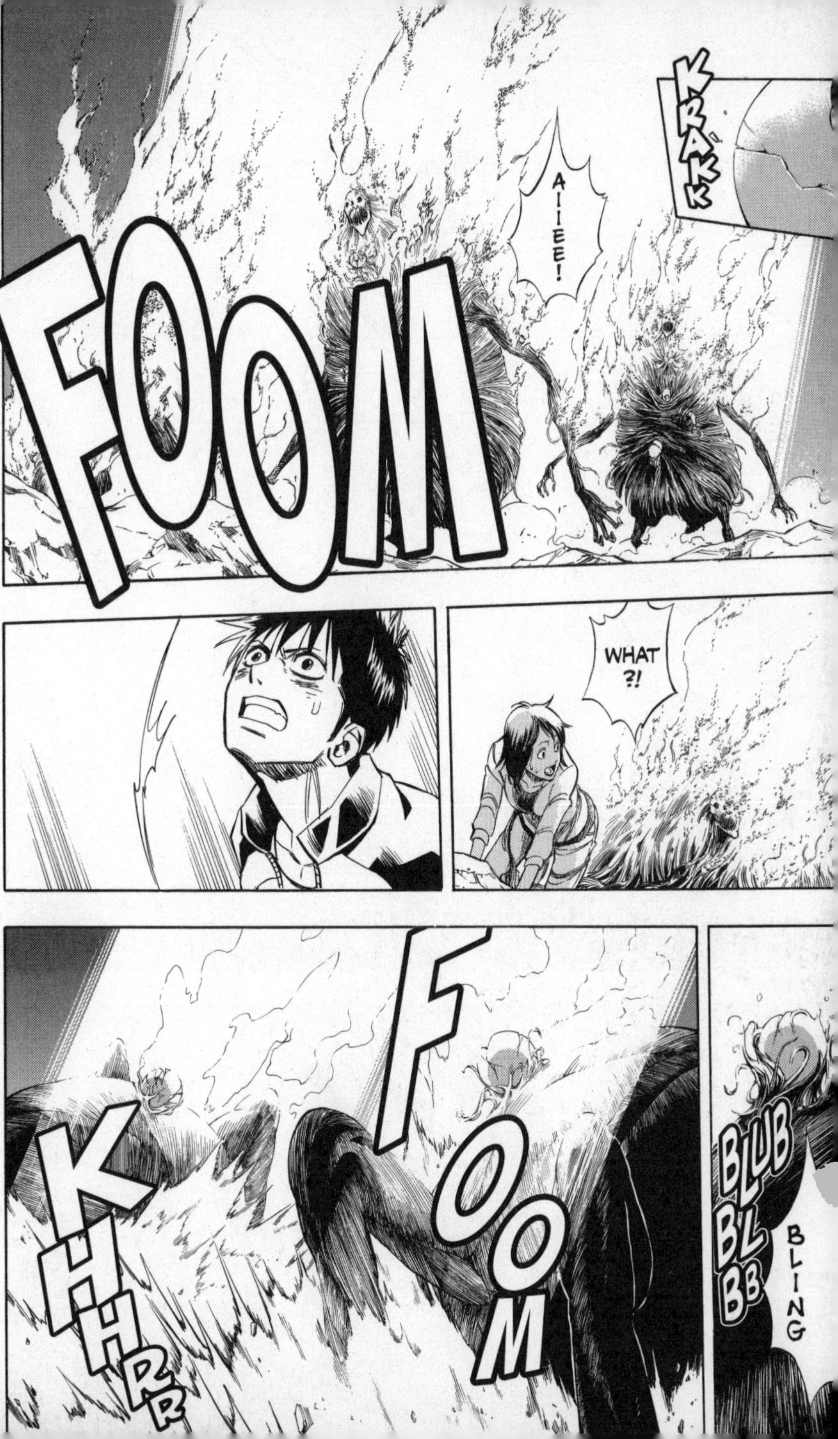
KRAKK
AIIEE!
FOOM
WHAT ?!
BLUB BLBLBB
BLING
FOOM
KHHRR

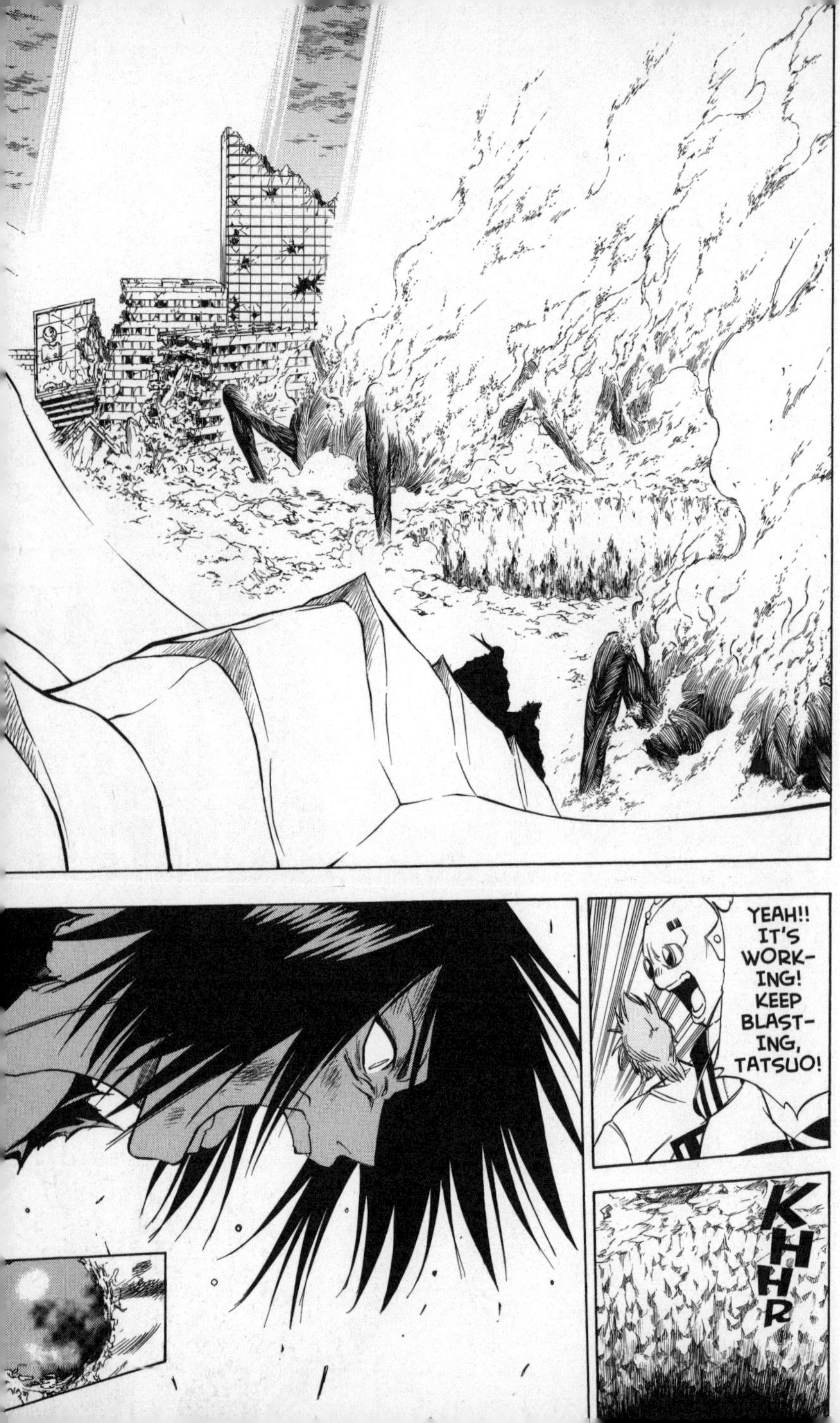
YEAH!! IT'S WORKING! KEEP BLASTING, TATSUO!
KHHR

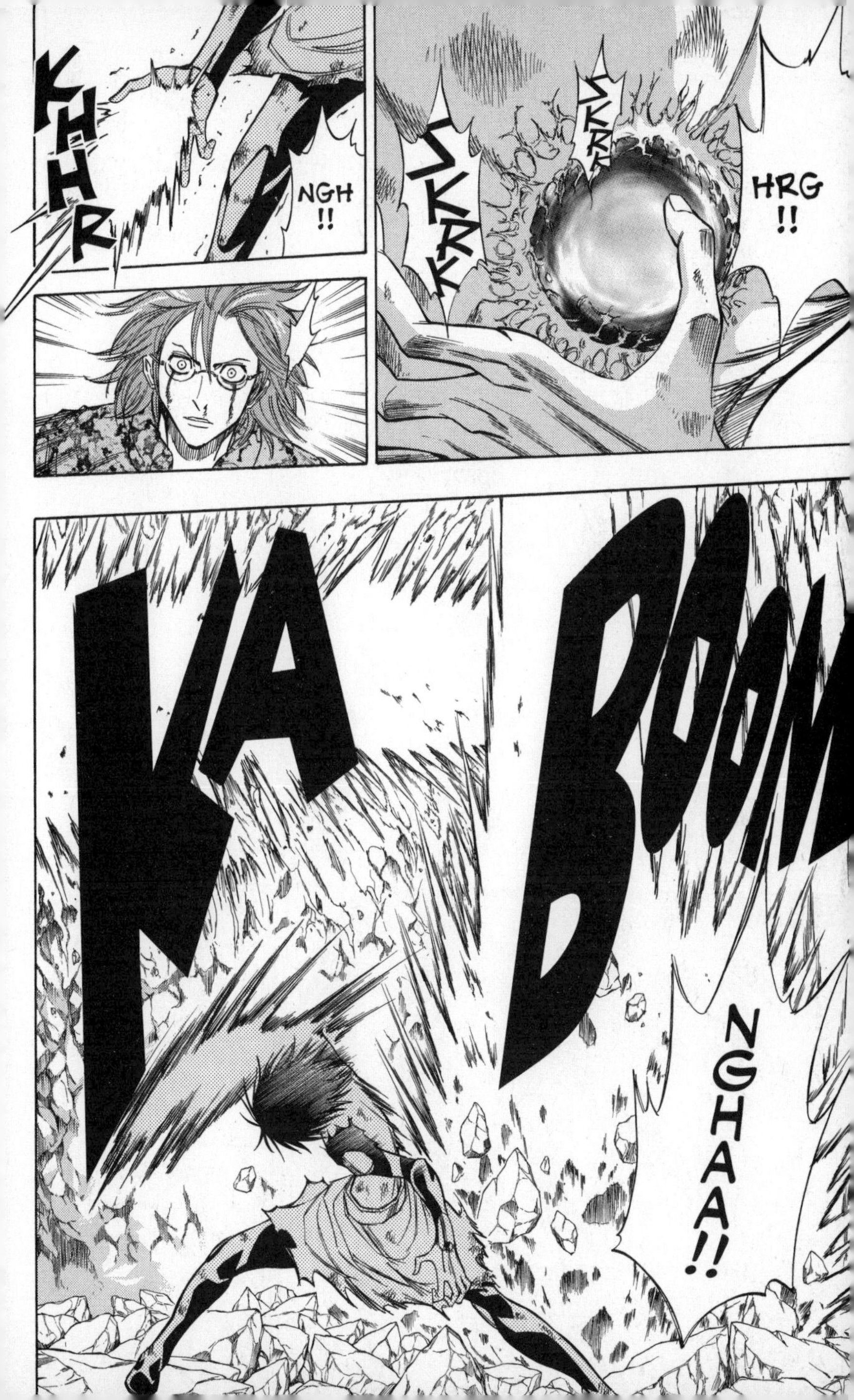
HRG !!
SKRK
SKRKRK
NGH !!
KHHR
KABOOM
NGHAA!!

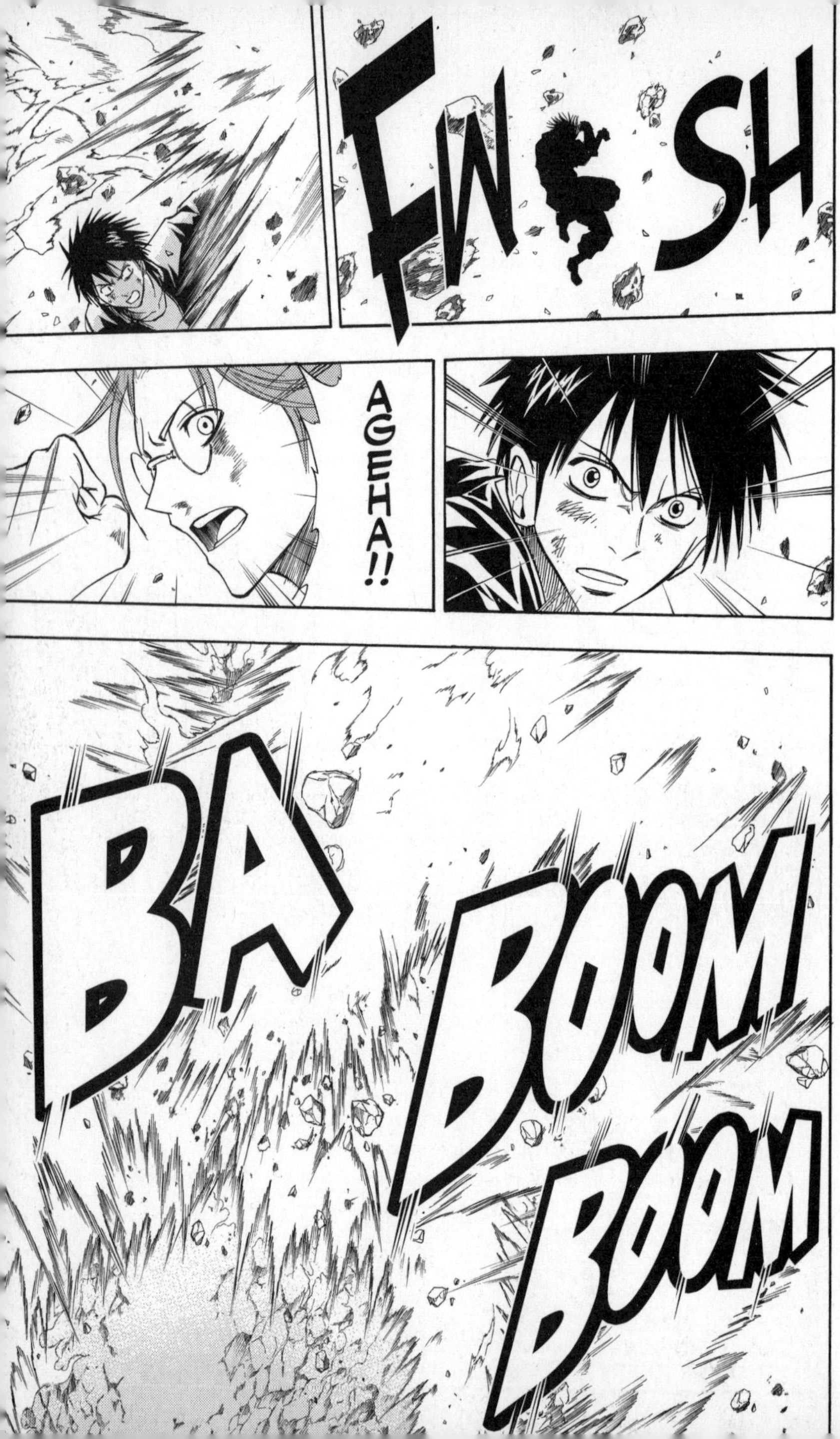
FWOOSH
AGEHA!!
BA-BOOM BOOM

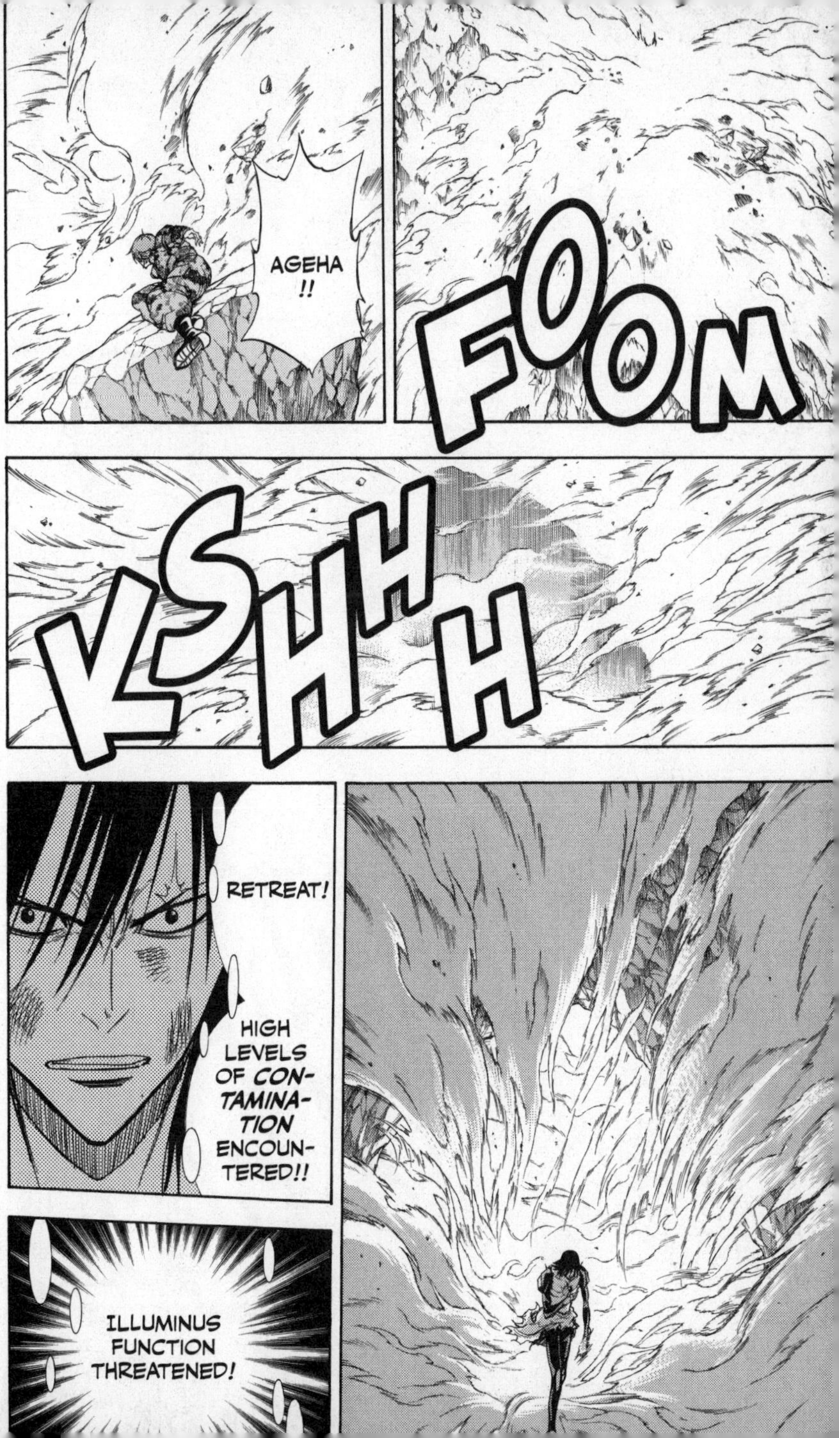
FOOM
AGEHA!!
KSHHHH
RETREAT!
HIGH LEVELS OF *CONTAMINATION* ENCOUNTERED!!
ILLUMINUS FUNCTION THREATENED!

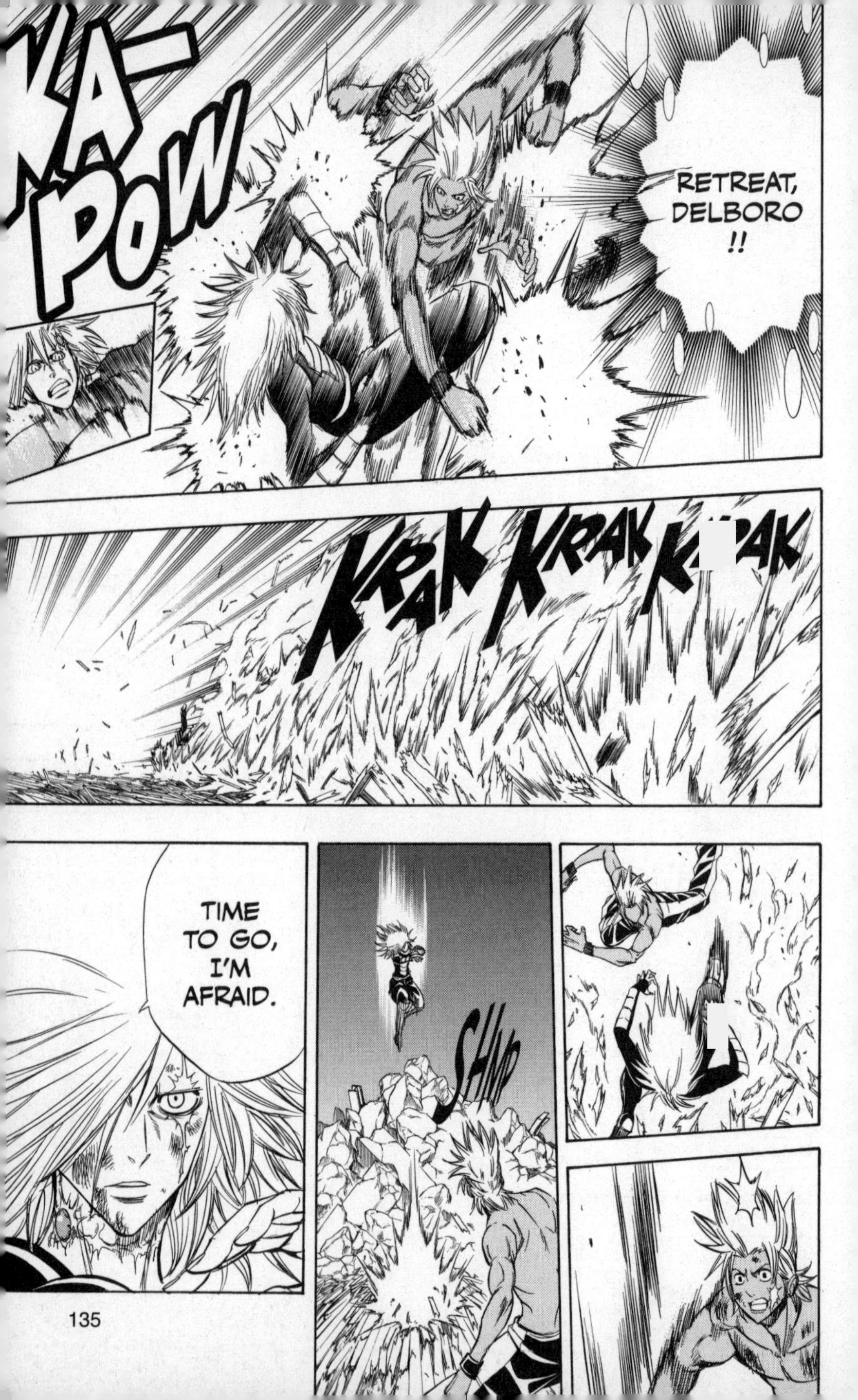
RETREAT, DELBORO!!
A-POW
KRAK KRAK
TIME TO GO, I'M AFRAID.

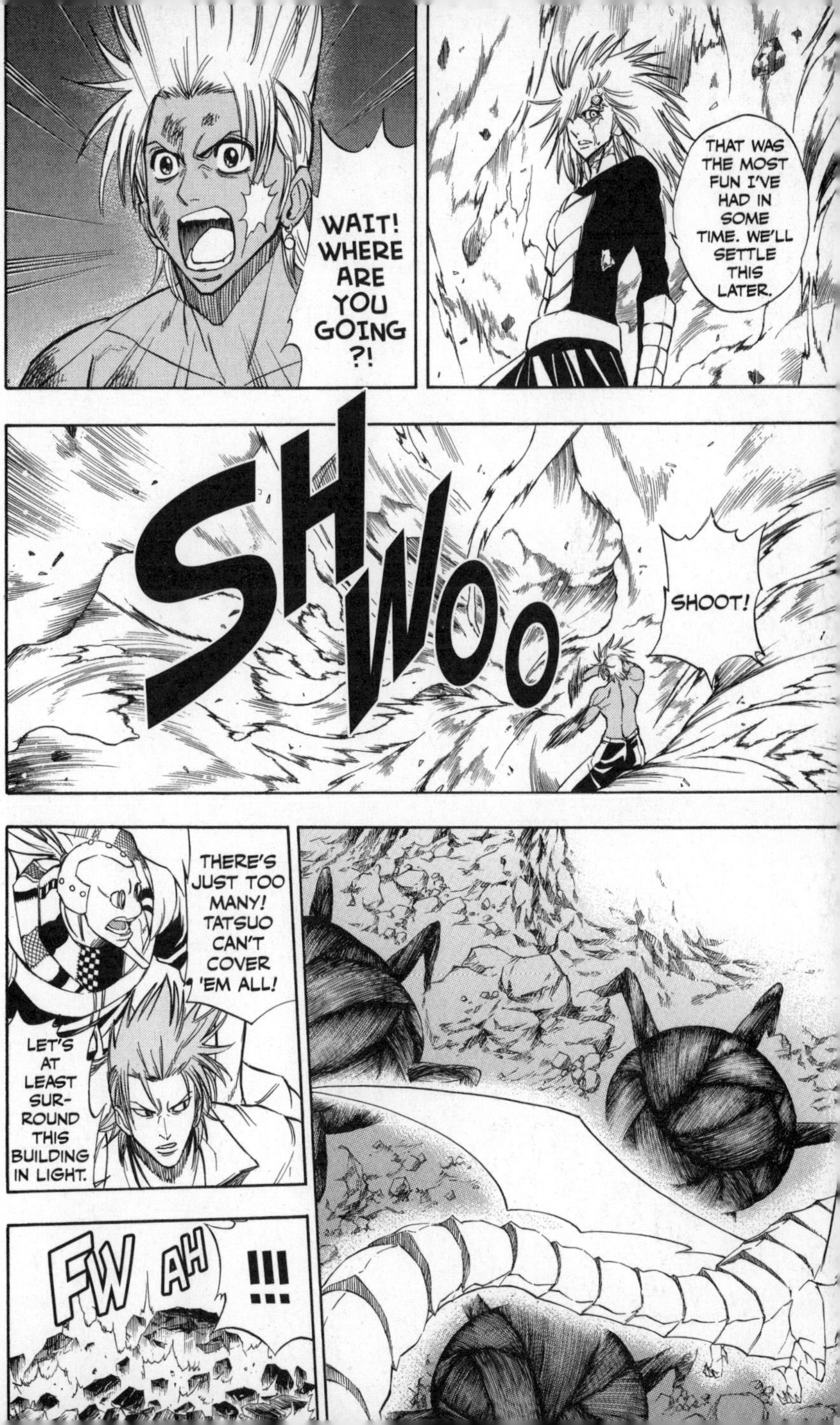
THAT WAS THE MOST FUN I'VE HAD IN SOME TIME. WE'LL SETTLE THIS LATER.
WAIT! WHERE ARE YOU GOING?!
SHWOO
SHOOT!
THERE'S JUST TOO MANY! TATSUO CAN'T COVER 'EM ALL!
LET'S AT LEAST SUR-ROUND THIS BUILDING IN LIGHT.
FWAH!!!

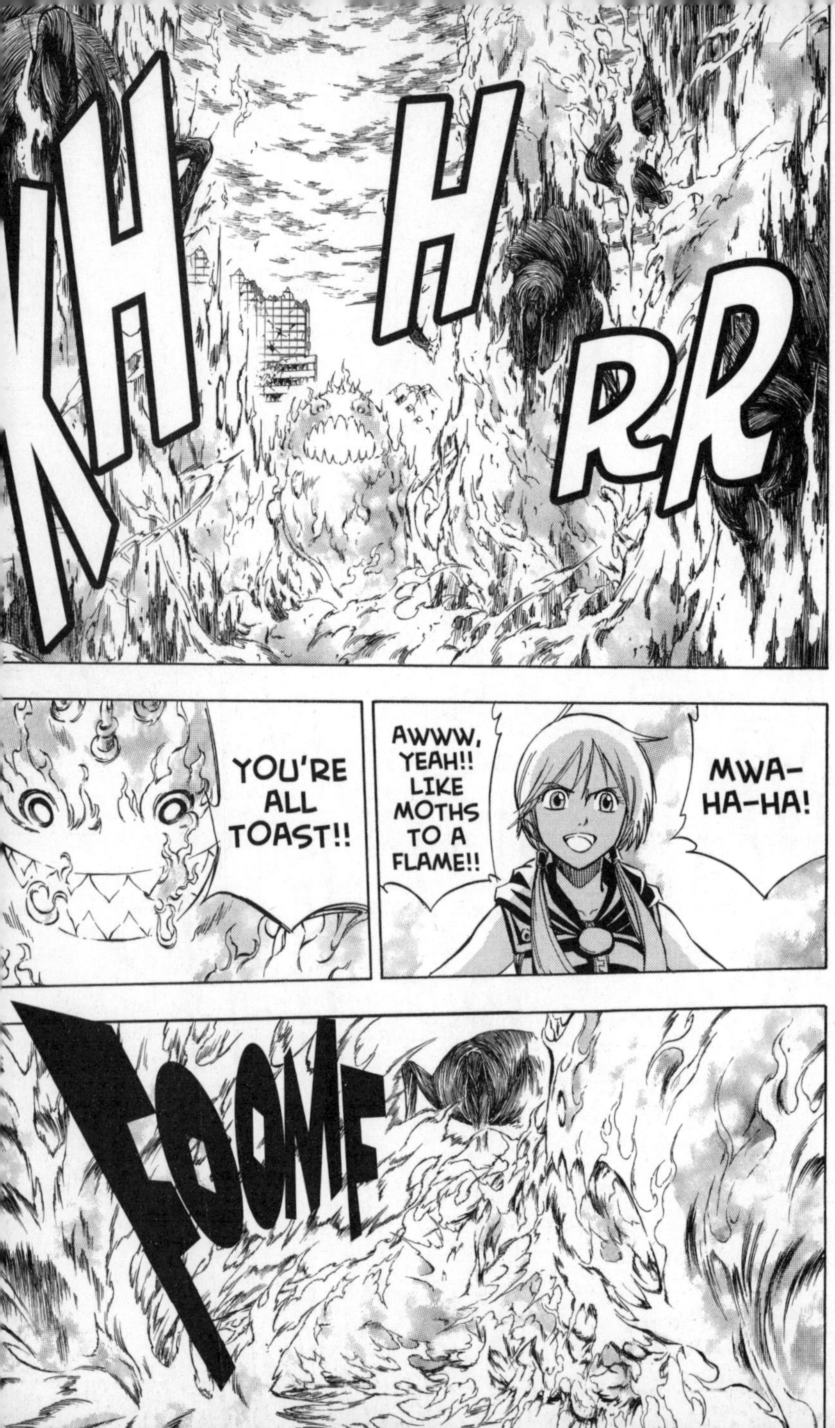
KHHRR
MWA-HA-HA!
AWWW, YEAH!! LIKE MOTHS TO A FLAME!!
YOU'RE ALL TOAST!!
FOOMF

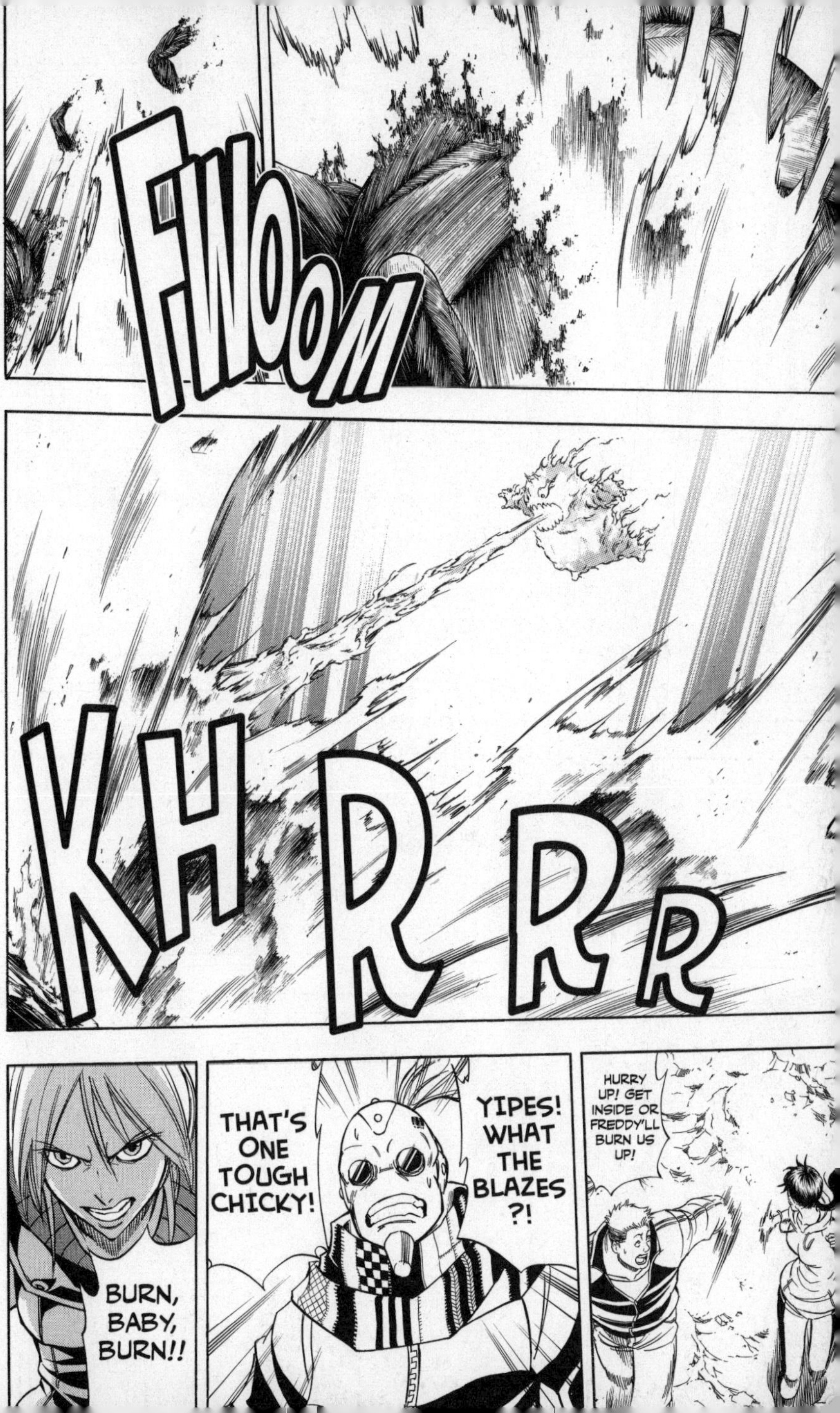
FWOOM
KHRRR
HURRY UP! GET INSIDE OR FREDDY'LL BURN US UP!
YIPES! WHAT THE BLAZES?!
THAT'S ONE TOUGH CHICKY!
BURN, BABY, BURN!!

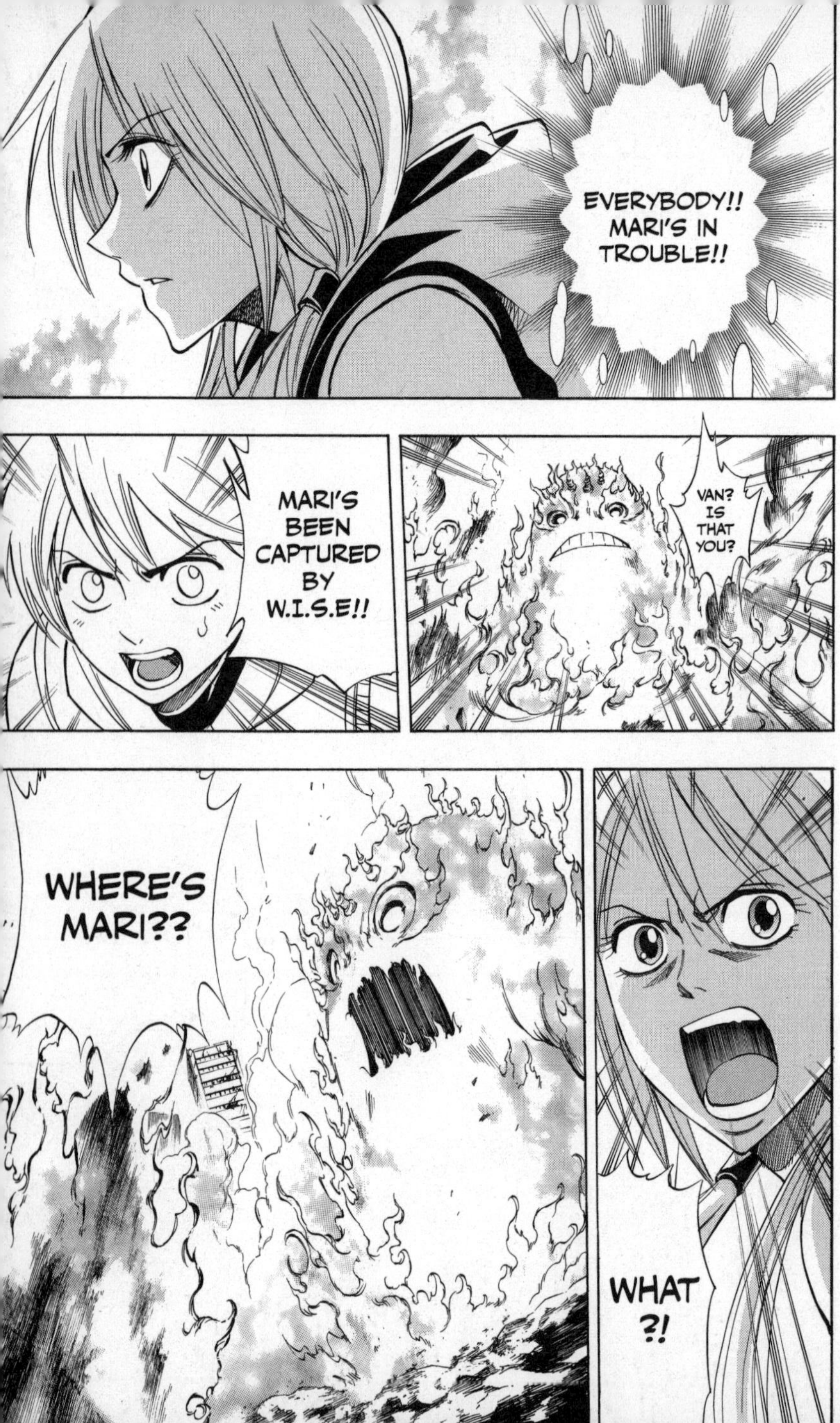
EVERYBODY!! MARI'S IN TROUBLE!!
VAN? IS THAT YOU?
MARI'S BEEN CAPTURED BY W.I.S.E!!
WHAT?!
WHERE'S MARI??

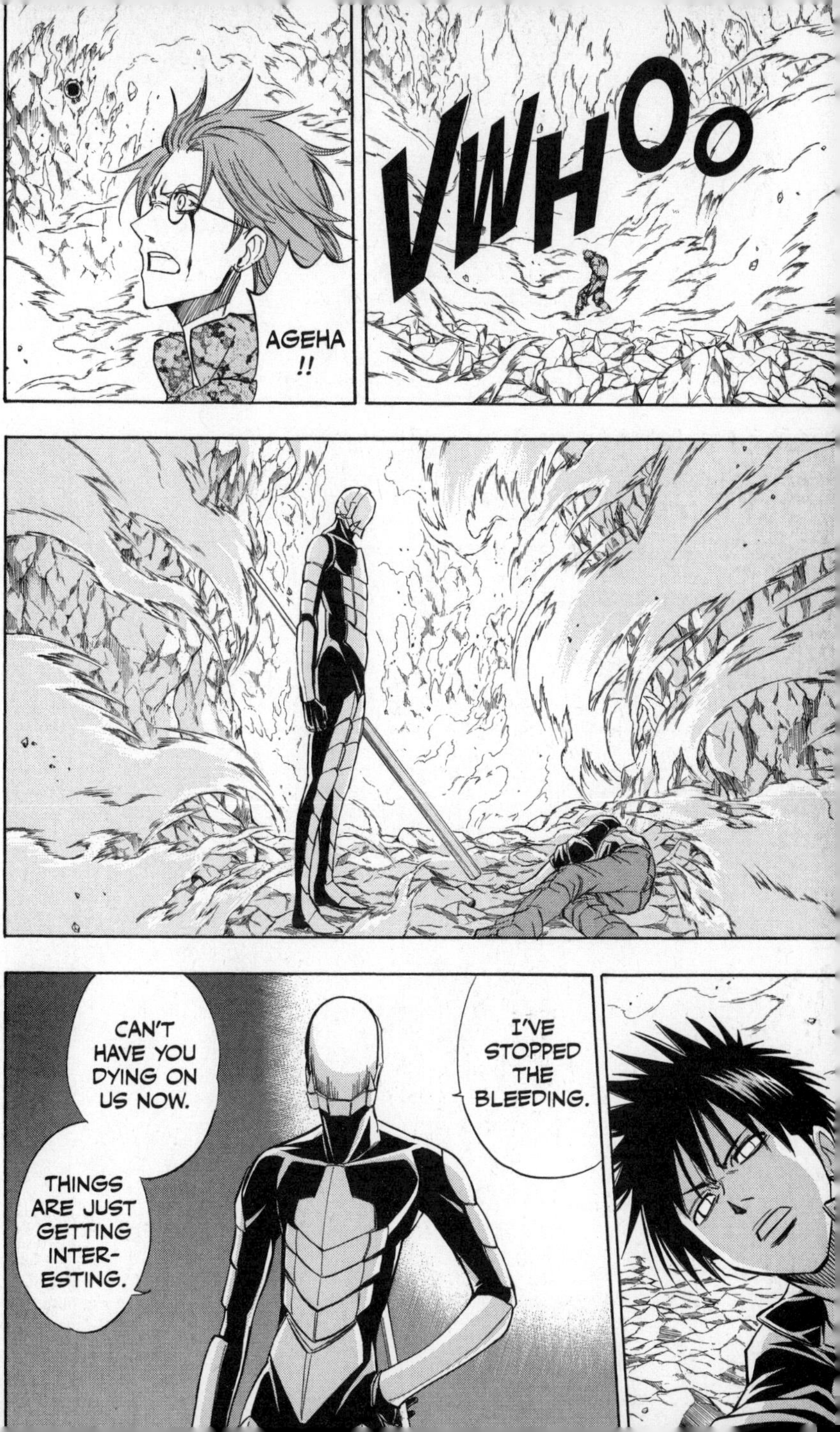
VWHOOo
AGEHA !!
I'VE STOPPED THE BLEEDING.
CAN'T HAVE YOU DYING ON US NOW.
THINGS ARE JUST GETTING INTER-ESTING.

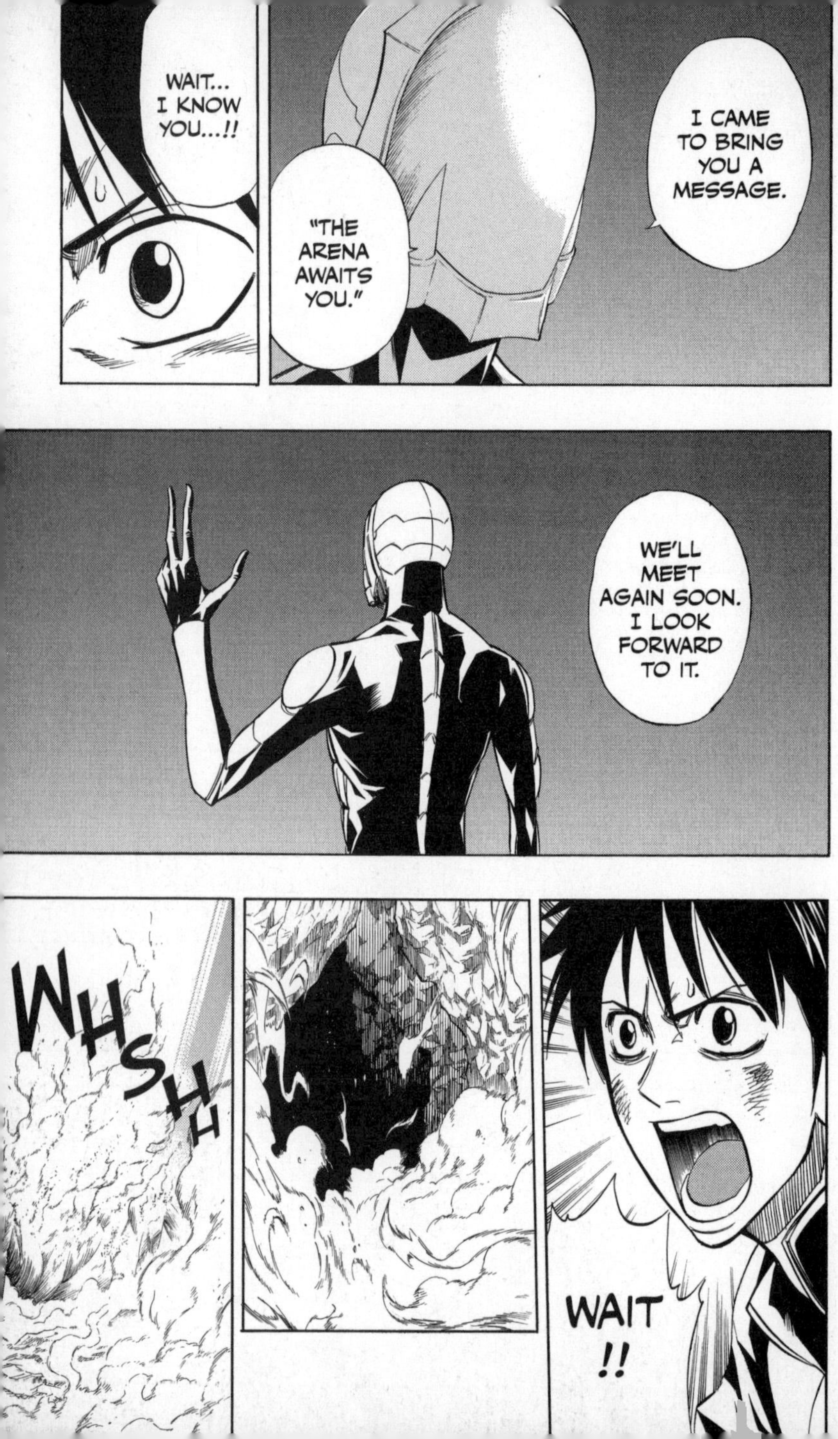
I CAME TO BRING YOU A MESSAGE.
"THE ARENA AWAITS YOU."
WAIT... I KNOW YOU...!!
WE'LL MEET AGAIN SOON. I LOOK FORWARD TO IT.
WAIT !!
WHSHH

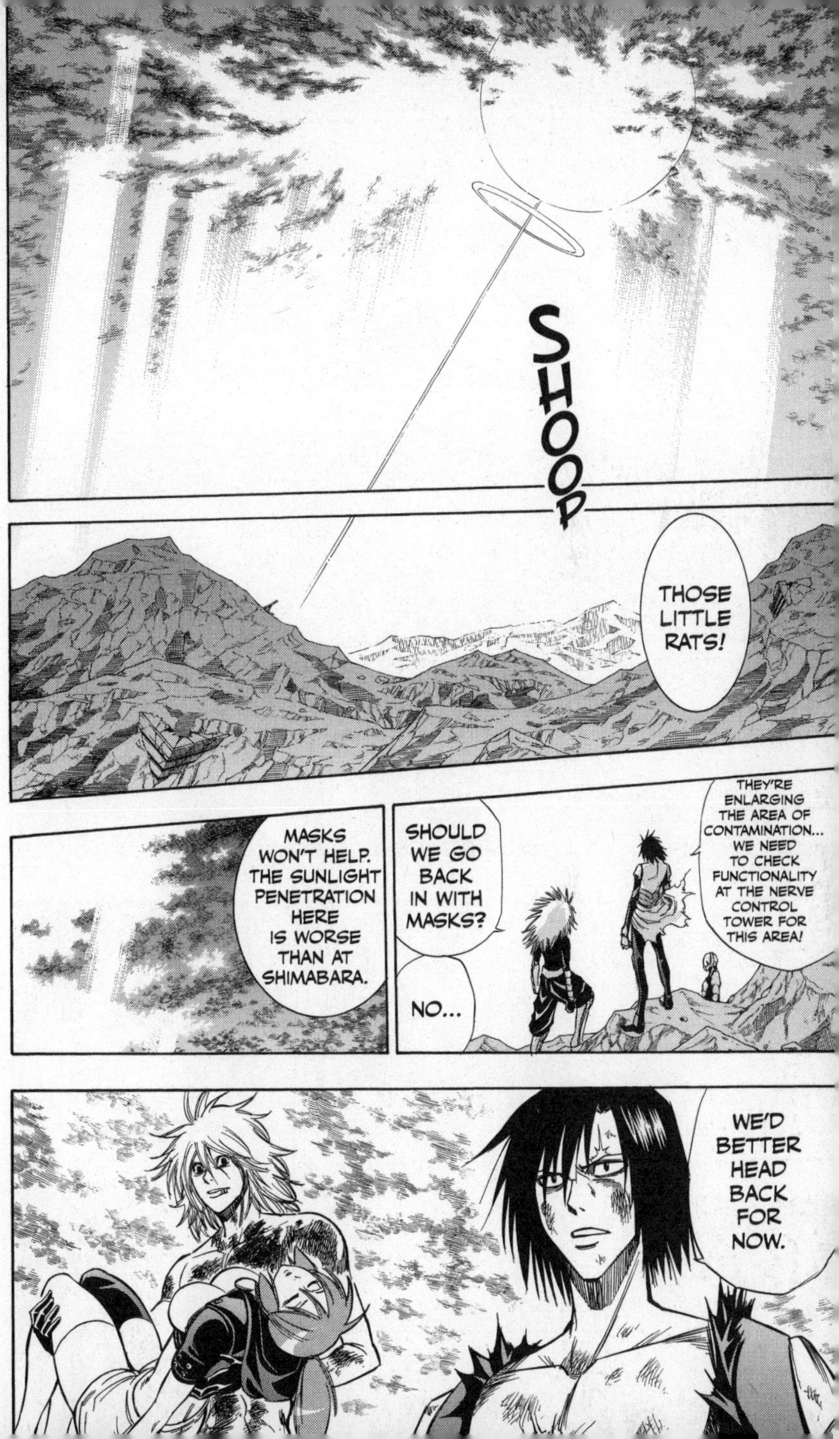
SHOOP
THOSE LITTLE RATS!
THEY'RE ENLARGING THE AREA OF CONTAMINATION... WE NEED TO CHECK FUNCTIONALITY AT THE NERVE CONTROL TOWER FOR THIS AREA!
SHOULD WE GO BACK IN WITH MASKS?
NO...
MASKS WON'T HELP. THE SUNLIGHT PENETRATION HERE IS WORSE THAN AT SHIMABARA.
WE'D BETTER HEAD BACK FOR NOW.

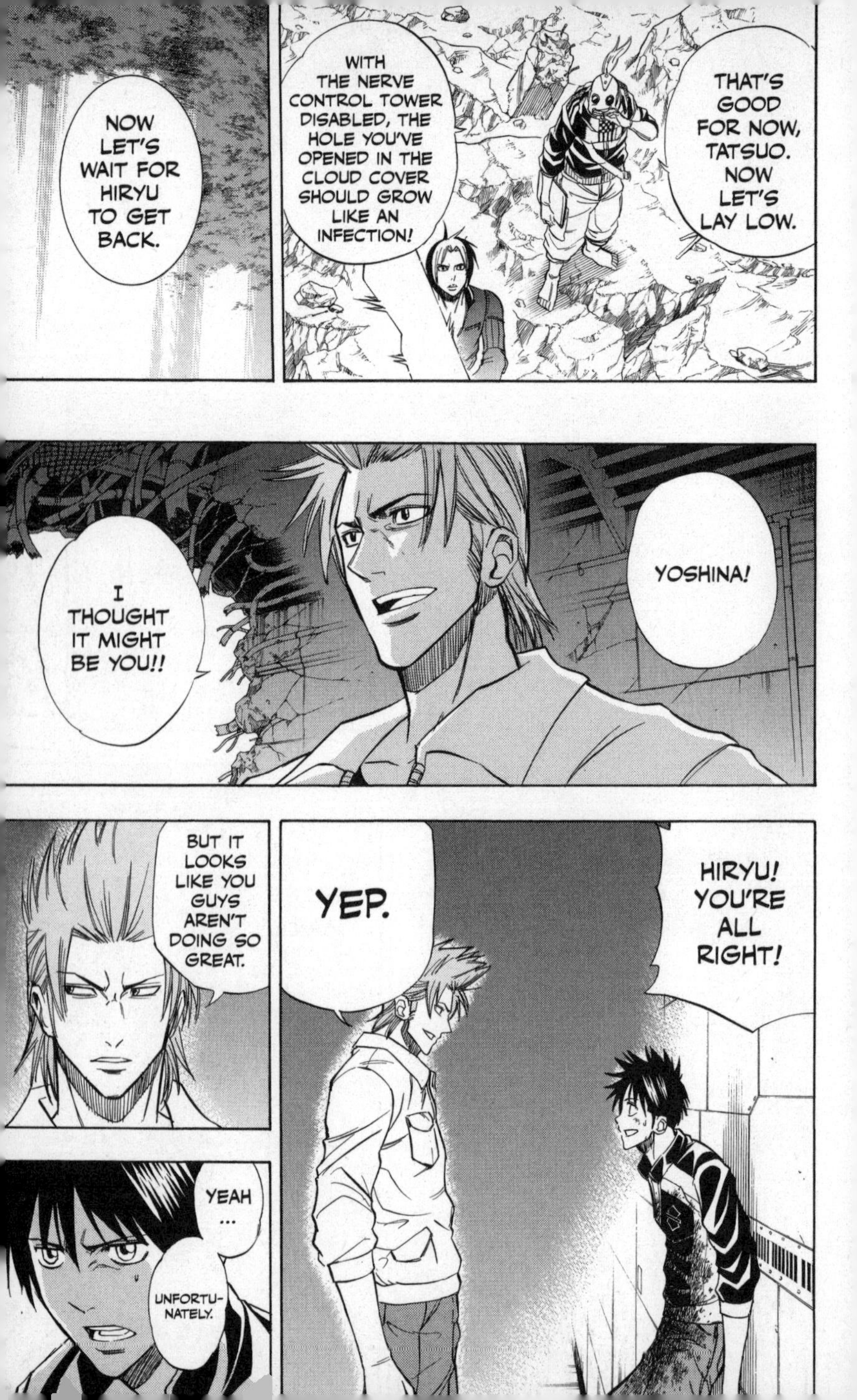
WITH THE NERVE CONTROL TOWER DISABLED, THE HOLE YOU'VE OPENED IN THE CLOUD COVER SHOULD GROW LIKE AN INFECTION!
THAT'S GOOD FOR NOW, TATSUO. NOW LET'S LAY LOW.
NOW LET'S WAIT FOR HIRYU TO GET BACK.
YOSHINA!
I THOUGHT IT MIGHT BE YOU!!
HIRYU! YOU'RE ALL RIGHT!
YEP.
BUT IT LOOKS LIKE YOU GUYS AREN'T DOING SO GREAT.
YEAH ...
UNFORTUNATELY.

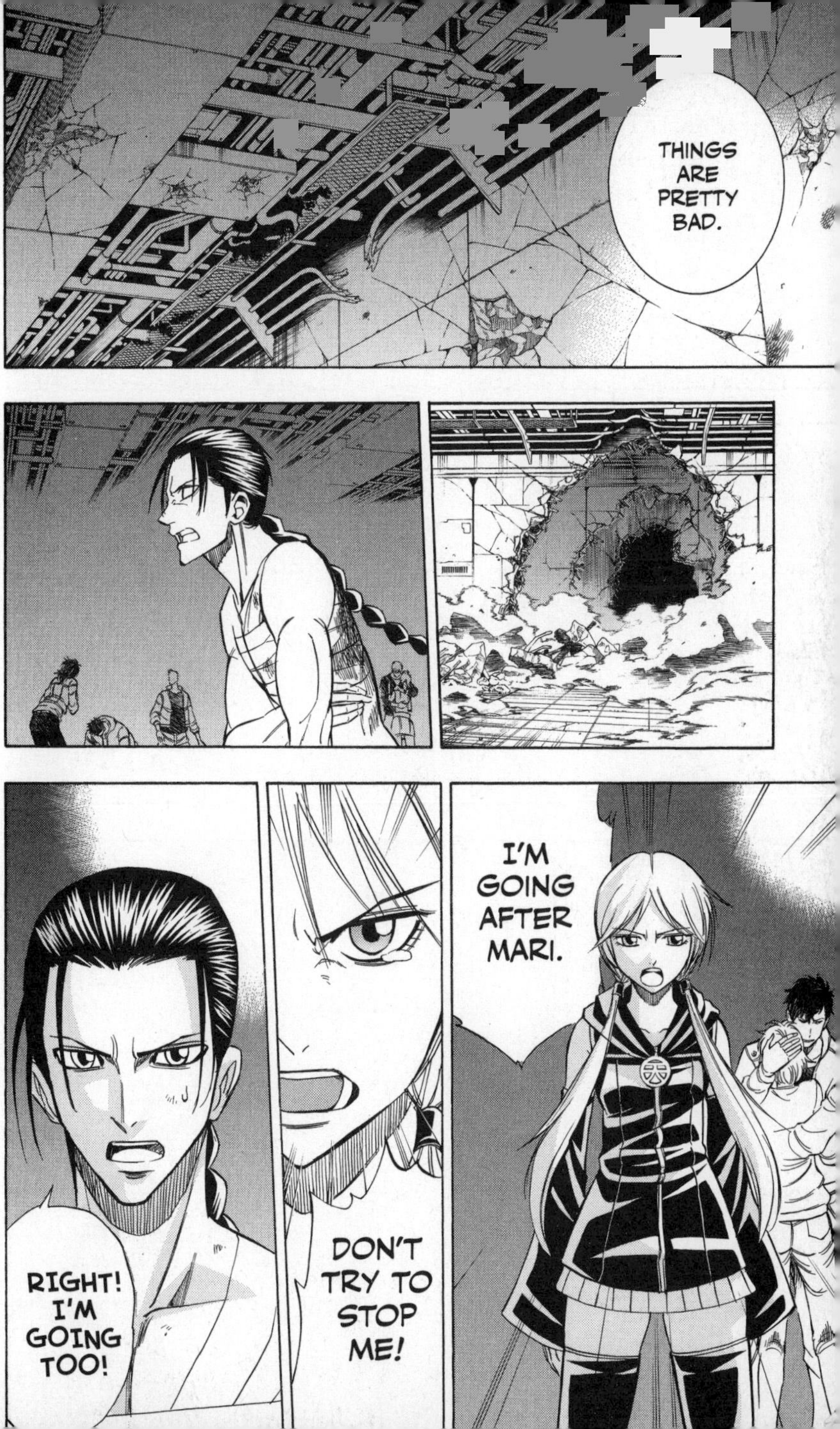
THINGS ARE PRETTY BAD.
I'M GOING AFTER MARI.
DON'T TRY TO STOP ME!
RIGHT! I'M GOING TOO!

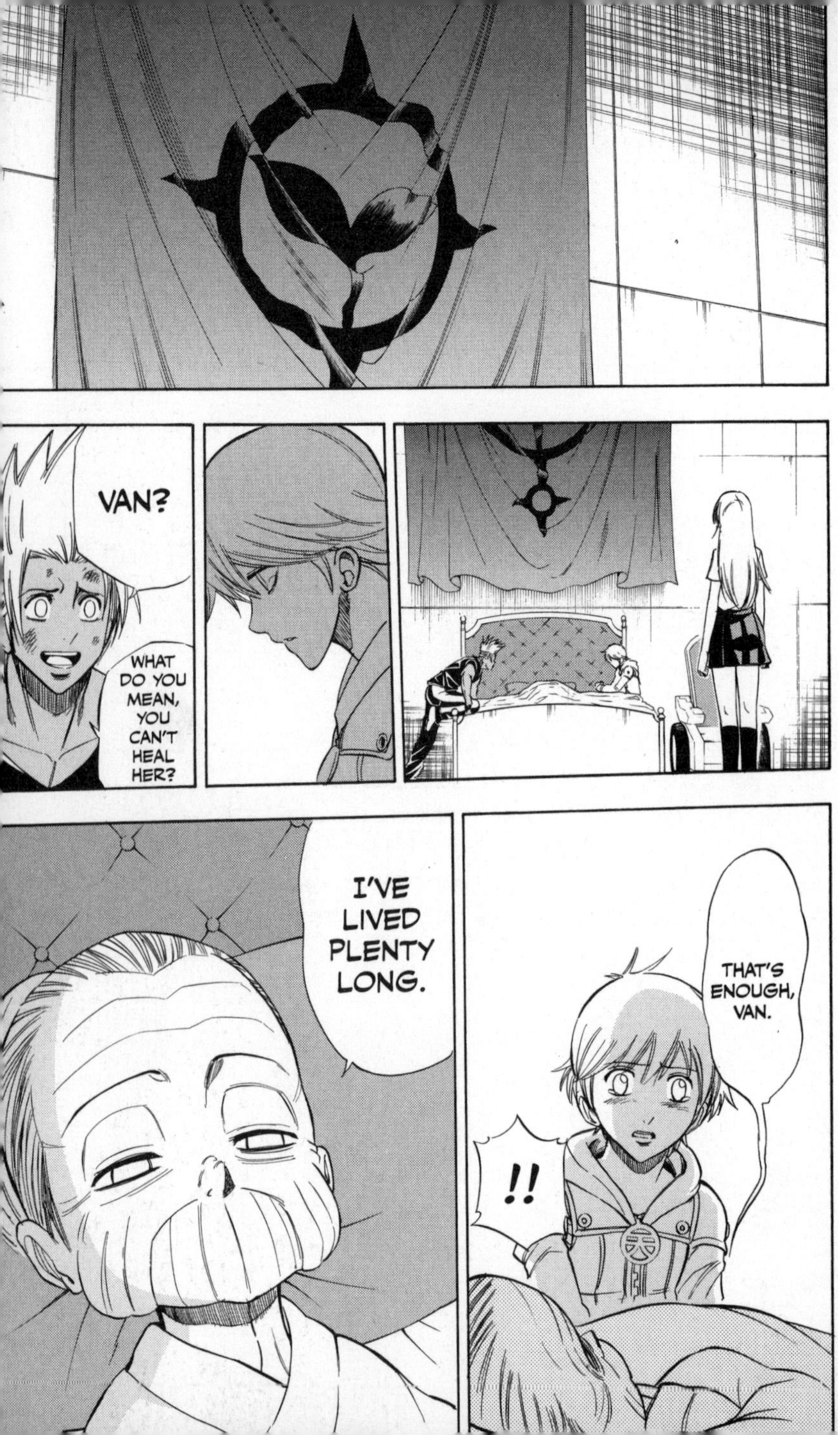
VAN?
WHAT DO YOU MEAN, YOU CAN'T HEAL HER?
THAT'S ENOUGH, VAN.
!!
I'VE LIVED PLENTY LONG.

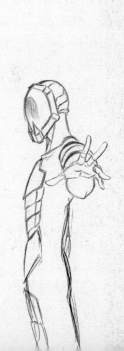

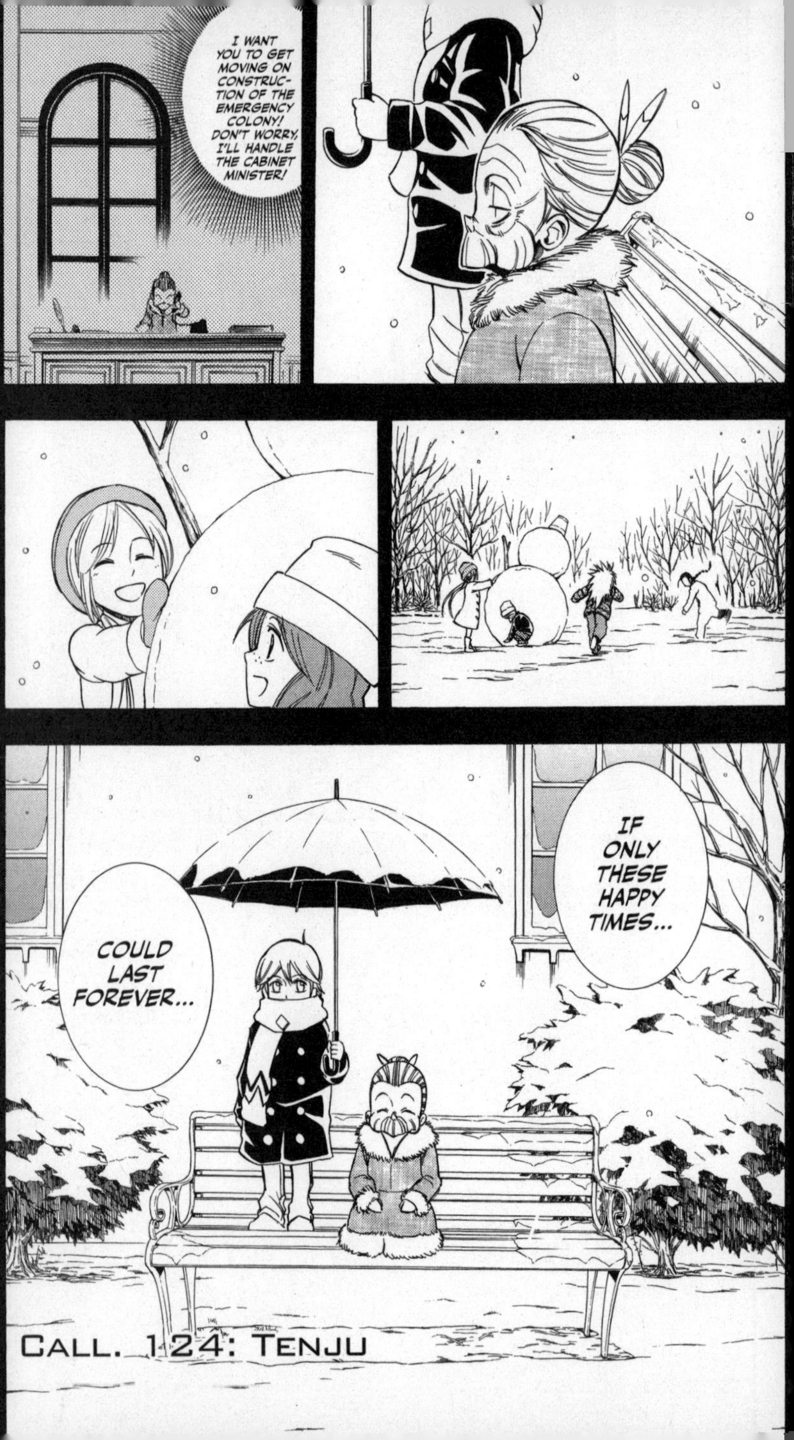
I WANT YOU TO GET MOVING ON CONSTRUCTION OF THE EMERGENCY COLONY! DON'T WORRY, I'LL HANDLE THE CABINET MINISTER!
IF ONLY THESE HAPPY TIMES...
COULD LAST FOREVER...
CALL. 124: TENJU

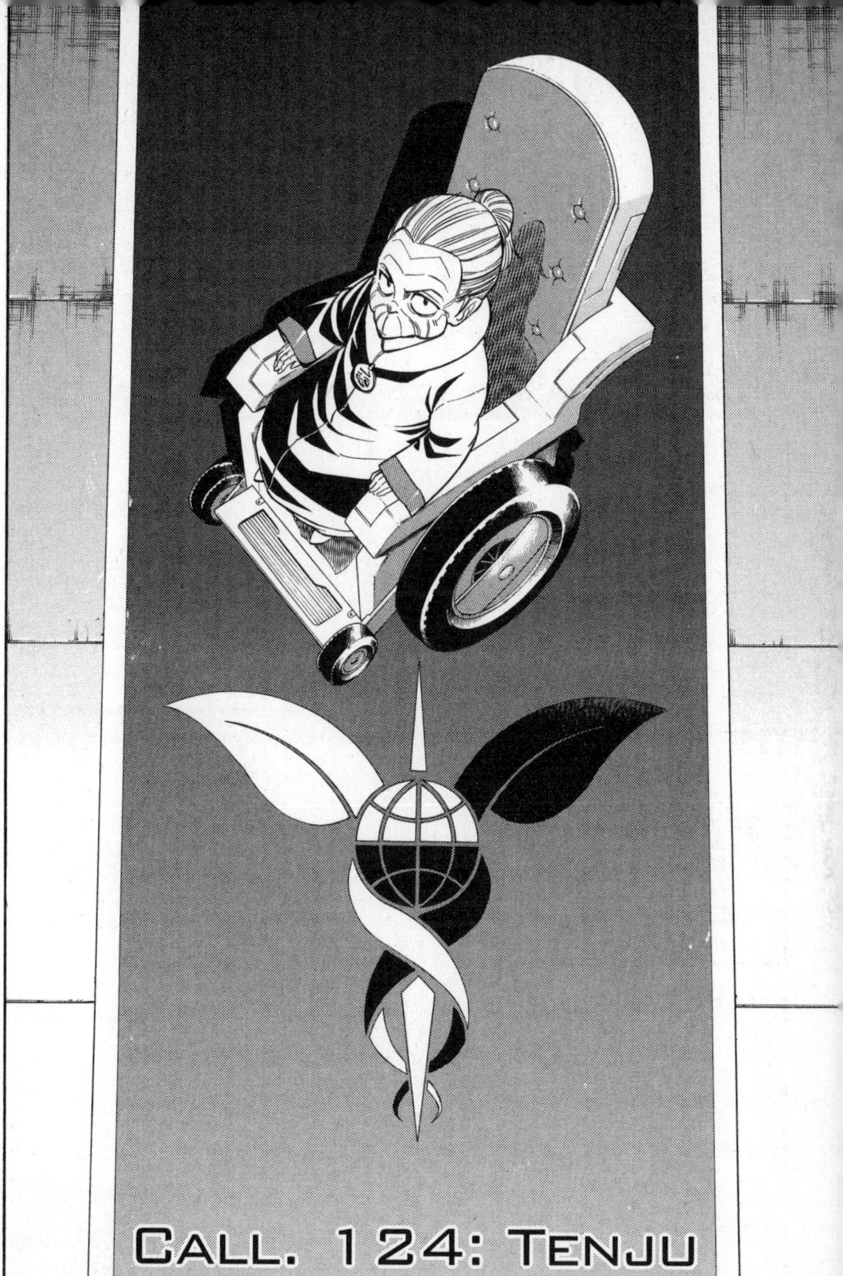

Call. 124: Tenju

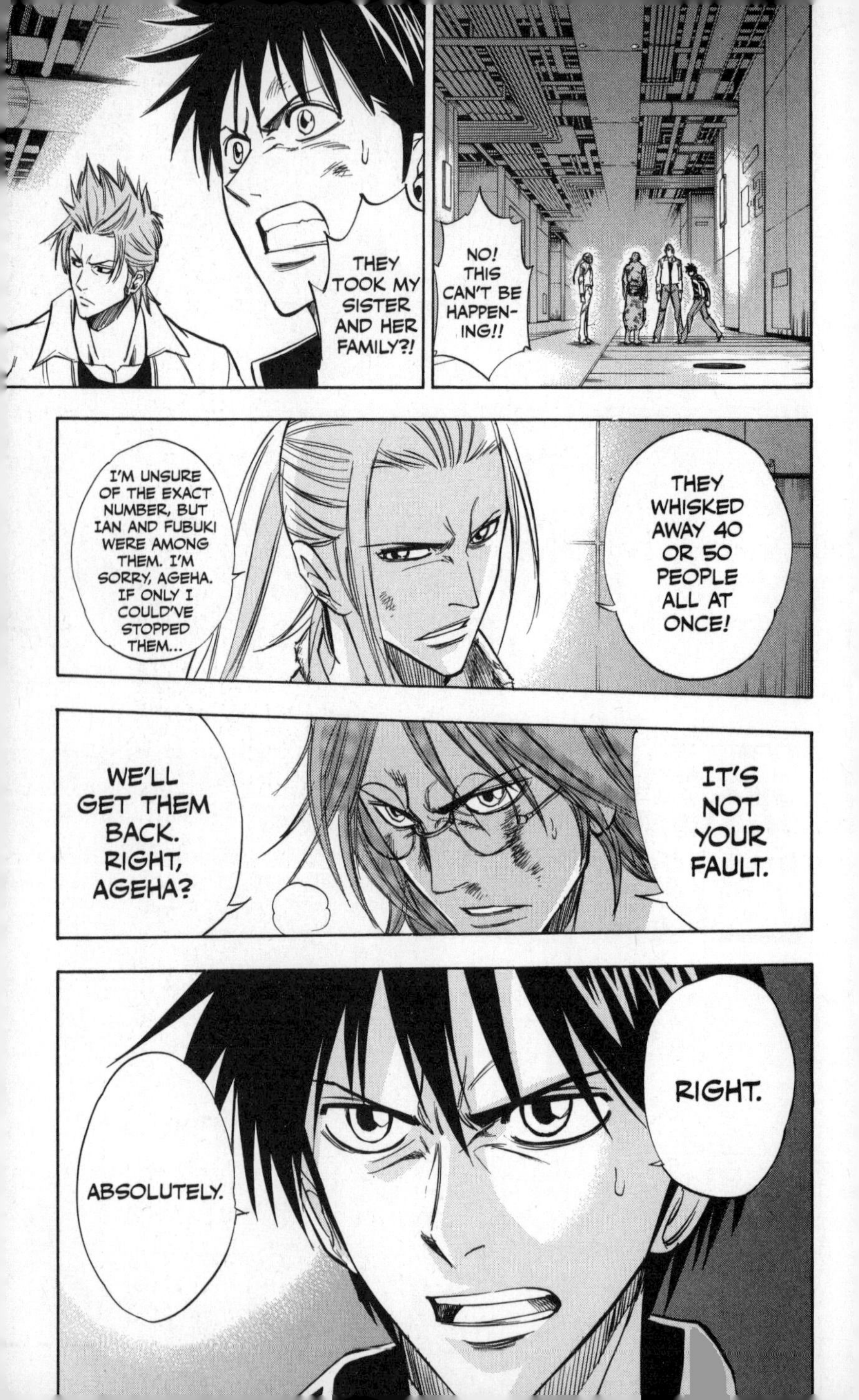
NO! THIS CAN'T BE HAPPEN-ING!!
THEY TOOK MY SISTER AND HER FAMILY?!
THEY WHISKED AWAY 40 OR 50 PEOPLE ALL AT ONCE!
I'M UNSURE OF THE EXACT NUMBER, BUT IAN AND FUBUKI WERE AMONG THEM. I'M SORRY, AGEHA. IF ONLY I COULD'VE STOPPED THEM...
IT'S NOT YOUR FAULT.
WE'LL GET THEM BACK. RIGHT, AGEHA?
RIGHT.
ABSOLUTELY.

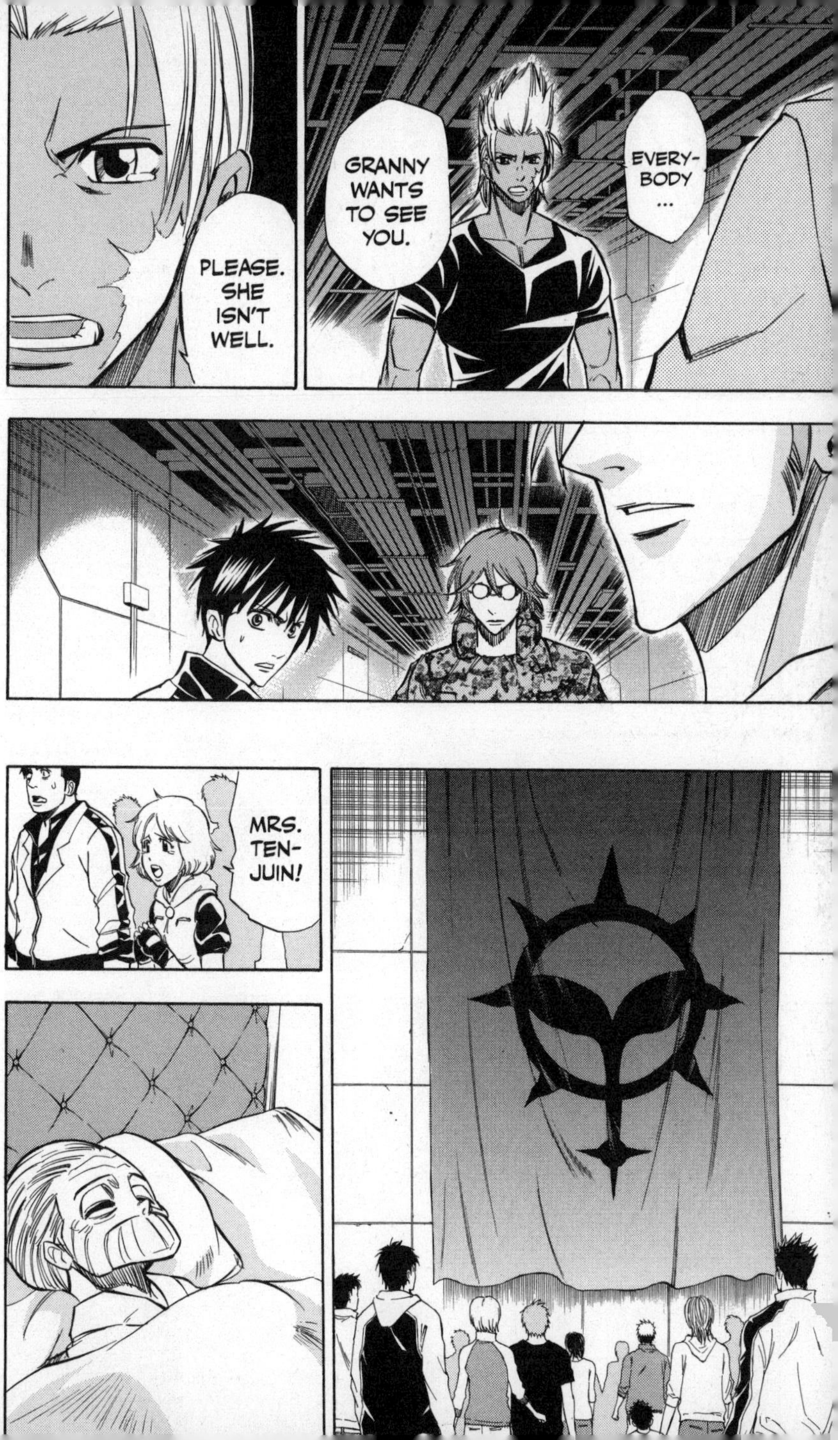
EVERY-BODY ...
GRANNY WANTS TO SEE YOU.
PLEASE. SHE ISN'T WELL.
MRS. TEN-JUIN!

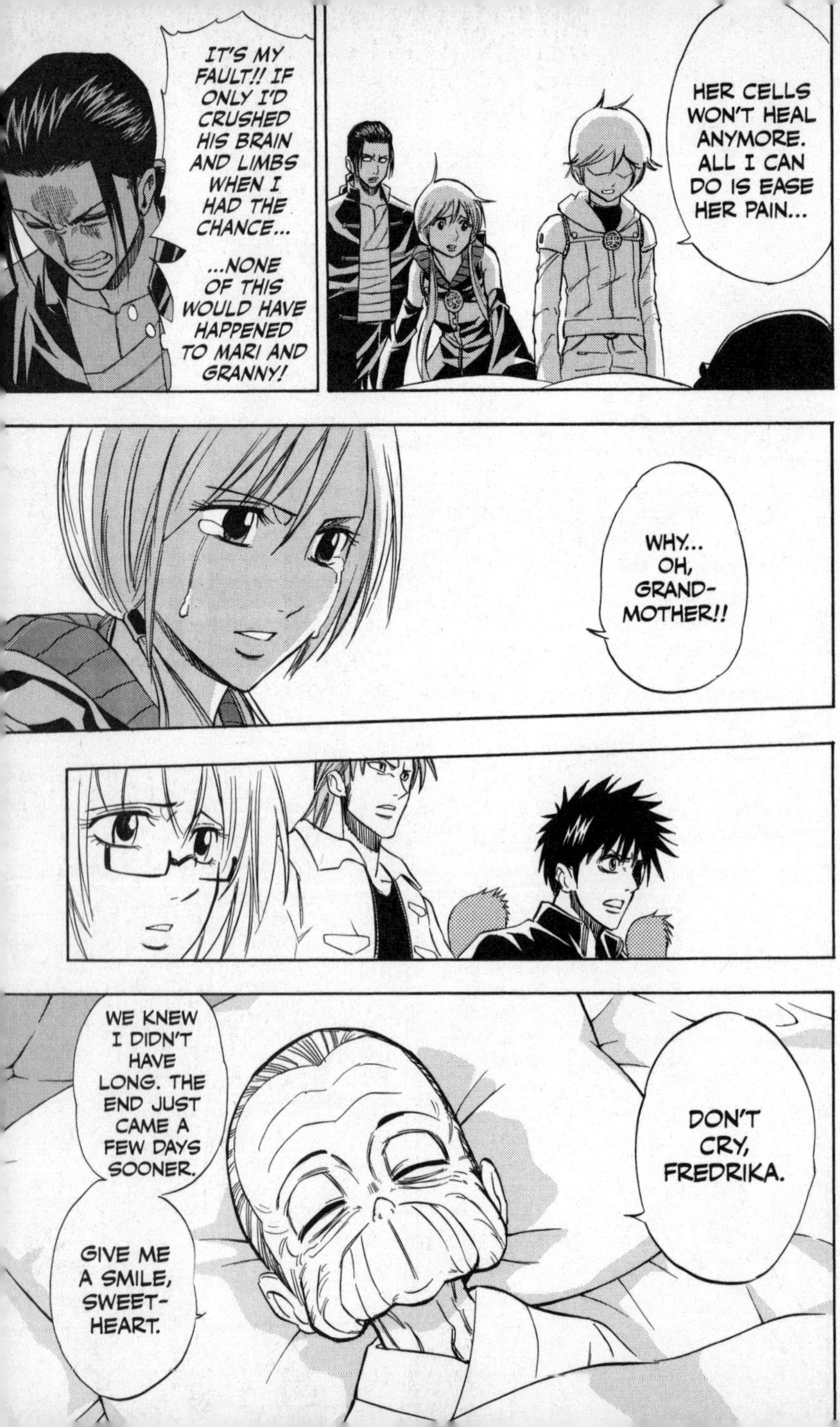
HER CELLS WON'T HEAL ANYMORE. ALL I CAN DO IS EASE HER PAIN...
IT'S MY FAULT!! IF ONLY I'D CRUSHED HIS BRAIN AND LIMBS WHEN I HAD THE CHANCE...
...NONE OF THIS WOULD HAVE HAPPENED TO MARI AND GRANNY!
WHY... OH, GRAND-MOTHER!!
DON'T CRY, FREDRIKA.
WE KNEW I DIDN'T HAVE LONG. THE END JUST CAME A FEW DAYS SOONER.
GIVE ME A SMILE, SWEET-HEART.

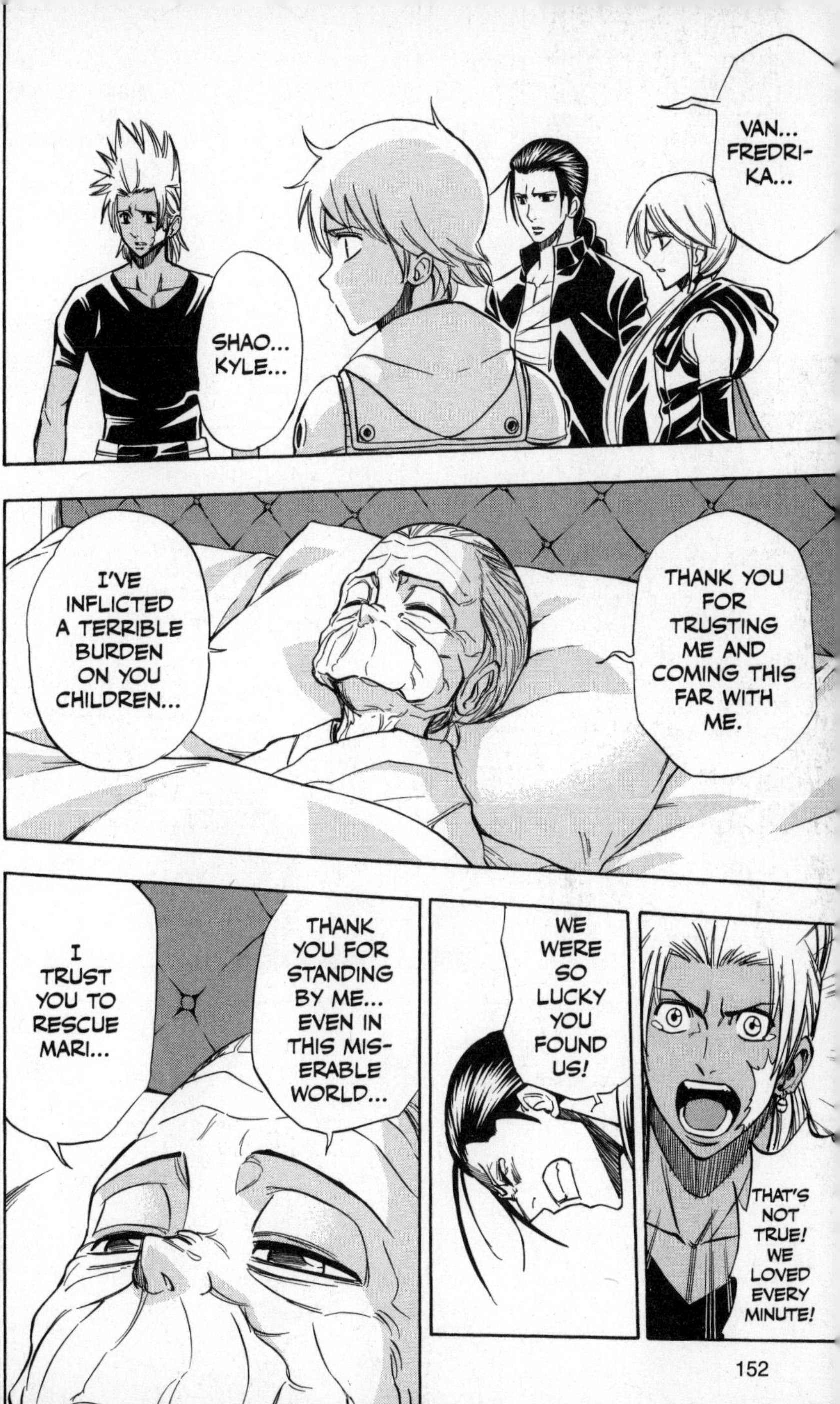
VAN... FREDRI-KA...
SHAO... KYLE...
THANK YOU FOR TRUSTING ME AND COMING THIS FAR WITH ME.
I'VE INFLICTED A TERRIBLE BURDEN ON YOU CHILDREN...
THAT'S NOT TRUE! WE LOVED EVERY MINUTE!
WE WERE SO LUCKY YOU FOUND US!
THANK YOU FOR STANDING BY ME... EVEN IN THIS MIS-ERABLE WORLD...
I TRUST YOU TO RESCUE MARI...

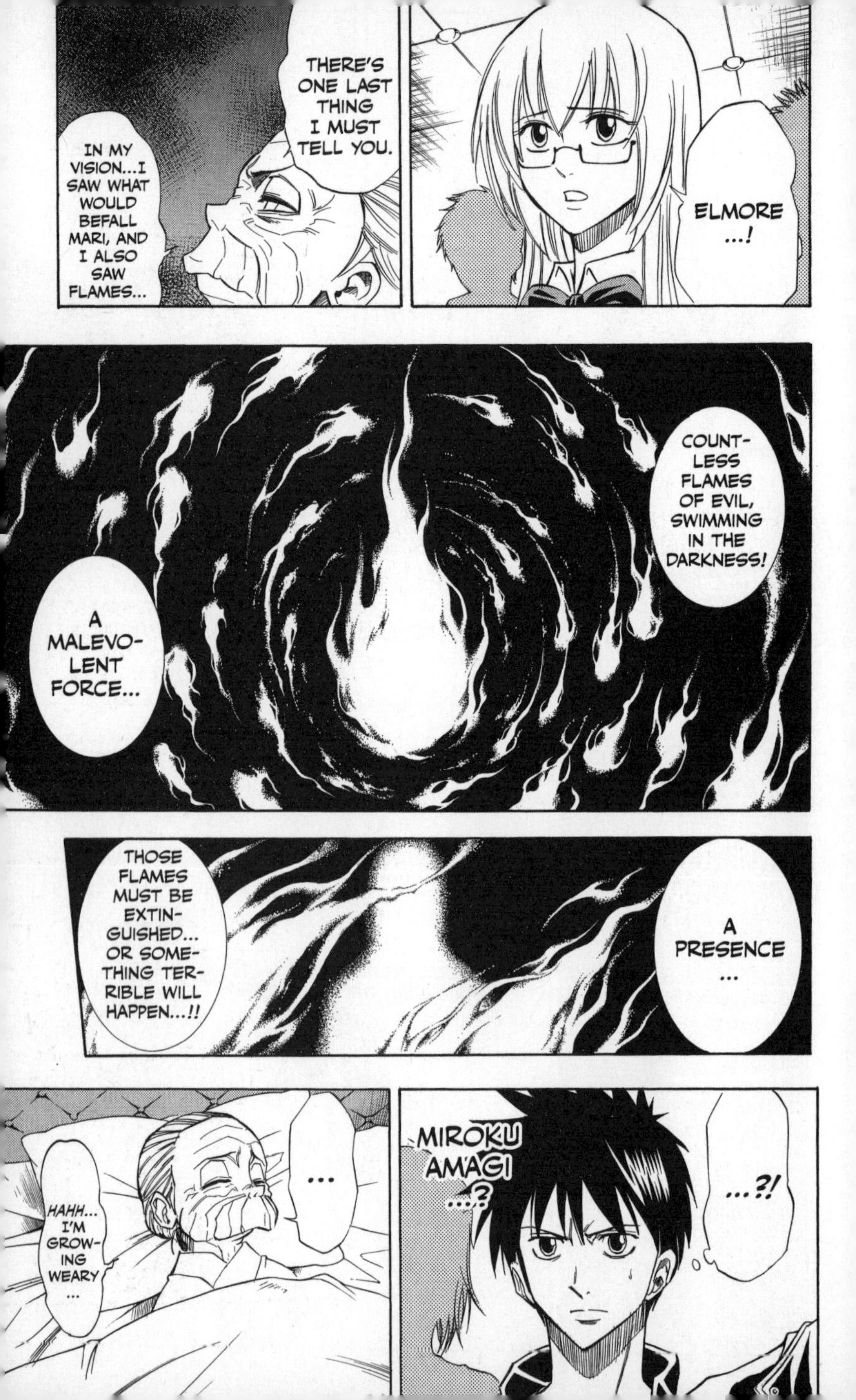
ELMORE ...!
THERE'S ONE LAST THING I MUST TELL YOU.
IN MY VISION...I SAW WHAT WOULD BEFALL MARI, AND I ALSO SAW FLAMES...
COUNTLESS FLAMES OF EVIL, SWIMMING IN THE DARKNESS!
A MALEVOLENT FORCE...
A PRESENCE ...
THOSE FLAMES MUST BE EXTINGUISHED... OR SOMETHING TERRIBLE WILL HAPPEN...!!
...?!
MIROKU AMAGI ...?
...
HAHH... I'M GROWING WEARY ...

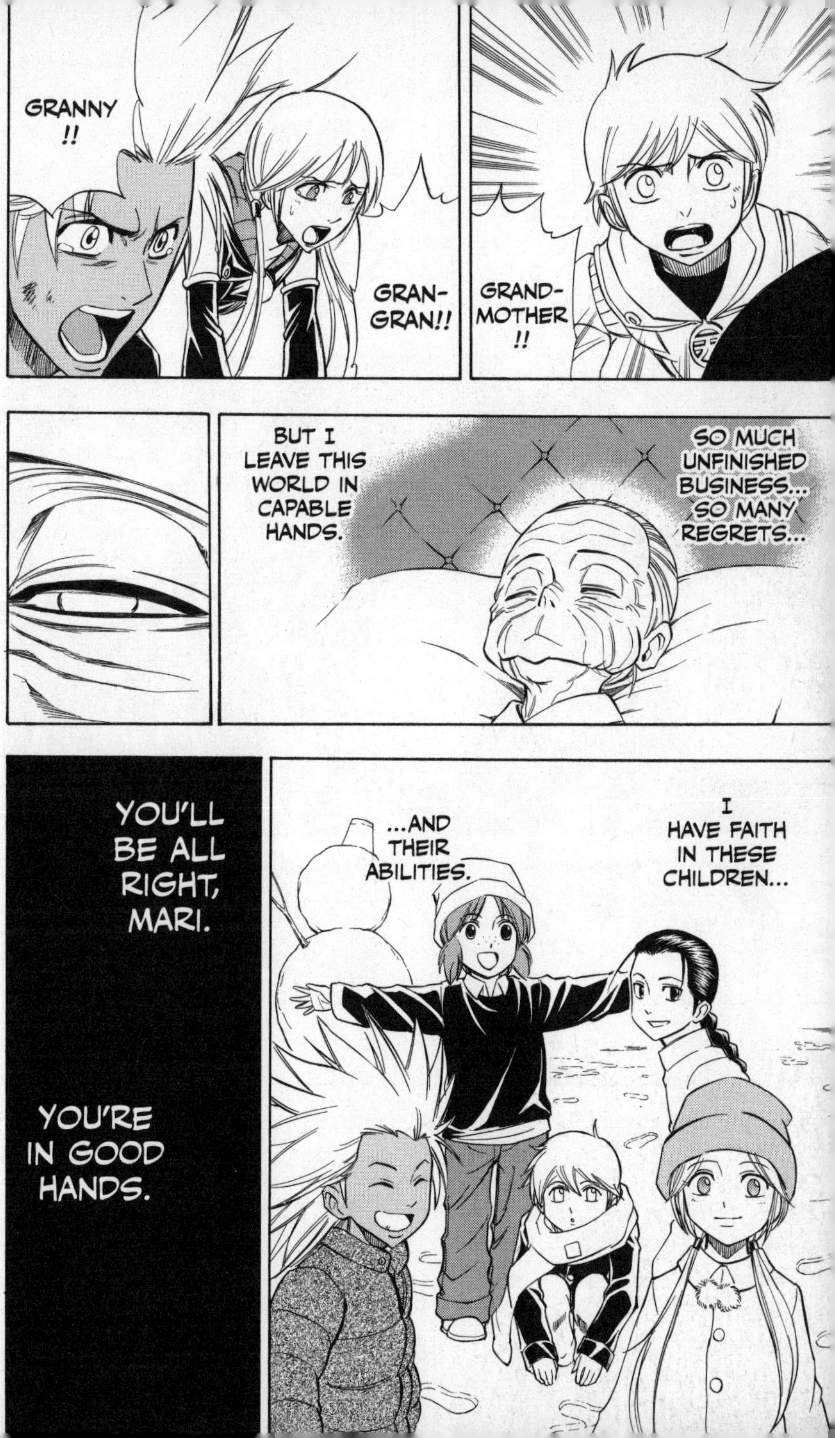
GRAND-MOTHER!!
GRAN-GRAN!!
GRANNY!!
SO MUCH UNFINISHED BUSINESS... SO MANY REGRETS...
BUT I LEAVE THIS WORLD IN CAPABLE HANDS.
I HAVE FAITH IN THESE CHILDREN...
...AND THEIR ABILITIES.
YOU'LL BE ALL RIGHT, MARI.
YOU'RE IN GOOD HANDS.

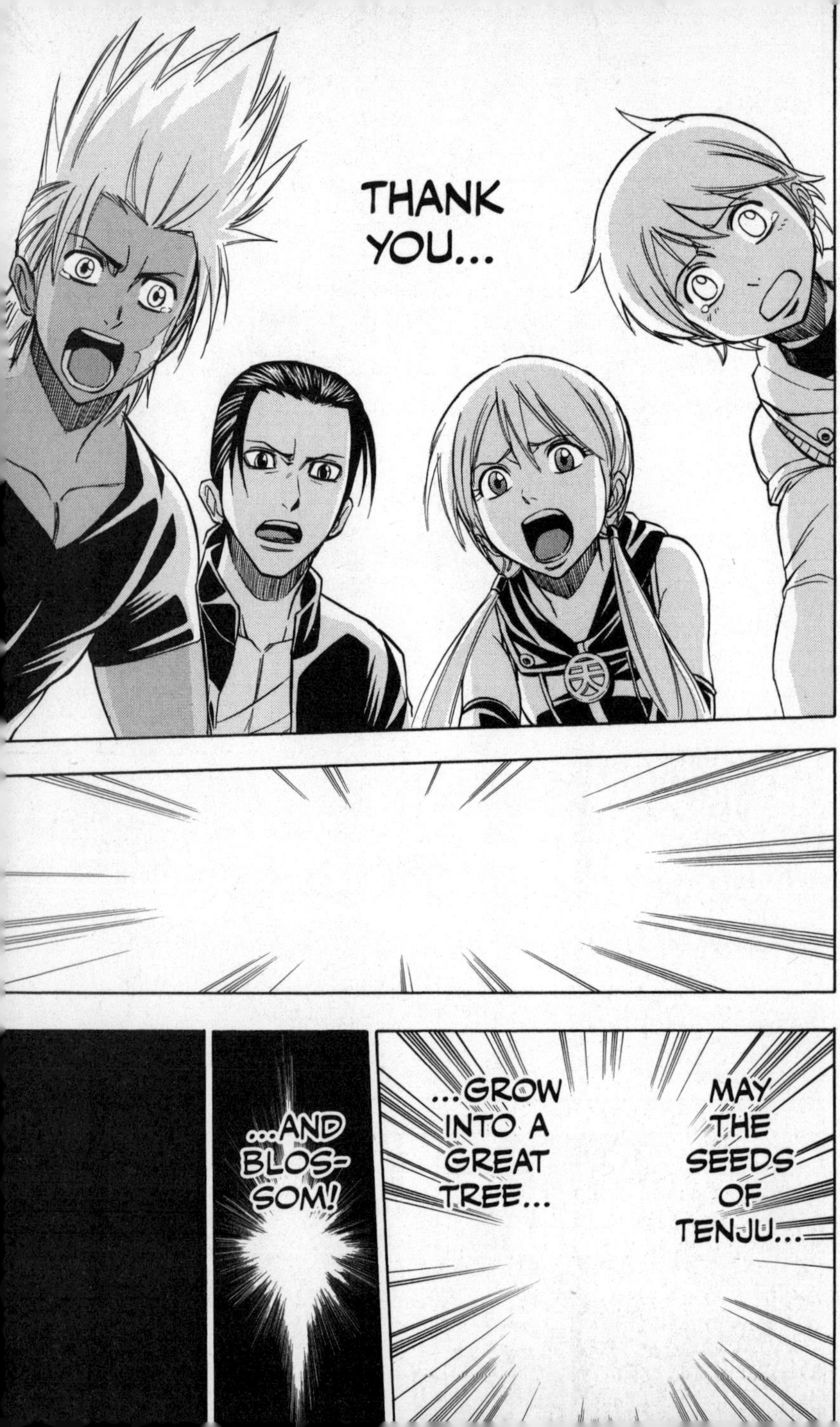
THANK YOU...
MAY THE SEEDS OF TENJU...
...GROW INTO A GREAT TREE...
...AND BLOS-SOM!

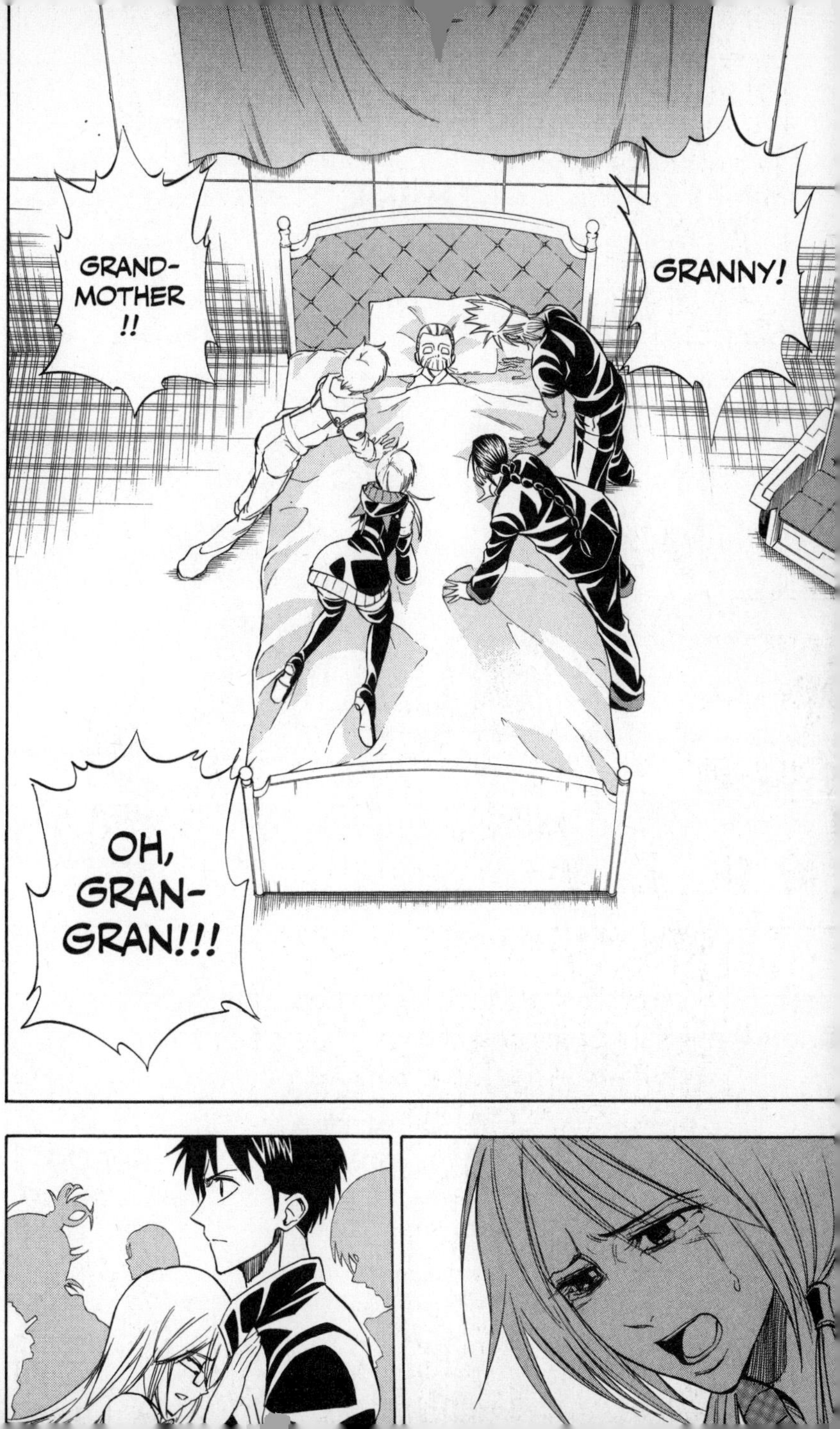
GRANNY!
GRAND-MOTHER!!
OH, GRAN-GRAN!!!

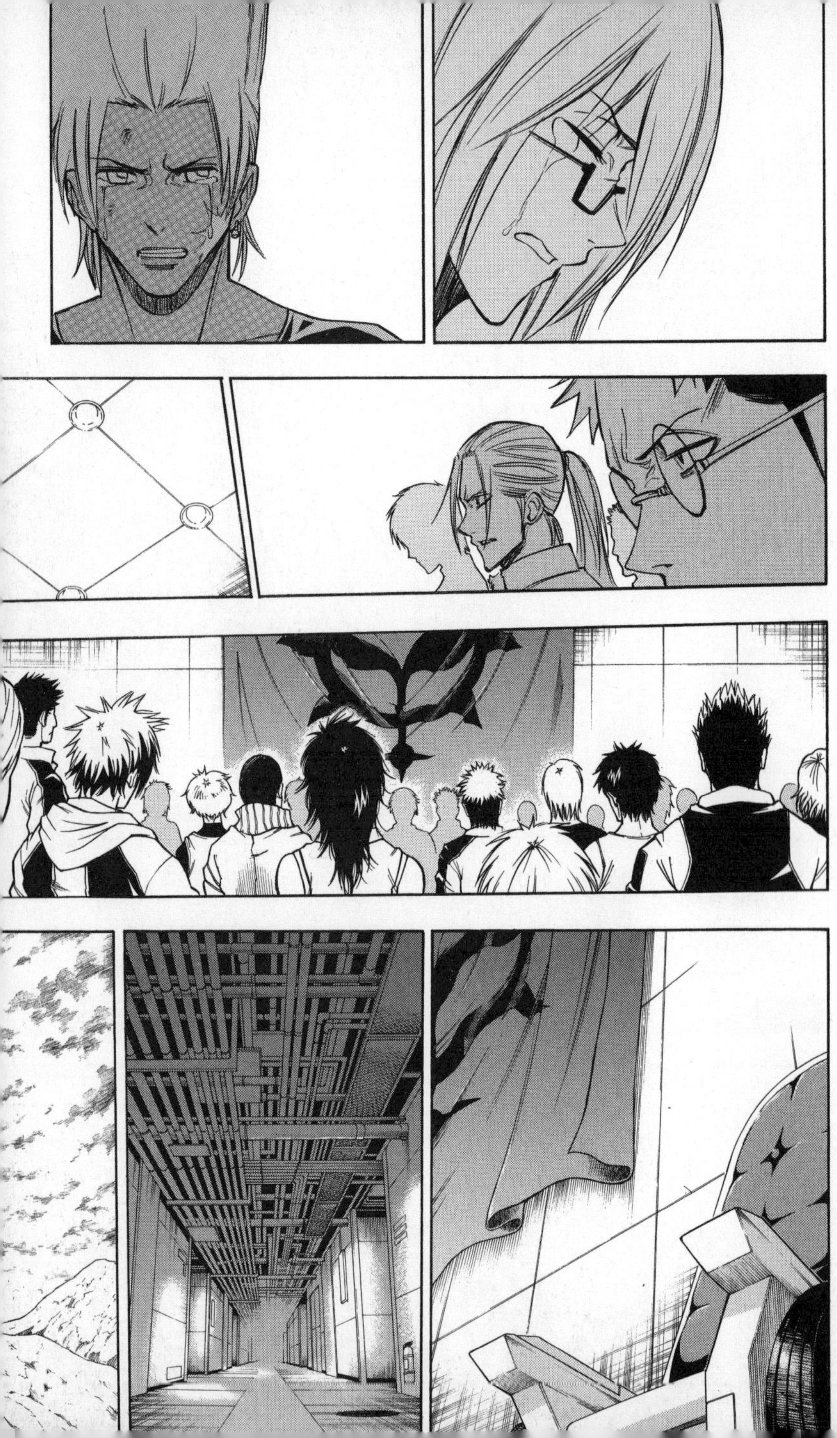

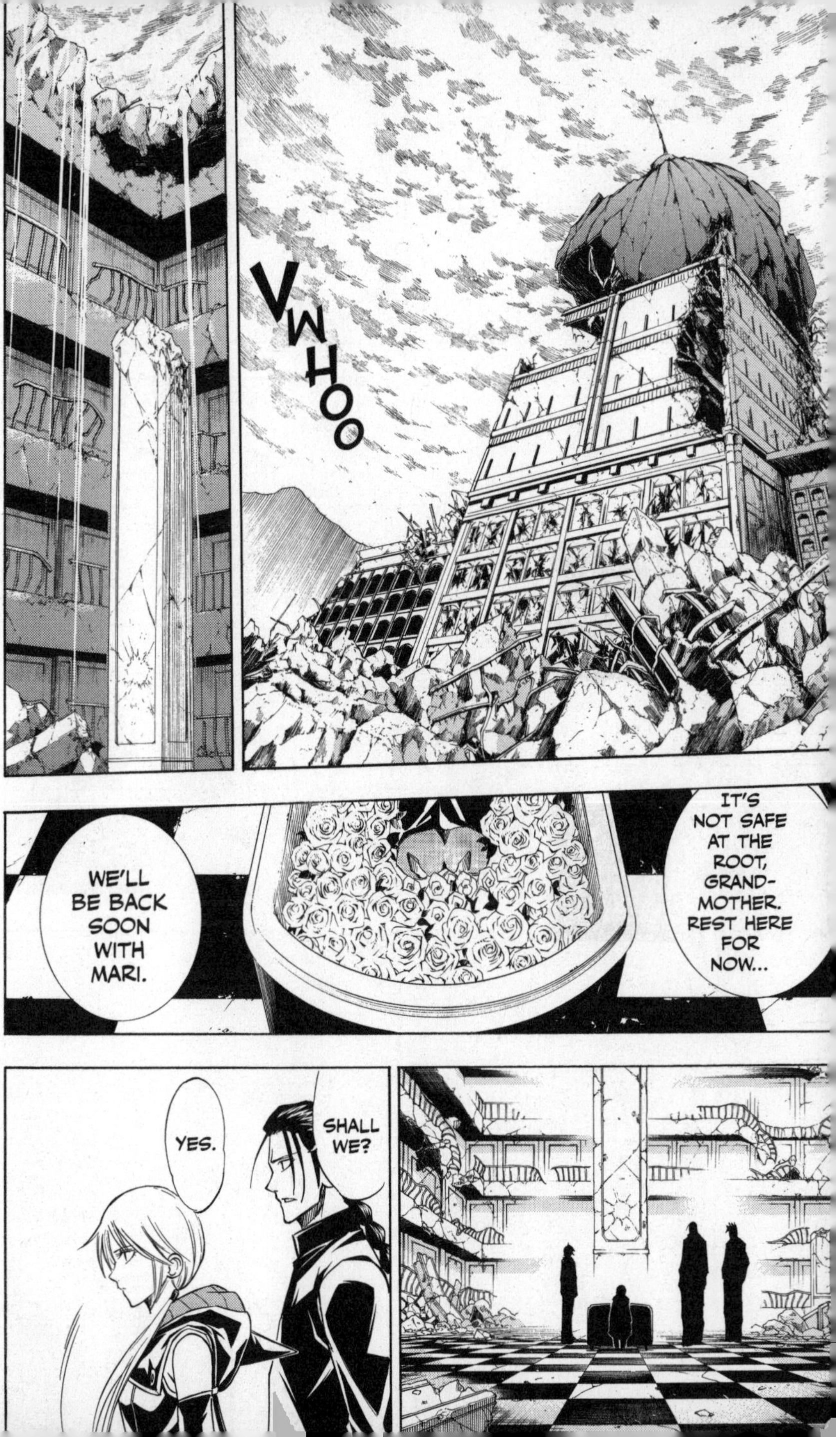
VWHOO
IT'S NOT SAFE AT THE ROOT, GRAND-MOTHER. REST HERE FOR NOW...
WE'LL BE BACK SOON WITH MARI.
SHALL WE?
YES.

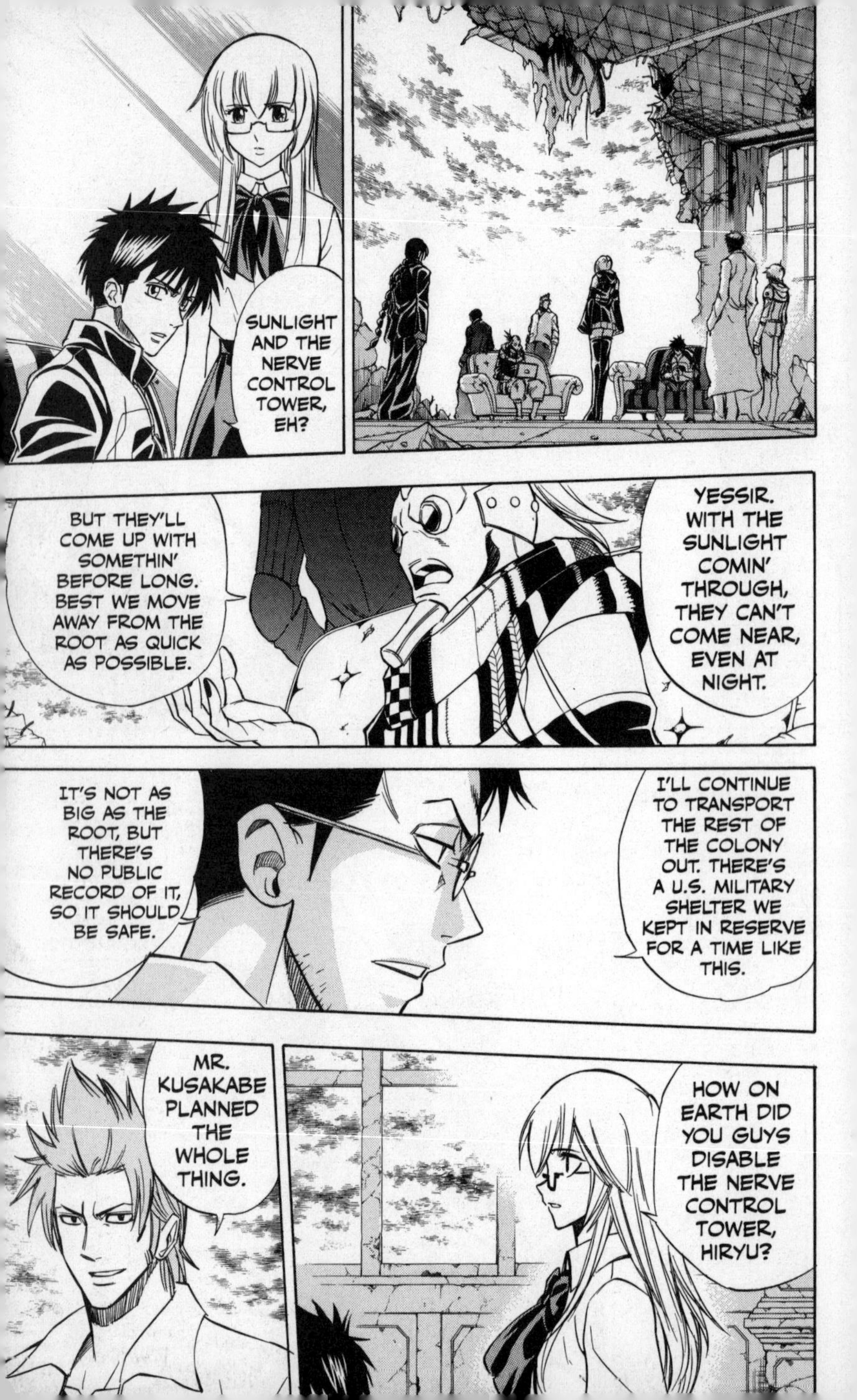
SUNLIGHT AND THE NERVE CONTROL TOWER, EH?
YESSIR. WITH THE SUNLIGHT COMIN' THROUGH, THEY CAN'T COME NEAR, EVEN AT NIGHT.
BUT THEY'LL COME UP WITH SOMETHIN' BEFORE LONG. BEST WE MOVE AWAY FROM THE ROOT AS QUICK AS POSSIBLE.
I'LL CONTINUE TO TRANSPORT THE REST OF THE COLONY OUT. THERE'S A U.S. MILITARY SHELTER WE KEPT IN RESERVE FOR A TIME LIKE THIS.
IT'S NOT AS BIG AS THE ROOT, BUT THERE'S NO PUBLIC RECORD OF IT, SO IT SHOULD BE SAFE.
HOW ON EARTH DID YOU GUYS DISABLE THE NERVE CONTROL TOWER, HIRYU?
MR. KUSAKABE PLANNED THE WHOLE THING.

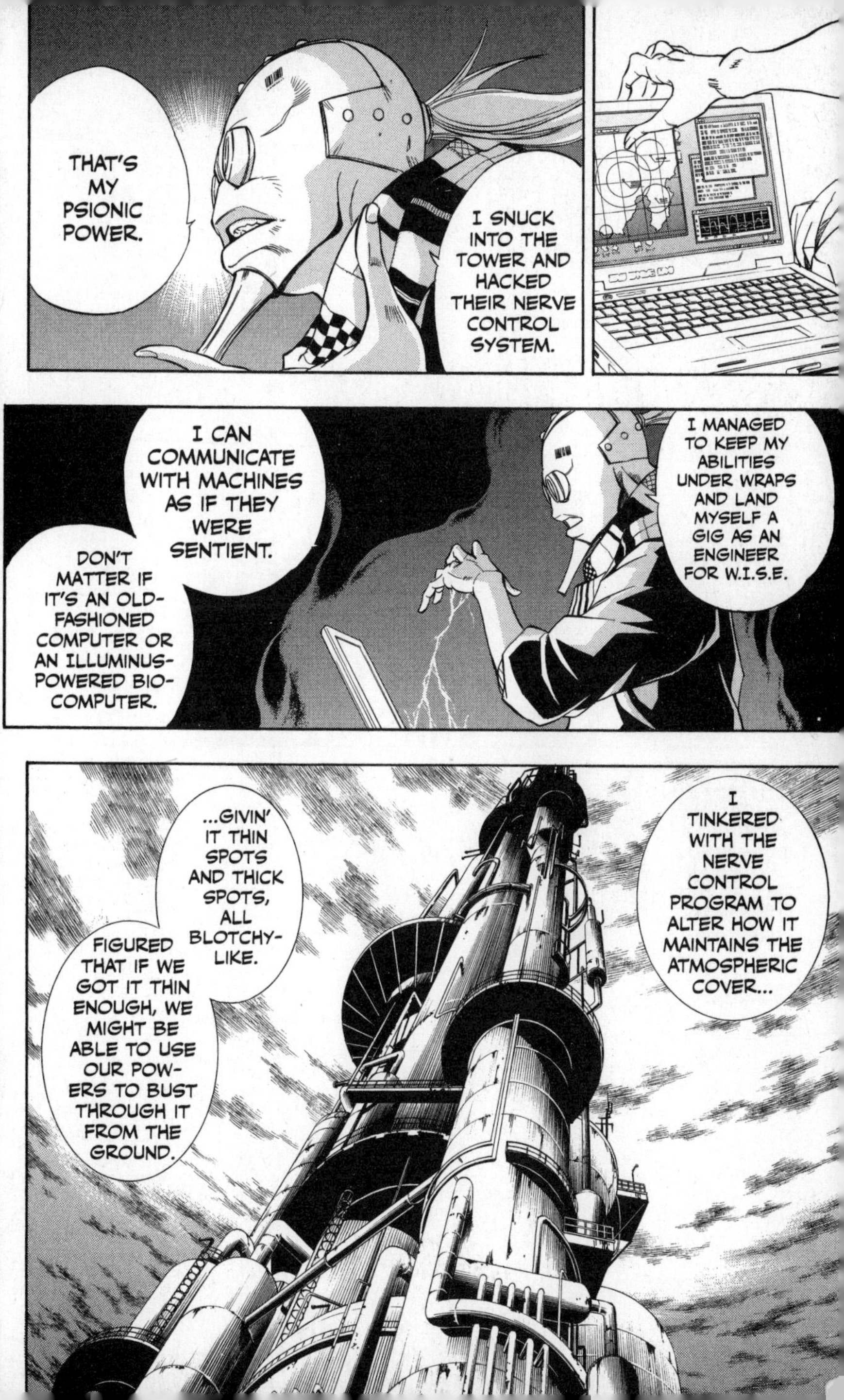
I SNUCK INTO THE TOWER AND HACKED THEIR NERVE CONTROL SYSTEM.
THAT'S MY PSIONIC POWER.
I MANAGED TO KEEP MY ABILITIES UNDER WRAPS AND LAND MYSELF A GIG AS AN ENGINEER FOR W.I.S.E.
I CAN COMMUNICATE WITH MACHINES AS IF THEY WERE SENTIENT.
DON'T MATTER IF IT'S AN OLD-FASHIONED COMPUTER OR AN ILLUMINUS-POWERED BIO-COMPUTER.
I TINKERED WITH THE NERVE CONTROL PROGRAM TO ALTER HOW IT MAINTAINS THE ATMOSPHERIC COVER...
...GIVIN' IT THIN SPOTS AND THICK SPOTS, ALL BLOTCHY-LIKE.
FIGURED THAT IF WE GOT IT THIN ENOUGH, WE MIGHT BE ABLE TO USE OUR POWERS TO BUST THROUGH IT FROM THE GROUND.

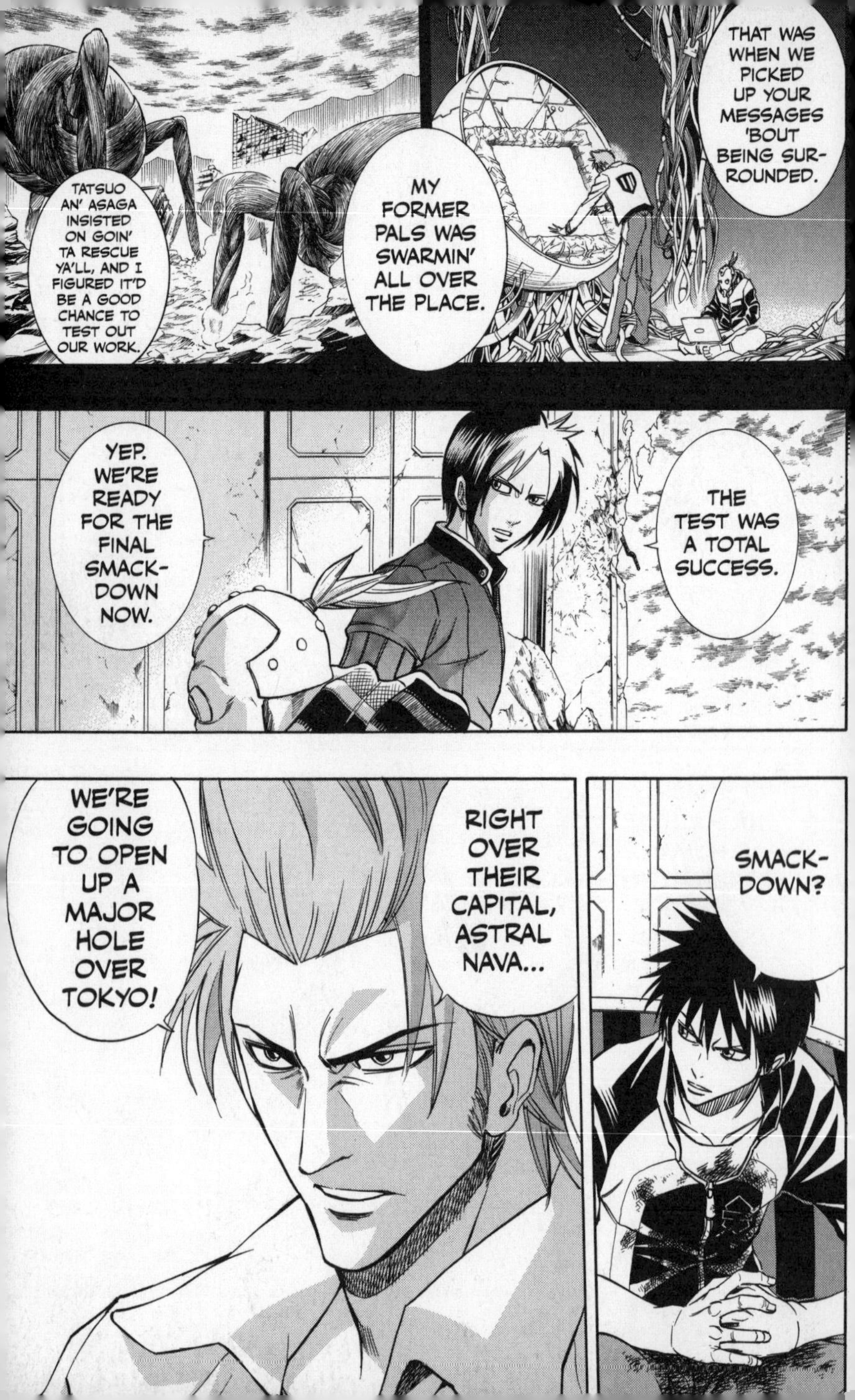
THAT WAS WHEN WE PICKED UP YOUR MESSAGES 'BOUT BEING SUR-ROUNDED.
MY FORMER PALS WAS SWARMIN' ALL OVER THE PLACE.
TATSUO AN' ASAGA INSISTED ON GOIN' TA RESCUE YA'LL, AND I FIGURED IT'D BE A GOOD CHANCE TO TEST OUT OUR WORK.
THE TEST WAS A TOTAL SUCCESS.
YEP. WE'RE READY FOR THE FINAL SMACK-DOWN NOW.
SMACK-DOWN?
RIGHT OVER THEIR CAPITAL, ASTRAL NAVA...
WE'RE GOING TO OPEN UP A MAJOR HOLE OVER TOKYO!

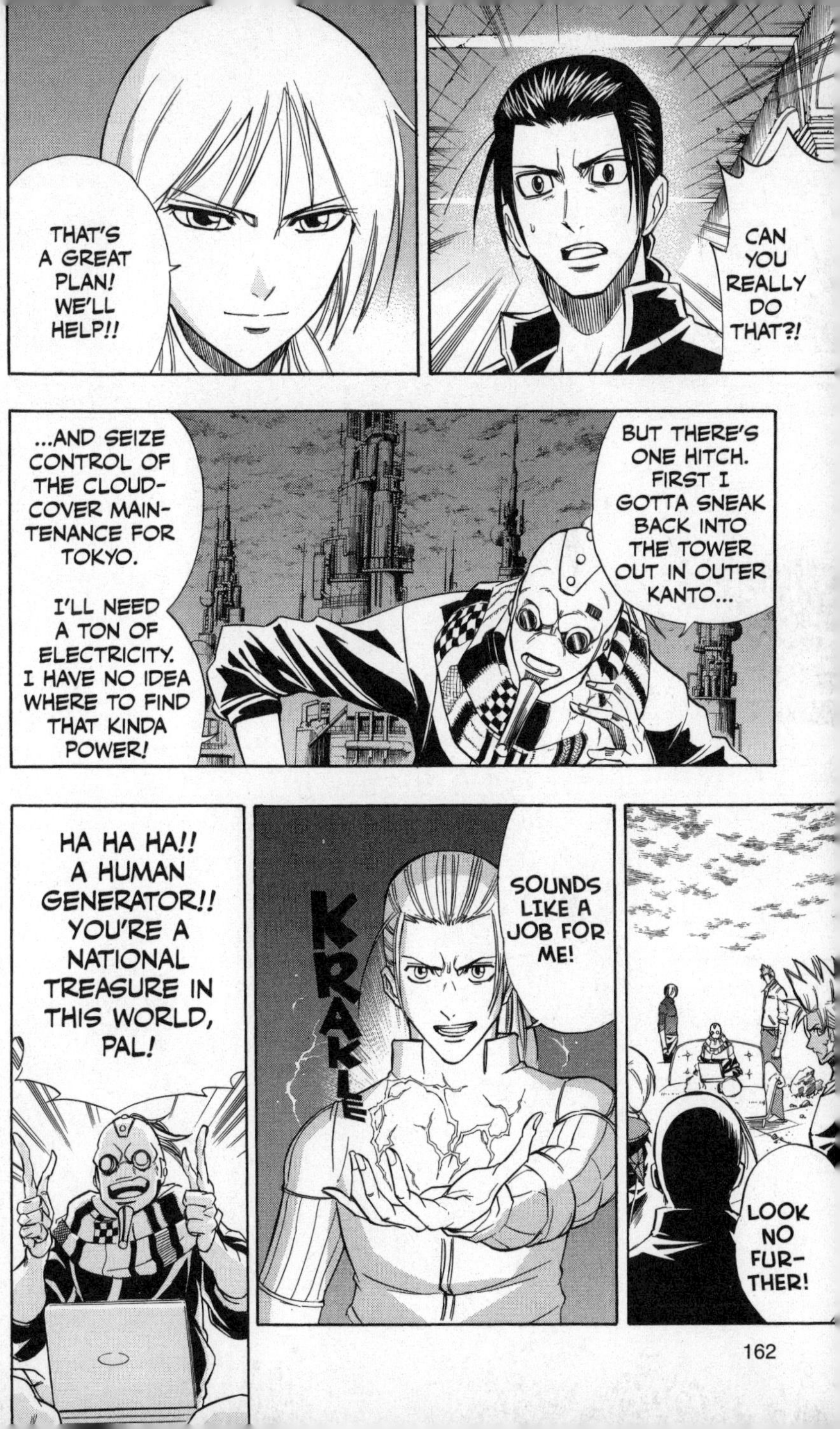
CAN YOU REALLY DO THAT?!
THAT'S A GREAT PLAN! WE'LL HELP!!
BUT THERE'S ONE HITCH. FIRST I GOTTA SNEAK BACK INTO THE TOWER OUT IN OUTER KANTO...
...AND SEIZE CONTROL OF THE CLOUD-COVER MAIN-TENANCE FOR TOKYO.
I'LL NEED A TON OF ELECTRICITY. I HAVE NO IDEA WHERE TO FIND THAT KINDA POWER!
LOOK NO FUR-THER!
SOUNDS LIKE A JOB FOR ME!
KRAKLE
HA HA HA!! A HUMAN GENERATOR!! YOU'RE A NATIONAL TREASURE IN THIS WORLD, PAL!

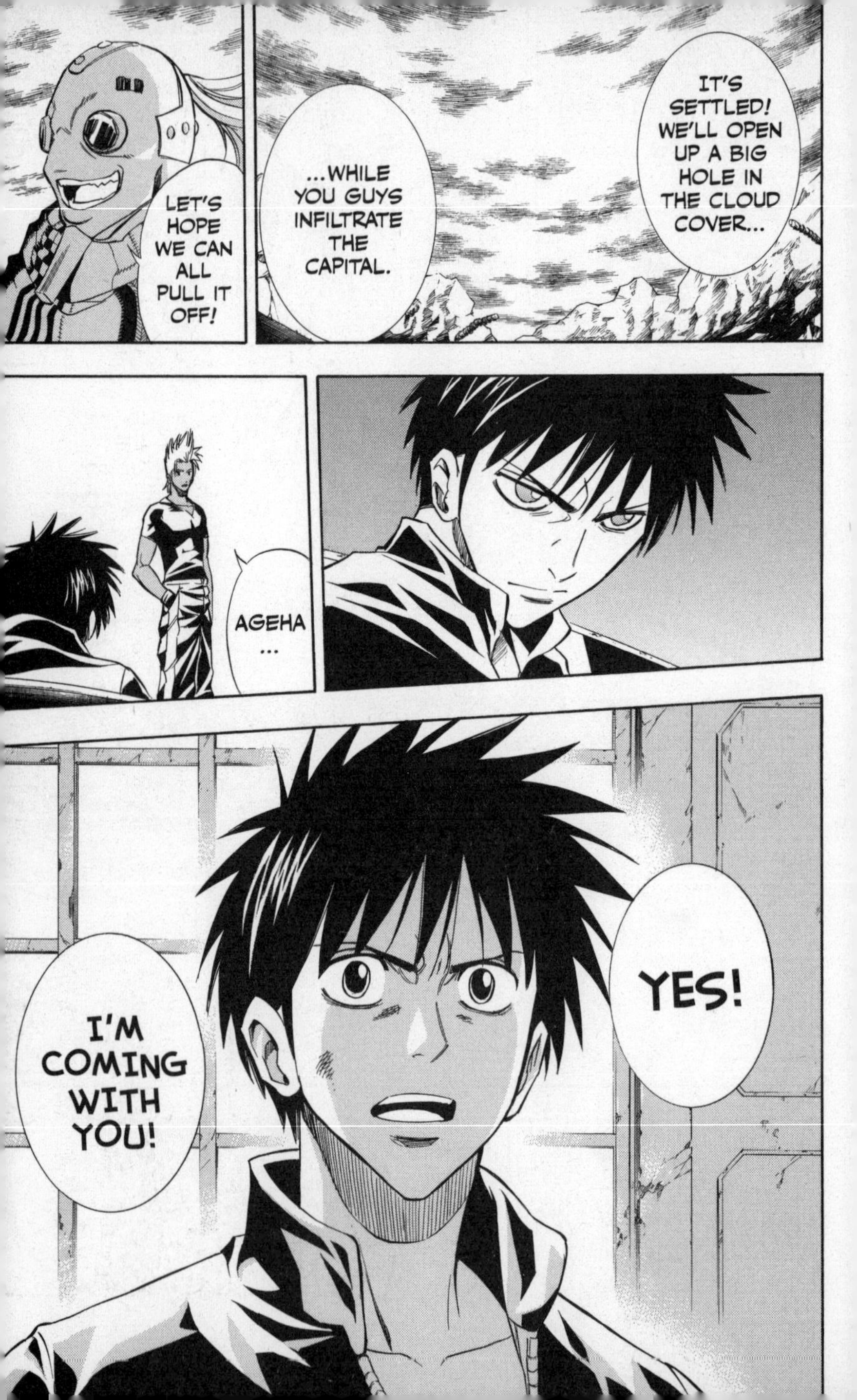
IT'S SETTLED! WE'LL OPEN UP A BIG HOLE IN THE CLOUD COVER...
...WHILE YOU GUYS INFILTRATE THE CAPITAL.
LET'S HOPE WE CAN ALL PULL IT OFF!
AGEHA ...
YES!
I'M COMING WITH YOU!

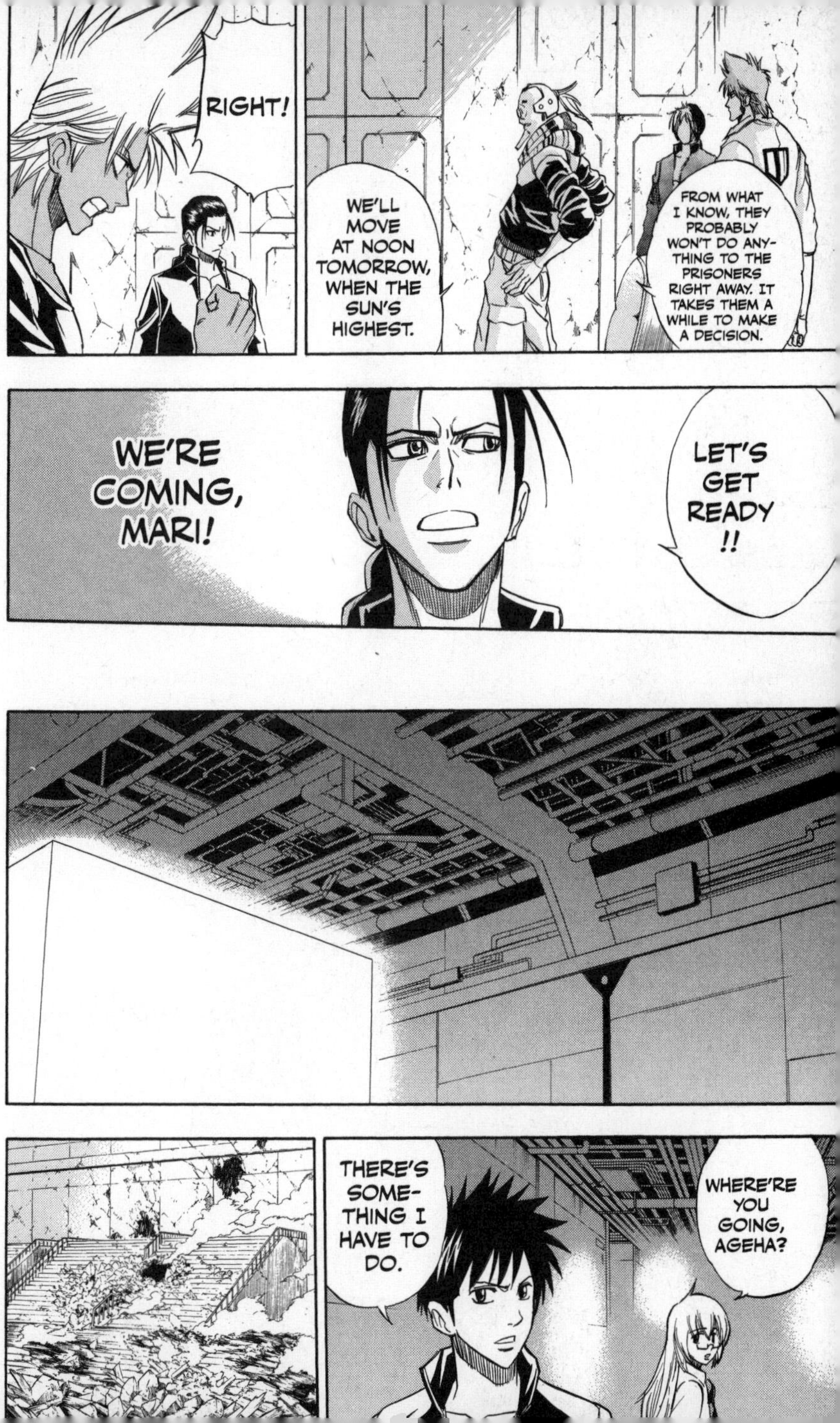
FROM WHAT I KNOW, THEY PROBABLY WON'T DO ANY-THING TO THE PRISONERS RIGHT AWAY. IT TAKES THEM A WHILE TO MAKE A DECISION.
WE'LL MOVE AT NOON TOMORROW, WHEN THE SUN'S HIGHEST.
RIGHT!
LET'S GET READY!!
WE'RE COMING, MARI!
WHERE'RE YOU GOING, AGEHA?
THERE'S SOME-THING I HAVE TO DO.

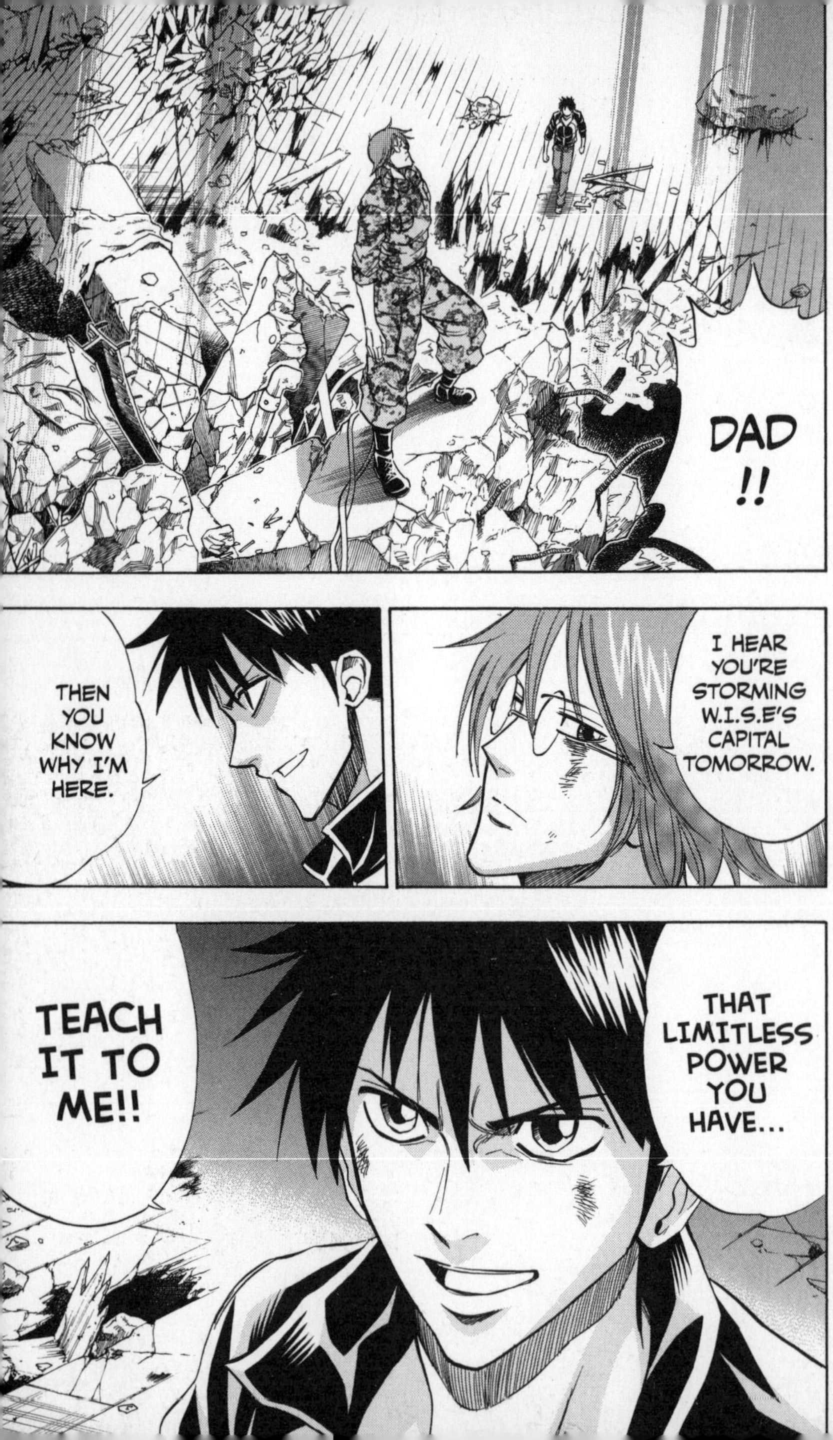
DAD !!
I HEAR YOU'RE STORMING W.I.S.E'S CAPITAL TOMORROW.
THEN YOU KNOW WHY I'M HERE.
THAT LIMITLESS POWER YOU HAVE...
TEACH IT TO ME!!

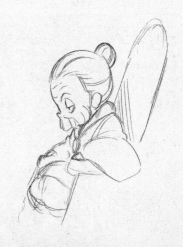

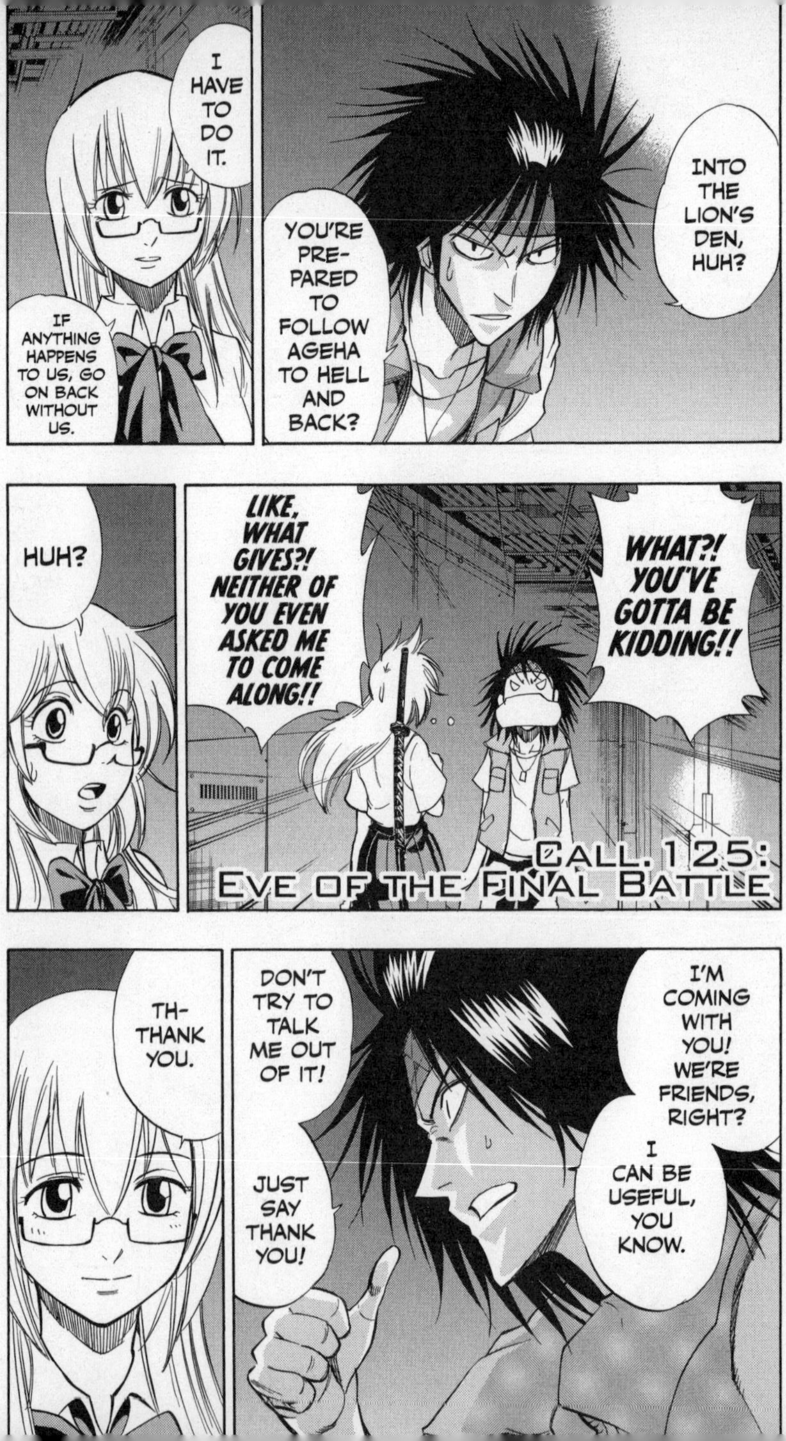
INTO THE LION'S DEN, HUH?
YOU'RE PRE-PARED TO FOLLOW AGEHA TO HELL AND BACK?
I HAVE TO DO IT.
IF ANYTHING HAPPENS TO US, GO ON BACK WITHOUT US.
WHAT?! YOU'VE GOTTA BE KIDDING!!
LIKE, WHAT GIVES?! NEITHER OF YOU EVEN ASKED ME TO COME ALONG!!
CALL. 125: EVE OF THE FINAL BATTLE
HUH?
I'M COMING WITH YOU! WE'RE FRIENDS, RIGHT?
I CAN BE USEFUL, YOU KNOW.
DON'T TRY TO TALK ME OUT OF IT!
JUST SAY THANK YOU!
TH-THANK YOU.

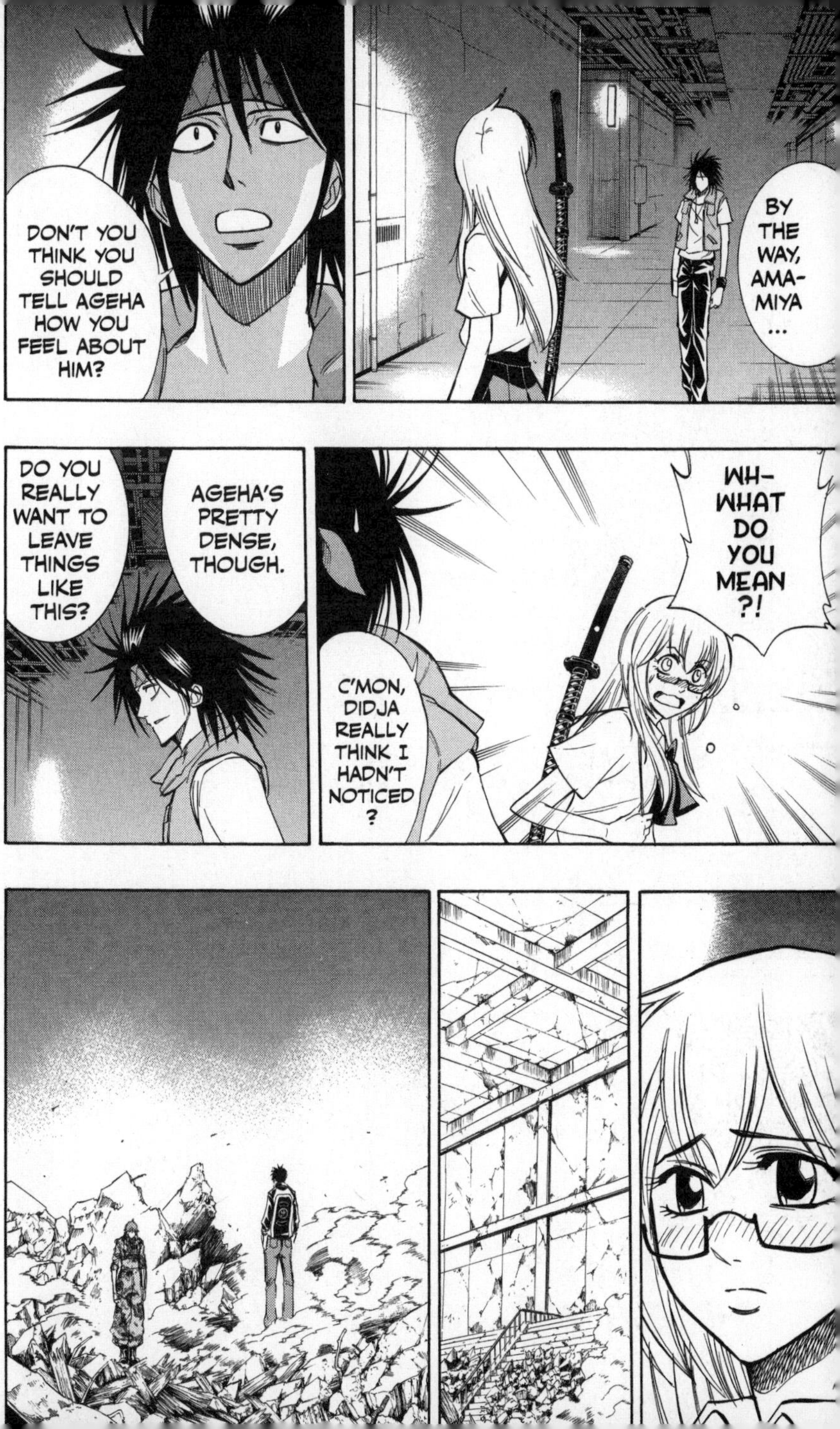
BY THE WAY, AMA-MIYA...
DON'T YOU THINK YOU SHOULD TELL AGEHA HOW YOU FEEL ABOUT HIM?
WH-WHAT DO YOU MEAN?!
C'MON, DIDJA REALLY THINK I HADN'T NOTICED?
AGEHA'S PRETTY DENSE, THOUGH.
DO YOU REALLY WANT TO LEAVE THINGS LIKE THIS?

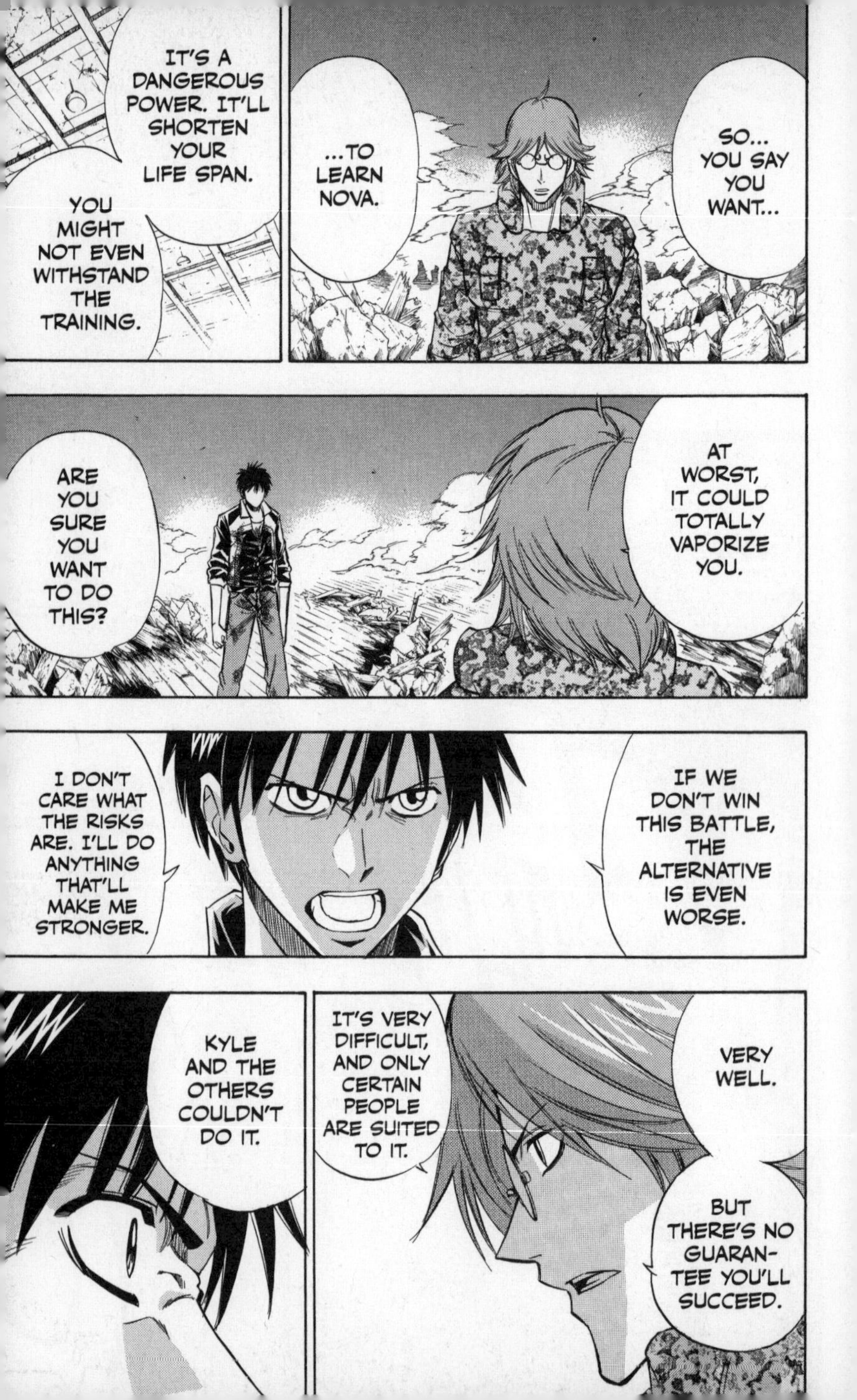
SO... YOU SAY YOU WANT...
...TO LEARN NOVA.
IT'S A DANGEROUS POWER. IT'LL SHORTEN YOUR LIFE SPAN.
YOU MIGHT NOT EVEN WITHSTAND THE TRAINING.
AT WORST, IT COULD TOTALLY VAPORIZE YOU.
ARE YOU SURE YOU WANT TO DO THIS?
IF WE DON'T WIN THIS BATTLE, THE ALTERNATIVE IS EVEN WORSE.
I DON'T CARE WHAT THE RISKS ARE. I'LL DO ANYTHING THAT'LL MAKE ME STRONGER.
VERY WELL.
IT'S VERY DIFFICULT, AND ONLY CERTAIN PEOPLE ARE SUITED TO IT.
BUT THERE'S NO GUARANTEE YOU'LL SUCCEED.
KYLE AND THE OTHERS COULDN'T DO IT.

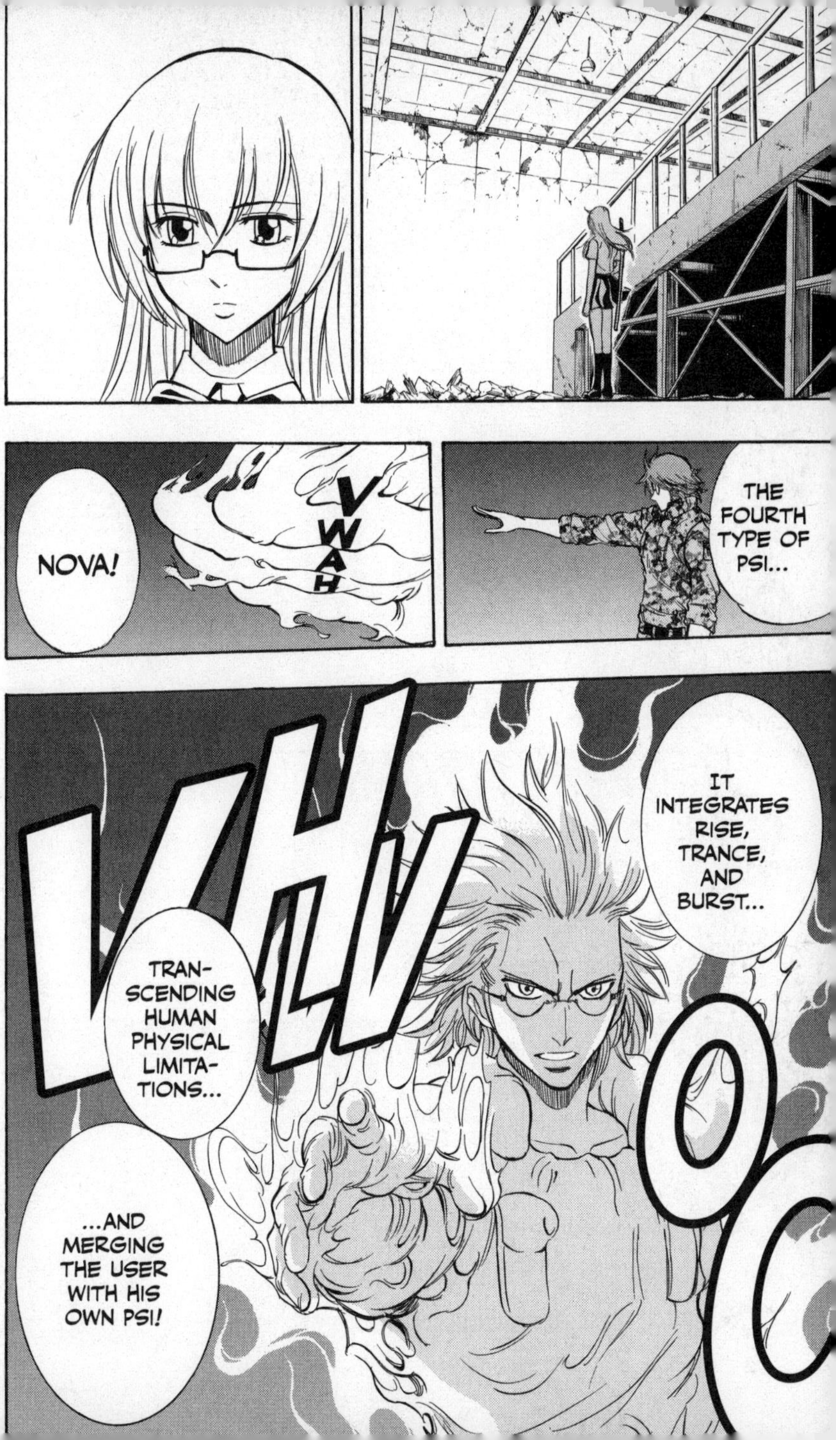
THE FOURTH TYPE OF PSI...
VWAH
NOVA!
IT INTEGRATES RISE, TRANCE, AND BURST...
VHV
OO
TRAN-SCENDING HUMAN PHYSICAL LIMITA-TIONS...
...AND MERGING THE USER WITH HIS OWN PSI!

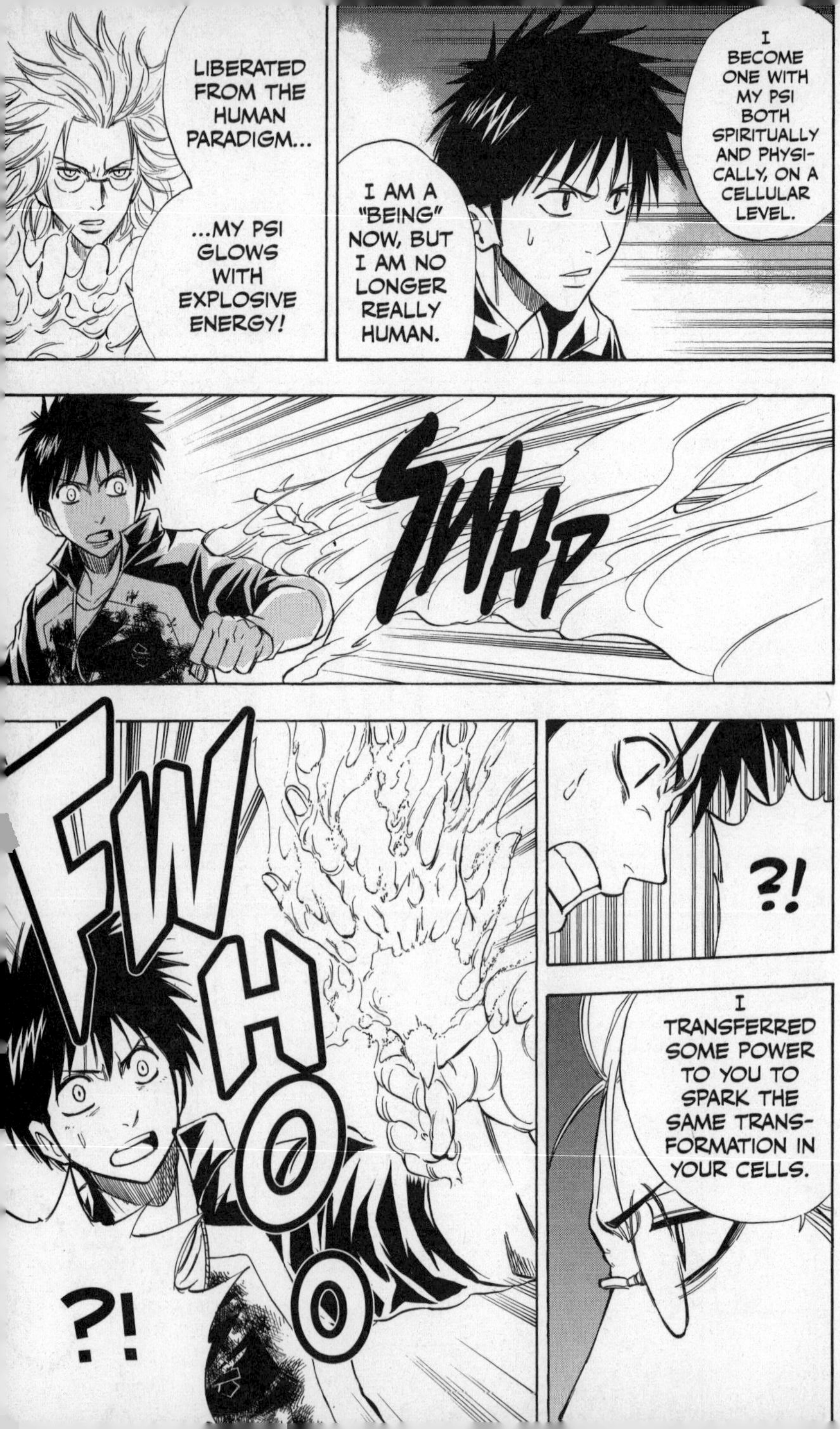
I BECOME ONE WITH MY PSI BOTH SPIRITUALLY AND PHYSICALLY, ON A CELLULAR LEVEL.
I AM A "BEING" NOW, BUT I AM NO LONGER REALLY HUMAN.
LIBERATED FROM THE HUMAN PARADIGM...
...MY PSI GLOWS WITH EXPLOSIVE ENERGY!
SWHP
?!
I TRANSFERRED SOME POWER TO YOU TO SPARK THE SAME TRANS-FORMATION IN YOUR CELLS.
FWHOO
?!

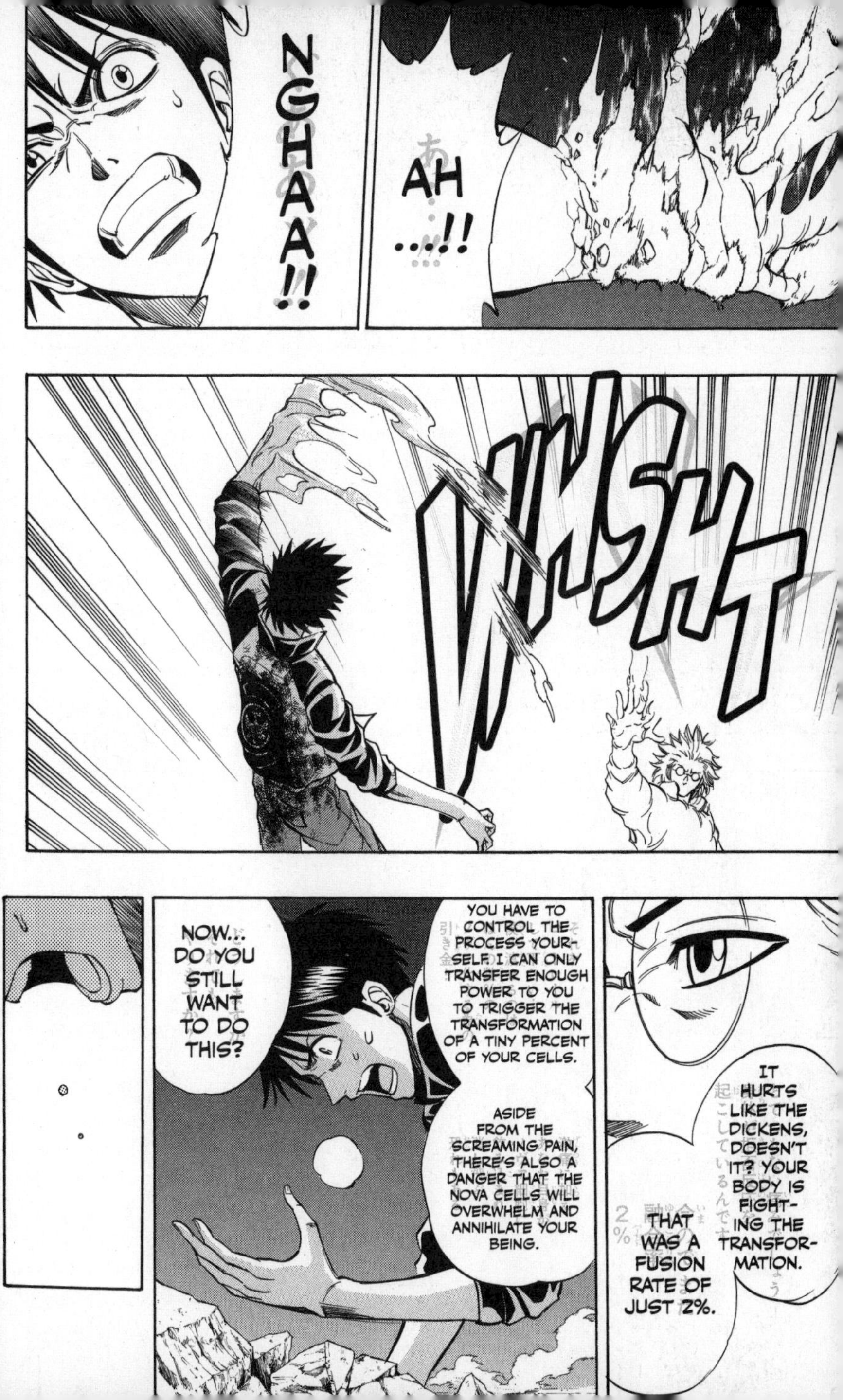
AH...!!
NGHAA!!
WHSHT
IT HURTS LIKE THE DICKENS, DOESN'T IT? YOUR BODY IS FIGHTING THE TRANSFORMATION.
THAT WAS A FUSION RATE OF JUST 2%.
YOU HAVE TO CONTROL THE PROCESS YOURSELF. I CAN ONLY TRANSFER ENOUGH POWER TO YOU TO TRIGGER THE TRANSFORMATION OF A TINY PERCENT OF YOUR CELLS.
ASIDE FROM THE SCREAMING PAIN, THERE'S ALSO A DANGER THAT THE NOVA CELLS WILL OVERWHELM AND ANNIHILATE YOUR BEING.
NOW... DO YOU STILL WANT TO DO THIS?

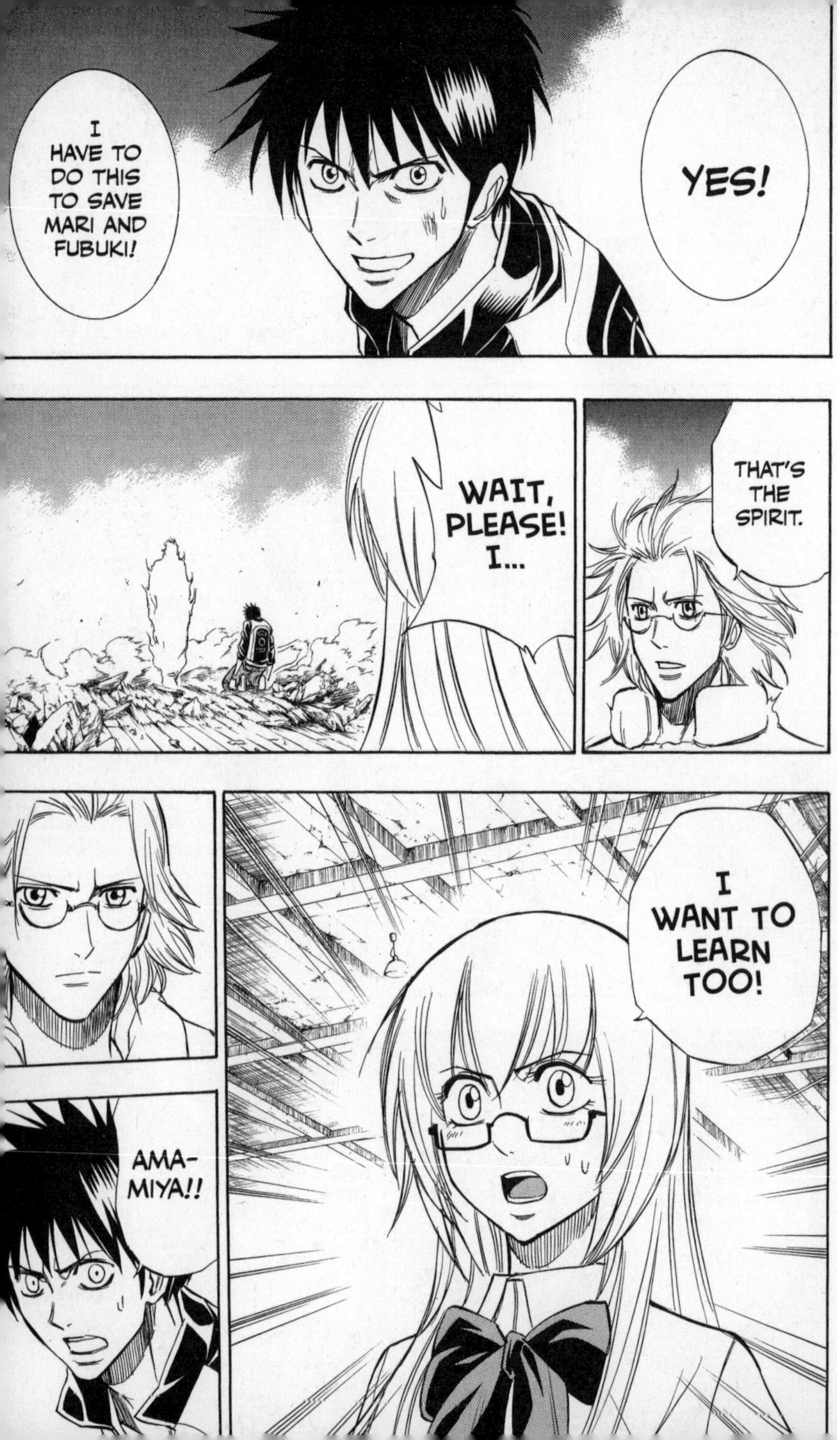
YES!
I HAVE TO DO THIS TO SAVE MARI AND FUBUKI!
THAT'S THE SPIRIT.
WAIT, PLEASE! I...
I WANT TO LEARN TOO!
AMA-MIYA!!

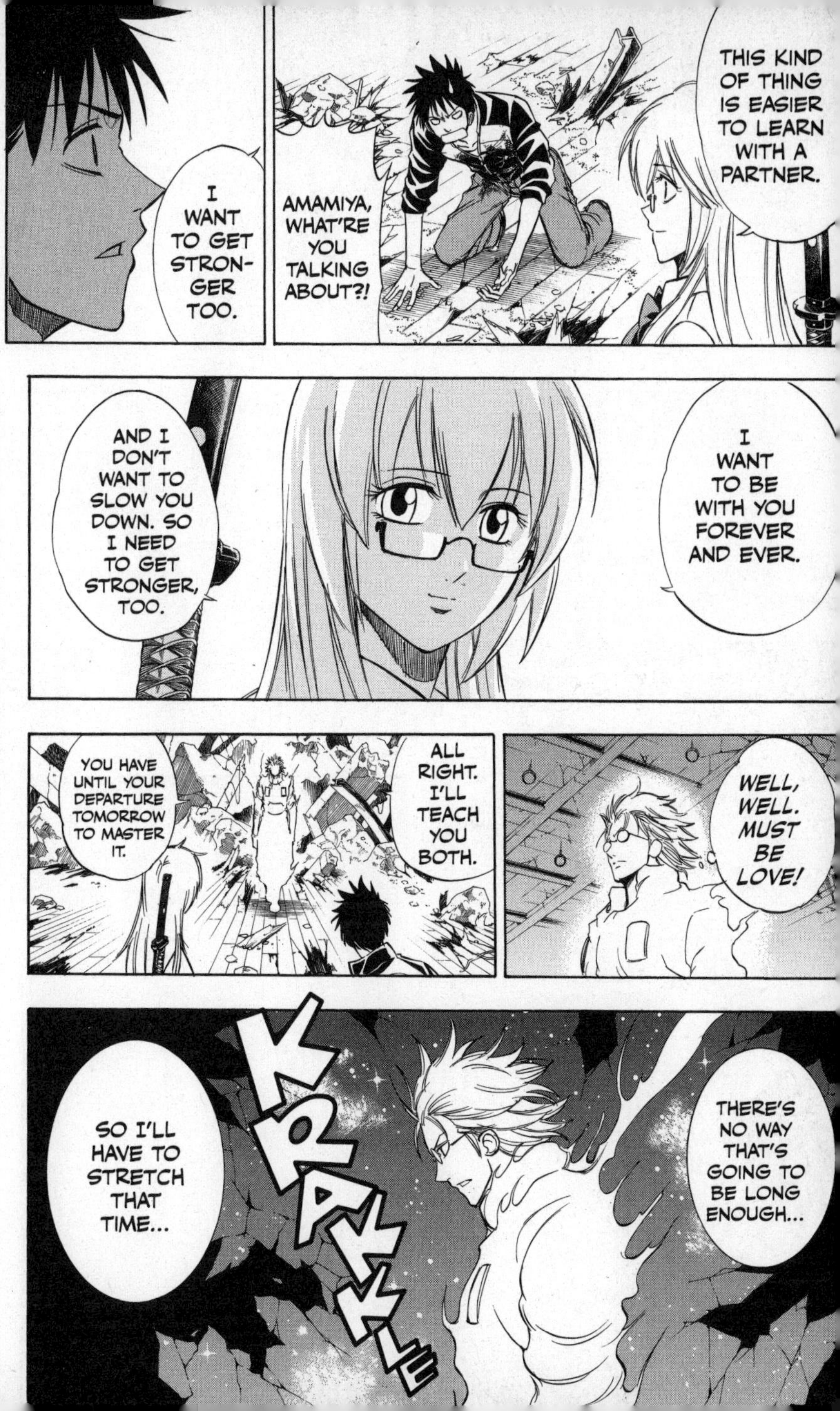
THIS KIND OF THING IS EASIER TO LEARN WITH A PARTNER.
AMAMIYA, WHAT'RE YOU TALKING ABOUT?!
I WANT TO GET STRON-GER TOO.
I WANT TO BE WITH YOU FOREVER AND EVER.
AND I DON'T WANT TO SLOW YOU DOWN. SO I NEED TO GET STRONGER, TOO.
WELL, WELL. MUST BE LOVE!
ALL RIGHT. I'LL TEACH YOU BOTH.
YOU HAVE UNTIL YOUR DEPARTURE TOMORROW TO MASTER IT.
THERE'S NO WAY THAT'S GOING TO BE LONG ENOUGH...
KRAKKLE
SO I'LL HAVE TO STRETCH THAT TIME...

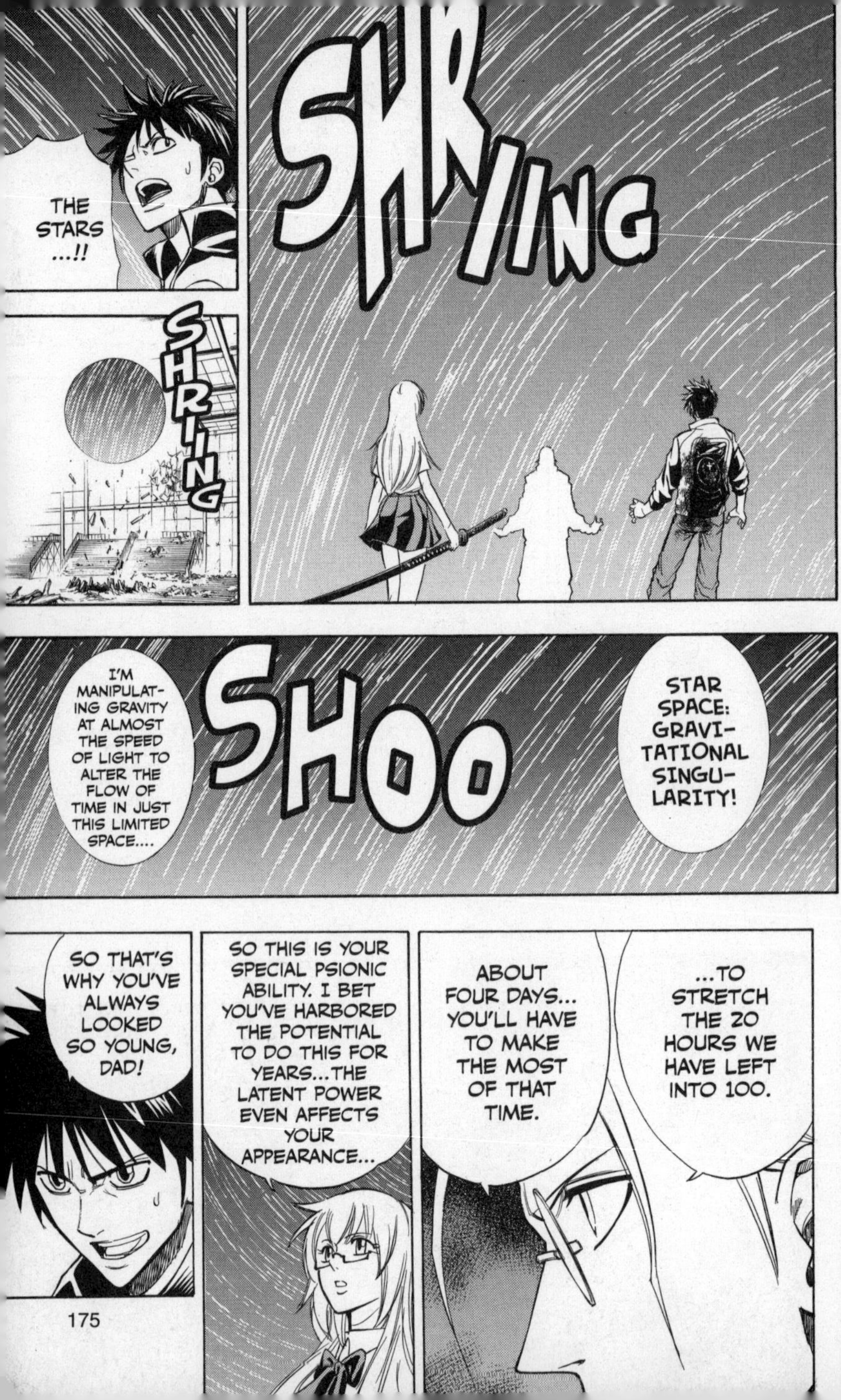
SHRYING
THE STARS ...!!
SHRING
STAR SPACE: GRAVITATIONAL SINGULARITY!
SHOO
I'M MANIPULATING GRAVITY AT ALMOST THE SPEED OF LIGHT TO ALTER THE FLOW OF TIME IN JUST THIS LIMITED SPACE....
...TO STRETCH THE 20 HOURS WE HAVE LEFT INTO 100.
ABOUT FOUR DAYS... YOU'LL HAVE TO MAKE THE MOST OF THAT TIME.
SO THIS IS YOUR SPECIAL PSIONIC ABILITY. I BET YOU'VE HARBORED THE POTENTIAL TO DO THIS FOR YEARS...THE LATENT POWER EVEN AFFECTS YOUR APPEARANCE...
SO THAT'S WHY YOU'VE ALWAYS LOOKED SO YOUNG, DAD!

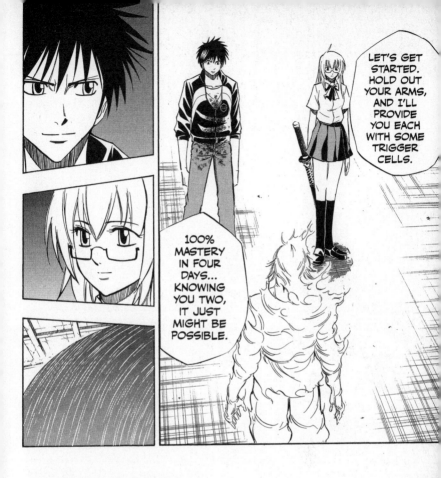

LET'S GET STARTED. HOLD OUT YOUR ARMS, AND I'LL PROVIDE YOU EACH WITH SOME TRIGGER CELLS.

100% MASTERY IN FOUR DAYS... KNOWING YOU TWO, IT JUST MIGHT BE POSSIBLE.

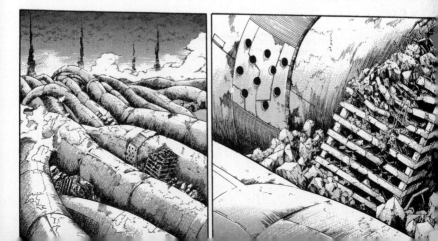

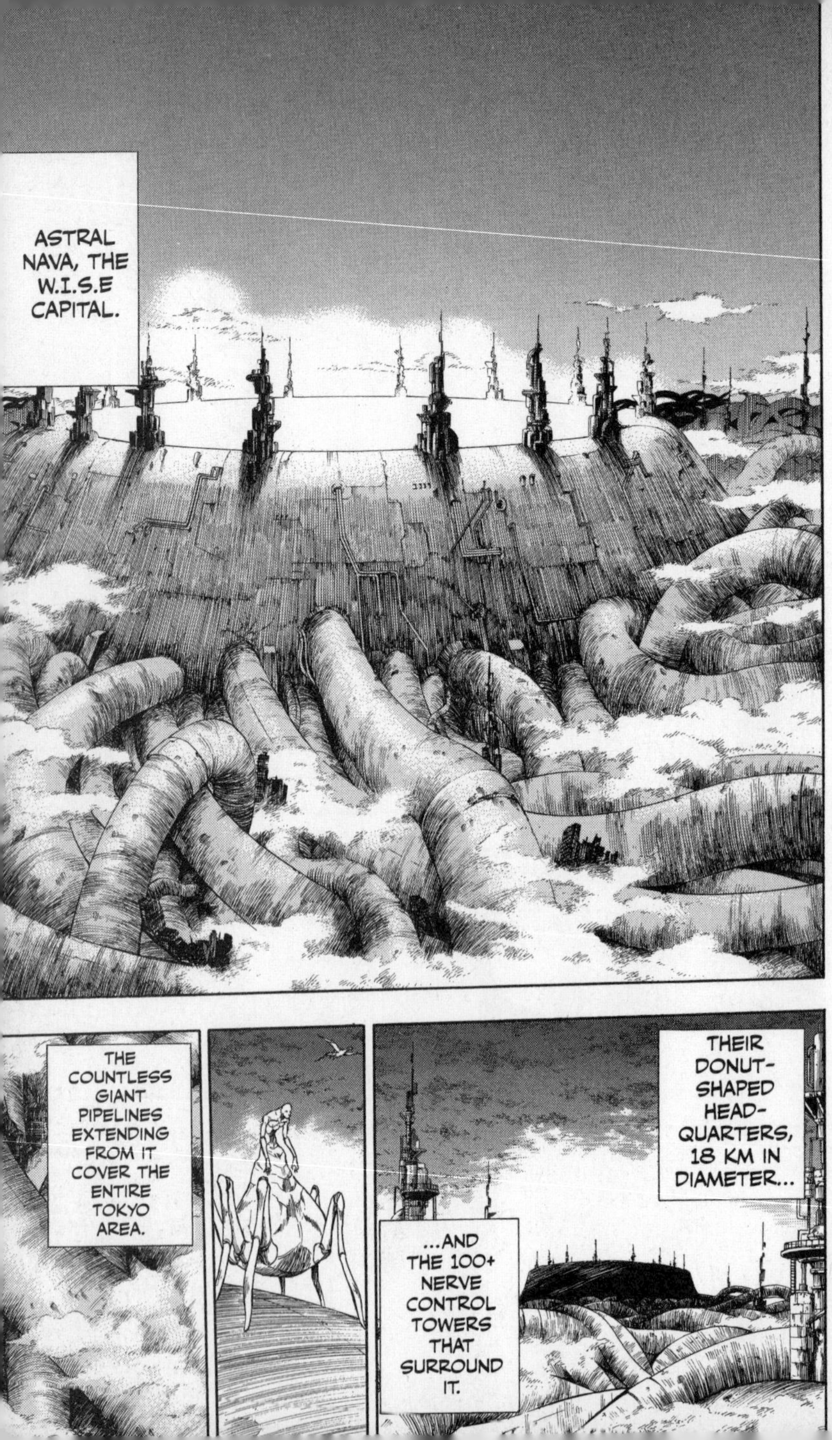
ASTRAL NAVA, THE W.I.S.E CAPITAL.
THEIR DONUT-SHAPED HEAD-QUARTERS, 18 KM IN DIAMETER...
...AND THE 100+ NERVE CONTROL TOWERS THAT SURROUND IT.
THE COUNTLESS GIANT PIPELINES EXTENDING FROM IT COVER THE ENTIRE TOKYO AREA.

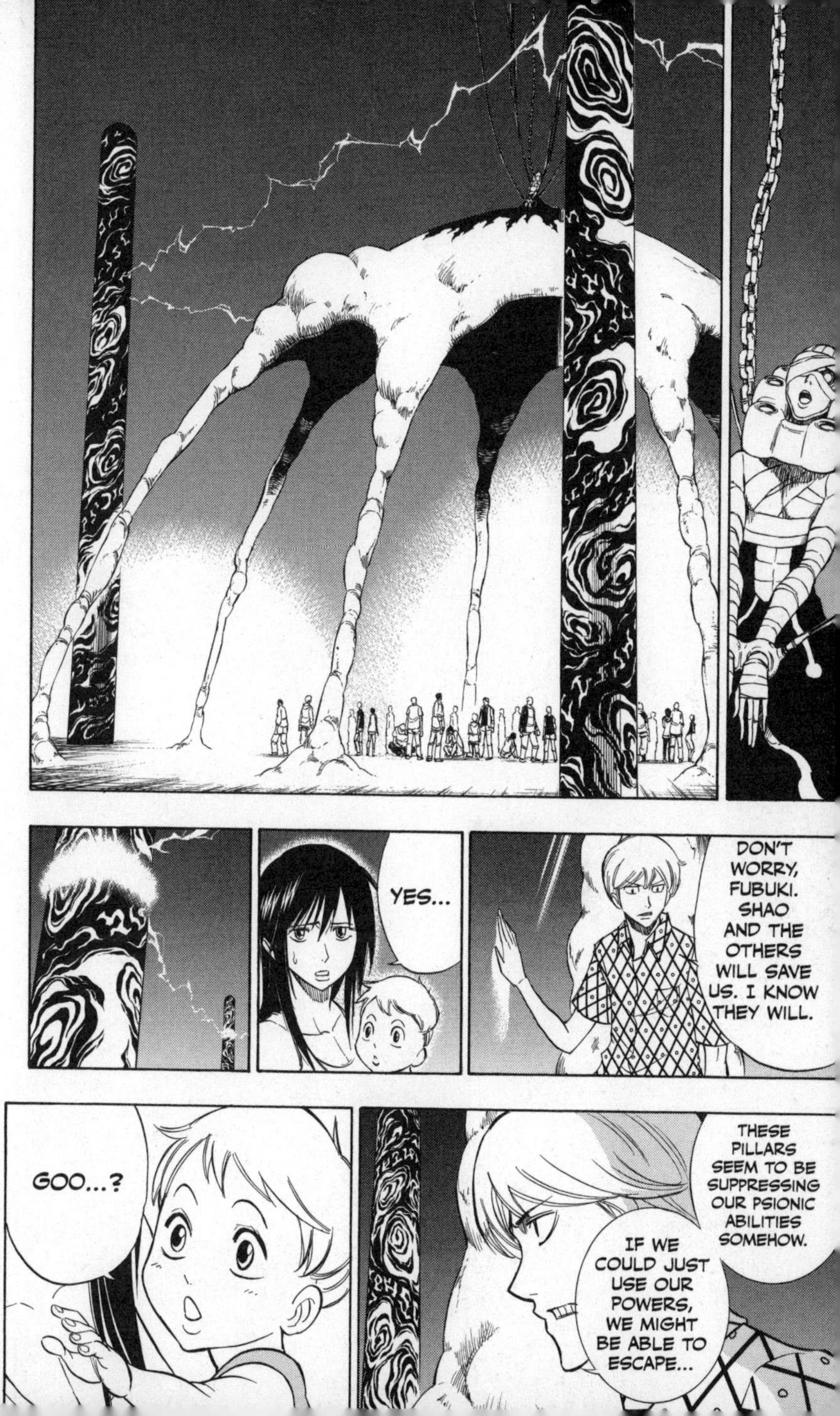
DON'T WORRY, FUBUKI. SHAO AND THE OTHERS WILL SAVE US. I KNOW THEY WILL.
YES...
THESE PILLARS SEEM TO BE SUPPRESSING OUR PSIONIC ABILITIES SOMEHOW.
IF WE COULD JUST USE OUR POWERS, WE MIGHT BE ABLE TO ESCAPE...
GOO...?

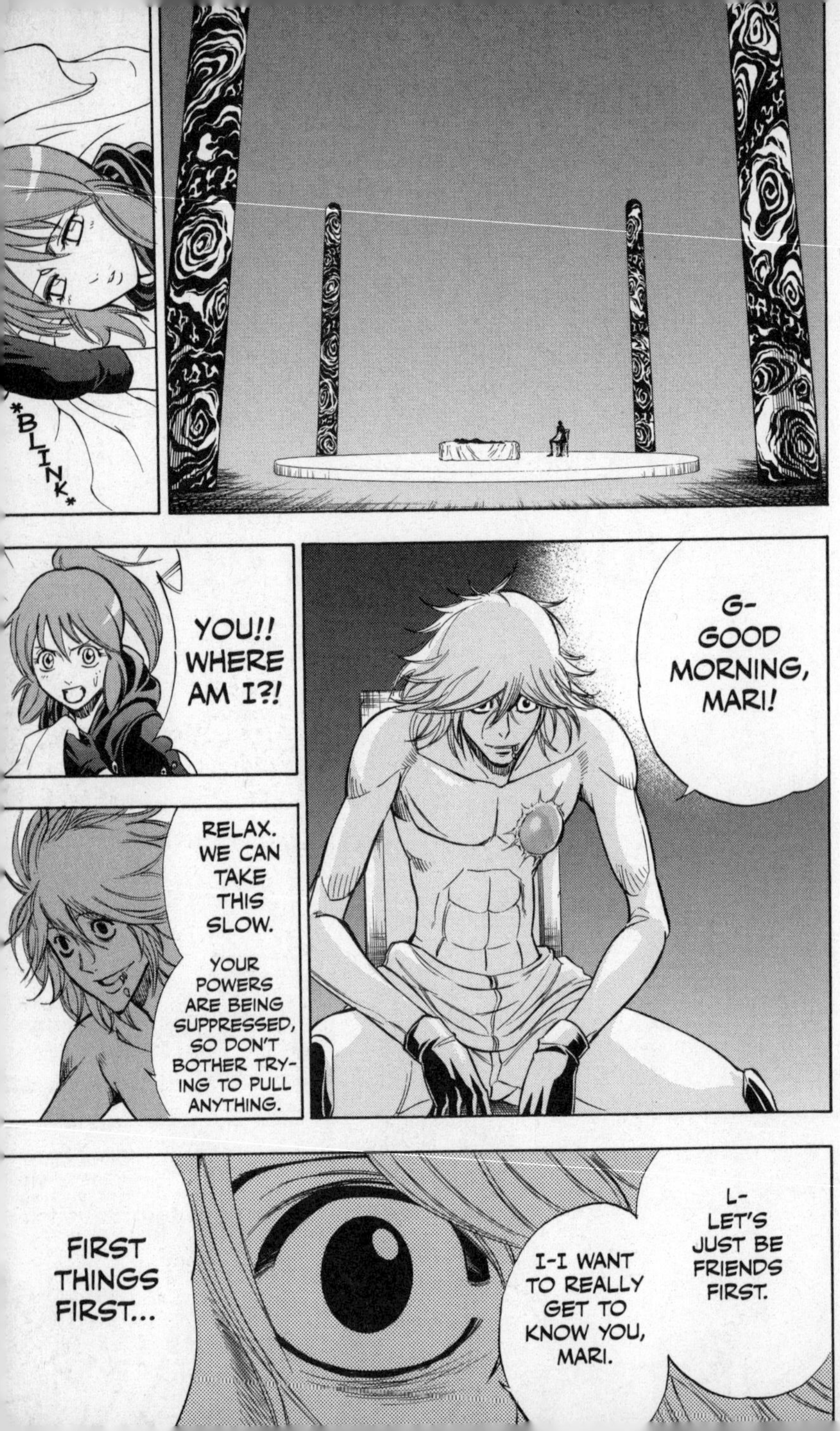
BLINK
G-GOOD MORNING, MARI!
YOU!! WHERE AM I?!
RELAX. WE CAN TAKE THIS SLOW.
YOUR POWERS ARE BEING SUPPRESSED, SO DON'T BOTHER TRY-ING TO PULL ANYTHING.
L-LET'S JUST BE FRIENDS FIRST.
I-I WANT TO REALLY GET TO KNOW YOU, MARI.
FIRST THINGS FIRST...

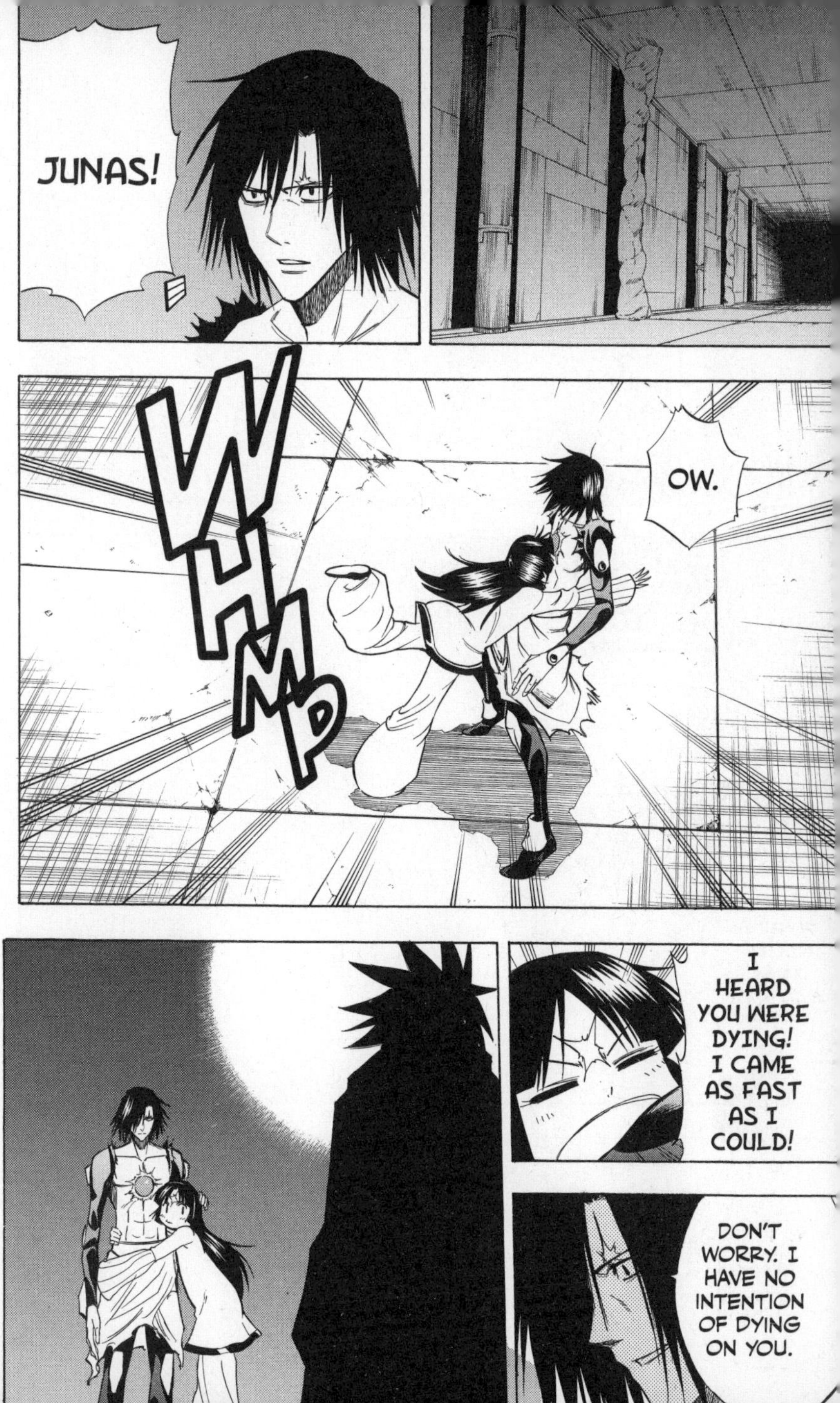
JUNAS!
OW.
WHMP
I HEARD YOU WERE DYING! I CAME AS FAST AS I COULD!
DON'T WORRY. I HAVE NO INTENTION OF DYING ON YOU.

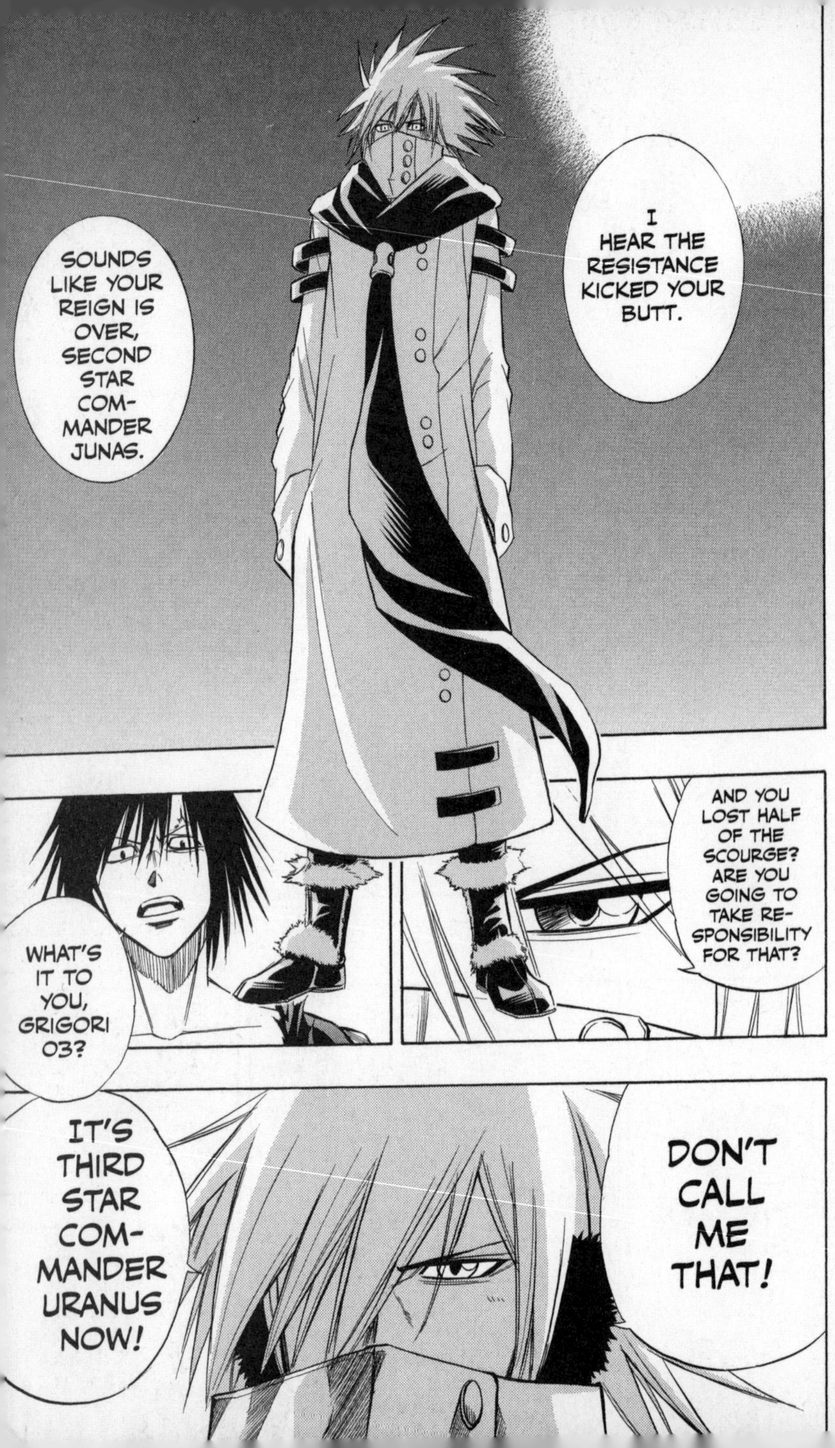
I HEAR THE RESISTANCE KICKED YOUR BUTT.
SOUNDS LIKE YOUR REIGN IS OVER, SECOND STAR COMMANDER JUNAS.
AND YOU LOST HALF OF THE SCOURGE? ARE YOU GOING TO TAKE RESPONSIBILITY FOR THAT?
WHAT'S IT TO YOU, GRIGORI 03?
DON'T CALL ME THAT!
IT'S THIRD STAR COMMANDER URANUS NOW!

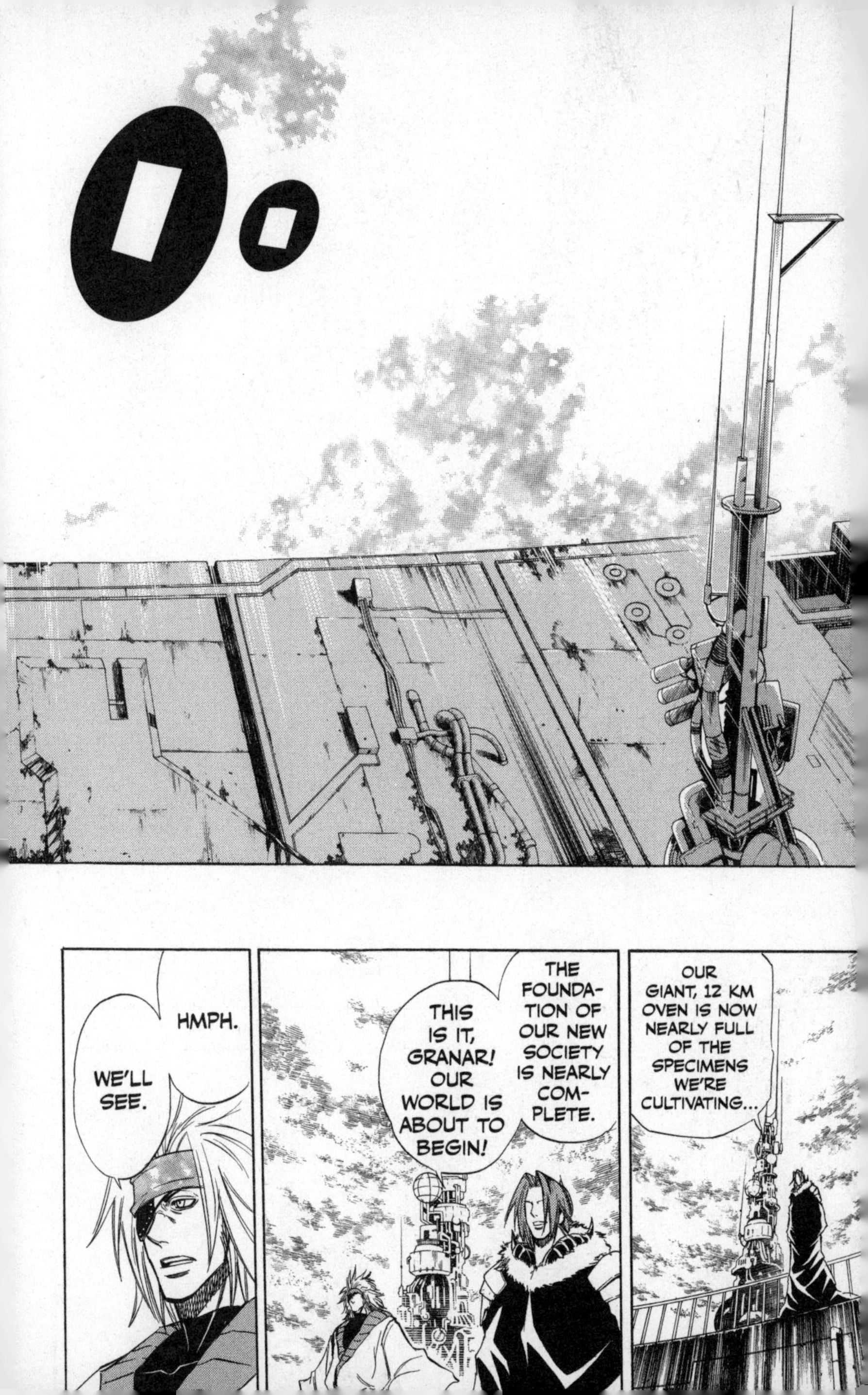
OUR GIANT, 12 KM OVEN IS NOW NEARLY FULL OF THE SPECIMENS WE'RE CULTIVATING...
THE FOUNDATION OF OUR NEW SOCIETY IS NEARLY COMPLETE.
THIS IS IT, GRANAR! OUR WORLD IS ABOUT TO BEGIN!
HMPH.
WE'LL SEE.

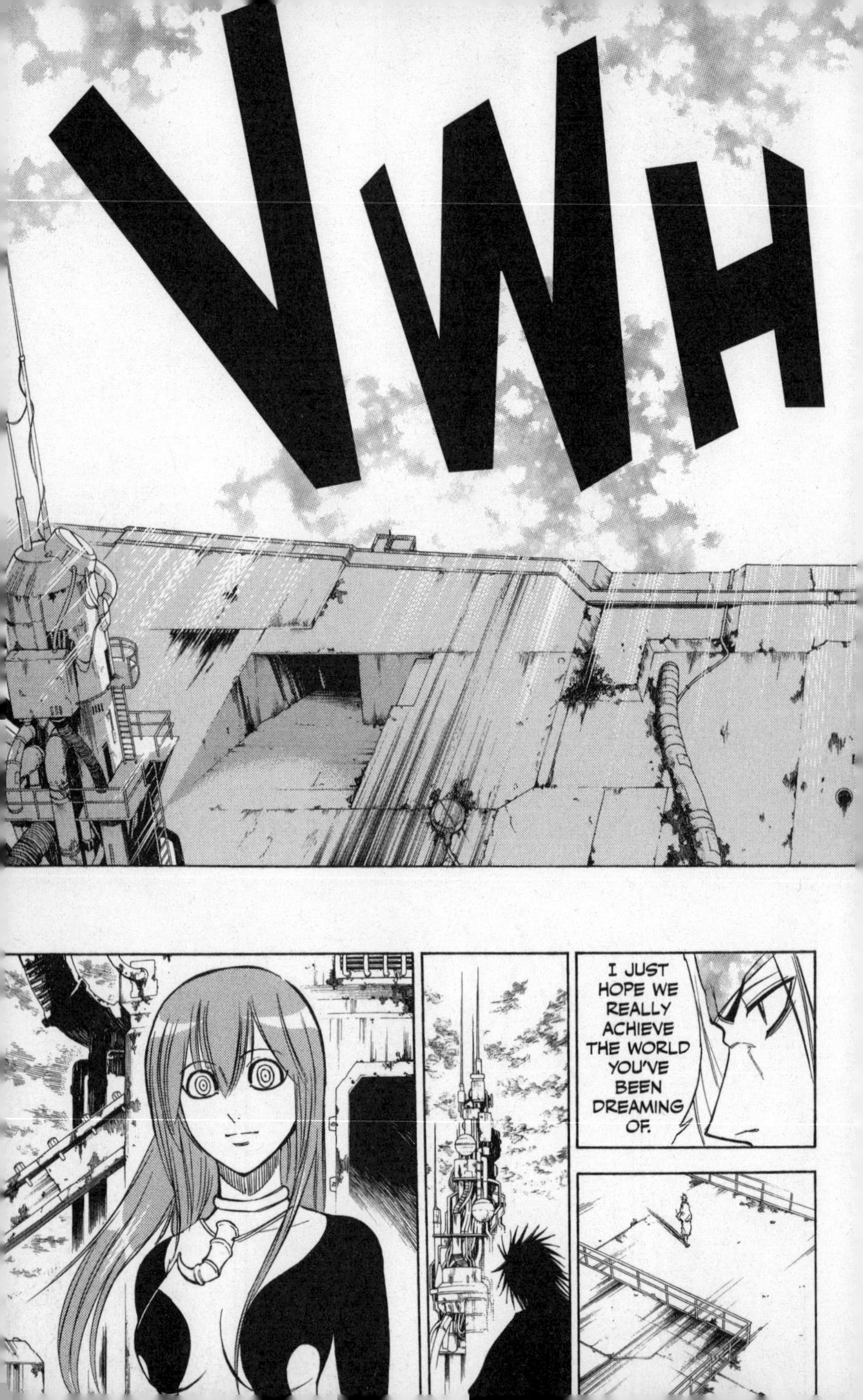
VWH
I JUST HOPE WE REALLY ACHIEVE THE WORLD YOU'VE BEEN DREAMING OF.

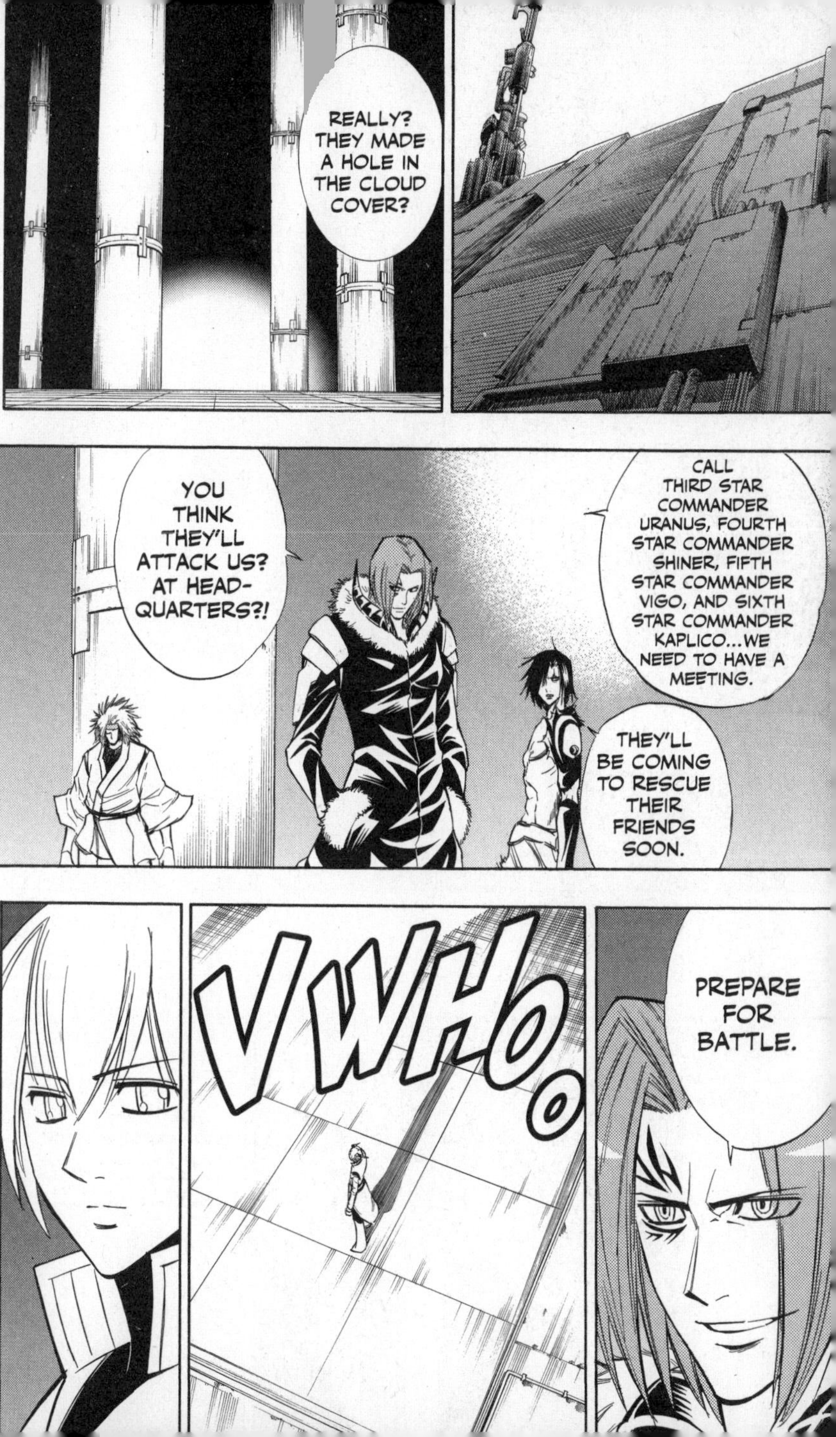
REALLY? THEY MADE A HOLE IN THE CLOUD COVER?
CALL THIRD STAR COMMANDER URANUS, FOURTH STAR COMMANDER SHINER, FIFTH STAR COMMANDER VIGO, AND SIXTH STAR COMMANDER KAPLICO...WE NEED TO HAVE A MEETING.
YOU THINK THEY'LL ATTACK US? AT HEAD-QUARTERS?!
THEY'LL BE COMING TO RESCUE THEIR FRIENDS SOON.
PREPARE FOR BATTLE.
VWHOO

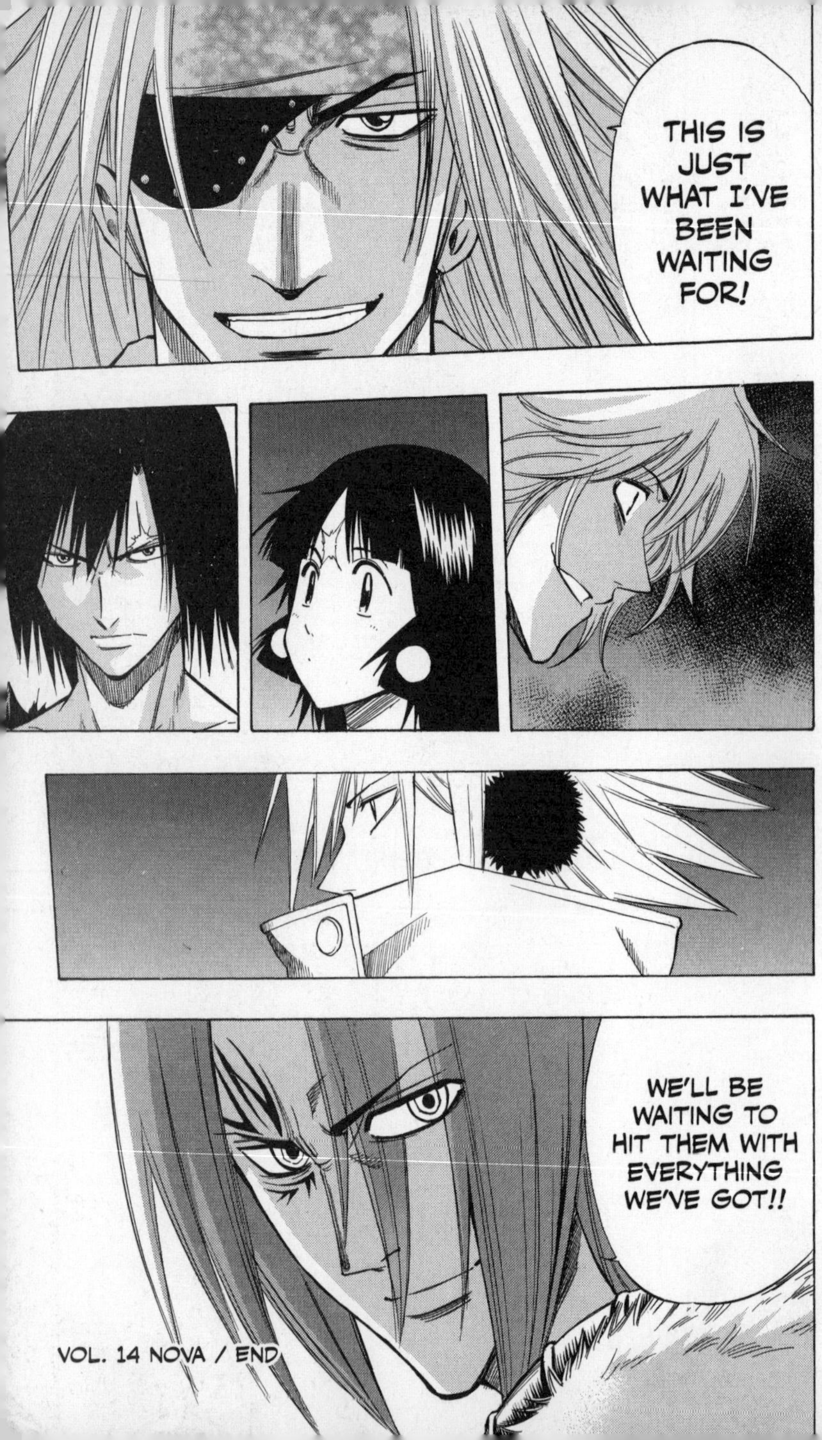
THIS IS JUST WHAT I'VE BEEN WAITING FOR!
WE'LL BE WAITING TO HIT THEM WITH EVERYTHING WE'VE GOT!!
VOL. 14 NOVA / END

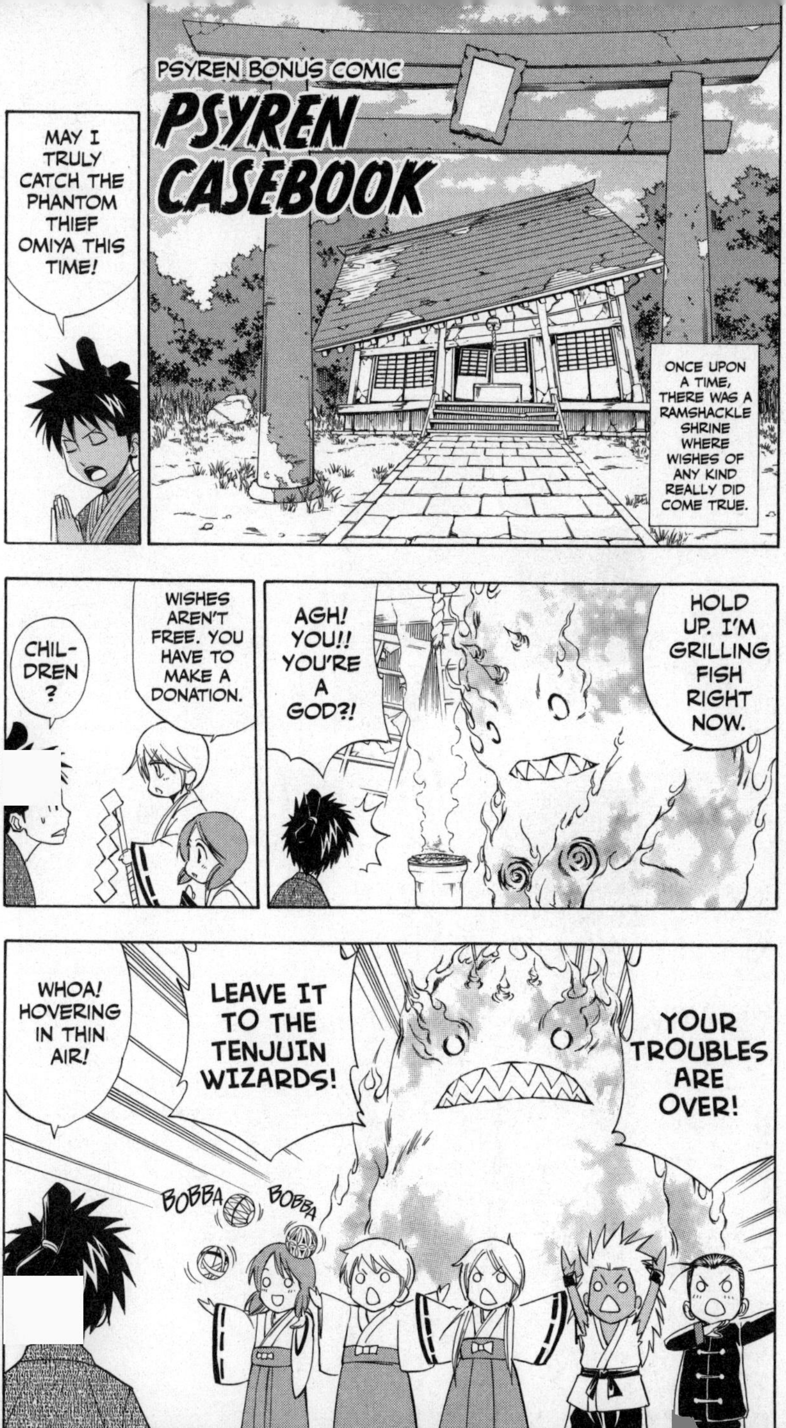
PSYREN BONUS COMIC
PSYREN CASEBOOK
ONCE UPON A TIME, THERE WAS A RAMSHACKLE SHRINE WHERE WISHES OF ANY KIND REALLY DID COME TRUE.
MAY I TRULY CATCH THE PHANTOM THIEF OMIYA THIS TIME!
HOLD UP. I'M GRILLING FISH RIGHT NOW.
AGH! YOU!! YOU'RE A GOD?!
WISHES AREN'T FREE. YOU HAVE TO MAKE A DONATION.
CHIL-DREN?
YOUR TROUBLES ARE OVER!
LEAVE IT TO THE TENJUIN WIZARDS!
WHOA! HOVERING IN THIN AIR!
BOBBA
BOBBA

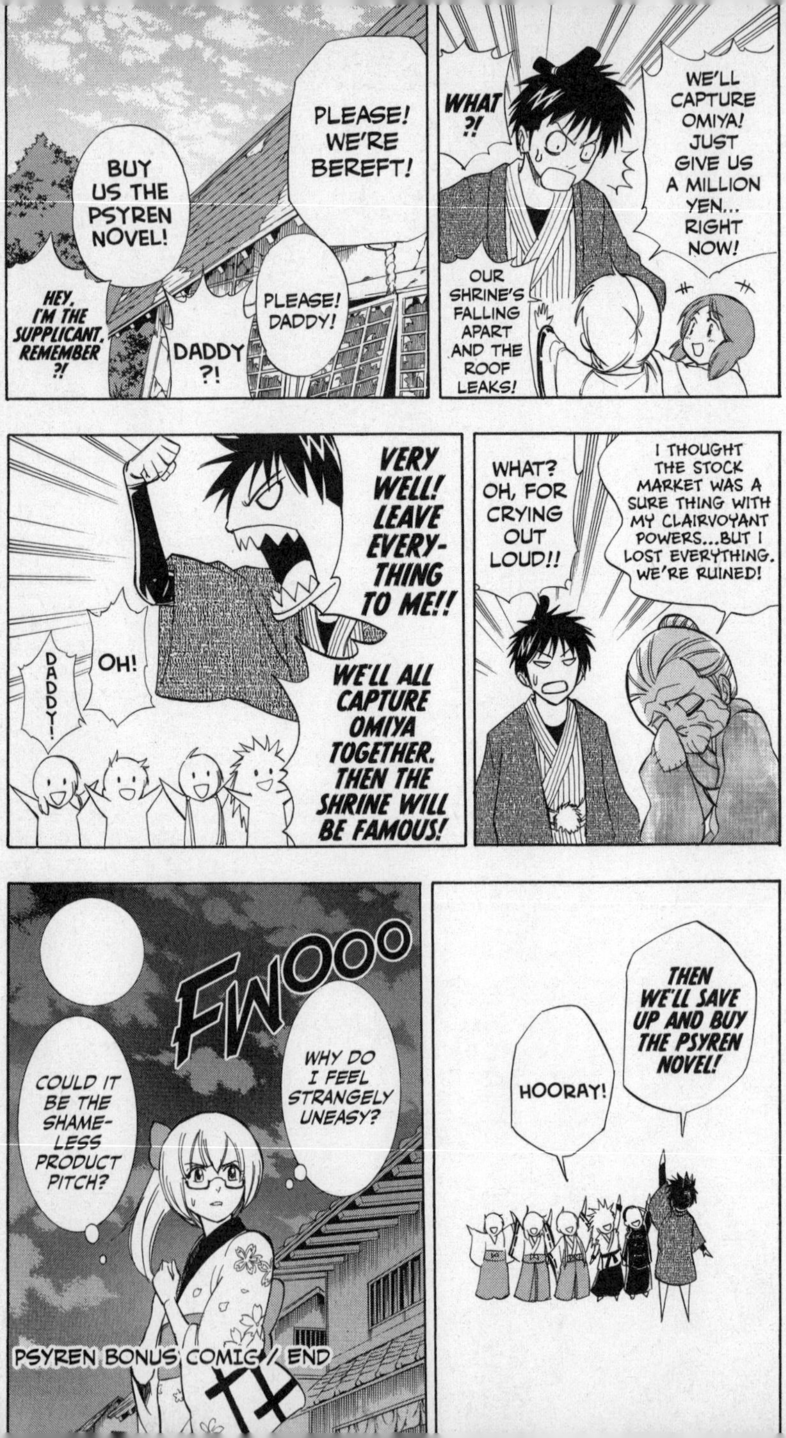
WE'LL CAPTURE OMIYA! JUST GIVE US A MILLION YEN... RIGHT NOW!
WHAT ?!
OUR SHRINE'S FALLING APART AND THE ROOF LEAKS!
PLEASE! WE'RE BEREFT!
BUY US THE PSYREN NOVEL!
PLEASE! DADDY!
DADDY ?!
HEY, I'M THE SUPPLICANT, REMEMBER ?!
I THOUGHT THE STOCK MARKET WAS A SURE THING WITH MY CLAIRVOYANT POWERS...BUT I LOST EVERYTHING. WE'RE RUINED!
WHAT? OH, FOR CRYING OUT LOUD!!
VERY WELL! LEAVE EVERY-THING TO ME!!
WE'LL ALL CAPTURE OMIYA TOGETHER. THEN THE SHRINE WILL BE FAMOUS!
OH!
DADDY!
THEN WE'LL SAVE UP AND BUY THE PSYREN NOVEL!
HOORAY!
FWOOO
WHY DO I FEEL STRANGELY UNEASY?
COULD IT BE THE SHAME-LESS PRODUCT PITCH?
PSYREN BONUS COMIC / END

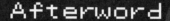

Afterword

THANK YOU FOR READING VOLUME 14!!

WHEN PSYREN WAS FIRST SERIALIZED,
I HAD PLANNED TO MAKE AGEHA'S
FATHER A BEEFIER, SWEATIER MIDDLE
AGED DUDE.

I DON'T KNOW WHO TAMPERED
WITH MY BRAIN, BUT INSTEAD HE'S TURNED
INTO THE MOST MYSTERIOUS CHARACTER
SINCE 07.

LATELY, WHEN I HAVE LUNCH WITH MY
ASSISTANTS, WE'VE BEEN GOING OUT TO EAT
INSTEAD OF ORDERING TAKE-OUT OR BUYING
READY-MADE LUNCHES. GETTING A
LITTLE FRESH AIR SEEMS TO MAKE A REAL
DIFFERENCE IN OUR MOTIVATION LEVELS.

ANYWAY, WE PROMISE TO KEEP
WORKING HARD ON THE MANUSCRIPTS!

IT'S COLD OUT THESE DAYS, SO TAKE CARE
AND DON'T GET SICK!

TOSHIAKI IWASHIRO, NOVEMBER 2010

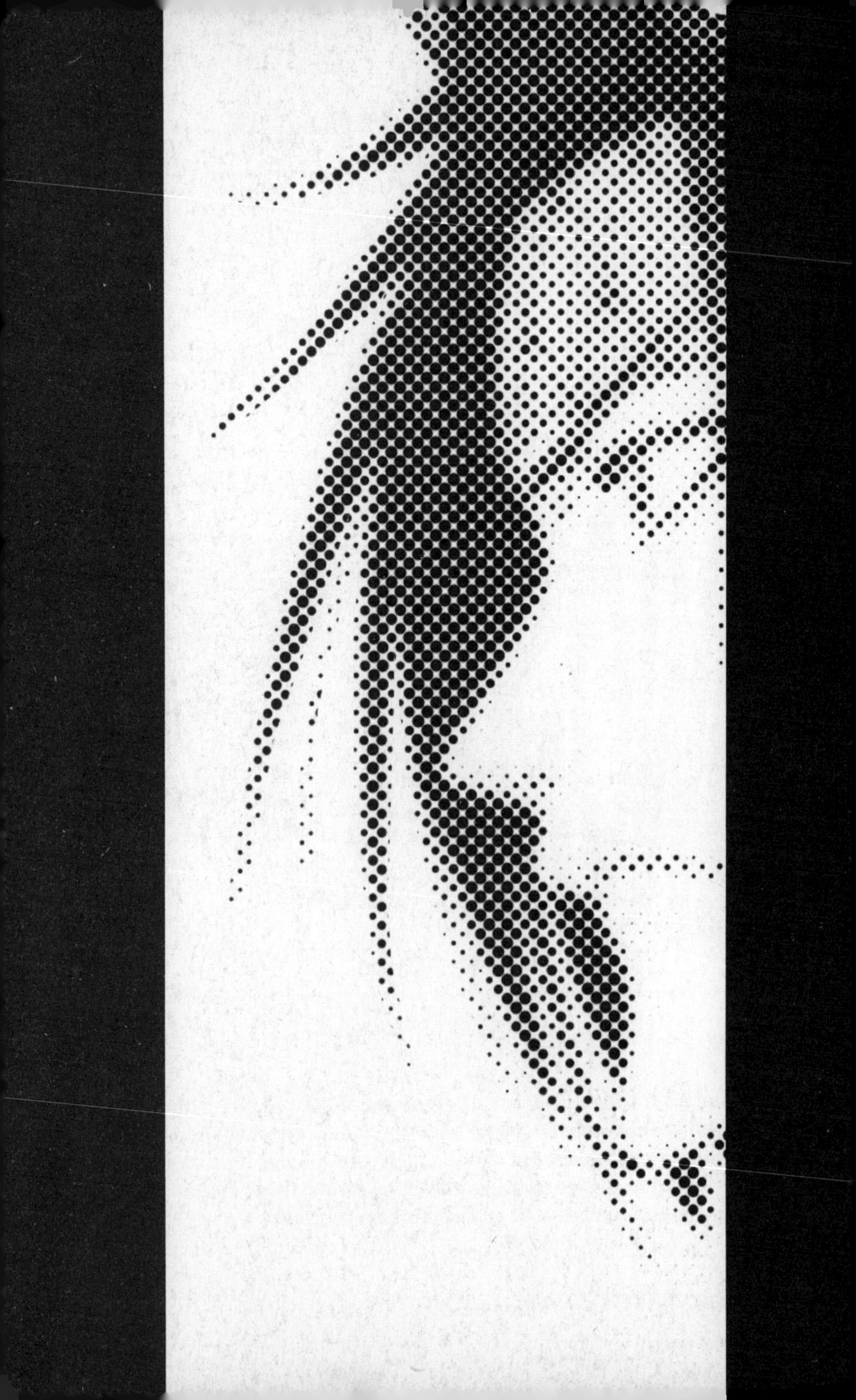

IN THE NEXT VOLUME...

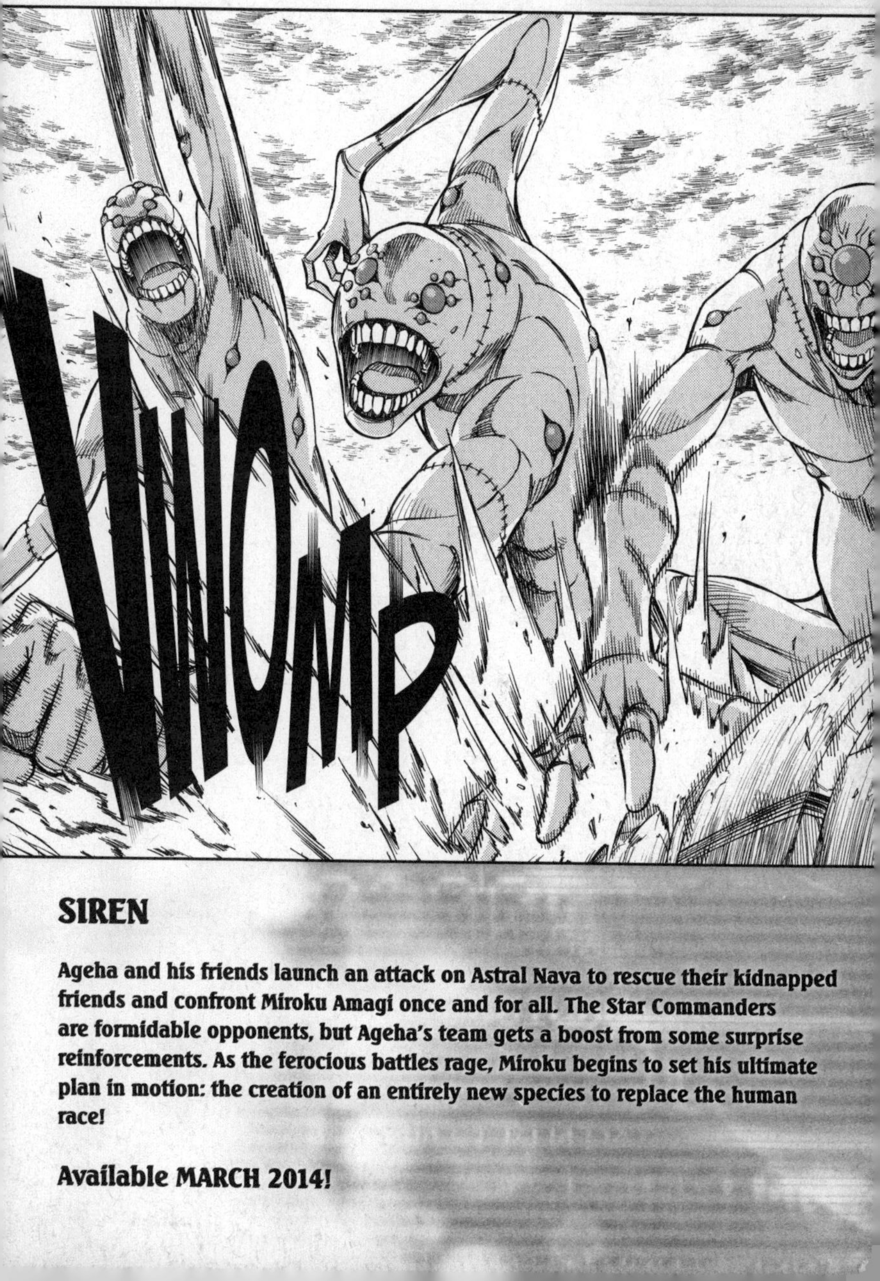
WHOMP

SIREN

Ageha and his friends launch an attack on Astral Nava to rescue their kidnapped friends and confront Miroku Amagi once and for all. The Star Commanders are formidable opponents, but Ageha's team gets a boost from some surprise reinforcements. As the ferocious battles rage, Miroku begins to set his ultimate plan in motion: the creation of an entirely new species to replace the human race!

Available MARCH 2014!

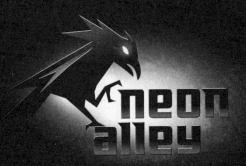
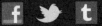

You're Reading in the Wrong Direction!!

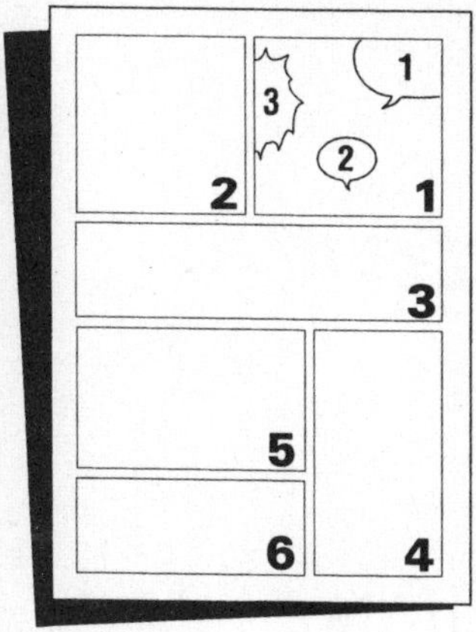

1
2
3
1
2
3
4
5
6

Whoops! Guess what? You're starting at the wrong end of the comic!

...It's true! In keeping with the original Japanese format, **Psyren** is meant to be read from right to left, starting in the upper-right corner.

Unlike English, which is read from left to right, Japanese is read from right to left, meaning that action, sound effects and word-balloon order are completely reversed—something which can make readers unfamiliar with Japanese feel pretty backwards themselves. For this reason, manga or Japanese comics published in the U.S. in English have sometimes been published "flopped"–that is, printed in exact reverse order, as though seen from the other side of a mirror.

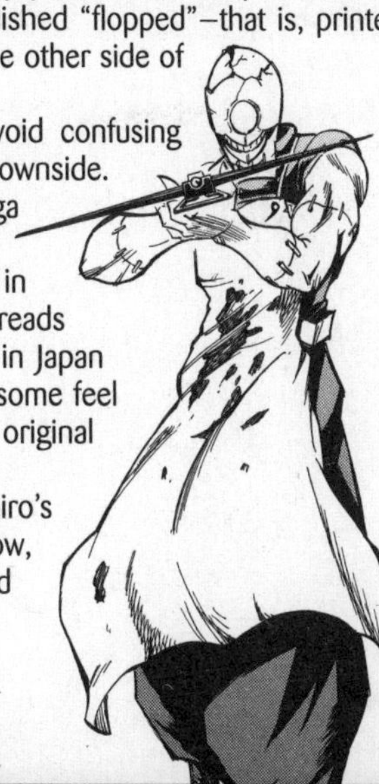

By flopping pages, U.S. publishers can avoid confusing readers, but the compromise is not without its downside. For one thing, a character in a flopped manga series who once wore in the original Japanese version a T-shirt emblazoned with "M A Y" (as in "the merry month of") now wears one which reads "Y A M"! Additionally, many manga creators in Japan are themselves unhappy with the process, as some feel the mirror-imaging of their art changes their original intentions.

We are proud to bring you Toshiaki Iwashiro's **Psyren** in the original unflopped format. For now, though, turn to the other side of the book and let the fun begin...!

–Editor